THE HARVEST OF TRAGEDY

MICHAELANGELO: *PIETÀ*
'The only great work of pity in all Rome'

THE HARVEST
OF TRAGEDY

by

T. R. HENN, C.B.E., M.A.

Fellow and Tutor of St Catharine's College, Cambridge
University Lecturer in English

METHUEN & CO. LTD
36 ESSEX STREET, STRAND, LONDON W.C.2

First published in 1956

CATALOGUE NO.

5848/U

PRINTED AND BOUND IN GREAT BRITAIN
BY BUTLER AND TANNER LIMITED, FROME AND LONDON

At the heart of the nature of things, there are always the dream of youth and the harvest of tragedy. The Adventure of the Universe starts with the dream and reaps tragic Beauty. This is the secret of the Union of Zest with Peace—that the suffering attains its end in a Harmony of Harmonies. The immediate experience of this Final Fact, with its union of Youth and Tragedy, is the sense of Peace. In this way the World receives its persuasion towards such perfections as are possible for its diverse individual occasions.

A. N. WHITEHEAD

Tragedy is clean, it is restful, it is flawless.

ANOUILH

To the thinker, feeling is a nuisance, except as it is exacted from other people . . . It is only when he can see that he must find salvation within himself, in taking responsibility for the archaic and irrational feeling elements in his own unconscious, that he can find the God within, the new value rising from the darkness.

F. G. WICKES

A. N. WHITEHEAD: *Adventures of Ideas*
ANOUILH: *Antigone*
F. G. WICKES: *The Inner World of Man*

Contents

Illustrations

Acknowledgements

I WISH to tender grateful acknowledgements to the following for their permission to quote or reproduce:

Mrs Frieda Lawrence Ravagli for two verses from D. H. Lawrence's *Eloi, Eloi, Lama Sabachthani*; George Allen & Unwin Ltd for the quotation from *My Life and Thought* by Albert Schweitzer; Bowes & Bowes Ltd for the quotation from Erich Heller's *The Disinherited Mind*; Jonathan Cape Ltd for the quotations from *Mourning Becomes Elektra* by Eugene O'Neill, Brieux's *The Three Daughters of Monsieur Dupont*, Strindberg's *Lady Julie*, and Jonathan Cape Ltd and the Executors of the James Joyce Estate for a quotation from *A Portrait of the Artist as a Young Man* by James Joyce; Columbia University Press, New York, for the quotation from *The Poetry of Thomas Hardy* by J. G. Southworth; J. M. Dent & Sons Ltd for the quotation from F. L. Lucas's translation of *Hippolytus*, and Ibsen's *Brand* (Everyman); Faber & Faber Ltd for the quotations from T. S. Eliot's Poetry, Drama and Prose; Hamish Hamilton Ltd for the quotation from J. Y. Cousteau's *The Silent World*; William Heinemann Ltd for the quotation from *John Gabriel Borkman* by Ibsen; The Hogarth Press Ltd for the quotation from F. L. Lucas's *Tragedy*; Longmans, Green & Co. Ltd for the quotation from *Shakespeare* by H. Fluchère; Macmillan & Co. Ltd for the quotations from Sir John Fortescue's *History of the British Army*, Butcher's translation of Aristotle's *Poetics* and Sean O'Casey's *Juno and the Paycock* and *The Silver Tassie*, and to Mrs Yeats and Messrs. Macmillan for the extracts from Yeats's Prose and Verse; Methuen & Co. Ltd for the quotations from *Antigone* by Jean Anouilh and G. Norwood's *Euripides and Shaw*; New Directions Inc., New York, for the quotations from *Three Tragedies of Lorca*, translated by James Graham-Luzan and R. L. O'Connell; James Nisbet & Co. Ltd for the quotations from *Beyond Tragedy* by Reinhold Niebuhr; The Oxford University Press for the quotation from *Archetypal Patterns in Poetry* by M. Bodkin; Penguin Books Ltd for the quotations from *The Greeks* by H. D. F. Kitto; Phoenix House Ltd for the quotation from Dr J. Bronowski's *The Face of Violence*; The Public Trustee and The Society of Authors for the quotations from Bernard Shaw's *St Joan*,

The Doctor's Dilemma and *Mrs Warren's Profession*; Routledge & Kegan Paul Ltd for the quotations from Jung's *Modern Man in Search of a Soul*, and *Introduction to the Science of Mythology* by Jung and Kerényi.

I wish to apologize for any accidental omissions that may be found in this list.

INTRODUCTION

§ i

THE object proposed in this book is to examine certain facts, theories and assumptions regarding the nature of the form which we term, loosely, Tragedy. To undertake such a task seems at first sight presumptuous, or otiose, or both. Much has been written on the subject, and much more is to come.[1] But it seems arguable that we have now reached a stage at which some fresh inquiry might be fruitful: particularly if the 'fact or experience' which we call Tragedy were to be examined, not as a stable compound, but as a highly complex, composite and active substance and form; with characteristic effects which can best be apprehended, because of their very nature, in religious or mystical terms.

Further, it appears probable that both the values and structures of the components of the form are themselves compound rather than simple: varying greatly in their composition according to the view of life presented by the individual writer of tragedies, himself a figure to be considered in some detail in the setting of his age. And if these terms are indeed compound and complex, it appears necessary to re-state the elemental and elementary problems of the subject; to consider how far philosophy, psychology and religion may now affect the triple thought that underlies them; and to attempt to relate or project the conclusions into some vital relationship with life and death.

§ ii

The student of such a subject as this becomes aware, from the very outset, of the gravest implications in his object of study. Tragedy, from its very nature, concerns itself continually with specific attitudes towards the widest possible range of moral problems. Such attitudes may be implicit or explicit; more often, perhaps, a complicated balance between the two. It may rely on paradox or antithesis for its typical statements, allowing no more than a momentary synthesis to emerge through image or symbol. When 'wrought to its uttermost' the

---

[1] While this book was in draft form, Dr Weisinger's work, *Tragedy and the Paradox of the Fortunate Fall*, appeared.

xi

essential problems converge rapidly upon religion and metaphysics. Yet it cannot seek its answers (since it moves too rapidly) through obscure definitions or even in terms of dogma. Its statement is 'philosophical' in the Aristotelian sense, in that tragedy can use for that purpose the resources of complex emotional communications, both in relation to its intellectual propositions and to the manner in which they may be interpreted. Its poetic resources are limited only by its intrinsic power to induce the audience to accept them, whether by Longinus's 'lightning flash', or by the gradual process of establishing a specific tradition. At its best it can create a moral homogeneity in the audience, and thereby acquire a power equalled only by the Epic at the height of its tradition, and by the greatest preachers of the seventeenth century. Because of the limitations of its form it cannot multiply entities, metaphysical or psychological, beyond a certain point; it must therefore achieve (at whatever cost in slow-developed subtleties of motive and character), a compression and energy that is found in no other form.

§ iii

I am aware both of those philosophies that find tragedy as a form to be either obsolescent or obsolete in the light of twentieth-century thought, and of those attacks, more specifically literary, which have formally dismissed it.

In this last category Mr J. W. Krutch may be quoted as typical:

> Tragedies, in that only sense of the word which has any distinctive meaning, can no longer be written in either the dramatic or in any other form, and the fact is not to be accounted for in any merely literary terms . . . [1] The tragic solution of the problem of existence, the reconciliation to life by means of the tragic spirit is, that is to say, now only a fiction surviving in art.[2] When that art has become, as it probably will, completely meaningless, when we have ceased not only to write but to *read* tragic works, then it will be lost and in all real senses forgotten, since the devolution from Religion to Art to Document will be complete.[3]

The implicit and explicit assumptions in this statement can be usefully contrasted with Nietzsche's view:

> . . . and this is the most immediate effect of the Dionysian tragedy, that the state and society, and, in general, the gaps between man and man give

---

[1] *The Modern Temper*, p. 118.
[2] 'The scholiast has hungrily misheard a dead man's toller as a muffinbell', *Finnegan's Wake*, p. 121, l. 30 (*cit.* L. A. G. Strong).
[3] *Ibid.*, p. 193.

way to an overwhelming feeling of oneness, which leads back to the heart of nature. The metaphysical comfort—with which, as I have here intimated, every true tragedy dismisses us—that, in spite of the perpetual change of phenomena, life at bottom is indestructibly powerful and pleasurable, this comfort appears with corporeal lucidity in the satiric chorus, as the chorus of natural beings who live ineradicable as it were behind all civilization, and who, in spite of the ceaseless change of generations and the history of nations, remain for ever the same.[1]

§ iv

We cannot escape this conflict; we may even use André Malraux's question [2] to state it more simply: 'On this soil of Europe, yes or no, is man dead?' In any consideration of tragic principles we shall be drawn into discussion of Existentialism, of Marxism, of Victorian optimism and of modern pessimism; as well as of the philosophies of Schopenhauer, Nietzsche, Kant, Hegel. For a framework to my own speculations I am profoundly indebted to the work of Reinhold Niebuhr; and I have therefore become involved, in varying degrees, in the rejection of the views of those who, through varying combinations of pessimism and materialism, have sought to show the irresponsibility of tragedy and the obsolescence of the values which it propounds.

§ v

As this essay progresses, it will, I think, be clear that I have reached a position in which anthropology and psychology appear to converge on, and blend with, modern 'Realistic' theology; [3] that I have been led to consider certain of the historical and political implications of my subject; and that the circle has returned to Shelley's aphorism: 'Poetry administers to the effect by acting upon the cause.' I do not apologize for this line of development. The implications of any discussion of the subject are such that moral questions are of the first importance. 'The literary critic is concerned rather with the wisdom *inherent* in literature, with the judgement of its ethical soundness, the firmness and range of its imitation of life.' [4]

It has therefore seemed essential to attempt to develop, in parallel rather than in series, the aesthetic and ethical aspects of the discussion;

[1] *The Birth of Tragedy*, pp. 60-1.
[2] In a lecture given at the Sorbonne, 4 Nov. 1946.
[3] That is, the branch of theology which has for its characteristic approach the rejection of the 'liberal' faith in the essential perfectibility of human nature and society; and which develops its position from a re-examination of the doctrine of the Fall and of original sin.
[4] Norman Foerster, *The Intent of the Critic*, p. 75.

to consider both the classical explanations of the nature and functions of tragedy, as well as those which have been put forward in the past half century; and not to evade such religious or mystical speculations which seem, of recent years, to have gone beyond what was once thought proper in orthodox theology. And if an interpretation of the nature and meaning of tragedy can be linked to the religious thought, not merely of the Greeks or Elizabethans, but of the contemporary world, it may be that some light—'though somewhat broken by the leaves'—can be thrown on some of its problems; nor is it, perhaps, entirely idle to see, in our interpretation of two great wars, some microcosm or macrocosm of the patterns that tragedy reveals.

Writers to-day, both on politics and on morals, lament the loss of the 'sense of tragedy' in the western world. They appear, in general, to attribute this to a corresponding loss of traditional values. But although we have irrefutable evidence of the de-sensitization, during and after each war, of the public and private conscience, its bearing upon the significance of tragedy is as yet by no means clear; and it will be suggested later that the problem can be shown to be one of varying doctrines of individual responsibility in the historical setting.

And if indeed counsels of despair prevail, if we are driven to deny what seem the deeper levels of human moral consciousness, we are denying not only tragedy but our response to a vast body of literature. We are exchanging what might move us to a greater wisdom for what merely titillates the surface; and we may suspect that this in turn is symptomatic of the atrophy of our general interest in ethical problems. The end is the decay of a sense of responsibility in many kinds of living.

In an attempt to impose some degree of unity upon so vast a subject, I have tried to follow out two main considerations: the formal features, qualities and effects of the tragic form, and that aspect of it which can be seen in terms of *hubris*, the sin of pride, and its counterparts in Christian philosophy. As touching this last, I do not see tragedy as the product of a wholly Christian faith, but as arising always out of the conflict (whether in the words of St Paul or of Sir Philip Sidney) between man's erected wit and his infected will. To these we may, perhaps, add a third component; the sheer complexity of the machinery of politics and government which (lacking any centre or power of simplification in existing systems) drives men to pitiless bewilderment, or to the irresponsibility of despair.

I have tried to achieve, though I know that I have failed, some balance between exposition and criticism, between recapitulation of plays that may be unfamiliar and the seemingly arrogant assumption of wider reading.

Not least among the difficulties of the subject is that of a critical terminology: its 'impure' nature, the danger of using traditional critical counters such as *hubris* and *katharsis*—though they appear inevitable; the indefiniteness of terms such as *pattern, rhythm, conflict*; the fact that we are dealing continually with qualities of persons and events that cannot be analysed directly, and with responses which can only be experienced and not argued over. Further, English is poor in some of the concepts that can be used with enlightenment in German. It is difficult, for instance, to find an exact equivalent to 'die tragische Erhebung'; '*Rührung*' in the sense of 'calm of mind all passion spent' or '*Teilnehmungsgefühle*' are untranslatable except by means of cumbrous paraphrases. *Todtentrieb* and *Schadenfreude*, though clearer in meaning because more familiar, are other instances. And the writer on tragedy lays himself open, at every turn, either to the charge of establishing new meanings upon an old terminology, or to losing himself in imprecision.

I am aware at every turn of my debts to many writers; among them Dr Ellis-Fermor for her *Frontiers of Drama*; F. L. Lucas for his *Psychology and Criticism*, and his *Tragedy*; Francis Fergusson for his *Idea of a Theatre*. On the philosophical and religious sides I owe much to the work and advice of Reinhold and Richard Niebuhr; to the writings of William Temple, Maud Bodkin, G. L. Bickersteth, and W. R. Matthews, Dean of St Paul's.

My thanks are due to the President and Fellows of Yale, the Administrators of the Fulbright Grant, and the Trustees of the Leverhulme Fund for the assistance which made it possible to complete this book, and for the opportunity of meeting many of the scholars to whose work and thought I am indebted.

Other debts I have tried to express in the text and in the footnotes; but I have drawn from many sources, and no doubt I have, unconsciously, re-cast much of the thought of others of my teachers and of my own pupils with whom I have talked. Among them, I am grateful in particular to Professor Basil Willey, Patric Dickinson, Dr R. T. H. Redpath, M. D. Brown, Professor A. E. Edinborough, the late Dr G. P. D. Allt, A. B. Wilkinson for assistance with the proofs and index, and to those who contributed to the views expressed in Chapter 22.

CAMBRIDGE–YALE 1952–5

–CAMBRIDGE

CHAPTER I

The Aristotelian Induction: and some Related Problems

IT is convenient to use certain extracts from the *Poetics*, both because of their familiarity and their central analysis of most dramatic writing, as a starting point: and to indicate briefly some of the questions that may arise. For this purpose Butcher's translation has been used, and I have not attempted to recapitulate the standard glosses upon it.

1. Tragedy, then, is an imitation of an action that is serious, complete, and of a certain magnitude; in language embellished with each kind of artistic ornament, the several kinds being found in separate parts of the play, in the form of action, not of narrative; through pity and fear effecting the proper purgation of these emotions.[1]

There is no agreement as to what an *action* is, or how it is to be defined. *Imitation* is perhaps the most debated word in the *Poetics*. *Serious* can be defined initially as 'that which matters' as opposed to that which is superficial, transitory: but its connotations have both narrowed and expanded throughout literary history. *Complete* is defined as that which has a beginning, a middle and an end. Both *beginning* and *end* raise dramatic problems. *Magnitude* is dealt with elsewhere. What, exactly, are *pity* and *fear* in tragedy, and what is *purgation*? in Aristotle's sense, or in ours?

2. Again, Tragedy is an imitation of an action; and an action implies personal agents, who necessarily possess certain distinctive qualities both of character and thought; for it is by these that we qualify actions themselves, and these—thought and character—are the two natural causes from which

What is the relationship of *thought* and *character* to action? And what is the relationship of both to personality? By what scales—religious, ethical, social, personal—do we reckon success or failure?

[1] *Poetics*, VI, 2.

actions spring, and on actions again
all success or failure depends.[1]

3. Hence, the Plot is the imitation
of the action:—for by plot I here
mean the arrangement of the
incidents.[2]

4. But most important of all is the
structure of the incidents. For
Tragedy is an imitation, not of
men, but of an action and of life,
and life consists in action, and its
end is a mode of action, not a
quality.[3]

5. . . . the most powerful elements
of emotional interest in Tragedy—
Peripeteia or Reversal of the Situation, and Recognition scenes—
are parts of the plot.[4]

6. But the limit as fixed by the
nature of the drama itself is this:—
the greater the length, the more
beautiful will the piece be by
reason of its size, provided that
the whole be perspicuous.[5]

7. As therefore, in the other imita-
tive arts, the imitation is one
when the object imitated is one,
so the plot being an imitation of

The Greek and the modern meanings
of *plot* appear to differ: for the
Greek dramatist is writing on the
foundation of an accepted myth,
which it is his business to re-time
and reorganize.

Aristotle's emphasis on plot is reasonable, since he has a biological
approach to tragedy, and the plot
is the skeleton of the animal. But
his second proposition raises metaphysical and ethical questions; both
absolutely, and in their relation to
Greek and Christian thought.

Peripeteia may, for the moment, be
defined as a 'turn' in the plot (to
use Dryden's phrase) which involves a recoil upon the inventor's
head; *Recognition* is 'the realization
that things are otherwise than they
were believed to be at some prior
stage in the plot'. But both terms
require amplification and discussion. *Recognition* in particular, in
view of its relationship to memory
as well as to inductive reasoning, is
of special interest in dramatic
criticism.

The question of length has, obviously,
other factors: probably the *momentum* which (it will be argued later)
must be generated in the action.
(But consider the problem of the
one-act tragedy—e.g. *Riders to the
Sea*.)

Assuming that we have defined *action*
and *imitation*, in what sense is the
unity of action to be understood?

[1] *Poetics*, VI, 5.　　　　　　　　　　　　　[2] *Ibid.*, VI, 6.
[3] *Ibid.*, VI, 9. Cf. Blake's: 'All that is not action is not worth reading.'
[4] *Ibid.*, VI, 13.　　　　　　　　　　　　　[5] *Ibid.*, VII, 7.

an action, must imitate one action and that a whole . . .[1]

8. Poetry, therefore, is a more philosophical and a higher thing than history; for poetry tends to express the universal, history the particular.[2]

Assuming again that history is the object of factual narrative—which is, of course, impossible—what is the sense of *more philosophical* and *universal*?

9. But tragedians still keep to real names, the reason being that what is possible is credible: what has not happened we do not at once feel sure to be possible: but what has happened is manifestly possible, otherwise it would not have happened.[3]

What are the advantages of the historical fable? It will, obviously, facilitate the task of exposition: but what effect has it on the credibility of the play? And is 'credibility' necessary? What is the relationship of the Past to the Present in the tragic structure?

10. Of all plots and actions the epeisodic are the worst. I call a plot 'episodic' in which the episodes or acts succeed one another without probable or necessary sequence.[4]

Is the 'epeisodic' plot necessarily bad? How are we to define *probable* and *necessary*? What is the distinction between the *probable* and the *improbable but possible*? What is the delicate balance between the criteria of our own reason, and the 'willing suspension of disbelief' that the dramatist enforces upon reader or audience?

11. But again, Tragedy is an imitation not only of a complete action, but of events inspiring fear or pity. Such an effect is best produced when the events come on us by surprise; and the effect is heightened when, at the same time, they follow as cause and effect. The tragic wonder will then be greater than if they happened of themselves or by accident; for even coincidences are most striking when they have an air of design.[5]

Is it true that *pity* and *fear*—whatever they may be—are best produced by surprise? And what is meant by *cause and effect*? What does *of themselves* mean? What is the part played by *accident*? and is it true that *coincidences are most striking when they have an air of design*? When does this *design* merge into Determinism?

12. . . . the change of fortune presented must not be the spectacle

Aristotle raises the whole question of the 'sinless hero'. As a further point

---

[1] *Ibid.*, VIII, 4.
[4] *Ibid.*, IX, 10.
[2] *Ibid.*, IX, 3.
[5] *Ibid.*, IX, 11.
[3] *Ibid.*, IX, 6.

of a virtuous man brought from prosperity to adversity: for this moves neither pity nor fear; it merely shocks us. Nor, again, that of a bad man passing from adversity to prosperity: for nothing can be more alien to the spirit of Tragedy; it possesses no single tragic quality; it neither satisfies the moral sense nor calls forth pity or fear. Nor, again, should the downfall of the utter villain be exhibited. A plot of this kind would, doubtless, satisfy the moral sense, but it would inspire neither pity nor fear; for pity is aroused by unmerited misfortune, fear by the misfortune of a man like ourselves. Such an event, therefore, will be neither pitiful nor terrible.[1]

13. Two parts, then, of the Plot—Reversal of the Situation and Recognition—turn upon surprises. A third part is the Scene of Suffering. The Scene of Suffering is a destructive or painful action, such as death on the stage, bodily agony, wounds and the like.[2]

14. (The tragic hero should be) . . . a man who is not eminently good and just, yet whose misfortune is brought about not by vice or depravity, but by some error or frailty. He must be one who is highly renowned and prosperous, —a personage like Oedipus, Thyestes, or other illustrious men of such families.[3]

of interest he appears to isolate the satisfaction of the *moral sense* from the emotional responses of pity and fear; the former being no doubt intellectual. Further, the partial definitions of *pity* and *fear* in the last sentence may seem to us to simplify these emotions to an undue extent.

What is the value of the *Scene of Suffering*? Is it an archaic survival, and no longer to be tolerated? Or has it sadistic or masochistic elements of possible therapeutic value? Is there a limit to dramatic toleration of suffering? How is it to be connected, if at all, with Christian values?

How far have the changes in the social and political pattern made obsolete the original symbolic values of the hero in his identification with the fate of his people? Are there any compensating factors in modern drama which produce the necessary sense of projected sympathy—if, indeed, this is the explanation of the tragic hero's stature and appeal? What is *error or frailty*? how is it to be reconciled

---

[1] *Poetics*, XIII, 2.   [2] *Ibid.*, XI, 6.   [3] *Ibid.*, XIII, 3.

with, e.g., the Hegelian theory? What is its connection with ethical and religious ideas of 'sin'—whatever definitions we may allow for that word? And how far do changing concepts of sin—as for instance those involved in the transition from Nineteenth Century Liberal thought to modern 'Realistic' theology—bear upon the question of tragic responsibility?

15. Those who employ spectacular means to create a sense not of the terrible but only of the monstrous, are strangers to the purpose of Tragedy; for we must not demand of Tragedy any and every kind of pleasure, but only that which is proper to it. And since the pleasure which the poet should afford is that which comes from pity and fear through imitation, it is evident that this quality must be impressed upon the incidents.[1]

Terrible — horrible — monstrous — grotesque—what meanings are we to give these words? And what kinds of 'pleasure' are *proper* to tragedy?

16. (The playwright) may not indeed destroy the framework of the received legends—the fact, for instance, that Clytemnestra was slain by Orestes and Eriphyle by Alcmaeon—but he ought to show invention of his own, and skilfully handle the traditional material.[2]

In view of the consistent appeal of the *received legends*—whether as archetypes or for some other reason— what are the limits that should be imposed on the playwright who handles them?

17. Now any speech or action that manifests moral purpose of any kind will be expressive of character: the character will be good if the purpose is good.[3]

Again this question of the relationship of *character* to *action*: with the need for reaching an understanding of *purpose*, or, perhaps, *will*.

18. The Chorus too should be regarded as one of the actors; it should be an integral part of

Enough has been written of the function of the Chorus in Greek drama; but the uncertain and variable

[1] *Ibid.*, XIV, 2. [2] *Ibid.*, XIV, 4. [3] *Ibid.*, XV, 1.

the whole, and share in the action . . .[1]

19. The perfection of style is to be clear without being mean. The clearest style is that which uses only current or proper words; at the same time it is mean:—witness the poetry of Cleophon and Sthenelus. That diction, on the other hand, is lofty and raised above the commonplace which employs unusual words.[2]

20. Accordingly, the poet should prefer probable impossibilities to improbable possibilities. The tragic plot must not be composed of irrational parts. Everything irrational should, if possible, be excluded; or, at all events, it should lie outside the action of the play . . . not within the drama.[3]

21. Again, in examining whether what has been said or done by some one is poetically right or not, we must not look merely to the particular act or saying, and ask whether it is poetically good or bad. We must also consider by whom it is said or done, to whom, when, by what means, or for what end; whether, for instance, it be to secure a greater good, or avert a greater evil.[4]

handling of it on the modern stage demands consideration.

The diction of tragedy, whether it attains its ends through 'that high breeding which is the essence of all style', or through the delineation of character through rhythm; or whether its poetic content should be unnoticeable, not raised above the commonplace — these are matters of importance.

A famous critical dictum, which has a good deal of bearing on the tragic form. Does this barrier of the *irrational* make the 'imitation' of religious material impossible?

A curious statement, which might be taken to imply a relativist view of morality. What is *poetically good or bad*? And is not this a starting point for an aesthetic of drama?

§ ii

It would, I think, be possible to project all, or all but all, the Aristotelian questions (with their inevitable Platonic background) into time and space in such a manner as to show their connections with the related problems of the tragic structure and content. But for convenience we may offer some of these problems in the following forms:

I. What bearing, if any, have current ideologies upon the emergence, at various periods, of tragedy, and upon its characteristic quality?

[1] *Poetics*, XVIII, 7.   [2] *Ibid.*, XXII, 1.   [3] *Ibid.*, XXIV, 10.   [4] *Ibid.*, XXV, 8.

II. What is the connection of rhetoric (in the true sense) with the tragic emotion; bearing in mind the modified attitudes towards rhetoric which can be inferred from recent experiments in poetic tragedy? [1]

III. What light, if any, does modern psychology or anthropology throw on the problem of the response to tragedy: bearing in mind the corresponding psychological theories of the Greeks and Elizabethans? [2]

IV. What moral connections can still be maintained as tragic values? Or does tragedy, as Macneile Dixon would have it, 'turn on a different axis'?

V. What cultural background on the part of his readers or audience may now be demanded, imposed or inculcated by the tragic writer?

VI. How can tragedy, to-day, recover its traditional functions and values?

[1] I have in mind, Mr Eliot's explanations of the purpose and characteristics of his verse.
[2] We may instance both the Freudian interpretations (Ernst Jones), the 'archetypal' approaches (Maud Bodkin).

CHAPTER 2

Some Historic Solutions

> Tragedy, indeed, carried the thoughts into the mythologic world, in
> order to raise the emotions, the fears, and the hopes, which convince the
> inmost heart that their final cause is not to be discovered in the limits of mere
> mortal life, and forces us into a presentiment, however dim, of a state in
> which those struggles of inward free will with outward necessity, which
> form the true subject of the tragedian, shall be reconciled and solved.
>
> COLERIDGE ¹

IN the preceding chapter we suggested a number of the fundamental
problems concerning the nature of tragedy that appear to have been
raised by Aristotle. It is no part of the present purpose to attempt
an historical treatment of them; but in order to carry the discussion
further, it is convenient to summarize some of the interpretations that
have been put forward and which would command some measure of
assent (in whatever form) from dramatic critics to-day. In the pages
that follow the sections correspond to those under which the questions
in the preceding chapter were set out.

§ i

1. *Imitation.* There is no question of the word denoting a flat or
slavish copy. Any such hypothesis is disproved by the text of the
Poetics.[2] Admittedly Greek criticism of art as well as of drama has a
substratum of *vraisemblance* which approved accurate likenesses. A valuable test of portraiture was the recognitional element: 'Ah, that is he!'
But the Aristotelian meaning of the word is intricately connected with
the controversy between Plato and his pupil Aristotle. It is sufficient
for our purposes to note that in the phrase 'Art imitates nature', the
term *nature* implies (and assumes) the perception of an order, pattern,
or harmony in the universe, which the artist, in view of his particular
sensibility, and synthetic or magical power, is able to seize and to
express within the limits of the object of imitation. At the same time,

---

[1] *Lectures and Notes on Shakespeare*, p. 10.
[2] For detailed arguments on this point, see, e.g., Margoliouth, pp. 43-4; Butcher,
pp. 121-62; Lucas, pp. 14-17.

the overtones of the Greek *mimesis* are such that we should probably
require a complex symbol of this order to approximate to its meaning:

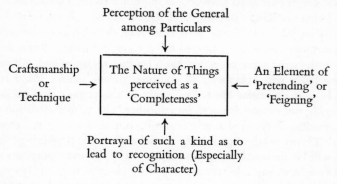

Perception of the General
among Particulars

Craftsmanship
or
Technique → The Nature of Things
perceived as a
'Completeness' ← An Element of
'Pretending' or
'Feigning'

Portrayal of such a kind as to
lead to recognition (Especially
of Character)

Imitation of an *Action*. The word Action is not defined except
through its qualities. It must have a beginning, a middle and an end;
conditions which Aristotle defines from a common-sense point of
view. The work, the play, existed in its own right, its structure following, by analogy, that of a vertebrate. The unity of an action does not
consist in the unity of the hero: e.g. the episodes of the *Odyssey* are
not, as a whole, a unity in virtue of having a hero in common. For the
moment, an *action* can be defined as the progress of an individual, with
his related or ancillary actors, from position A, one of temporary
stability, to position B; at which he either dies, or becomes involved in
an entirely new set of circumstances. We can agree with Fergusson [1]
that the term 'action' is an analogical concept, and can only be understood with reference to particular 'actions'. In its broadest sense it
would cover, not only the 'shape', 'rhythm' and duration of a sequence
of events, but its components in so far as these are separable into the
actions of individuals, their speech and characterization, and even the
dramatist's manipulation of the main action by his selection of
the setting as well as by his stage directions for it. [2] The power of the
dramatist to impose formal characteristics on the raw material is almost
unlimited.

The *beginning* of an action might thus be perceived as a sort of
momentary slack water before the turn of the tide. At the opening of
Hamlet there is every indication that, if it were not for the appearance

[1] *The Idea of a Theatre*, p. 230.
[2] Ibsen's work, particularly as studied by J. R. Northam in *Ibsen's Dramatic Technique*,
will illustrate this point.

of the Ghost, events in Denmark would have settled down into a
period of rest; Hamlet himself would have gone to Wittenberg, and
the kingdom enjoyed a period of tranquillity under a sufficiently wise
and judicious King. Events in *A Doll's House* are stimulated into
activity by the forged letter, now emerging, through a combination of
circumstances, from the past into the present and future. But it is clear
that in the strict sense no action has a beginning, or an end. All events
spring from past causation; all continue through time. 'Man is not
simply *in* a situation. He is "in" only in the respect that he is just
emerging out of one situation into another. The human situation consists *simultaneously* of what it is emerging out of and what it is moving
into.'[1] The methods of providing a link between the Beginning and the
Past will be discussed in the next chapter. For dramatic purposes there
is obvious a strong selective and rejecting element in the playwright's
'imitation'. An action in time is selected and reorganized in obedience
to whatever time-scale the dramatist may select. In the process incidents
may be transposed to provide the desired concentration; the whole will
be re-focused in terms of the dramatist's personality and tradition, the
resources of his theatre and actors, and the spirit as well as the problems
of his age.[2] He must establish a definite relationship between past and
present; a relationship which (we may suspect) has itself the peculiar
dream-like qualities of which we are conscious when we attempt to
analyse this relationship in our own lives. This dream-like aspect
appears to have some bearing on the use that is made of various aspects
of the supernatural.

'Imitation of an Action that is *Serious*.' Endless controversy has
ranged round this word. It is best translated as *something that matters*,
concerned with important values and hence of a permanent character;
as opposed to what is slight, trivial, transitory, or of the surface. But it
should not be limited to Matthew Arnold's *high seriousness*, *high and
excellent seriousness*, as suggesting Jahveistic, stoic, 'sublime' or 'grand
style' values. Eighteenth-century criticism, with a background of
Poussin, Salvator Rosa and Milton, made the same kind of mistake
over 'Longinus' and his sublime.

'. . . Serious, complete and of a certain magnitude.' *Complete* demands
a discussion of the nature of finality, and the dramatic value of death as
a terminal point. *A certain magnitude* is again defined qualitatively: the

---

[1] P. Wheelwright, *Sewanee Review*, Winter, 1953 (p. 58): quoting Julián Marías.
[2] e.g. the important social and political questions that underly Greek and Elizabethan
drama.

'larger the better, provided that the whole be *perspicuous*'. This per-
spicuousness, a capacity for adequate communication and integration
of the artistic experience, remains a standard criterion; on which
centres, for example, much of the controversy over Shaw's *Back to
Methuselah*. In general, it seems as if this magnitude may be determined
partly by physiological necessity, partly by an empirically-ascertained
norm beyond which the audience's attention cannot be satisfactorily
held, and partly by sheer force of custom which has set up a standard
'expectation' for the length of a play.

There is, however, another consideration; that of the length of play
which is necessary to build up what we may call the tragic momentum.
This momentum appears to require the following conditions:

1. Unless the characters of the protagonists are sufficiently established
   in the known fable there must be sufficient length of development
   in order to enlist the sympathy and interest of the audience.
2. With the same exception the plot-pattern must be sufficiently long
   to produce the impression of a full, and sufficiently complex,
   pattern in operation.
3. The establishment of *depth*, whether through chorus, sub-plot,
   symbolism or language, appears to demand a certain amount of
   space to produce its effect; often by liturgical or repetitive
   methods.

It is a debatable question how far a miniature tragedy of the type of
Riders to the Sea can achieve momentum. The lack of it is possibly to
blame for the comparative failure of Maeterlinck's work, though the
extreme subtlety of his medium and his technique of inference from
the unspoken, is perhaps unfitted, in any event, to the normal theatre.

§ *ii*

. . . through pity and fear effecting the proper purgation of these emotions.[1]
. . . indirectly through pity and terror righting mental disorders of this type.[2]

It seems arguable that the preferable translation is *of this type* or *of these
and such-like emotions*. This is, perhaps, the most discussed sentence in
the *Poetics*, and a starting point for most aesthetic speculations. Margoliouth quotes from the *Politics* of Aristotle.[3]

The ailment which befalls some minds severely is to be found in all, only
differing in intensity; viz. pity, fear and religious excitment: for to this last

---

[1] Butcher transl.   [2] Margoliouth transl.   [3] *Op. cit.*, p. 57.

ailment, too, some are liable; and we see that these persons when treated with the melodies which ordinarily excite the mind orgiastically *kathistamenoi* as though they had undergone the medical operation called *katharsis*. The same must be possible with the pitiful, the timid, and in general the emotional, viz. there must be some pleasurable mode of *katharsis*, i.e. being relieved, for all.

Now *katharsis* is a medico-psychological term, implying a homoeopathic treatment. Galen describes it as 'qualitative evacuation of what is troublesome'. A regular cure for madness was purgation by vapour baths and hellebore.[1] Excess of heat or cold in the black bile is the cause of depression and fear. Tragedy appears to be the purgative remedy against excessive cold; the external chill drives out the internal cause of the malady.[2]

Before going a stage further it is well to recall certain aspects of the Greek temperament. What evidence we possess suggests that the response to tragedy was violent in the extreme. It was in part a religious ritual; the chant and dance of the Chorus contained an element of stimulation to a state of ecstasy which requires the utmost imaginative effort to recapture now.[3] Kitto reminds us of what many readers of Greek drama are apt to forget:

> The doctrine of the Mean is characteristically Greek, but it should not tempt us to think that the Greek was one who was hardly aware of the passions, a safe, anaesthetic, middle-of-the-road man. On the contrary, he valued the Mean so highly because he was prone to the extremes. . . . He sought control and balance because he needed them; he knew the extremes only too well. When he spoke of the Mean, the thought of the tuned string was never very far from his mind. The Mean did not imply the absence of tension and lack of passion, but the correct tension which gives out the true and clear note.[4]

The term *fear* is apt to be somewhat blurred in meaning because of the Aristotelian linkage with pity. Aristotle in the *Ethics* speaks of the 'nobility of fear'. We may distinguish the following kinds:

1. Fear or *Angst*, centred on the individual, in the form of a vague

---

[1] Margoliouth, *op. cit.*, p. 58.
[2] Cf. Browning, *Aristophanes' Apology*:
> 'The warm spring, traveller, dip thine arms into,
> Brighten thy brow with! Life detests black cold!'

[3] Yeats's insistence on the value of the dance in his miniature plays, and the purity of its communication, is of interest here.
[4] H. D. F. Kitto, *The Greeks*, p. 252. This 'correct tension' may be thought of in connection with I. A. Richards's view of the 'balance' resulting from the aesthetic experience. See pp. 14, 90, *infra*.

general anxiety as to future security. This is perhaps the commonest source of neurotic states.

2. Fear which arises out of disinterested concern for relatives or friends; or in certain cases, for a society or state.

3. Fear which arises out of confrontation with

   (a) events which contain an element of the inexplicable, such as the supra-natural. This includes the element of the numinous. 'A spirit passed before my face, and the hair of my flesh stood up.'

   (b) events (such as ruin or destruction) perceived as awe-ful in themselves, probably without specific reference (other than that of *scale*) to ourselves.

4. Fear which arises out of the recognition, in ourselves, of guilt or sin, which we perceive in the actions of others and equate in some manner with our own. Questions of the *origins* of guilt or sin, or of present or future judgement, are for the moment irrelevant.

It seems clear that one or more of these kinds can exist simultaneously in the response to tragedy. As regards pity, an interesting and profitable definition—but one which is a great deal less than Christian—is Bergson's:

> True pity consists not so much in fearing suffering as desiring it. The desire is a faint one, and we should hardly wish to see it realized; yet we form it in spite of ourselves, as if Nature were committing some great injustice and it were necessary to get rid of all suspicion of complicity with her.[1]

At the same time Bergson carries the development of this emotion through a series of stages: from repugnance to fear, from fear to sympathy, and from sympathy itself to humility. The increasing intensity of pity thus consists in a qualitative process. The final stage may be thought of as containing some element of the perception of scale; humility experienced as a result of comparisons, implicit or explicit, with the emotions of the spectator. On the other hand, it should be remembered that Kierkegaard regards pity as a form of contempt; and while admitting that this may be so, on occasion, we must again regard it as 'impure' form, utterly removed from the idea of the Christian *caritas*.

At this stage it is desirable to attempt to summarize the main interpretations that have been placed on *katharsis*.

[1] *Time and Free Will*, transl. F. L. Pogson, p. 19.

A. The 'Joyful Safety' Theory, as stated by Freytag.[1]

The spectator's tears flow more easily and his mouth twitches more readily than in ordinary life; yet this pain is accompanied with a vigorous sense of pleasure;—after the fall of the curtain, in spite of the effort of attending for hours,(!) he feels an intensification of vital power, his eye sparkles, his step is elastic, every movement is firm and free. His agitation has been succeeded by a feeling of joyful safety.

Part of this description is summed up in a cruder formulation: 'There but for the Grace of God go I.'

B. The Theory of Balanced Forces: best summarized by I. A. Richards, and consonant with his aesthetic theory. In brief, Pity is the impulse to advance, Fear is the impulse to retreat. When both are experienced a system of balance replaces the existing emotional excess. This theory is attractive, but breaks down as soon as we admit into the tragic range emotions other than Pity and Fear. And I think they must be so admitted. At the same time, Richards appears to be ready to admit a wider range provided that these two emotions remain as dominants.

The extraordinarily stable experience of Tragedy, which is capable of admitting almost any other impulses so long as the relation of the main components is exactly right, changes at once if these are altered. . . . Tragedy is perhaps the most general, all-accepting, all-ordering experience known . . . It is invulnerable; there is nothing which does not present to the tragic attitude *when fully developed* a fitting aspect and only a fitting aspect.[2]

Richards's whole account of the tragic response is of great importance, and we shall return to it later.

C. James Joyce's Theory has connection with that of Richards, but is a philosophical rather than a psychological formulation.

Pity is the feeling which arrests the mind in the presence of whatsoever is grave and constant in human sufferings and unites it with the human sufferer.[3]

Terror is the feeling which arrests the mind in the presence of whatsoever is grave and constant in human sufferings and unites it with the secret cause.

---

[1] *Teknik des Dramas.* Quoted Margoliouth, *op. cit.,* pp. 154–5.
[2] *Principles of Literary Criticism,* p. 247.
[3] We may compare with this Miguel de Unamuno: 'For to love is to pity; and if bodies are united by pleasure, souls are united by pain.' *The Tragic Sense of Life,* p. 135.

The tragic emotion, in fact, is a face looking two ways, towards terror and towards pity, both of which are phases of it. You see I used the word *arrest*. I mean the tragic emotion is static. Or rather the dramatic emotion is. The feelings excited by improper art are kinetic, desire or loathing. Desire urges us to possess, to go to something; loathing urges us to abandon, to go from something. The arts which excite them, pornographical or didactic, are therefore improper arts. The aesthetic emotion (I used the general term) is therefore static. The mind is arrested and raised above desire and loathing.[1]

D. The 'Inoculation' Theory: that is, that tragedy provides small and harmless doses of passions which can be indulged in harmlessly in the theatre, whereas they might become dangerous obsessions in the world of reality. As a variant of this, tragedy may be seen as a kind of ritual prophylaxis. If we enact the evil thing often enough, it will not happen.

E. The 'Reduction to Scale' Theory: the spectator, witnessing large-scale suffering and catastrophes on the stage, is made aware of the tiny scale of his own emotions, and hence perceives them in proportion. The best-known formulation is in Browning's *Aristophanes' Apology*:

> Small rebuked by large
> We felt our puny hates refine to air,
> Our prides as poor prevent the humbling hand,
> Our petty passion purify its tide.

This is, in many ways, an attractive solution, and one to which individual experience lends some support. At the conclusion of a tragedy which has produced a full response we seem momentarily stunned, and often desire to be peaceful and silent for a time. A complex readjustment of values seems to take place. In particular, there is a tendency to modify the leaning towards self-pity, or vanity, which no doubt Aristotle would have included among the 'vicious' emotions. We have been enabled to see ourselves as individuals in proportion against a larger pattern. A similar therapeutic value is found in mountaineering, sailing, and such occupations which confront man with the immense, the permanent, the fearful. 'Fear is God's Grace.'

F. Sadistic-Masochistic Theories ⎫ These are considered in a sub-
G. The Schadenfreude Theory   ⎬ sequent chapter, *The Shadow*
                                ⎭ *of the Pleasure.*

[1] *A Portrait of the Artist* (1924), pp. 232–3.

H. Myth-Ritual Theories   These are also considered in the
chapter of that title.

J. The theory which I shall call Lucas's Theory. It is given as the
conclusion of Chapter II of his *Tragedy*.[1] I have selected certain
sentences in an attempt to state his case.

> The function of tragedy is simply and solely to give a certain sort
> of pleasure, to satisfy in certain ways our love of beauty and of truth,
> of truth to life and about it.[2]

> Life is fascinating to watch, whatever it may be to experience. And
> so we go to tragedies not in the least to get rid of emotions, but to
> have them more abundantly; to banquet, not to purge.[3]

> To be 'tragic', however, the experience must have in addition a
> certain peculiar quality—'must', not for moral or philosophical
> reasons, but because if the experience were not of that kind, we should
> use a different word for it. It is a matter of vocabulary, not of meta-
> physics. Some other forms of Art may be merely beautiful; by
> Tragedy, I think, we imply also something fundamentally true to life.
> It need not be the whole truth, but it must be true.[4]

> It is dangerous to generalize too precisely about the spirit of
> tragedy; but we can say that there the problem of evil and suffering
> is set before us; often it is not answered, but always there is something
> that makes it endurable.[5]

Now we may agree with Lucas's remarks in their entirety without
necessarily holding that there *is* no kathartic effect. The fact that the
achieving of such an effect was neither the overt intention of the
dramatist, nor the object of the spectator in going to the theatre, is
irrelevant to the consideration of what the response may be, whether
historically, or in the present. As in so many instances the response is
certain to be highly complex;[6] it may well contain elements of most of
the explanations offered above. Nor is Lucas's view so divergent from
the tradition as at first appears. If we banquet on emotions—the image
of that and of the alternative purge is not quite applicable—we shall

---

[1] Hogarth Press, 1927. I am indebted, as every writer on the subject must be, to the
scholarship and sanity of this book.
[2] *Ibid.*, p. 51.   [3] *Ibid.*, p. 52.   [4] *Ibid.*, pp. 52–3.
[5] *Ibid.*, pp. 56–7. This view suggests a modification of Stoicism.
[6] 'When we respond to *Hamlet* or *Lear*, countless emotions are embodied in the
aesthetic impression which the tragic developments of these plays make upon us. These
emotions do not arise directly out of the Tragic as such, but are part of the whole tragic
impression . . .' Volkelt, *Aesthetik des Tragischen*, p. 268.

presumably exhaust our capacity or appetite for such emotions, for some time at least.[1]

A further discussion of the pleasure-aspect is reserved for a subsequent chapter.

There is one word in the quotation from the *Politics* [2] which has received little attention. Aristotle speaks of emotions being purged *orgiastically*. The implication is that of a violent spasm or shock reaction: not unlike the various kinds of shock treatment now employed in psychotherapy. We need not presuppose that such a spasm will always be evident in the theatre, as it was among the women who viewed the performance of the *Eumenides*. But it is possible that there may be some sudden recognition, among the audience as on the stage, that amounts to a complete reorientation of personality through powerful emotional shock. Some analogy with this orgiastic 'shock' may be found in modern electrical or insulin treatment for depressive disorders. Among the results we find an obliteration of memory in so far as it relates to the period leading up to the illness, and an emotional exhaustion which passes slowly. The mind is then ready to receive fresh perceptions, and to readjust them in a new pattern of values.

§ *iii*

Aristotle stresses repeatedly the importance of plot. The Greek dramatist, working on a known fable, selected and re-timed the progress of his protagonists between Points A and B. The plot is the railway-line over which the trucks pass. Those trucks may be, in theory, empty; hence Aristotle's peculiar statement that there may be a plot without Character, a dictum to which no critic would subscribe to-day.

There are certain commonplaces to note at the outset. The characters in a Greek drama are far more definitely 'fixed' as typical figures, both because of the nearness of their sources, the conventions of the stage,[3] and the selection of the action at its point of ripeness: which left little room to show character-development by its reaction to a wide range of circumstances. Further, if the classical drama had included character delineation on any intricate scale, it would have tended to obscure the clear-cut issues raised by the plot. In other words, the enclosing net is more strictly defined; the amount of freewill given is minimized in

---

[1] Dame Sybil Thorndike has said that she never slept so well as when she was playing in Grand Guignol.
[2] p. 11, *supra*.
[3] Notably the religious character of the whole performance, the masked actors, and the presence of the Chorus.

3

comparison with the *illusion* of freedom, which the five-act Elizabethan form can give.

The relationship between Plot and Character is one of the most
fascinating aspects of dramatic history. To-day we regard them as far
more closely interwoven than Aristotle would have done, since we do
not admit the possibility of a 'good' man engaging in evil actions, or
the reverse. Further, we are divided as to the possibility of belief in
the classic concept of temperament, the natural endowments of personality, and character as the modification of temperament by the
will, or by virtue, or perhaps by the Christian concept of grace. It is
in fact a species of fatalism, or at worst a line of defence, to fall back
on temperament as determined by heredity and environment to explain the evil that we do, or even to exculpate ourselves from responsibility. In this respect it is important to remember the Elizabethan
concern, in terms of their psychology, with types who were tempera-
mentally prone to psychological aberrations (e.g. the Jealous, the
Wrathful, the Choleric) and whose failure to achieve a balance through
the cultivation of virtue is a precipitating cause of catastrophe.[1]

§ *iv*

Reversal and Recognition. These are the leading tests, in Aristotle's
view, of the dramatist's artistic competence: they are, primarily, the
results of his skill in re-timing and reorganizing of the plot. The
reversal arises when the action which we take to safeguard ourselves
betrays us and brings about our downfall. The recognition comes when
we realize how we have been deluded (this is the mental kind); or
when in a physical demonstration, we recognize by material evidence
that a thing is so. In the one case there is an awakening from the 'strong
delusion' that has brought us to belief in the lie; in the second, a physical
event produces a specific kind of knowledge.[2]

Now there are three ways in which a man comes to misfortune:

(a) By the action of his enemies. This is not tragic, for he should have
been forewarned against them.[3] (There is a limited sense in which
ignorance may produce a slight flavour of tragedy: as when, for

---

[1] See, e.g., L. B. Campbell's *Shakespeare's Tragic Heroes*, and R. L. Anderson, *Elizabethan
Psychology and Shakespeare's Plays.*

[2] As, for example, the lock of hair on the tomb in the *Choephoroë*, by which Elektra
recognizes her brother.

[3] He may, however, if his enemies are those of his state, be left without possibility
of defence or evasion.

example, a peaceful and respected king is murdered by a madman, under circumstances which could not have been foreseen.)

(*b*) By sheer chance. This is not in itself tragic, though popular
usage tries to make it so. (On the other hand, chance may
shade into some form of pattern, Aristotle's 'air of design'; particularly through such repetition as Hardy uses in his novels and
short stories.[1])

(*c*) By the action which we take to safeguard ourselves, or to ensure
that we pursue a particular course of action without danger to
ourselves or to others.

§ *v*

The *length* of the plot. No one can quarrel with Aristotle's demand
for perspicuity in the drama; though we may note that Elizabethan
practice appears at times to work toward a deliberate sense of confusion, often suggesting a corresponding response to the events taking
place on the stage. (Certain critics of *King Lear* and of *Antony and
Cleopatra* stress this aspect of these plays). His idea of *magnitude* probably has religious and ethical overtones, quite apart from the question
of the plot-dimensions.

Of modern drama we can say that

1. It appears to demand a certain length in order to bring the Past
   into alignment with the Present, for the purpose of developing
   both.
2. A certain element of preparation is necessary before the audience
   can warm up to 'the willing suspension of disbelief'.
3. Sympathy with the characters, and understanding of them, cannot
   be built up rapidly, since the lights must be turned on them from
   different angles.
4. Reversal and recognition are definite points in a dramatic rhythm.
   The plot cannot be hurried if the formal qualities of structure are
   to be perceived in their microcosmic significance.[2]

The exceptions are perhaps to be found when

1. The groundwork of the plot is so simple, or so familiar, as to
   demand little exploration.
2. The action proceeds so rapidly, and is so much more important
   than the character, that no development of the latter need take
   place.

---

[1] The problem of the admissibility of chance is discussed later.   [2] See Chapter 3.

In theory, these conditions are fulfilled when a plot is taken at its climax. But in general it seems as if the momentum which gives the full illusion requires the conventional length; which is partly the product of custom, partly (we may suspect) the result of physical and psychological limitations.

§ vi

One action and that a whole. No action can be said, speaking accurately, to have initial and terminal points; nor, it is suggested, can any action be completely isolated in time and space. Perhaps the best image is that of a funnel or cone, representing the notional limits of the action. Within the cone, the separate threads of the action progress; Past meeting the Present, coalescing with it, a number of separate plot strands converging and narrowing to the end. I shall suggest later that it is the character of the *end* which gives the plot its distinctive quality of a symmetrical narrowing or focusing; and that the *end* in its turn is present in the structure, language, and imagery of the play.

§ vii

A more philosophical and a higher thing than history; for poetry tends to express the universal, history the particular.

This sentence is the nucleus, as it were, of an infinity of controversy:[1] not only as to the qualities and function of drama, but those of poetry in general. It interlocks with other statements in the *Poetics* as part of the general refutation of the Platonic propositions that poetry is twice removed from reality.

I do not wish to recapitulate the historical arguments that have centred on this passage. On it hang the 'golden world' of Sir Philip Sidney, the many definitions on 'Nature' in Augustan literary theory, the metaphysics of Coleridge. It is sufficient to point out two things. The term 'a more philosophical and a higher thing'—φιλοσοφώτερον και σπουδαιότερον should be taken as relating to the poetic statement of those elements in the past, as re-presented by the dramatist, which can be shown in a significant relationship to the present and future. For if Epic, Myth, Fable or History, representing as they did the religious and cultural heritage of the Greeks, were a living and continuous force in the present, the business of the dramatist was to communicate them so that, in the pattern of their interrelationships,

---

[1] An admirable historical consideration is to be found in J. Bronowski's *The Poet's Defence*.

they formed as it were components or facets of a total sum of *wisdom*. Poetry was not to be moulded into any formal philosophy; since a connected framework of beliefs belonged to others. It was only to be *more philosophical* than history: 'history' being perceived—quite wrongly, but understandably for the purpose of the argument—as the record of *fact*. It was to be a 'higher' thing—more intense, more significant—partly because its object was to impart this wisdom, partly because poetry could excise the trivial or superfluous detail perceived in the flat mirror of history. In all its functions the traditional manner and materials supported this activity. The myth or fable could often be seen in a certain perspective as concerning political or social problems in contemporary Athens. The disorders of the State could be perceived as mirrored in a past event, and achieve a certain scale or dignity, or even a solution, by that comparison. (We may consider, as some kind of parallel, the significance of *Richard II* in 1601, the interest in that play and in *Richard of Bordeaux* at the time of the abdication of King Edward VIII, the relevance of *Julius Caesar* to the régime of Mussolini.) Reference to the past, by myth, epic, genealogy, and by genealogical or geographical synonyms, was rich and continuous. In such a context Aristotle's statement is clear.

This concern with a world in transition, the attempt to relate past and present, appears to be a continuing aspect of tragedy.

§ *viii*

. . . *What has happened is manifestly possible, otherwise it would not have happened.*

In the *Poetics* the apparent glimpses of the obvious are always worth considering. The adherence of the Greeks to the material of myth, fable, epic and ballad gave a particular sanction, weight and foreknowledge to the whole structure of the drama. Any miraculous or supernatural events, if they *had* happened, were possible. In our own time we can note one kind of advantage enjoyed by writers using religious or Biblical subjects, and the varying degrees of success achieved by, say, *Murder in the Cathedral* compared with John Drinkwater's *Abraham Lincoln*. There are probably advantages in using material so well known, yet so inaccurately chronicled, that liberties may be taken with regard to the plot without any sense of misuse of holy writ.

It is also enlightening to compare the Greek attitude to the Homeric legends, with, say, the Elizabethan attitude to Holinshed or Plutarch. *Antony and Cleopatra* stands as a story familiar in broad outline to the audience, but which lent itself to alteration in a variety of ways without any sense of distress to them. A fable which has a vague popular basis probably offers the best prospects to the dramatist; the story has popular sanction, is received unhesitatingly as having happened; yet is not too intractable to be remoulded completely.

In the circumstances, it is surprising that there are so few good historical tragedies, and such an inordinate number of bad ones; though the badness can often be explained—as in the work of the Romantic Movement—by a slavish adherence to the Elizabethan-Jacobean form, and to an archaic technique which was utterly alien to contemporary thought.

§ ix

Of all plots the epeisodic are the worst.

The epeisodic plot is one composed of fortuitous incidents which do not conform, as a composite whole, to any coherent pattern. In order to achieve this coherence the sequence must be 'necessary' or 'probable'. Events are classified under four groups:

1. The necessary.
2. The probable.
3. The improbable but possible.
4. The impossible.

—according as they happen always, generally, occasionally, or never.

Now the *necessary* can always be accounted for, either in terms of the fulfilment of a prophecy, or in a tragedy which adheres strictly either to past history, or to fable accepted by the audience as historical; 'for what has happened is credible, otherwise it would not have happened'. Both *Oedipus* and *Julius Caesar* have their firm roots in history; though Thornton Wilder's introduction to *The Ides of March* shows the foreshortening in time that was necessary for the purposes of that ingenious plot.

The *probable* can be surmised; given the initial factors and some information as to the Past-Present relationship at the outset of the play. Both the *necessary* and the *probable* imply that the scheme of events can be reduced to an intelligible system. Coleridge noted that Shakespeare's greatness lay, in part, in his use of expectation in preference to surprise.

The *improbable but possible*, and the *impossible*, are grouped together in opposition to the first two types of events. They are τὸ ἄλογον, the illogical or irrational element in things. But the *improbable possible* is so important in the structure of tragedy as to require discussion.

§ *x*

The place of accident in tragedy.

We can say in general that accident is admissible in tragedy, and indeed in all drama, under the following conditions:

(*a*) Provided it is used as an accelerating, and not a determining factor: that is, if a given situation would arise out of given characters and plot, but later rather than sooner, then it is legitimate to make use of chance to bring the particular situation within the time-place scale of the play.

(*b*) Provided it is used in conformity with a recognizable rhythm in the play: that is, if the 'coincidences have an air of design'. This design usually produces the impression of outside powers taking a hand in the game. The star-crossed lovers in *Romeo and Juliet* remain star-crossed till the end; so that the various malignant coincidences are, as it were, awaited by the audience. The Elizabethan and Jacobean practice of supplying sub-titles to amplify the plays may have emphasized this expectation.

(*c*) Provided the dramatist can disguise, or gloss over, the improbability of the event. The classical instance of this is Hamlet and the pirate-ship.

Thomas Rymer is known for his perversity as a Shakespearian critic, but his remarks on the dropping of Desdemona's handkerchief will serve to illustrate the different uses of accident. Rymer attacks the whole incident; why is so remote a trifle given so important a function? Presumably there is a moral connected with it. 'This may be a warning to all good wives, that they may look to their linen.' The jest, to the Restoration reader, is sufficiently apparent; but the various functions of the handkerchief are of some interest.

As it stands in the play, we may regard it as an accelerating factor in the plot. Given the plot and characters, the handkerchief merely brings matters to a head. It serves to precipitate Othello's jealous seizure; it also shows Desdemona another side of her husband's barbaric superstition—the only way of accounting for the value he places upon it—and this leaves Desdemona still more bewildered and more incapable than ever of dealing rationally with the whole situation.

But we can imagine other situations; one in which the dropping of the handkerchief and its recovery provided the sole motive for Othello's jealousy. In this case it would be pure and, dramatically speaking, unjustified accident.

Alternatively, Desdemona's enemies might have noticed in her an innate carelessness, manifested in the tendency to lose handkerchiefs; a failing symptomatic of a levity, perhaps, akin to that of Milton's Eve; a tragic flaw perhaps to be compared with Cordelia's tactlessness. To her enemies, then, the loss of the handkerchief would have appeared a likely accident, and Rymer's criticism would have contained a shadow of truth.

We can imagine also a situation in which Desdemona is aware from the outset of the magical properties of the handkerchief, as a pledge of faithfulness. In such a case it would have acquired a high symbolic value, preparing the minds of the audience for the tragic consequences of its loss.

As a further case we can imagine some oracular doom pronounced on Desdemona's life which had warned her to beware of handkerchiefs. She had, in spite of the curse, accepted the gift against her own judgement. It therefore became heavy with destiny, and its loss a prelude to catastrophe.

In any of these cases we are removed from the realms of accident into those of the necessary and probable.

§ *xi*

The Flaw. Aristotle has eliminated the non-tragic cases: it remains to consider what he means by *error* or *frailty*.

Macneile Dixon is typically frank:

> 'Whether it means a moral or intellectual error, of the heart or head, no one has yet discovered . . .'

As a short answer I suggest that it may be, in different tragedies, either; or both combined.[1] Consider first some of the explanations.

(a) As applied to a single act, it denotes an error due to inadequate knowledge of particular circumstances.[2] These circumstances are, strictly, such as might have been known. This kind of error introduces an element of guilt; as, for example, when a military commander chooses to disregard the intelligence available to him.

(b) As applied to unavoidable ignorance, or 'misfortune'.[3] In these

[1] Both moral and intellectual error appear to be involved in *Oedipus*.
[2] Butcher, *Aristotle's Theory of Poetic and Fine Art*, pp. 317–18.   [3] *Ibid.*, p. 318.

cases the error is blind; and raises the secondary question; how far the individual is to be held responsible for his ignorance. A consideration of the ignorance of Othello suggests that we are driven back from this point into psychological assessments of character, race and environment; and thence to problems which involve psychology and criminology.

(c) The fault or error where the act is conscious and intellectual but not deliberate.[1] This suggests at once the moral questions raised by, e.g., *crime passionnel.*

(d) A defect of character proper;[2] the joint in the harness, the vulnerable spot in the body; the flaw which is not in itself vicious, and which will only become vulnerable and destructive through the 'unfortunate' setting of the tragedy. The matter is not simplified for the modern reader by the absence in Greek thought of anything approaching the Christian doctrine of intention, though it is true that a clear-cut distinction exists between culpable and innocent ignorance.[3] But the fact—what had happened, and was credible, otherwise it would not have happened—was part of the pattern of things, of the inevitable structure of events. The doer must suffer. It is true that the full rigour of retribution may be averted by the god from the machine, or by vicarious sacrifices; but this compromise appears alien to the full tragic response.

Some further developments of the tragic character are suggested in the chapters—*The Ethical Problem* and *Let Man's Soule be a Spheare.*

[1] *Ibid.*, p. 319.　　　　　　　　　　　[2] *Ibid.*, p. 319.
[3] Sikes, *The Greek View of Poetry*, p. 141, quoting *Ethics*, N. iii, 2.

CHAPTER 3

The Structure of Tragedy

Memory and imagination give the past and future a shape; contemplative awareness of them reduces their power over us—or at any rate over that part which matters most. Thus metaphorically we can say that human existence, so far as we live it on the human level, is an interweaving not only of moment with moment, but of the transiency of moments with the permanency of that which sustains us in their passage.

WHEELWRIGHT [1]

Given a description of an isolated part of the physical universe in the most complete terms that have physical meaning, that is, down to the smallest elements of which our physical operations give us cognizance, then the future history of the system is determined within a growing penumbra of uncertainty, this penumbra growing broader as we penetrate to finer details of the structure of the system or as time goes on, until eventually all but certain very general properties of the original system, such as its total energy, are forever lost in the haze, and we have a system which was unpredictable.

P. W. BRIDGEMAN [2]

IF we accept this first statement provisionally, as a definition, we have to consider a sequence of events in space and time, isolated from the past except in so far as the dramatist desires to show a connection with the past, and terminated upon an object which is perceived as a convergent point of that sequence and of its ancillary sequences. Such actions are confined within a formal space-time framework. While the framework has definite aesthetic qualities, and can be shown to possess qualities for which the light and shade, massing and colour, of a picture provide the roughest of analogies, it is never susceptible of satisfactory analysis. In its specific quality of an action subjected to the process of imitation it must possess the attribute of completeness or wholeness which the latter term implies.

In this system the unity of action, which is the only unity that Aristotle postulates as a law of tragedy, is felt rather than perceived; not as something peculiar to tragedy, but an essential of all aesthetic form. ' "Unity of action" is not properly a rule, but in itself the great end, not only of the drama, but of the epic, lyric, even to the candle-flame of an epigram—not only of poetry, but of poesy in general, as

[1] *The Burning Fountain*, p. 11.   [2] *The Logic of Modern Physics*, p. 210.

the proper generic term inclusive of all the fine arts, as its species.'[1] In the *Poetics* it is defined negatively: it does not consist in the Unity of the Hero. It is recognizable in the manner by which the action is artistically completed, even though that completion can have only an aesthetic validity. Within its peculiar form, elements which are apparently discordant or incongruous can be seen to be coexistent with the unity of action; provided that they can be perceived, at some stage during the tragedy, or even after its conclusion, as subserving a single specific end. In rare instances they may juxtapose a number of discrete or heterogeneous experiences or images in such a manner that they can be seen to illustrate a common thesis or idea. In certain tragedies, as we shall suggest later, the heterogeneous can be carried to a point where the Irrational must be perceived as an aspect of the 'imitation'.

Any such sequence or system will rely to a greater or less extent on the events preceding it. The implication of the past in the present will vary directly in accordance with the dramatist's stage tradition and his mechanical resources, and the conditions that differentiate, say, the Greek from the Elizabethan drama in this respect are commonplaces of dramatic criticism. What is, perhaps, less frequently stressed is the bearing of the past-present relationship on the metaphysical content of tragedy. It is probably true to say that the greater the proportion of 'past' that is allowed to impinge upon, or to modify, the present, the easier it is to give the impression of a rigid or semi-rigid structure enclosing the action, and the larger the apparent content of determinism. Where the past is common property, as in mythology or religion or the better-known historical events, it has, paradoxically, a number of apparently contradictory effects. While it frees the dramatist from the need for extended exposition, it gives less play to his protagonists in their relationships. The common symbols which he uses may liberate the imagination of his audience; but unless his use of them is both subtle and arresting he will run the risk of a failure of communication. If he wishes to present a deterministic pattern—with whatever modifications, such as might be found in a spiral rather than in a repetitional interpretation of history—he will show the past linked to, or dependent from, the continuous present of the play. Such technique is common in Ibsen's plays.

If it then be accepted, for the moment, that the basis of tragedy is an action, a sequence of events in time related to an object, or complex of objects, which is capable of being perceived as a termination of that

[1] Coleridge: *cit.* Francis Fergusson, *The Idea of a Theatre*, p. 4.

particular sequence, the problem of the tragic playwright would appear to be to refract, condense, and reorganize that experience in accordance with certain empirical laws. The method of the reorganization will depend on the limitations of the theatre for which it is designed, the crudities inherent in the communication by the spoken word, and the particular intention of the dramatist. This last, again, is probably highly complicated; in its simplest form it may be Tendenz-drama (such as that of Hauptmann), religious or pseudo-religious, or mere entertainment-pleasure; though this will in turn become 'impure' under the stimulus of the poetic excitement, the 'inspiration', which is fired by the frictions set up in the structural hinges of the tragedy.

To symbolize this structure we can modify such well-known figures as the isosceles triangle of Freytag's Cone into the upper half of an oval figure,[1] so that the 'action' can be conceived as curvilinear. It is, almost certainly, perceived in relation to a norm, implicit or explicit in the tragedy; and the norm is often conveyed by such characters as Kent, Enobarbus or Horatio, or in a more subtle manner by Ranke of *A Doll's House*. In the lower half of the oval we may sometimes perceive a complementary, or counterpointing, curve or curves; in its simplest form that of a sub-plot, giving depth and meaning to the upper curve; and presenting at its most involved the symbols and imagery which serve—among other ends—to produce this particular effect.

We are then left to consider the two terminal points of our schematic oval or perhaps egg-shaped figure. At first sight its end presents no particular difficulty, though we shall find later that the conventional aspects of the 'end' involve certain assumptions about, or attitudes towards, the nature of death. The 'beginning', however, must be a point which at first sight appears arbitrary. For example, it may seem natural to question, as did Gordon Bottomley,[2] what train of events preceded the strange and violent openings of *Lear*, or of *Othello*: the Messenger or the Watchman of Greek Drama have much to tell in a manner which may appear to be tedious, but which has in fact important epic and ritualistic aspects in relation to the antecedent action and its national implications. These aspects are shared by the audience as intimately as the audience of *Henry V* may be thought of as sharing the glory of Agincourt.[3] We may be confronted with the need to interpret plays in altogether differing ways according as to whether we take

---

[1] Cf. 'Bergson's theory that a concept of time, as distinguished from pure experience of it is, always built on a space-like model.' (Philip Wheelwright, *Sewanee Review*, LXI, 1, p. 58.)

[2] In the play *King Lear's Wife*.   [3] As well as the topical interest of Essex' expedition.

them singly or as components of a trilogy. There is no action that may not be seen to start *ab ovo*, traced back and back to its origins. In what sense, then, is there a 'beginning'?

We may suppose, for convenience, a universe in which the stream of events, though in reality continuous, is apprehended as falling into groups. This process is familiar to the historian. Events tend to group themselves in clusters, time-sequences in which the seriousness of the issues arising from them appear to be intensified. The history of the House of Atreus, of Coriolanus, or of Rosmer shows such a grouping, and the 'beginning' appears to be the point at which the wheel has momentarily slowed down preparatory to an acceleration under the impact of some unforeseen stimulus, the fall of Troy or the coming of a ghost.

The conical or pyramidal development of complication, crisis, and resolution, familiar in all expositions of dramatic theory, appears to be, generally speaking, valid, though it must be interpreted in different minor curves for each play. The 'action' is scaled down, reorganized, re-timed into the plot; which must undertake, more or less simultaneously, three tasks.

1. It must reveal the effect and pressure of the past upon the present and future. But it must not do this with too palpable a design. Nietzsche has put the matter forcefully: 'The Aeschyleo-Sophoclean tragedy employed the most ingenious devices in the first scenes to place in the hands of the spectators as if by chance all the threads requisite for understanding the whole: a trait in which that noble artistry is approved, which as it were 'masks the *inevitably* formal, and causes it to appear as something accidental'.[1]
2. It must establish the characters in a relationship, first of potential and then of actual conflict or tension.
3. It must show in this conflict a rhythm,[2] which in turn probably has these aspects:
   (*a*) the recognition of the similarity of the rhythm either to an

---

[1] *The Birth of Tragedy*, p. 99.
[2] There are clearly aspects of rhythm and of structure in drama that have never been adequately explored, but which are of importance in the tragic effect. The accelerations and retardations of the action and of the pace of the speech can be noted in a few separate aspects, but cannot be explained, as organic wholes, on the different levels at which they are distributed. As potent, but as much beyond the power of analysis, is the musical pattern of verse drama; which, since it is itself its own direct mode of communication, is not susceptible of other statement. Only in a small-scale one-act verse tragedy one may sometimes feel that the sense of this musical pattern is within one's grasp.

actual, or imagined, rhythm in life.[1] This similarity is often
emphasized, or made credible, either by deliberate symbolism (Ibsen's *Master Builder*), by a repetitive pattern linking past and present (*Ghosts*) or by an emphasis on certain
aspects of common life; which may in their turn be perceived as a direct, or ironic, commentary on the events of
the main plot.

(b) a stimulus to accept certain complicated propositions, conscious and unconscious, in the poetry, imagery, symbolism.

(c) a calculated increase in the emotional or intellectual excitement, achieved by the imposition of a steadily-mounting
series of 'peaks' within the main oval or conical structure.

It seems probable that the artistic finality of a tragedy is to be explained in terms of a combination of these factors. But the plot does
not merely seek to impose order upon event-sequences as motivated by
the past and by character; it relies for its effect on a series of statements
concerned, in the broadest terms, with moral philosophy. Such statements may be explicit, as in the tedious morality of the Senecan drama,
or implicit in the dramatist's attitude or in his poetic statement; more
commonly, perhaps, they are to be found in a series of opposing statements or paradoxes, which we may regard as the poles of a morality
which is, as it were, *projected* outside our immediate consciousness of
the work, and which can only be apprehended as a moving point in
time. And these contradictions or paradoxes may become, as in *King
Lear*, a vital part of the conflicting rhythms of plot and character. The
provisional answers to the question 'What rules the world?' are given
differently by Edmund, Gloucester, Kent, Edgar and Lear: for the
reader, perhaps even for the audience, it is completed only by his own
extended response—itself modified by the individual acceptance or
rejection of (for example) the symbolism—to the total statement of
the play. Such a response seems to be projected as a moving and
growing conception, developing itself in space and time, and therefore capable of fruitful re-interpretation in successive periods of
civilization.

But the plot must also be designed to offer a quality which has been
variously discussed in terms of 'depth', 'universality', 'empathy', and
so on. The dramatist's problem is to extend the significance of the play

---

[1] It seems arguable that there are, in fact, *two* rhythms in a play, that which the dramatist
imposes in accordance with his own perception of order, and a secondary rhythm resulting from the interaction of his characters (in so far as they 'talk themselves into life').

beyond that of an individual or domestic system of references. Such extension is readily available in various kinds of 'fable', where their very character presupposes a significance beyond the immediate personalities involved. To the Greek city state the death of the hero was an event of immense importance for its welfare and safety: and we need not, at present, go beyond the political considerations into those of anthropology. The death of Oedipus, or Creon, or Hippolytus will serve as example; while the problems of kingship and succession raised by *Richard II* needed no emphasis. But any 'fable' limited, whether intrinsically or by the passing of time, to narrowly historical or personal interests, must be so handled as to provide some quality of universality. The most convenient summary is given in W. B. Yeats's essay *The Emotion of Multitude*:

> The Greek drama has got the emotion of multitude from its chorus, which called up famous sorrows, even all the gods and all heroes to witness, as it were, some well-ordered fable, some action separated but for this from all but itself. The French play delights in the well-ordered fable, but by leaving out the chorus it has created an art where poetry and imagination, always the children of far-off multitudinous things, must of necessity grow more important than the mere will. This is why, I said to myself, French dramatic poetry is so often rhetorical, for what is rhetoric but the will trying to do the work of the imagination? The Shakespearean Drama gets the emotion of multitude out of the sub-plot which copies the main plot, much as a shadow upon the wall copies one's body in the firelight. We think of King Lear less as the history of one man and his sorrows than as the history of a whole evil time. Lear's shadow is Gloster, who also has ungrateful children, and the mind goes on imagining other shadows, shadow beyond shadow, till it has pictured the whole world. In *Hamlet* one hardly notices, so subtly is the web woven, that the murder of Hamlet's father and the sorrow of Hamlet are shadowed in the lives of Fortinbras and Ophelia and Laertes, whose fathers, too, have been killed. It is so in all the plays, or in all but all, and very commonly the sub-plot is the main plot working itself out in more ordinary men and women, and so doubly calling up before us the image of multitude. Ibsen and Maeterlinck have on the other hand created a new form, for they get multitude from the wild duck in the attic, or from the crown at the bottom of the fountain, vague symbols that set the mind wandering from idea to idea, emotion to emotion.[1]

Though we need not at once subscribe to all the values implied in this extract, it appears that the main contention is sound. For the

---

[1] *Essays*, pp. 265–6.

'archetypal' fables require (whether because of their familiarity or because of their correspondence to archetypal psychological patterns) no more shadow-work than is strictly proper to them. Less familiar fables, such as those of Sejanus, Aureng-Zebe, Hernani, Empedocles on Etna, and perhaps Abraham Lincoln, require more skilful handling.

Now if the extension of significance is achieved by means of the sub-plot, or by a dominant symbol, we may consider this as the complementary half of our schematic oval figure, or as two pyramids with a common base.[1] These components will be complementary to the upper, or main curve, and will have a complex harmonic relationship to it. The sub-plot in *Lear* involves, for example, a series of linkages to different critical points of the same action, but is in fact a self-sufficient entity. The dominant symbol of *The Wild Duck* pervades more than one level of the play. (We may suspect that its unsatisfactory character is partly explained by the fact that, like a decadent Metaphysical image, it is drawn out artificially from one level to another and its effectiveness diffused or dissipated thereby.)

Some such harmonic figure, severely limited by space and time but forced by these considerations to present the supreme virtue of perspicuity, may be visualized as the typical tragic pattern. It will satisfy, as an artistic entity, what seems to be a fundamental human desire for an apparently complete and self-contained section of an *action* bounded by *time*, in which causation can be apprehended—part intuitively, part emotionally—as capable of being mastered (however momentarily) by man. It is the cry of Sir John Davies:

> O could we see how cause from cause doth spring,
>   How mutually they linkt and folded are,
> And hear how oft one disagreeing string
>   The harmony doth rather make than mar!

From yet another point of view the tragic pattern can be considered as representing, again for the moment, man's conquest of time. That eternal problem, which occupies so much of the attention of poets throughout history, is susceptible of a satisfactory statement only in Epic and Tragedy; perhaps because work of some massiveness in scale is essential to give the impression of a relationship between the finite and the infinite. The lyric may achieve it by the expansive qualities of the symbol, the burning city, the lamp, the tower, the golden cock, the swan; but its communication has not, perhaps, the continuing quality

---

[1] This is, in fact, a development of Freytag's Cone.

of the larger forms. Man's cry for the stability of all sensuous pleasure is recalled by Faust's words:

> Werd, ich zum Augenblicke sagen:
> Verweile doch! du bist so schön!
> Dann magst du mich in Fesseln schlagen,
> Dann will ich gern zu Grunde gehn.
> Dann mag die Todtenglocke schallen,
> Dann bin ich deines Dienstes frei,
> Die Uhr mag' stehn, der Zeiger fallen,
> Es sei die Zeit für mich vorbei!

Time implies mutability. The poet's search for a symbol that will afford some sheltering island in the river is a commonplace of literature: whether it be the Grecian Urn, or Spenser's *Epithalamion*, or Mr Eliot's *Four Quartets*. Tragedy appears to offer such a moment; prolonged through the course of the play, apprehended intuitively at its conclusion, often above the tomb:

> For one throb of the artery,
> While on that old grey stone I sat
> Under the old wind-broken tree,
> I knew that One was animate,
> Mankind inanimate phantasy.[1]

That the experience is illusory is not, for the moment, the point at issue: though we may note that the accessory-aspects of the drama—clowns, processions, battles and the like—may, by their very theatrical nature, emphasize and re-inforce the nature of the momentary perception of reality at the conclusion. It is here that Shaw's notorious criticism of *Antony and Cleopatra* might appear to break down: 'Shakespeare finally strains all his huge command of rhetoric and stage pathos to give a tragic sublimity to the whole wretched business, and to persuade foolish spectators that the world was well lost by the twain.'

Many factors contribute to the final unity. Among them are the traditional features: consistency and credibility of character; the use or misuse of chance or coincidence; the sense by which the interaction of the past with the present is conveyed; the use of imagery in poetic language, with or without the additions of symbol, to provide extension, universality, or the emotion of multitude. The organism is a delicate one, and easily distorted by under-emphasis or falsity of tone. Too strong an emphasis on a rigid connection between cause and effect

---

[1] Yeats, *A Meditation in Time of War.*

4

will tend to eliminate any 'play' in the framework, and may produce an unacceptable didactic element; the intrusion of this last into a tragic concept which saw emotion as valuable for itself alone, and which perceived the tragic utterance as something which could be isolated in its purely rhetorical qualities from the inmost qualities of the verse, may be thought to be responsible for the distorting sentimentalities of Eighteenth-century Tragedy. Its unity, its organic character and the sense of inevitability which it conveys are among the more important qualities which differentiate tragedy from melodrama. Finally, the ending and the 'end' are perhaps more important than any other factors in producing a sense of completeness in the pattern. These aspects or factors will be discussed in subsequent chapters.

CHAPTER 4

The Nature of the Net

Know now that God hath overthrown me, and hath compassed me with
his net.

Job

> . . . if the assassination
> Could trammel up the consequence, and catch
> With his surcease success. . . .

Macbeth

§ i

THE structure of a play may be considered from three possible points
of view. The spectator perceives it in varying degrees of 'aesthetic
distance', oscillating between some measure of 'willing suspension of
disbelief' and his knowledge that 'from the first act to the last, the stage
is only a stage, and the players merely players'. His view of the outcome of the action will vary in accordance with his mood, the expecta-
tions aroused by the known conventions within which the dramatist
is working, the extent to which his awareness of the plot is counter-
balanced by the success in emotional communication, and the significant momentum which the fable, if known, may have acquired in
his mind. He will be aware of a movement in time and space controlled and terminated by the dramatist; but it seems likely that—particularly in tragedy—the emotional response will produce a further
oscillation. He knows that the outcome will obey a predetermined
pattern: yet as he watches he becomes aware (as many have testified)
that he hopes for a different solution. There is just the possibility that,
this time, Desdemona will not be murdered, nor Antony be betrayed.
This excited hope carries an intermittent suggestion of free will, the
momentary illusion of a self-generating self-determining action that
can perhaps be modified, as in the *Eumenides*, by the intrusion of the
irrational.

The dramatist himself is aware of the overriding framework, the
compulsions of his form: which, if we are to judge by the accounts
of dramatists who have described their own creative activity, modifies
and re-shapes itself continually during that process. It may, indeed,

become almost a purgatorial experience, as Goethe testified: 'I am ter-
rified at the idea of undertaking to write a tragedy, and I am almost
convinced that I might destroy myself by that very effort.'[1] He is con-
trolling the destiny of his characters, allowing them the sense of
momentary escape, and of glimpses of a compulsive pattern which is,
in varying degrees and in varying civilizations, of their own making.

If it were possible to perceive the play (in the manner of Pirandello)
from the viewpoint of certain of the leading characters, they would
become progressively aware of a rigid structure, built up from character and the impact of the Past upon the Present, enclosing a more
flexible structure which 'gives' momentarily to the demands of *immediate* action. This flexible structure, the illusion of escape which it gives,
is the instrument of one kind of dramatic irony, its recoil in obedience
to the outer structure one source of the Reversal of the Situation. And
the protagonists—or the Chorus—will perceive intermittently the
nature of the outer compulsive structure, and the fact that this nature
is, *from their point of view in the space-time continuum of the play*, beyond
explanation save that afforded by momentary intuitions.

In the following pages I have attempted to show, by two images,
some qualities of the tragic structure. That of the net is a frequent
metaphor in tragedy; as regards its application here I have in mind two
forms. The first is the seine, which consists of a long wall of netting,
deeper at the middle than at the sides; the wall being extended ver-
tically by a lead-line below, and a cork-line above. The ends are
extended by wooden posts, weighted at the foot, and attached by a
bridle to hauling-ropes. It is 'shot' from the stern of the boat, one
hauling-line made fast to a man on shore. Once the net is extended,
the boat returns to the shore in a half-circle, the net being dragged
both by the boat and by the helper on the shore. The two meet, and
the net is drawn slowly, horse shoe-wise, so that its middle, where
the purse is formed, comes in last. The fish are enclosed, and as the
purse or belly of the net comes nearer, the fish can be seen struggling
in the diminishing space. It was this image that Yeats had in mind
when he wrote:

> Shakespearean fish swam the sea, far away from land;
> Romantic fish swam in nets coming to the hand;
> What are all those fish that lie gasping on the strand?[2]

---

[1] Quoted by Volkelt, *op. cit.*, p. 267 n. See also Erich Heller, *The Disinherited Mind*:
and in particular the very illuminating chapter 'Goethe and the Avoidance of Tragedy'.
[2] *Three Movements*.

There is yet another projection of the thought. Certain kinds of fish—grey mullet, for example, will jump the cork-line as the purse diminishes. A single fish tries; the rest follow. Sometimes straw is floated on the surface of the water to give the illusion of a net above as well as in front; in some parts of the world a raft is placed behind the purse, and on it the leaping fish fall.

The second type is the trammel; a wall of large-meshed heavy netting, forming a wall with lead-and cork-lines, moored across the current. On either side of the main wall hang, loosely, walls of much finer mesh. Fish that move with the current strike the wall, thrust the fine mesh into a bag through the squares formed by the wall of the coarse mesh, and are caught in the purse which they themselves have formed.

Both images are applicable to certain kinds of tragedy.

For the seine net, the lead-line of Fate moving onwards disturbs the fish lying on the bottom, or swimming in mid-water: the power applied at either end moves it onwards steadily, yet shapes it intelligently into the horseshoe form. There is no escape above or below; though there may be, for a time, an illusion of freedom, of space to manœuvre, even a sense of companionship with others in misfortune,[1] and a strengthening of courage thereby. (Webster's tragedies give some sense of this.) But the progress towards the shore is inexorable; the open space contracts; the meshes stifle the struggles; and with a final motion the fish are flung upon the beach, great and small together.

As to the analogy of the trammel, the workings of destiny are more crude, the current and the instinct to stem it or to follow it, are more compulsive, the self-enmeshing more dramatically the outcome of the struggle to escape.

There is often in tragedy just this sense of the symmetrical tightening of the plot-ropes, the narrowing of the circle in the final stages of the

---

[1] Cousteau in *The Silent World* (pp. 112–13) has a description of a herd of tunny fishes that have been trapped in the inner chamber of a maze of nets because of their habit of swimming, during the spawning-season, with their right eyes towards the shore: as if the left were blind. The last stages before the kill in the *corpo* are described thus by the divers among them:

'Life took on a new perspective, when considered from the viewpoint of the creatures imprisoned in the *corpo*. We pondered how it would feel to be trapped with the other animals and have to live their tragedy. Dumas and I were the only ones in the creeping, constricting prison who knew the outcome, and we were destined to escape. Perhaps we were over-sentimental, but we felt ashamed of the knowledge. I had an impulse to take my belt knife and cut a hole for a mass break to freedom.

'The death chamber was reduced to a third of its size. The atmosphere grew excited, frantic. The herd swam restlessly faster, but still in formation. As they passed us, the expression of fright in their eyes was almost human.'

play. Oedipus for long preserves the illusion of freedom, and builds up the continuous irony of the play by his ignorance of the outcome. Macbeth is aware of the narrowing circle, and uses images of a familiar kind to express his own fierce despair:

> . . . I am in blood
> Stepp'd in so far, that, should I wade no more,
> Returning were as tedious as go o'er.[1]

and

> I am tied to a stake; I cannot fly,
> But, bear-like, I must fight the course.[2]

There are, of course, degrees in this illusion of freedom, in the possibility of escape. And the tensions often appear to be distributed among the victims themselves:

> Will you, I pray, demand that demi-devil
> Why he hath thus ensnar'd my soul and body? [3]

§ ii

We can carry some of the images of the net a stage further if we imagine the tragic structure as composed of a series of concentric yielding circles, which gradually diminish in size. For the outer ring we may postulate the First Cause, under whatever name it may be recognized: imperceptible, stable, within the awareness of the spectators and the protagonists; the presence that is felt, for example, throughout the *Iliad*, the object of prayers or imprecations in *King Lear*. Within it there is the ring of Present Action, shifting and changing in its points of pressure, yet linked to a ring immediately outside it, between it and the First Cause, which is the Determining Past. (Perhaps the gods in Homer, themselves symbolizing man's dilemma, lie between the two rings; and there also Irony has its first growth.) It is, obviously, in close sympathy with the ring of the First Cause; the connection is a matter for philosophical speculation. Within the third circle, yielding perpetually to their struggles, yet doubly constricted by the two outer circles, the protagonists of the tragedy may be thought to move. Their circle is flexible, giving the illusion of control over the present action and even providing glimpses, through the mesh-wall of the Past, that enable the protagonists to speculate, intuitively or by analogy, on the nature of the First Cause.

---

[1] III. iv, 136.   [2] v. vii, 1.   [3] *Oth.*, v. ii, 299.

THE CIRCLES OF TRAGEDY

The conformation of the circles to the movements and pressure may be seen at their simplest in Greek Drama. The First Cause is not subject to speculation; we do not know why Thyestes was doomed to eat of his children's flesh, or even why the curse should have lighted on the House of Atreus. The Determining Past is stayed and bolted to it; Iphigenia has died at Aulis, and Clytemnestra nurses her wrongs. Within the next ring, Agamemnon is free to refuse to walk on the purple carpet, to commit *hubris*; yet the illusion has only a pathetic value, for Cassandra is prophesying that he must be slain in the Palace. Out of the past the Messenger comes to rob Oedipus of his last hope; and indeed the Messenger is often both the remembrancer of the Past and the architect of the present. In *A Doll's House* the Past is pushed forward intermittently, until the pattern that it is forming becomes clear to the protagonists who might once have altered that past, for Nora Helmer might have left her husband; and this pattern from the past is horribly projected into, and beyond, the Present, even the Present of the final scene. In *Ghosts* the home on Captain Alving's Foundation belongs to the future as much as the champagne and the incestuous kiss belong to the past. Once the final ring has narrowed on the protagonists and crushed them, it expands again and becomes in its turn part of the Determining Past; perhaps to repeat its pattern of nemesis, as in Shakespeare's history plays, upon a fresh shoal of characters round whom the net has again been shot.

§ iii

There are several methods of emphasizing the linkage between past and present. The Greek Chorus has among many functions that of conveying the sense of past momentum, and an artificial helplessness dissociated from the spectators. They are in one sense the guardians of the past, mediating, interpreting it, moralizing upon it, but never developing it into an authoritative pattern that may affect the present. The symbol, confirmed and sanctioned by the past, achieves a growing validity from that fact; and the revelation of its progression is a powerful emotional agent as we view the closing of the net. The pattern may be conveyed, as in Shakespeare's Historical Plays, by a recurrent sense of the nemesis of Kingship, of a repeating intermittent perception of crime and punishment against a patient background which reflects, almost casually, and in minute particulars, the politics of the great. It seems likely that the *sententiae*, and the proverbial lore of Elizabethan drama, served to establish a similar continuity.

A more subtle linkage takes place when the title and framework of a myth is projected into the present, as in Anouilh's *Eurydice*, or O'Neill's *Mourning Becomes Elektra*. The intellectual appeal of 'recognition', whether of similarities or of differences in relation to the source-play, is an obvious appeal; yet it is probable that the fable is strongly re-inforced in its re-creation, not only by the scholar's recollection of the earlier pattern, but by the validity attaching to the archetypal qualities of the original formulation. Even more complex patterns are formed by the counterpointing of a Biblical narrative against a classical or modern setting. The 'reversed' passage from Ezekiel in O'Casey's *The Silver Tassie* is a case in point, crude but dramatically effective:

> And the hand of the Lord was upon me, and carried me out in the spirit of Lord, and set me down in the midst of a valley.
> And I looked, and saw a great multitude that stood upon their feet, an exceeding great army.
> And he said unto me, Son of man, can this exceeding great army become a valley of dry bones? . . .
> And I answered and said, O Lord God, thou knowest. And he said, prophesy and say unto the wind, come from the four winds a breath and breathe upon these living that they may die . . .
> And I prophesied, and the breath came out of them, and the sinews came away from them, and behold a shaking, and their bones fell asunder, bone from his bone, and they died, and the exceeding great army became a valley of dry bones.

§ *iv*

In the seine-net image we can communicate the sense of an inexorable external pressure in the progress of tragedy; the progressive constriction of the individual's power of choice; the symmetrical narrowing of the horseshoe; the illusion of liberty in the meshes, or above the cork-line; the final catastrophic hauling of the purse to land. It is applicable to those forms in which there is a strong deterministic aspect.

The image of the trammel is more valid for the self-wrought tragic situation. Fish progress with or against the current,[1] athwart the line of the net. They push forward towards a particular objective. The first obstacle is soft, yielding: they thrust against it, and in so doing push the sagging net through the large heavy meshes of the centre net. Once in the purse which they themselves have formed, the smaller meshes

[1] Cf. Cousteau, p. 37, *ante*.

close about them. The further they thrust forward the more secure the trap becomes. They hang in the purse, perhaps to drown in the current, perhaps precariously alive, till the net is hauled and re-set. The responsibility of the presence of the net belongs to the life above the surface of the water. The thrust into the trap is (whatever instinct may drive him forward) the responsibility of the individual fish. So it is, perhaps, in the tragedy born of self-will, or of the sexual instinct, or of the will to power. The victims do not always question what power has set the net across the flood.

It will be seen that in developing this image I have implicitly rejected the proposition that the entire responsibility for tragedy rests upon the protagonists. To Hegel's proposition that 'the dramatic character plucks for himself the fruit of his own deeds' I assent, but in a strictly limited sense. The dramatic character, it seems to me, has a limited amount of free-will. For the sake of dramatic consistency he possesses the potency to follow Course A or Course B. He chooses B, either through his *hamartia*, or because of his *hubris*, or both. But, from the spectator's point of view, the action is in a sense predetermined. The plot or net is secured to the Past, and to the principle of evil, that, when once it is loosed, is self-generative. The ending (given the genre) is inevitable, if the mechanics of the net stand the strain of the hauling. If a rent is made deliberately (as perhaps in *Measure for Measure*) or if its shape is changed (as in *The Winter's Tale*) it ceases to function. But to attribute free-will to characters within the given structure as ordered by the dramatist appears to me inconsistent, and to demand presuppositions as to the rationality of character which causes us, too often, to lose sight of the compulsive nature of the pattern, and to lose ourselves in the subtleties of motivation. Yet Fate must not be wholly malignant, and the weakness of *Romeo and Juliet*, as of Hardy's *Weltanschauung*, is that complete malignity makes tragedy without meaning. Man's struggle with himself and with circumstances must have its own virtue; whether in the hope that the net may one day be broken, or in the good that accrues through suffering. The malignant fate may arouse pity and fear; it denies all possibility of purgation,[1] though it may rid the writer of some 'imposthume in his brain'. It is here that the net image, which I have used in order to suggest a particular aspect of the tragic response, ceases to be useful. To cry out, with Job, against the

[1] That Hardy obtained a characteristic purgation from his own pessimism is clear. 'He is now—this afternoon—writing a poem with great spirit; always a sign of well-being with him. Needless to say it is an intensely dismal poem.' (Mrs. Hardy to Sir Sydney Cockerell: quoted J. G. Southworth.)

compassing of God's net, is human and necessary to convey that agony of apparent entanglement. But the meshes are slashed across in death, and its resolution; and there is sometimes a strange feeling that the victims are returned to reabsorbtion in a new life in the sea.

CHAPTER 5

The Shadow of the Pleasure

Our sympathy in tragic fiction depends on this principle; tragedy gives delight by affording a shadow of the pleasure that exists in pain.

SHELLEY, *Defence of Poetry*

For we are not to expect any and every kind of pleasure from tragedy, but only that which is proper to it.

ARISTOTLE

§ i

FOR some five hundred years the commentators on Aristotle have put forward explanations of the pleasure experienced in tragedy. To recapitulate these would be tedious and not very profitable: it is sufficient to note the main headings of the apologetics. One important group finds the tragic pleasure closely linked to the Aristotelian pleasure in *learning or inferring*. So the generalization of Scaliger: 'Pleasure does not reside in joy alone, but in everything fitted to instruct.' Thus, since tragedy deals with high moral issues, it affords a corresponding pleasure. And in the tragic representation the artistry of the playwright is an important source of pleasure: a view no doubt deriving from the Aristotelian 'Objects which in themselves we view with pain, we delight to contemplate when imitated with minute fidelity: such as the forms of the most ignoble animals and of dead bodies'.[1] A purely aesthetic approach is thus grafted, as it were, on to the moral one, a view which is linked to the later view of the 'distancing' of the spectator. Castelvetro [2] gives us what is virtually a hedonistic view; we find pleasure in tragedy because our own moral sense is flattered. The spectator infers that fate has been unjust; 'we realize that unjust things displease us; this realization is a very great pleasure to us because of the natural love we have for ourselves'. This is a somewhat unctuous solution.

Subsequent theorists of the eighteenth century, assuming a greater degree of empathy in the audience, found a pleasure-value in the spectacle of virtue triumphant over evil in spite of physical disaster. 'Virtue, ever lovely, while labouring under distress appears with a

[1] *Poetics*, IV, 3.   [2] *Poetica d'Aristotele* (2nd Edn.), p. 36.

double lustre.—Constrained by its attractions, we run to the theatre, and embrace objects of distress, notwithstanding the pain they afford us.'[1] In this last there is a hint of the theory of contradictory impulses that was to be developed later by Nietzsche, and which begat a host of psychological elaborations on the theme.

A further school of critics rely on the general proposition that any harmonious stimulation of man's spiritual faculties is pleasurable, and is indeed the sole source of the pleasure. Among these emotions pity and fear occur, but are moderated into pleasure by the unreality of the drama. (Again the question of aesthetic distance is brought in.) So Rapin: 'of all Passions Fear and Pity are those that make the strongest Impressions on the Heart of Man . . . In effect, when the Soul is Shaken, by Motions so Natural and so Humane, all the Impressions it feels become Delightful; its Trouble pleases, and the Emotion it finds, is a kind of Charm to it.'[2] Descartes distinguished between the passions excited by external stimuli, and the interior emotions. This dichotomy has important consequences in tragedy: since the soul, secure in its own virtue, finds that the impact of the external world, however violent, merely serves to increase its own 'inward joy'.[3] Pleasure attends all the passions so long as the passions do not impinge on the inner virtue of the soul. And since a kind of inner fortification is thus provided, the individual is free to seek out, deliberately, experiences which are gloomy, awe-ful, lamentable, and so forth: since the effect of this individual security is to hold them, as it were, at arm's length even if these occurrences are real, and not distanced by artistic representation. It is, perhaps, converging on a Stoic view, and we may remember Campion's rendering of Horace:

> The man of life upright,
>   Whose guiltless heart is free
> From all dishonest deeds,
>   Or thought of vanity;

> That man whose silent days
>   In harmless joys are spent,
> Whom hopes cannot delude,
>   Nor sorrow discontent;

.   .   .   .   .

---

[1] Anonymous, 1770. Quoted by E. R. Wassermann, ELH, Vol. 14, No. 4. I am indebted in this chapter to this writer's admirable summary in *The Pleasures of Tragedy*.
[2] Quoted by Wassermann, *op. cit.* It is curious to find Nietzsche using the same term, *Charm*, of the tragic experience.
[3] Descartes, *Works*, I, 373.

He only can behold
With unaffrighted eyes
The horrors of the deep
And terrors of the skies.

And he may even go forth to seek those horrors deliberately, secure in his own divided and controlled emotions, to provide a thrilling experience. He can analyse and observe such emotions with dispassionate passion. Such is the genesis of the Romantic outlook. But the most convenient summary, a sort of drag-net that gathers something from the turbulent schools of his predecessors, is that of Hurd:

> . . . not only our attention is rouzed, but our moral instincts are gratified; we reflect with joy that they are so, and we reflect too that the sorrows which call them forth, and give this exercise to our humanity, are but fictitious. We are occupied, in a word, by a *great* event; we are melted into tears by a *distressful* one; the heart is relieved by this burst of sorrow; is cheered and animated by the finest moral feelings, exults in the consciousness of its own sensibility; and finds, in conclusion, that the whole is but an illusion.[1]

The term *Mitleid*, so common in German writers on tragic theory, is perhaps a more precise term than our 'sympathy'. It is of such importance that the doctrines of the eighteenth century on the subject are worth noting. Sympathy is defined by Campbell as 'that quality of the soul which renders it susceptible of almost any passion, by communication from the bosom of another'.[2] Hume remarks on its universality:

> In general, 'tis certain, that wherever we go, whatever we reflect on or converse about; every thing still presents us with the view of human happiness or misery, and excites in our breasts a sympathetic movement of pleasure or uneasiness. In our serious occupations, in our careless amusements, this principle still exerts its active energy.
> A man, who enters the theatre, is immediately struck with the view of so great a multitude, participating of one common amusement; and experiences from their very aspect, a superior sensibility or disposition of being affected with every sentiment, which he shares with his fellow-creatures.[3]

According to Burke, it is a social passion, whereby 'we enter into the concerns of others'. But the desire to concern ourselves thus is part of the divine plan—*Love one another*—and has thus been made pleasurable. This view leads logically to the conclusion that real suffering is more effective than that represented on the stage. Burke therefore introduces

---

[1] Hurd, Edn. of Horace's *Ep*. ad. Pisones, pp. 101–2: *cit*. Wassermann.
[2] Campbell, *The Philosophy of Rhetoric*: *cit*. Wassermann.
[3] *Works*, Vol. IV, Section V: *Why Utility Pleases*.

the aesthetic pleasure of 'imitation' as a component, acting as it were a brake upon the impact of the painful experience which must be communicated as realistically as possible upon the stage. But if this sympathy is considered as a dominant aspect of the tragic experience, it tends to deny the requirement that the tragic protagonists should be of high estate (since pure sympathy can be more readily aroused for the misfortunes of men like ourselves, or of lower rank), and at the same time excludes the emotion of fear. Hence arises a distinction between 'pathetic' and 'moral' tragedy, the latter only exciting both pity *and* fear. In this unhappy division we may see the failure of Eighteenth-century Tragedy.

§ *ii*

But in all the welter of theory the Scene of Suffering, as such, received little attention; and the light that modern psychology has thrown upon its potentialities on the stage makes it of particular interest. Since it is closely bound up with questions of ethical values, of cathartic and expiatory effects, of the dissociation of the spectator's sympathy, and of the more primitive sacrificial aspects that appear to be involved, we must consider it in some detail.

No reaction is more complicated or more variable than that of individual humanity to suffering. Of all responses it appears to be that most readily dulled by usage, distorted by various degrees of egotism, modified by different social backgrounds. 'Conduct which at one stage produces its measure of harmonious satisfaction, in other surroundings or at another stage is destructively degrading.' [1] The gradual elimination of overt cruelty in national life is a commonplace of social history; the failure to eliminate it in war, its recrudescence under such conditions with every ingenious accessory of torture that imagination can devise, always comes as a temporary but apparently evanescent shock. The extent to which it enters into tragedy raises the following important questions:

1. What is the limiting factor, if any, of pain which is effective in the Scene of Suffering? Or, perhaps, in another form, at what stage does terror pass into horror? [2]

2. Under what poetic conditions does the Scene of Suffering achieve its maximum effect?

[1] Whitehead, *Adventures of Ideas*, p. 334.
[2] Cf. Rowe, *Preface to Shakespeare*. 'This is to distinguish rightly between *Horror* and *Terror*. The latter is a proper Passion of Tragedy, but the former ought always to be carefully avoided.'

3. What is the validity of those theories which have found in tragedy elements of sadism, or of masochism, or of *schadenfreude*—sometimes of all three?

4. Does the pattern of tragedy in itself react upon the Scene of Suffering, in its individual setting, in such a way as to produce a special kind of appeal?

At the outset it would appear that *any* physical suffering depicted on the stage runs a grave risk of failure in communication. It was for this reason, among others, that Lamb preferred to read *King Lear* in the study rather than to see it on the stage. The boundary between the effective and the ridiculous, the point at which the emphatic response is dissolved in laughter or rejected by the sheer physical revolt of the entrails, is thin and wavering. Attempted verisimilitude in blood, strangling, beheading, mutilations, is very apt to break down in ridicule. 'La grande principe de ne pas ensanglanter la scène' contains much sense; even the matter of Caesar's wounds requires tact in production and speech, and Lavinia's entrance in *Titus Andronicus* is an object lesson in the purely revolting; unless it is played as 'historic' comedy. Torture-scenes as such are degrading, and easily become comic; Shaw's account of Joan's burning reflects the horror, but avoids transgressing the limit of pain. In the epic wounds are not essentially painful, because of their relation to the intention of the poetic structure.

It is clear that certain types of physical violence produce that kind of intestinal reaction which we call horror. Both Oedipus and Gloster with their empty streaming eye-sockets have caused endless controversy, and the descriptions are usually toned down in production. Sword or rapier deaths as in *Hamlet*, *Romeo and Juliet*, *Coriolanus*, are effective because the death-wound is the climax of the sword-play, itself an aesthetic activity, perhaps a ritual, of notable dramatic appeal to an Elizabethan audience, and sometimes even to us. The strangling of Desdemona is perhaps on the border line of horror, and is made possible only by the remoteness of the inner stage or its equivalent. Cleopatra's death at the teeth of the asp remains the most artistically satisfying of all deaths, for it has been prepared, metaphysically, in the text of the play. It is not only

> the lover's pinch
> That hurts and is desired

but is sublimated into the peace of the wife and the mother, with all its implications of these images in relation to Cleopatra's transfiguration:

> Peace, peace,
> Dost thou not see my baby at my breast
> That sucks the nurse asleep? [1]

In general it appears as if the Scene of Suffering varies in its effectiveness with the background of the audience. A taste for public executions, for bear-baiting, for the dismembering insults to the dead body, might enable an Elizabethan audience to contemplate Lavinia raped, her tongue torn out, her lopped and bleeding wrists, with a certain excitement which no doubt had its sexual component. Euripides' description of the corpse of Hippolytus, mangled (like Hector's) by being dragged behind the horses, is given with tact and the minimum of display of the wounds.[2] But in Jacobean tragedy, in Webster, Ford, Tourneur, death which is contrived so as to stimulate factitious and perhaps unfamiliar emotions is, to modern taste, either offensive or ridiculous.

It would seem that, so far as physical suffering is concerned, there is a definite boundary (as there is in Comedy) which the dramatist must not transgress. The crossing of it will often be signified by violent physical reaction, vomiting and nausea. Horror, indefinite in its nature, appears to occur when the balance is upset in the direction of this intestinal spasm; itself accentuated by the absence of any corresponding imaginative balance in the preparation for, or the imaged description of, the scene itself.

The point will perhaps be clearer if we take the well-known torturers' scene from the Wakefield Miracle Play of the Crucifixion. The whole hideous act is stressed at length in the dialogue, to the accompaniment of some mechanical comedy. The cross is dropped violently into its socket. And then, from the figure against the sky (as in Blake's drawing of that event) there is the supreme lyric set against the rough dialogue that preceded it:

> My folk, what have I doon to thee
> That thou all thus shall torment me?
> Thy sin bear I full soon.

---

[1] *A. & C.*, V. ii, 306.

[2] As a modern example of such tact (and of the recurrence of an historical situation) I quote from a letter from W. B. Yeats to Sir Herbert Grierson: 'In my own neighbourhood the Black and Tans dragged two young men, tied alive to a lorry by their heels, till their bodies were rent in pieces. "There was nothing for the mother but the head", said a countryman, and the head, he stated, was found on the roadside. The one enlivening truth that starts out of it all is that we may learn charity after mutual contempt.' (Letter hitherto unpublished.)

How have I grieved thee? answer me.
That thou thus nailest me to a tree,
  And all for thine errour.
Where shalt thou seek succour?
This fault how shalt thou amende
When that thou thy saviour
Drivest to this dishonoùr
  And nail'st through feet and hende.
All creatures whose kinds may be trest,
Beasts and birds, they all have rest
  When they are woe begone.
But God's own son, that should be best
Has not whereon his head to rest,
  But on his shoulder bone.

It seems arguable that here the liturgical complexity of the lyric has cancelled out the previous suggestion of horror. The act of the Crucifixion remains the supreme example of the Christian Scene of Suffering; but it is likely that its 'terror' aspects have long since been merged in other religious emotions. That the degree of sympathetic suffering encouraged by the Church has itself changed greatly is a commonplace of history.

§ iii

The Scene of Suffering achieves its maximum effect when its composition, technically, is impure: that is, when its setting involves a series of other adjustments in the spectator. The mental sufferings of Othello after his 'recognition', of Mrs Alving as she watches the unfolding of her son's tragedy, of Maurya's lament over her dead sons in *Riders to the Sea*, are highly complex and differ widely in their system of references.[1] If we are to find any common ground in this type of scene, we may isolate the following elements which modify and control the suffering into a larger framework:

1. A strong link with the past, expressing itself in an elegiac mood:
   Macbeth's

         She should have died hereafter

   Lear's

              Thou'lt come no more,
      Never, never, never, never, never!

---

[1] A simple instance would be the difference in these 'adjustments' as between a Jacobean and a modern audience regarding Othello's suffering: in particular their views of his reactions regarding Desdemona's chastity.

Beatrice Cenci's

> Here, Mother, tie
> My girdle for me, and bind up this hair
> In any simple knot; ay, that does well.
> And yours I see is coming down. How often
> Have we done this for one another; now
> We shall not do it any more.

2. A poetic statement embodying *either* the summit of that play's characteristic rhetorical impetus *or* a simplicity and flattened language, in obedience to the emotional pressure.
3. A connection established with one or more dominant themes of the play through the imagery of the passage:

Lear's

> Why should a dog, a horse, a rat, have life,
> And thou no breath at all?

Othello's

> Here is my journey's end, here is my butt,
> And very sea-mark of my utmost sail.

§ *iv*

Before we consider other elements in the Scene of Suffering, and the dramatic theories associated with them, it is well to attempt to define certain terms.

Sadism is the pleasure directly experienced from the pain of others; with the important proviso that the resultant pain must be the result of actions by the person experiencing that pleasure. In a wider sense, perhaps too wide—it has been defined as 'the pleasure felt from the observed modifications on the external world produced by the observer'.[1]

Masochism denotes the pleasure experienced from the voluntary submission to pain. Both sadism and masochism are often connected with sexual perversions. It is enough for the moment to remark that, as regards both elements, they become perversions only when they are stressed to the exclusion of normal emotions, or become substitutes for them. In moderate proportions, for instance, both are consistent with normality in the sexual act. Sartre's definition is of interest:

> Masochism is a perpetual effort of a person to reduce his subjectivity

[1] Gorer, *Revolutionary Ideas of the Marquis de Sade*, p. 220.

to nothingness through its assimilation by another [i.e. the complete surrender to domination or physical pain]. This attempt is accompanied by an exhausting but delightful experience of defeat, and the individual finishes by seeking defeat as his principal end.[1]

Algolagnia is the term used to denote 'the intimate connexion between sex and pain . . . it is the meeting place of the sexual and constructive-destructive instincts.'[2]

Schadenfreude can best be defined as 'the opposite face of pity'. It is not merely a pleasure in destruction or death for its own sake, but involves a deliberate withholding of compassion. This produces various kinds of psychic compensation in the beholder. Nietzsche defines it thus:

> Malicious joy arises when a man consciously finds himself in evil plight and feels anxiety or remorse or pain. The misfortune that overtakes B makes him equal to A, and A is reconciled and no longer envious.—If A is prosperous, he still hoards up in his memory B's misfortune as a capital asset, so as to throw it into the scale as a counterweight when he himself suffers adversity. In this case too he feels 'malicious joy'. This thought, directed towards a 'levelling-up' process applies in the same way to matters of fortune and fate. . . . Malicious joy is the commonest expression of victory, and restoration of equality, even in a higher state of civilization.[3]

Sadism, masochism and *schadenfreude* have at various times attracted writers on tragedy as offering explanations of the 'pleasure' derived from the scene of suffering. The explanations cover a wide range, from the most exalted to the most material. Some of them can be summarized briefly here.

The pleasure experienced in suffering may be expiatory in character, as in the meditations on the suffering Christ, and, for example, such as lead to the production of the phenomena of the Stigmata. Its validity depends on the current doctrines of the Church as to its spiritual value. It is not easy to say, in such instances, where masochism begins or sadism ends. As a well-defined step in mystical experience the pleasure-aspect is undoubted, though highly complex and subject to rationalizations of various kinds. For our present purposes we shall expect to find it only in religious drama.

[1] Quoted by Dempsey, *The Psychology of Sartre*, p. 43.
[2] Gorer, p. 237.
[3] Works, Vol. VII, p. 207. (*Human, All-Too-Human.*) We may note that the distress of others is in some measure a reassurance as to our own security. But it does not necessarily imply malice.

A second view seems to postulate sympathetic suffering that alternates with an artistic distancing of that suffering through the conditions of the theatre. This is Freytag's principle of 'joyful safety': the spectator sympathizes with the protagonists, yet continually recalls the world of make-believe and his own security in the theatre. In this instance the elements of true sadism or masochism are probably slight. As a subdivision of this view, there can be a strong *moral* aspect of the pleasure-pain: perhaps best summarized in the phrase 'There but for the grace of God go I.' (The meaning of this sentence may vary a good deal according to which words we stress.) The weakness of this view is perhaps its dependence on the applicability of the positive and negative virtues of the play to the spectator himself. Full identification is, on the whole, improbable,[1] though Coleridge's criticism of *Hamlet* from this point of view is well known.

A third view, and one of the utmost importance, is that which finds in sadism or masochism a fulfilment of the unconscious sense of guilt, and/or desire for punishment; feelings of which the conscious mind may be completely unaware. It is possible that a 'sacrificial' component of many tragedies may be perceived in response to such a demand.

Now the unconscious sense of guilt, the satisfaction in punishment, is of sufficient importance to require consideration here. Nietzsche's analysis of the matter is relevant. Punishment can be regarded

1. As rendering the criminal harmless and incapable of further injury.

   (Some such response may occur in *Macbeth*, and in the holocausts of the 'glorious villains' of Webster.)

2. As compensation for the injury sustained by the injured party.

   (This does not seem applicable to tragedy.)

3. As an isolation of that which disturbs the equilibrium.

   (This is not far off the Bradleian view of expelling the poison from the body politic.)

4. As a means of inspiring fear of those who determine and execute the punishment.

   (Such a view may have been more relevant in Elizabethan-Jacobean tragedy when the absolute power of the governor was more a matter of normal experience and importance.)

5. As a compensation for the advantages which the wrong-doer has hitherto enjoyed.

   (Is not some such feeling possible on viewing *Dr Faustus*?)

[1] See Chapter 22, *infra*.

6. As the elimination of an element of decay, hence as a means of purification.

(This appears to overlap with No. 3 above, and again with No. 11 below. It is perhaps of more importance in Greek drama.[1])

7. As a festival, of the violent suppression and humiliation of an enemy that has at last been subdued.

(Not, I think, very relevant; except for the modern emphasis on the ritual elements in drama.)

8. As a mnemonic, whether for him who suffers the punishment or for him who witnesses it.

> Faustus is dead: regard his hellish fall.

Perhaps the commonest aspect of tragedy in medieval thought.

9. As the payment of a fee stipulated for by the power which protects the evil-doer from the excesses of revenge.

10. As a compromise with the natural excesses of revenge.

(I do not find these relevant; except in so far as we shall have occasion to discuss revenge later.)

11. As a declaration and measure of war against an enemy of peace, law, order, authority.

(To be considered with 3 and 6 above: which, indeed, say much the same thing in different versions of the Nietzschean language.[2])

As regards *Algolagnia*, it is impossible to say, with any certainty, that it is a feature of any specific tragedy. The nearest approach might be found in *Hamlet*, where the insulting and rejection of Ophelia by Hamlet might under certain conditions provide a response of this kind. Sex is seen in a specific relationship to pain. Construction and destruction meet in the bawdry, the violent revulsion; the deliberate brutality may well represent, for a portion of the audience, a vicarious psychic revenge. The long train of denunciation of women in Shakespeare, upon which certain biographical fictions have been built, does suggest, at moments, a sadistic pleasure. Berowne's indictment in *Love's Labour's Lost*, Iago's strange half-comic insults to Desdemona, Troilus's warning

---

[1] Cf. Strindberg, Preface to *Lady Julie*: of the half-woman: 'It is not a good type—for it does not last—but unfortunately it transmits its own misery to another generation . . . Fortunately, these women perish, either through lack of harmony with reality, or through the uncontrolled mutiny of the suppressed instinct, or through the shattering of their hopes of keeping up with the men.'

[2] *Genealogy of Morals*, pp. 94-5.

to Cressida, all contain some element both of sadism and masochism
blended with sexuality.

At the same time it is of interest to note the number of minor figures
in the tragic structure who appear to fulfil some kind of sacrificial
function, passive or semi-passive in character; Hedvig in *The Wild
Duck*, Lady Macduff's children, the Princes in *King John* and in
Richard III. That they have other dramatic purposes is clear; they are
a certain method of eliciting pathos. But they may also on occasion
suggest other archetypal values, which will be discussed in a subsequent
chapter.

§ *v*

The Schadenfreude theory appears to split into two groups: that
which assumes a *malicious* pleasure in the suffering, and that which finds
a more ennobling exaltation in cosmic ruin. Of the first type a moderate expression is La Rochefoucauld's 'We bear with equanimity the
misfortunes of others'; or Macneile Dixon's quotation from Burke, 'I
am convinced we have a degree of delight, and that no small one, in
the real misfortunes and pains of others.'[1] The point, of course, is
whether the 'pleasure' arises out of malignity or out of sympathy.
Once admit sympathy, and we are back to some modification of the
theories of empathy and perhaps of masochism. The true exponent of
Schadenfreude would rely entirely on malignity; although if pressed
he might appeal to the satisfaction of this aspect of Original Sin, and be
compelled, therefore, to acknowledge its cathartic value.

We must return again to Nietzsche and his comments on Schadenfreude. 'How excellent a thing it is that mankind has discovered so
many joys in the contemplation or experience of pain! Man has also
grown in stature through his recognition of Schadenfreude. (He finds
joy, too, in his own pain: and this is a motivating force in many moral
and religious systems.)'[2]

And again:

> Joy in the injuries done to others is something quite other than the mor-
> bid: it is the enjoyment in sympathy, and reaches its peak when that
> sympathy is greatest—that is, when we torture those whom we love. If some-
> one else causes suffering to someone we love, then we rage with anger, and
> sympathy becomes wholly painful. But it is we who love him, and *we* who
> cause him to suffer. For that reason sympathy becomes a most delectable

[1] *Tragedy*, p. 16.   [2] Works, XII, p. 90.

thing; it is a clash between two opposing and powerful impulses, and has the most powerful effect upon us.[1]

It may be doubted whether this Schadenfreude is as powerful as Nietzsche would have us suppose; but elements of it no doubt exist in tragedy, whether in the purer form of Oscar Wilde's *Ballad of Reading Gaol*

> For each man kills the thing he loves

or in Blake's *Sick Rose*, or as some impure compound with *Algolagnia*.

§ vi

The Schadenfreude idea may contain a considerable element of this *Todtentrieb*, the desire for death and destruction. It is often associated with a state of exaltation, particularly in a culture influenced by Fascist ideals. The principle of self-immolation, either for the sake of the State, or because of the failure of a political ideal, is obvious both in Wagner, and in Hitler's orders for the destruction of the German State. The Twilight of the Gods, the last stand in the Festung-Europa, are perceived as abstract heroic conceptions which have in them strong nihilistic elements. It appeared in German patriotic songs:

> Es zittern der Morschen Knochen der Welt vor dem grossen Krieg.
> Wir haben den Schrecken gebrochen: für uns war's ein edler Sieg.
> Wir werden weiter marschieren, wenn alles in Scherben fällt;
> Denn heute gehört uns Deutschland, und morgen die ganze Welt.

A less violent expression is found in Yeats:

> And I would have all know that when all falls
> In ruin, poetry cries out in joy,
> Being the scattering hand, the bursting pod,
> The victim's joy among the holy flame,
> God's laughter at the shattering of the world.[2]

It will be seen that this last statement implies both a sacrificial element not unlike the *Todtentrieb*, as well as the mystical death-and-resurrection of the seed. Nietzsche's account is worth noting:

> The affirmation of life, even in its most familiar and severe problems, the will to life, enjoying its own unexhaustibilities in the sacrifice of its highest types,—that is what I call the Dionysian, that is what I divined as a bridge to a psychology of the tragic poet. Not in order to get rid of terror and pity, not to purify from a dangerous passion by its vehement discharge (it was thus

---

[1] *Ibid.*, pp. 90 f.   [2] *The King's Threshold*, (Works, p. 193).

that Aristotle misunderstood it); but beyond terror and pity, to realize in fact the eternal delight of becoming, that delight which even involves in itself the joy of assimilating.[1]

Much has been written regarding the 'pure' or 'stage' villains of Elizabethan and Jacobean drama: but through it runs a certain incredulity as to the characters that stand for revenge, however motiveless. Yet the existence of such mental states is indisputable, and is of interest in all 'gangster' psychology. There is a convincing statement in Bronowski's *The Face of Violence*:

> *Man*   Which of us has not cried, Revenge!
> Which of us has not felt
> A liberation in the act of anger.
> Which of us has never said
> 'I'll show 'em yet!'
> *Woman* Who has not hoped
> To outrage an enemy's dignity.
> Who has not been swept
> By the wish to hurt.
> And who has never thought that the impersonal world
> Deserves no better than to be destroyed
> By one fabulous sign of his displeasure.[2]

Here both sadism, Schadenfreude, and the power-compensation are clearly shown. From another point of view revenge is shown as a rationalization of cumulative frustration:

> You and I are looking for a deed in the past
> When the moment of hate suddenly becomes solid,
> And we're wonderful at kidding ourselves that fate
> With a great show of innocence
> Has picked us only to dispense
> A more respectable brand of hate,
> An extra special brand they call revenge.[3]

> But deeper under every human heart
> Rise the thwarted passions
> And the springs of jealousy,
> And they in secret build a flood
> Whose violence is charged with power.[4]

This formulation is helpful to our perception of the appeal of so much

[1] *The Twilight of the Idols*, p. 139.   [2] p. 55. Note the infantile power-urge.
[3] p. 18.   [4] p. 39.

'violent' literature. It is clear that it is not merely escapist in character, but offers a somewhat complicated formulation and discharge of psychological pressures. It can be made a direct and valuable link between the practical and the poetic life. Iago, Bosola, Byron and Pinky of Graham Greene's *Brighton Rock* have much in common. And all such characters illustrate (from another angle) the self-propagating aspect of evil, particularly when it has been accumulated over a long period, and is therefore in a state of tension. So in Chapman's *Hero and Leander*:

> The more ill threats us, we suspect the less:
> As we grow hapless, violence subtle grows,
> Dumb, deaf and blind, and comes when no one knows.[1]

There are, no doubt, other components of pleasure-pain; an exacerbative element may exist in certain tragedies. This feeling of superiority on the part of the spectator may be increased by a kind of double consciousness: that of superiority which has been achieved *in spite of* the heroic flaw, and increases thereby the stature of the protagonist towards whom identification extends. To accept a purely pessimistic interpretation, and to assume, however temporarily, some form of stoicism, may on occasion be astringently healthy, though it may balance on a knife-edge dangerously near self-pity.

We have, then, a vast number of explanations for the 'shadow of the pleasure'. Those that seem of most interest to-day are, perhaps, the evaluation and comparison of the characteristic moral questions of tragedy with our own (whether we regard them as 'recognitions' of our own experiences, or as new aspects of knowledge); an acknowledgment of our own pleasure in pain, whether it gratify a revenge instinct (with or without an element of sexual pleasure) or some common latent instinct for the macabre; the unconscious recognition of a 'sacrificial' principle at work in the world, whether as mere propitiation or as an aspect of the expulsion of evil. And, at the last, there is probably a joy, as Yeats pointed out, in the sheer sight of destruction; which may be unalloyed by moral or malicious considerations, and be in fact one road to a state of exaltation. On the stage a great personality meets destruction. His fall may be like the destruction of a great tree

> . . . And this pine is bark'd
> That o'er-topped them all.

[1] *Fourth Sestiad.*

Thus the sinking of a ship, a great fire, or an explosion, or Wordsworth's storm in *The Prelude*.[1] The sense of the numinous is present. So Chesterton—

> There lives one moment for a man
> When the door at his shoulder shakes,
> When the taut rope parts under the pull,
> And the barest branch is beautiful
> One moment, while it breaks.[2]

[1] II, 306.   *The Ballad of the White Horse.*

CHAPTER 6

The Spring and the Trigger

The spring is wound up tight. It will uncoil of itself. That is what is so convenient in tragedy. The least little turn of the wrist will do the job. Anything will set it going; a glance at a girl who happens to be lifting her arms to her hair as you go by; a feeling when you wake up on a fine morning that you'd like a little respect paid to you to-day, as if it were as easy to order as a second cup of coffee; one question too many, idly thrown out over a friendly drink—and the tragedy is on.

ANOUILH [1]

Ce n'est pas par des crimes qu'un peuple se met en situation fausse avec son destin, mais par des fautes. Son armée est forte, son caisse abondante, ses poètes en plein fonctionnement. Mais un jour, on ne sait pourquoi, du fait que ses citoyens coupent méchamment les arbres, que son prince enlève vilainement une femme, que ses enfants adoptent une mauvaise turbulence, il est perdu. Les nations, comme les hommes, meurent d'imperceptibles impolitesses.

GIRAUDOUX [2]

§ i

WE may perceive in both these statements by French dramatists a certain cynicism as to the releasing of the tragic force; yet they express accurately what many critics have felt, and tried to rationalize, in their theory of tragedy. From another point of view, their complaint is an expression of the moral discrepancy felt between the first or second causes of a tragedy and the outcome. If they are indeed right, the *hamartia* is reduced purely to an error of judgement, but an error which possesses an appalling element of the irrational or the capricious both in its inception and its fulfilment. It is therefore necessary to examine the apparent motivations in the tragic action.

It is, I think, true to say that the majority of writers have found the mainspring of tragedy to lie in the Will. Schopenhauer, deriving from Kant and followed by Brunetière, gives us a typical statement of his destructive pessimism:[3]

It is the Will which constitutes the fundamental reality of the Ego. The Will as a thing in itself constitutes the mind, true and indestructible essence

---

[1] *Antigone*, p. 34. [2] *La Guerre de Troie n'aura pas lieu*, p. 188.
[3] Any evaluation of Schopenhauer's views would, I think, start with a detailed consideration of his life; and would need to explain his idea of beatitude through negation.

of the will . . . The Will to live is the substance and nucleus of all reality. But it has neither consciousness nor knowledge; it is a blind dynamic urge. The Will is irrational. It acts at random.

This immediately raises the question of the whole moral conscious-ness in relation to tragedy. If this force is a blind dynamic urge (as we may sometimes feel in the plays of Marlowe or Webster) the tragic feeling will break down unless we can counterweight it with some moral principle. If we split this 'urge' into its possible components, we are in a position to consider Nietzsche's account, perhaps the most original and influential analysis of the tragic energy. We must first consider his use of the words *Apollonian* and *Dionysian*:

> The word 'Apollonian' stands for that state of rapt repose in the presence of a visionary world, in the presence of a world of *beautiful appearance* designed as a deliverance from *becoming*; the Dionysos, on the other hand, stands for strenuous becoming, grown self-conscious, in the form of the rampant voluptuousness of the creator, who is also perfectly conscious of the violent anger of the destroyer . . .[1]

> The antagonism of these two attitudes, and the *desires* that underlie them. The first would have the vision it conjures up *eternal*; in its light man must be quiescent, apathetic, peaceful, healed, and on friendly terms with himself and all existence; the second strives after creation, after the voluptuousness of wilful creation, i.e. constructing and destroying. Creation felt and explained as an instinct would be merely the unremitting inventive action of a dis-satisfied being, overflowing with wealth and living at high tension and high pressure—of a God who would overcome the sorrows of existence by means only of continual changes and transformations,—appearance as a transient and momentary deliverance; the world as an apparent sequence of godlike visions and deliverances.[2]

Beneath this curious language we can discern Nietzsche's psycho-logical dualism. Dionysian man is the creator and destroyer, the sinner. He must, in the fashion of Marlowe's Faustus, challenge the gods: he commits sin that good may eventually come. Nietzsche contrasts the Promethean myth with that of the Fall; the first is the heritage of the Aryan, the second of the Semitic.[3] The Promethean action affords a typical illustration of the *pecca fortiter* theme. Fire is of transcendent value to man: but it is given by the gods only as lightning or as the sun, and neither can be under man's control. Therefore Prometheus robbed the gods, and had to suffer; but his sin is active and dignified

[1] *The Birth of Tragedy*, p. xxv.
[2] *Ibid.*, p. xxvi.   [3] *Ibid.*, p. 78.

as compared with the feminine sin of the Fall.   Hence 'the necessity for crime imposed upon the Titanically-striving individual' and

> this Titanic impulse, to become as it were the Atlas of all individuals, and to carry them on broad shoulders, higher and higher, farther and farther, is what the Promethean and the Dionysian have in common.[1]

And the final end is

> . . . *the mystery doctrine of tragedy*: the fundamental knowledge of the oneness of all existing things, the consideration of individuation as the primal cause of evil, and art as the joyous hope that the spell of individuation may be broken, as the augury of a restored oneness.[2]

But in this world, with its strange blend of superhuman energy with reflective mysticism, pain is perceived as a condition of knowledge. (We should remember that *The Birth of Tragedy* was originally entitled *The Birth of Tragedy out of the Spirit of Music*.)

> The formless and intangible reflection of the primordial pain in music, with its redemption in appearance, thus generates a second mirroring as a concrete symbol or example.[3]

And again:

> Indeed he [the Apollonian Greek] had to recognize . . . that his entire existence, with all its beauty and moderation, rested on a hidden substratum of suffering and knowledge, which was again disclosed to him by the Dionysian.[4]

So Nietzsche takes Raphael's *Transfiguration* to illustrate the upper Apollonian world of beauty, with its substratum, the 'terrible wisdom' of Silenus. In his desire to give further application to the Prometheus-image, he turns to Oedipus:

> because of his excessive wisdom, which solved the riddle of the Sphinx, Oedipus had to plunge into a bewildering vortex of monstrous crimes: thus did the Delphic god interpret the Grecian past.[5]

Such a position is of course quite untenable; Oedipus' sequence of crimes is not intrinsically connected with his wisdom. It seems that we must look elsewhere for our explanation of the trigger, if not of the spring.

[1] *Ibid.*, p. 80.   [2] *Ibid.*, p. 83.   [3] *Ibid.*, p. 45.
[4] *Ibid.*, p. 41.   [5] *Ibid.*, p. 40.

§ ii

As usual, we must return to Aristotle. The Fall takes place: through some error or frailty. The wholly sinless hero appears impossible, unless we set up a counter-puppet by dividing the ethical substance. We are left with the following logical possibilities.

1. We may use Anouilh's image, and assume that there is in the universe this coiled-spring tension, ready at any moment to release its destructive-tragic forces, regardless of the kind or quality of the force that touches the trigger to release the detaining sear. (A development of the image into weapon-detail is, for the moment, useful.) The explosion thus has a completely irresponsible character: and we are compelled to suppose a complete though momentarily static tension as a normal condition of events. We are not, however, given any explanation of how the state of tension has arisen; it is apparently implicit in the nature of the universe. And so we are in a room full of hidden wires connected to booby-traps set by jealously-watching gods, a room in which we must go about our daily business, moving most delicately and invoking the element of luck. But the threat remains. Both explanations, the arbitrary spring and the capricious trigger, seem to me unsatisfactory.

2. Alternatively, we may reverse the hypothesis, and consider Giraudoux's thesis that nations 'meurent d'imperceptibles impolitesses'. In such a case catastrophe might arise from cumulative inattention to what Chapman called 'ceremony'. Life is seen as ordered, 'pious', disciplined; unceremonious clumsiness may shatter it. One aspect of such a state of mind will be the sin of levity, which Tillyard finds at the centre of Eve's sin in *Paradise Lost*. Any lapse from grace will be cumulative, produce a condition in which the cup will suddenly brim over from an apparently trivial addition. A civilization, when it reaches a certain state of deterioration, is ready to be precipitated into tragedy. Something is rotten in Denmark, or in the world of Coriolanus, or in mid-nineteenth-century Norway, or in the Ireland of O'Casey.

This hypothesis is in some ways attractive; but it results inevitably in a drastic reduction of the 'seriousness' of tragedy, and blurs the tragic issues. Yet both quotations, Anouilh's and Giraudoux's, have this in common: we *feel* that the tragic action releases a powerful force of sheer evil: that this force has been in a preparatory state of extreme tension: that the initiating action, the trigger, is often unrelated in its seriousness to the force released; and that the pressure upon it may be trivial or capricious. In considering this situation we are touching the problem of evil from another aspect, though we are not concerned with any final evaluation of cause and effect. It is probably best to examine certain tragic openings to see whether any light is thrown on the problem.

Romeo and Juliet affords a simple instance. The tension in the spring is the hatred between the houses of Capulet and Montague; demonstrated at a low level in the opening scene, and on various planes afterwards. The trigger releasing it is Romeo's sudden and seemingly arbitrary infatuation for Juliet. Thereafter the spring expands, as it were, in jerks. In *Macbeth*, as in *Lear*, a series of new political adjustments are taking place. Whether the Witches embody Macbeth's thoughts of ambition, which are suddenly half-confirmed by events, or whether the action of Lear presupposes a cumulative hatred on the part of Goneril and Regan such as Gordon Bottomley imagined, there appears to be enough *potential* disruption in the mere political setting. In Ibsen, and perhaps in Chekhov and Strindberg, we sometimes appear to have two springs, one within the other; a general setting of corruption or ineffectiveness that is not specifically limited to the characters of the play, and a more immediate and personal tension created by the past actions of the characters themselves. It is this inner spring which uncoils, but its action is governed and reinforced by the outer one; and it would appear that the trigger-force is part of a larger decisive pattern rather than an arbitrary or casual action such as Anouilh describes. There is a sense of ripeness, of a saturation point in the cloud of nemesis.

It appears that in general the 'trigger' shows a principle in common with that of accident in dramatic structure. Both are legitimate devices, in so far as the apparent arbitrariness of either factor may be considered as tightening or accelerating, or precipitating at a given moment, a train of circumstances which would, without such intervening, have occurred *sooner or later*, but which occur when they do because of the characteristics of the dramatic structure. Within the general circle of causation, the preliminary tension, its capacity for releasing evil or destruction, may be thought to build up, by the mere act of delay, an increasing explosive quality. This impression is given very strongly in the work of Chekhov, whose world of *accidie* and listless romantic despair is shown, by his use of the past in the present, to have accumulated steadily over a long period.

§ iii

It seems that we can best meet the known conditions by the following hypotheses:

1. A general moral Law, on whose component parts we can speculate in detail but whose total operation and pattern is *ex hypothesi* unknowable, orders and controls events.
2. The outcome of that Law, its system of rewards and punishments, *as we understand them*, is also unknown and unknowable.
3. Within its system, and on a lower level than that system, man's will is free to operate on its proper levels, and in obedience to his known ethic.
4. But is therein subject to the Pauline paradox

> 'For the good that I would, that I do not: but the evil which I would not, that I do.' [1]

5. The *reasons* for the operation of this law may arise from any of the following features, or from any combination of them:
    (*a*) The influence of past evil upon the active present; the quantitative and qualitative connection between the two being unknowable; since the higher system, which operates less unclearly in the past than in the present, is (at best) perceived intermittently: through processes which we can describe in terms of faith, or of mysticism, or of the poetic statement.
    (*b*) the individual will to evil, or to what, in a given sociological context, is perceived as evil.
    (*c*) the accumulation of past evil set into activity by a breakdown of the ceremonial order of society, and thus generating a favourable condition for a catastrophic cycle.

It will be seen that this position involves the rejection of the Hegelian division of the ethical substance in favour of a relativist doctrine of evil; that is, evil perceived as operative against both a fixed body of ethic, *and* as against a contemporary or local situation which might modify such an ethic.[2]

---

[1] Rom. vii, 19.
[2] A number of anthropological examples will occur to the reader.

CHAPTER 7

The Ethical Problem

A play which is entirely explained is simply a morality play; a play which is all inexplicable is only a meaningless photograph of the surface chaos of life.

E. M. MATTHAEI [1]

Diminish evil, and it will go hard with the tragic poets.

NIETZSCHE

–And take upon's the mystery of things,
As if we were God's spies.

King Lear

THE central problem of Tragedy, from Aeschylus onwards, has always been the moral or religious problem of the place of evil and suffering in the world. From Prometheus on the Rock to Othello's crucifixion of repentance, from Lear's madness to the dusty horror of *The Wild Duck*, the mystery of evil is continuously presented; and with it the cognate problem, the relationship between crime and punishment in the tragic structure. The pretext or circumstances under which evil may be released was considered in the previous chapter, *The Spring and the Trigger*: it is now necessary to remind ourselves of the main philosophical answers to the problem of its existence. We can consider them under four classic headings.

§ *i*

The first is Determinism. God is the responsible author of good and evil alike. Sin and suffering are necessary parts of the divine plan, which He has predestined. There is thus no free-will, whether in fact or as illusion; action is part of a total pattern, rigid in character, but incomprehensible to the mortal spectator. There is thus no element whatever of individual responsibility, nor even—in a strict interpretation—of a redemptive aspect in suffering. The failure of medieval drama to produce a tragedy from its material was due to two causes; a deterministic view of the Christian story, and a failure—for any

[1] *Greek Tragedy*, p. 158.

such attempt would have been blasphemy—to set up even an opponent
of straw (such as a Roman Security Council) to provide some kind
of balance. And the Christian projection of life, redemption and
reward beyond the grave weighted the scales unduly. As an extreme
instance we may consider the dramatic situations constructed in George
Moore's *The Apostle*, and in Yeats's *Calvary*.

§ ii

A second solution rests on the hypothesis that sin and suffering are
an earthly illusion. Evil has no existence for God who is above space and
time. Man is incapable of perceiving this: though he may attain through
contemplative and spiritual exercises a position above all considerations
of evil, and is unaffected either by the fact or by the knowledge. But
this again is foreign to the spirit of tragedy; for it leaves unexplained
man's moral sense, annihilates his potential conflict with evil, and
renders impossible any bond between the actor and the audience.
The solution of tragedy in

> Calm of mind, all passion spent

is an ending, and not a state.

§ iii

A third solution, that of a clear-cut dualism, has something to com-
mend it from the point of view of the tragedian. There is war in
heaven. God's omnipotence is only partial, or He may have withdrawn part of His omnipotence so as to clear the battleground for man.
The fortunes of the battle may then ebb and flow according to man's
virtus, his fortitude and integrity of soul. His stature as a tragic hero
depends, not on the guardianship of Faustus' Good and Bad Angels,
but upon the qualities which he exhibits in the course of his conflict.
We are then confronted with a highly complicated series of problems.
Does the *virtus* of Macbeth, the poet-king tied to the stake of his own
evil deeds, *and* his credulity in the interpretation of illegitimately invoked prophecy, outweigh the moral sins of his bloodshed? How far
is Horatio's speech

> Good night, sweet prince,
> And flights of angels sing thee to thy rest!

a monstrous assumption as to the future of Hamlet's murderous soul,

even though it is based on the words of the Committal Service?
Antony among the Elysian fields we can approve:

> Stay for me:
> Where souls do couch on flowers, we'll hand in hand,
> And with our sprightly port make the ghosts gaze;
> Dido and her Aeneas shall want troops,
> And all the haunt be ours.[1]

but the Roman heroes are at least consistent in their attitude to suicide,
and to the eternal night that must be slept.

But if we postulate a dualism, the existence of a free evil abroad,
many familiar aspects of tragedy fall into place. If the evil is like a
thundercloud, the slightest change in its system of tensions will suffice
to precipitate the storm.[2] The pattern admits and accounts for Satan,
or the tragic villain, given power to cause consternation among men:

> I am mightily abus'd. I should even die with pity
> To see another thus.[3]

And the tragic villains reply, some one thing, some another, from
Aegisthus to Bosola, from Richard III to Byron's Cain. His reasons
may be the intellectual enjoyment of the Fox at his power over the
Lion; or a revenge for bastardy, or neglect, or the effect of some mole
of nature in the man. The women villains are notably more pure in
villainy, more single-souled in their rejection of good, since it is a
single current only that has been turned against morality.

The Manichaean heresy has its attractions if we demand a positive
and exciting explanation. It fits well enough into the Stoic pattern, and
it receives some support in terms of psychology for the distortion and
personification of evil in the villains. True, the Christian philosophy
may return to bring a whimper into the dying speech of Faustus—

> The stars move still, time runs, the clock will strike
> The devil will come, and Faustus must be damn'd.

And it does not exclude the idea of virtue in that conflict, even if the
setting is entirely pagan:

> Because Euripides shrank not to teach,
> Though gods be strong and wicked, man, though weak,
> May prove their match by willing to be good.[4]

---

[1] IV. xii. 51.
[2] It is of interest to note that Hebbel considers the fundamental characteristics of
tragedy as related to a metaphysical conception of original or cumulative guilt.
[3] *Lear*, IV. vii. 53.   [4] Browning, *Aristophanes' Apology*.

§ *iv*

There is a fourth way of considering evil, on the hypothesis that the world is purposeless and chaotic. What is left is a residue in a stoicism of varying degrees of resignation or bitterness. The free evil is in itself the product of chance. It obeys no laws but those of probability. The end is a spiritual nihilism, which, under certain conditions, is not without its value:

> The sense that every struggle brings defeat
> Because Fate holds no prize to crown success
> That all the oracles are dumb or cheat
> Because they have no secret to express;
> That none can pierce the vast black veil uncertain
> Because there is no light beyond the curtain:
> That all is vanity and nothingness.[1]

There are many variants of the attitude: as, for example, that which runs through so much of Housman's poetry, often shading into Manichaeism:

> We for a certainty are not the first
>   Have sat in taverns while the tempest hurled
> Their hopeful plans to emptiness, and cursed
>   Whatever brute or blackguard made the world.

Such a view eliminates all mystery concerning evil, which is both dominant and arbitrary. To confront it in a mood of pessimism does, without question, bring a temporary psychological satisfaction, at intermediate levels, not unlike that afforded by revenge, real or imagined. The frequency of such attitudes during adolescence, and the studies of them both in novels and in the drama, is sufficient proof. It is also well to note that pessimistic feelings can exist simultaneously with those which are basically moral. But we are left with the problem of reconciling such an attitude with the sense of good, the sense of a world evolving creatively, of a sum total of evil which, for all the intermittent evidence to the contrary, is steadily decreasing in the world.[2] We have to account for the facts of happiness, of a moral sense, of the existence of that which Synge postulated in drama as 'reality and joy'. Our judgements are inevitably moral, and Elizabethan tragedy is, however we may palter about it, founded on such

---

[1] James Thomson, *The City of Dreadful Night.*
[2] Also the conditions under which what we may call 'the communicable hysteria of evil' may arise seem also to be diminishing.

judgements; on volition rather than motivation. Yet we may remind ourselves of the words of an historian of the British Army, as embodying a sane and normal view of a single evil:

There is talk of universal brotherhood, yet the quarrels of brethren are proverbial for their bitterness. There has been talk of a reign of the saints, yet in the earliest days of Christianity St Paul contended against St Peter. There are those who maintain that human nature can be changed; and there can be no question of their sincerity and good intent. But there can also be no question that, notwithstanding all their efforts, a month's starvation—always possible through some catastrophe in nature—would turn not a few members of the most highly civilized community into something akin to savages. There is so much that is hidden even from the most steadfast view; there are so many human reactions which, if not called into play, are forgotten. With an eye and a heart fixed aloft upon the known good, yet with a wasting downward tendency to evil, this human nature of ours, if viewed in all its latent powers, its possibilities and its activities, remains for ever unchanging and perhaps unchangeable. To our imperfect understanding war may well seem horrible, lamentable, an accursed thing to be utterly abolished; yet there it is—perhaps, if we are to judge from history, the oldest and most persistent of human institutions. We trust that it has its high purpose in the divine scheme which passes our intelligence, but we may not end it. Man cannot alter his essential nature, nor can he load the balances of God.' [1]

§ v

In Job's answer, and in the Christian one, there are such balances, and they are not to be loaded. It is well to re-state the divisions of the problem as it affects our purpose here.

1. Why does evil exist at all in an evolutionary and *on the whole* beneficent universe?
2. Why is there, in drama as in life, such an observed lack of proportion between sin or error and the resultant evil?
3. Are pain and suffering (*a*) in themselves evil?
   (*b*) of immediate *or* of ultimate value?
   (*c*) of value as having a sacrificial aspect?
   (If this last is true, what is the value of sacrifice in terms of individual or cosmic morality? Does an element of atonement, direct or vicarious, find a place?)
4. Why is there an apparent capriciousness of rewards and punishments? (We have all seen the righteous forsaken, and his seed begging their bread.)

[1] Sir John Fortescue, *History of the British Army.*

The Christian statement of the philosophical position may be grouped under the following headings:

(a) Moral evils, which constitute the problem of sin.
(b) Physical evils, which constitute the problem of suffering.

Neither in Christian philosophy, nor a tragic theory which takes account of Christianity, is there any causal connection between these two. The tragedy of *Job* is in some sense the examination of this inconsistency; it resolves the problem by an approach, not to reason, but to experience. A single experience is reduced to scale against the complexity of God's creation. The violent storm of misfortune passes as soon as the experience is recognized for what it is.

But Christianity does explain a large proportion of moral evil in terms of collective sin; and since collective sin is itself beyond any possible computation in terms of human values, its implications and results are also beyond assessment in past, present or future action. Ignorance and stupidity on the one hand, and the lack of repentance, or the will thereto, on the other, create the conditions for the liberation of a great cloud of accumulated evil. The trigger that sets off the charge may be, from the theological point of view, the confirming act that places the agent beyond the divine grace (this is the Macbeth situation when *Amen* sticks in his throat); or, from a wider point of view, it may be any act of *hubris*. (I shall suggest later that the explanation of *hubris* cannot be excluded from a Christian philosophy.) Greek tragedy, by the very nature of its fabulous material, conveys just this sense of accumulated evil, sometimes visibly augmented in the present by impiety of many kinds. The curse that hangs over the Palace of the Atridae has its roots in past sin. The threat implicit in the second Commandment, however much we ridicule it to-day, contains the germ of an impressive doctrine of transmitted responsibility. In *Macbeth* and *Julius Caesar* the omens, the supernatural events, are the distant lightnings that show, as it were, the changing potentials in the charges, built up in the past, of the shadowing storm. In Ibsen the idea of sin in the past, whether collective or individual, is all-pervading; again it is reinforced, as in Greek drama and in Shakespeare, by the course to which the protagonists are committed. That sin, as in *Ghosts*, may be in terms of the second Commandment, or of some family curse, as in *Rosmersholm*. It is always, I think, complicated by other factors—environment, social conventions, stupidity, greed, self-interest. In both Ibsen and Brieux the most terrible of the accumulated sins is heredity. 'The scientific principle of heredity is Nemesis without her mask. It is the last of the Fates, and the most terrible. It is the only one of the gods whose real name we know.' [1]

Neither in Christian philosophy, nor in the observed practice of Greek tragedy, is there any consistent suggestion of a just proportion in retribution for sin. 'Those eighteen, upon whom the tower in Siloam fell, think ye that they were sinners above all men that dwelt in Jerusalem?' [2]

§ vi

Before we consider the Christian position, we may notice certain 'intermediate' solutions, which will be dealt with in a subsequent chapter. Those of interest are:

1. The Marxist position, which makes evil a consequence of the distortion, through the temporary breakdown of the social system, of man's social and economic environment. Underlying it we have, of course, the romantic fallacies of the dominance of reason and the perfectibility of man.

2. Freudianism; which, as commonly misunderstood, effects a partial or complete transference of individual responsibility to environment and upbringing.

3. All systems that exonerate man's virtue by lowering the standards by which he is to be judged. Under this heading come the 'moral realists', Nietzschean, Neo-Machiavellian, Syndicalist and Freudian. [3]

4. Hegelianism and its modifications which regard the ethical substance itself as capable of internal division or fission; in certain circumstances resolving that substance into two or more conflicting claims, each justified in itself, but bringing about destruction when one is pushed to the exclusion of the other. [4]

5. Combinations of these; of which one variant is romantic nationalism, as expressed in all 'power' philosophies, which also seek to externalize responsibility, [5] and which are rooted in what Jaspers calls 'the margin of awareness beyond power'.

[1] Oscar Wilde, *The Critic as Artist.*
[2] Luke xii, 4.
[3] M. F. Thelen, *Man as Sinner*, p. 23.
[4] Cf. Bradley, *Hegel's Theory of Tragedy*, in *Oxford Lectures on Poetry.*
[5] A particularly effective Nazi poster of 1939 showed a map of Germany ringed with menacing guns: the enemies who sought to annihilate a contented defenceless Germany. (Consider also the demand for *Lebensraum.*)

We may remember that immature tragedy, such as *Romeo and Juliet*, and immature characters in the greater tragedies, seek relief in just such a transference. The stars look down on the psychiatrist's consulting-room.

> This is the excellent foppery of the world, that, when we are sick in fortune, often the surfeit of our own behaviour,—we make guilty of our disasters the sun, the moon and the stars: as if we were villains by necessity, fools by heavenly compulsion, knaves, thieves and treachers, by spherical predominance, drunkards, liars and adulterers, by an enforced obedience of planetary influence; and all that we are evil in, by a divine thrusting on: an admirable evasion of whoremaster man, to lay his goatish disposition to the charge of a star! [1]

§ vii

The tragic theory of Hardy is important, not because of its embodiment in *The Dynasts*, but as offering the sole consciously-formulated 'philosophy' of a poet.

> In a dramatic epic—which I may perhaps assume *The Dynasts* to be— some philosophy of life was necessary, and I went on using that which I had denoted in my previous volumes of verse (and to some extent prose) as being a generalized form of what the thinking world had gradually come to adopt, myself included. That the Unconscious Will of the Universe is growing aware of Itself I believe I may claim as my own idea solely—at which I arrived by reflecting that what has already taken place in a fraction of the whole (i.e., so much of the world as has become conscious) is likely to take place in the mass; and there being no Will outside the mass—that is, the Universe—the whole Will becomes conscious thereby: and ultimately, it is to be hoped, sympathetic . . .
>
> This theory, too, seems to me to settle the question of Free-Will vs. Necessity. The will of a man is, according to it, neither wholly free nor wholly unfree. When swayed by the Universal Will (which he mostly must be as a subservient part of it) he is not individually free; but whenever it happens that all the rest of the Great Will is in equilibrium the minute portion called one person's will is free, just as a performer's fingers are free to go on playing the pianoforte of themselves when he talks or thinks of something else and the head does not rule them. [2]

Elsewhere Hardy speaks of 'It' as the Prime Cause or Invariable Antecedent. It seems probable that neither this theory, nor the illustrative simile that concludes the passage, is entirely satisfactory. 'It' is too

---

[1] *Lear*, I. ii. 122.   [2] *Cit.* Southworth, pp. 215–16.

abstracted, too ponderously distant in its operation, to satisfy our minds: nor does a growth of collective will into a harmony (still less a sympathetic one) find supporting evidence in history. If 'It' or the Prime Cause is felt to explain Hardy's tragic vision in the novels, its operation appears to sway between impassivity and malice. It is a tragic vision that sees human frailty, lust, cruelty, the transitoriness of man set against the miracle of the countryside, beautiful or menacing, in a style of scrupulous austerity. The Immanent Will gives no hope, and its world is full of pity and fear, but without resolution. So of Tess walking at night:

> It is then that the plight of being alive becomes attenuated to its least possible dimensions. She had no fear of the shadows; her sole idea seemed to be to shun mankind—or rather that cold accretion called the world, which, so terrible in the mass, is so unformidable, even pitiable, in its units . . .

Yet it is difficult to deny the title of tragedy to the great novels; but it seems to me a tragedy which grows out of their background in Wessex, and the curiously remote viewpoint of their creator. It is a tragedy that drifts, a little hopelessly, on a grey current, pausing for a moment to find, in its eddies and backwaters, those qualities of nobility, patience, charity; but it is not concerned to show those qualities vindicated in conflict.

§ viii

The Christian solution will depend largely on the views of the nature of sin which emerge in the course of theological evolution; a process which may be thought to show something of a circular tendency. The absolute prohibitions of the Decalogue gave way in nineteenth-century Liberal Theology to a concept verging on the relativist. Tennant, because of his great influence, is a useful starting point:

> Non-Christian or non-theistic philosophy is free, if it choose, to employ a single term for both imperfection and sin.[1]

> It is not every unfaithfulness to God that constitutes a violation of the rights of men, and gives them a title to reproach us.[2]

So we have his definition of sin:

> Sin will be imperfect compliance (in single volitional activity or in character resulting from such activities) with the moral idea—in so far as this

[1] *The Concept of Sin*, p. 48.   [2] *Ibid.*, p. 22.

THE HARVEST OF TRAGEDY

is, in the sight of God, capable of apprehension by an agent at the moment of the activity in question both as to its content and its claim upon him; this imperfect compliance being consequent upon the choice of ends of lower ethical worth when the adoption of ends of higher worth is possible, and being regarded in its religious aspect (which may in some cases be wanting).[1]

It will be seen that the effect of Tennant's definition is, in Thelen's words, 'to reduce sin to one of the many evils which plague human existence. A good part of the evil which Augustinian theology has relied upon in establishing the truth of original sin is found by Tennant not to be sinful because not done in full responsibility.' [2] On the other hand, Tennant insisted that 'science does not imply that sin is merely the survival of necessary appetites or habits'.[3]

Against this we may set the view of Reinhold Niebuhr, as representative of modern 'Realistic' theology:

> The temptation to sin lies . . . in the human situation itself. This situation is that man as spirit transcends the natural and temporal process in which he is involved and also transcends himself. Thus his freedom is the basis of his creativity but it is also his temptation.[4]

Niebuhr's statement is so profound, and is sufficiently borne out by tragic experience, as to require further consideration. It can be shown to account both for human guilt, the splendour of the heroic effort in defeat, the characteristic impatience of the hero with the observed realities, with time and space. Man is perceived as sinning through his effort to raise himself above the norm, the man of great stature who cannot perceive his own limitations or those of the world which he desires to re-shape. So Antigone, Faustus, and Faust, Macbeth and Peer Gynt, in as many different ways. Niebuhr thus agrees, in part, with Julius Bab: 'Tragic guilt is not ethical, it is on the contrary, metaphysical, that is to say, innate.' [5] In an earlier work Niebuhr develops the idea in another direction:

> The pretensions of human cultures and civilizations are the natural consequences of a profound and ineradicable difficulty in all human spirituality. Man is mortal. That is his fate. Man pretends not to be mortal. That is his sin. Man is a creature of time and place, whose perspectives and insights are invariably conditioned by his immediate circumstances . . . Thus man builds

---

[1] *The Concept of Sin*, p. 245.   [2] Thelen, *op. cit.*, p. 21.   [3] *Ibid.*, p. 22.
[4] *Nature and Destiny of Man*, p. 266.
[5] Quoted by Volkelt, *op. cit.*, p. 140: who cites Hebbel in the same sense: 'The absolute *qua* absolute, is guilt-laden in the metaphysical sense.'

towers [1] of the spirit from which he may survey larger horizons than those of his class, race and nation. This is a necessary human enterprise. Without it man could not come to his full estate. But it is also inevitable that these towers should be Towers of Babel, that they should pretend to reach higher than their real height; and should claim a finality which they cannot possess ... The higher the tower is built to escape unnecessary limitations of the human imagination, the more certain it will be to defy necessary and inevitable limitations. Thus sin corrupts the highest as well as the lowest achievements of human life. Human pride is greatest when it is based on solid achievements; but the achievements are never great enough to justify its pretensions. This pride is at least one aspect of what Christian orthodoxy means by 'original sin'. It is not so much an inherited corruption as an inevitable taint upon the spirituality of a finite creature, always enslaved to time and place, never completely enslaved and always under the illusion that the measure of his emancipation is greater than it really is.[2]

§ ix

The Christian answer is implicit in the assumption that, while the world is evolutionary in character, it is not designed for 'the greatest happiness of the greatest number'. Any assumption that it is leads to moral confusion in face of the observed facts. The pleasure-pain system has no place in it. Its retributive processes are far from being mechanical; since, as Niebuhr points out, a divine judgement includes redemption and resurrection, and so cannot be purely retributive. If the highest good is to be attained, pain and suffering are natural and logical aspects of the system, of birth and re-birth, symbolized in the Crucifixion and Resurrection. I believe that, with certain modifications, Niebuhr's position is capable of representation in such a manner as to show that it covers most of the 'tragic fact', and that it does, on the whole, fall within most of the traditional metaphysical explanations.

1. *Spirit* is the term used for 'the impulse to subject the individual or social ego to the universal even to the point of self-annihilation or absorbtion'.[3] *Spirituality* is not merely rationality but reason, will and emotion acting together to see life in its total relationships and also to 'feel' an obligation toward the whole of life.[4]

2. *Nature* is the impulse to universalize the ego even to the point of destroying or enslaving all competing forms of life.

[1] The Tower image is archetypal, and endless examples in poetry will be recalled. The Lightning-Struck Tower, which symbolizes the defeat of human aspirations by the Incalculable, is the Thirteenth Card of the Tarot Pack.

[2] *Beyond Tragedy*, pp. 28 ff.   [3] *cit.* Thelen, p. 72.

[4] What follows is entirely from this source.

3. These two contradictory impulses lie at the root of the human situation.

4. The ethic of Jesus *taken by itself* is an inadequate guide for the problems of to-day.

5. We must therefore be supplemented by a restoration of the concept of two kinds of natural law

> *jus naturale* and *jus gentium*, the former embodying the absolute demands of equality and freedom and the latter regulating the government, coercion, conflict, and slavery existing in the historic institutions of society.[1]

This immediately suggests the Greek dichotomy:

> To any rational thinker it is at once clear that Dike, Natural Order, and Themis, Social Order, are not the same, nay even they are not mother and daughter; they stand at the two poles remote and even alien. Natural Law is from the beginning; from the first pulse of life, nay even before the beginning of that specialized movement which we know as life, it rules over what we call the inorganic. Social Order, morality, 'goodness' is not in nature at the outset; it only appears with 'man her last work'.[2]

6. Man is infinite in the sense that his mind constantly seeks to relate all particular events to the totality of the real. He is finite in that this same mind is itself 'embedded in the passing flux, a tool of a finite organism, the instrument of its physical necessities, and a prisoner of the partial perspectives of a limited time and space'. [3]

7. The origin of sin arises from man's pretensions by denying his own finiteness.[4] From this arises personal, national and international conflict.

> Ideally men seek to subject their arbitrary and contingent existence under the dominion of absolute reality. But practically they always mix the finite with the eternal, and claim for themselves, their nation, their culture, or their class the centre of existence. This is the root of all imperialism in man and explains why the restricted predatory impulses of the animal world are transmuted into the boundless imperial ambitions of human life.[5]

8. It is this very blindness and self-deception which constitute the

---

[1] *N. & D.*, p. 143: Thelen, p. 76.   [2] Jane Harrison. *Themis*, p. 534.
[3] *N. & D.*, p. 66: Thelen, p. 78. Hamlet's thoughts on the matter will be remembered.
[4] Thelen, p. 80.   [5] *Cit.* Thelen, p. 80.

mystery of sin. For it is really a mystery. No one, not even the most astute psychologist, has ever made a perfectly convincing analysis of the comparative degrees of ignorance and dishonesty which enter into it.[1] (Consider Donne's 'Nequissima animae ignorantia' and the aphorism 'God sends on men strong delusion that they shall believe a lie.')

Actually, man always deceives himself into believing that evil is good before he is able to choose it. This self-deception is partly unconscious, as Freud and Marx discerned; but it is also partly deliberate, as is proved by the fact that in his regret or remorse after the deed man confesses that he was not fully deceived; and so man cannot be absolved from responsibility for his Fall.[2]

§ x

This position, which does not (in my view) exclude a theatre which accepts some or all of the traditional elements of tragedy, may be summarized as follows:

1. There are three forms of evil.

   (a) Intellectual Evil or Error.
   (b) Emotional Evil or Suffering.
   (c) Moral Evil or Sin.[3]

2. Error consists in unwarrantable synthesis: a failure, not in the emphasis placed upon a judgement, but in a failure to distinguish the qualities of things. From another point of view we may quote Martin Buber: 'There is no evil impulse but that which is separated from the whole being.'

3. Emotional Evil or suffering. This, when it befalls the innocent or noble, *and only then*, is seen at its purest and highest, and most terrible. It is the cry of the Agony in the Garden, of Job confronting his friends; in both cases it is the momentary failure of the conscience under agony, and is the prelude to enlightenment.

4. Moral Evil is a direct and willed violation of a known and accepted law, which is abrogated for a variety of reasons under the direction of the Will.[4]

---

[1] Thelen, p. 85.   [2] Thelen, p. 95.
[3] Cf. Temple, *Mens Creatrix*, p. 273. I am indebted in many ways to this book.
[4] The psychology of dictatorship is of interest here: as of all theories that glorify the Will as an absolute.

5. In all three cases 'affliction' [1] is a real aspect of the human situation.

6. This human situation is under God. Therefore, ultimately, it must be good. But, because of our finite nature, our faith can never be sufficiently perfect to prevent our awareness of this conflict: as between the finite and immediate experience and suffering, and its ultimate resolution in time.

7. The awakening, or recognition of this human predicament, projected, as it were outwards (as against the normal response to personal suffering, which is egocentric) in compassion in its literal sense: co-suffering, embracing pity and fear.

8. This compassion lies at the heart of Christianity, since it is through the recognition of, and unity with, the fact of Christ crucified that the ultimate redemption of man's sin is perceived. But the ultimate reconciliation is only made possible by love (itself the last perfection of compassion, and transcending it), and therefore compassion comes to have a value in and of itself.

9. The awareness of the tragic fact depends both upon an intellectual acceptance of the human predicament, and a spiritual perception of its resolution in suffering.

10. The statement of the tragic theatre enables us to perceive in a focus that differs sufficiently from real life to present an ordered and progressive induction to this compassion. *For this purpose it may and often does show evil as 'isolated' or 'pure'.* [2]

11. By its formal qualities, or by the 'hint of reconciliation', or by both the play is perceived, both in its immediate aspect as rousing 'compassion', and in its wider aspect as *sub specie aeternitatis*.

12. The combination of these two responses, both aspects of man as the creature of God, destined by Him to attain love through compassion, and in faith of ultimate union with Him. There are thus co-existent in the tragic response a sense of suffering, and of a deep serenity for which 'pleasure' is an inadequate term. We may approximate to it in the term 'satisfaction' in the most profound sense; but we are thus confronted with a number of problems of character, which are discussed in the next chapter.

---

[1] In the sense used by Simone Weil, *Waiting on God*, pp. 63 ff. 'Affliction is an uprooting of life, a more or less attenuated equivalent of death, made irresistibly present to the soul by the attack or immediate apprehension of physical pain.'

[2] It appears from the practice of the theatre that attempts to show 'neutral' or highly complex shades of evil are generally ill-suited to the tragic rhythm.

I have not at this stage attempted to consider Niebuhr's views of Atonement and Redemption as essentials of the Christian position. All I would suggest at present is that the views presented afford an adequate explanation of the fact and experience of tragedy; of the generation of evil through man's infinite desire, and of his blindness to his situation. It is thus that we can account for the failure of the tragic hero to perceive his place and function in *time*, and hence the ultimate consequence of his actions. They cover, under the term 'presumption',[1] the commonest form of *hubris*. They account for the internal conflict, in that the two sides of man's nature are in a constant state of tension: for the Internal-External conflict in so far as he seeks to change the image of the external world, in obedience to what Niebuhr calls 'imperialism'. If, for the moment, the problem of evil can be viewed in this light we can go on to consider some anthropological elements that may be apparent in Tragic Man.

[1] Cf. Shaw's *St Joan*.

CHAPTER 8

Myth, Ritual and Release

(Richard II) is typical not because he ever existed, but because he made us know something in our own minds we had never known of had he never been imagined.

W. B. YEATS [1]

The conflict of the material and spiritual aspects of life only shows that the psychic is in the last resort an incomprehensible something.

JUNG [2]

§ i

MY purpose in this chapter is to suggest that a proportion of the pleasure and the effect of tragedy is to be accounted for by its impact, mainly unconscious, upon certain activities of the mind. The dangers of such a subject are many. Anthropology that leads to religious and philosophical speculation is all too easily misused, too readily filed and adjusted in order to fit subjective presuppositions. On the other hand the evidence for the myth, and for its expression through the archetypal image, seems now to be acceptable as a basis for discussion. We may quote at the outset Kerényi's formulation of the nature of the myth: since the connotations of that word in dramatic theory are both vague and unfortunate:

The word 'myth' [says Kerényi] is altogether too equivocal, blunted and hazy for our purpose; it does not give us as much of a start as the expressions that combine the word μῦθος with the word λέγειν, meaning 'to put together', 'say'. Plato, himself a great 'teller of myths', teaches us from his own experience something of the vitality and mobility of what the Greeks called μυθολογία. This is an art alongside and included within poetry (the two fields overlap), an art with a special assumption as regards its subject-matter. A particular kind of material determines the art of mythology, an immemorial and traditional body of material contained in tales about gods and god-like beings, heroic battles and journeys to the Underworld—mythologem is the best Greek word for them—tales already well known but not unamenable to further reshaping. Mythology is the *movement* of this

[1] *Plays and Controversies*, p. 93.
[2] *Modern Man in Search of a Soul*, p. 219.

material: it is something solid and yet mobile, substantial and yet not static, capable of transformation . . .

In a true mythologem this meaning is not something that could be expressed just as well and just as fully in a non-mythological way . . . Just as music has a meaning that is satisfying in the sense that every meaningful whole is satisfying, so every true mythologem has its satisfying meaning. This meaning is so hard to translate into the language of science because it can be fully expressed only in mythological terms.[1]

The evidence for the existence of such mythological material on a world scale, a material which is 'self-born, born anew' because it corresponds to deep-seated human needs, is sufficiently strong:

In the dream, as in the products of psychoses, there are numberless combinations to which one can find parallels only in mythological associations of ideas (or perhaps in certain poetic creations which are often characterized by a borrowing, not always conscious, from myths). Had thorough investigation shown that in the majority of such cases it was simply a matter of forgotten knowledge, the physician would not have gone to the trouble of making extensive researches into individual and collective parallels. But, in point of fact, typical mythologems were observed among individuals to whom all knowledge of this kind was absolutely out of the question, and where indirect derivation from religious ideas that might have been known to them, or from popular figures of speech, was impossible. Such conclusions forced us to assume that we must be dealing with 'autochthonous' revivals independent of all tradition, and, consequently, that 'myth-forming' structural elements must be present in the unconscious psyche.[2]

We can use for this collective unconscious the term 'The Great Memory', as Yeats uses it. But it is important to note that, as myth evolves in history, it is Protean and regenerative in its forms—

> Those images that yet
> Fresh images beget.

and this fact adds immeasurably to the difficulties and uncertainties of interpretation. So—

These products are never (or at least very seldom) myths with a definite form, but rather mythological components which, because of their typical nature, we can call 'motifs', 'primordial images', types or—as I have named them—*archetypes*. . . . In the individual, the archetypes occur as involuntary manifestations of unconscious processes whose existence and meaning can

---

[1] Jung and Kerényi: *Introduction to a Science of Mythology*, pp. 3 ff.
[2] *Ibid.*, pp. 99 f. (G. C. Jung).

7

only be inferred, whereas the myth deals with traditional forms of incalculable age.[1]

Here we must note specifically the nature of the archetypes, for they can be easily misunderstood. They are not the *idées innées*: they are only dispositions to the formation of images, which are only encountered directly through their manifestations. They have something in common with Goethe's 'Eminent Instances'. A general image may be expressed symbolically in many ways. It seems likely that a disposition to expand and express consciousness through their means is inherited, and that like many normal inherited gifts, it can be cultivated.[2] At the same time we must proceed very cautiously: for the exegetical process as applied to this subject may easily become confusing and may (unless we are careful to return continually to each mythologem in its particular setting) render it desiccated and impotent. All images are sensitive, as it were, to their context. The life blood of a conception grows thinner as it becomes more universal.

The presence of mythological elements in tragedy will be apparent in two ways:

1. From the occurrence of certain root situations, whether overtly in a multitude of disguises, as corresponding to a recurrent communal problem. These can be further subdivided into

    (*a*) the relationship of the leader to the community, including his power, mediatorship or priesthood, death and sacrifice, and

    (*b*) his relationship to individuals who are closer than the community, involving specific relationships with which his obligations as a leader may conflict.

2. From the emergence of certain archetypal images, modes of language originally involved in such myths but surviving as keys to the latent emotion that once adhered to them, and which are still apparent through the pressure of the unconscious as shown in various manifestations.

§ *ii*

For the moment, if we accept this position, we can proceed to further propositions as they affect the tragic form.

[1] Jung and Kerényi: *Introduction to a Science of Mythology*, pp. 99–100 (Jung).
[2] Consider Yeats's experiments with the stimulation of 'visions', clearly archetypal in their nature, by means of 'triggers' of various kinds.

1. All dramatic performances, and particularly tragedy, have a well-defined ritual aspect, which has tended to become overlaid with the passing of time. It is most strongly marked in Aeschylus, negligible in Ibsen except perhaps in *Brand* and *Peer Gynt*, recovered (in part) by Synge, Eliot and Yeats. Recent critics of Elizabethan and Jacobean tragedy find that ritual occurs extensively in them. The further these roots are traced back the more strongly this ritual element appears. Such ritual is a disguised and at the same time formal version recalling or commemorating or connected with archetypal experiences. The chief among these experiences are as follows:

2. The Hero, in his birth, upbringing, kingship, death and burial, can be shown to follow a pattern which is common, or largely so, to a large number of typical figures. Lord Raglan [1] enumerates twenty-two steps in what we may call the standard fable, and finds that most of them are, in one form or another, included in his selection of Heroes. He takes his examples from (among others) Oedipus, Theseus, Romulus, Herakles, Perseus, Jason, Bellerophon, Pelops, Asclepios, Dionysus, Apollo, Zeus, Joseph (son of Jacob), Moses, Elijah, Sigurd, Arthur, Robin Hood.

3. The slaying of the Old King has a well-defined ritual value. It does not matter whether he is perceived as the Father, or the Old Year, or Pharmakos the Scapegoat. From the point of view of the worshipper, or of the spectator, the measure of identification achieved with him offers a release to the commoner power-fantasies originally repressed. (Instances from child and adult psychology, and from the history of magic and fairy tales, are too numerous to quote.) His death affords a satisfactory termination to those fantasies (as the natural processes of adolescence demand) without impairing the self-esteem of the spectator: who thus obtains relief from the burden of jealous emulation, envy, and the feeling of helplessness before superior strength now obeying its cyclic decline. *King Lear* is typical of such a pattern; the waning powers of the Old King afford the normal pretext for his dethronement and death. Lear is at once the egoist, the breaker of the social order, a kind of 'imperialist' (in Nietzsche's sense) in reverse, and finally, a violator of the fundamental law of self-knowledge. 'He hath ever but slenderly known himself.'

[1] *The Hero*, Chapters XVI–XVIII.

4. At the same time the King's death has a primitive sacrificial value; not merely for the community who find in it the scape-goat-function as well as a fertility-value linked to their welfare, but for the individual who has already made his psychological transference to a greater or less degree. (Consider Strindberg's *The Father*.) In civilized communities this sacrifice may achieve high ethical levels, as it does in most of Greek Tragedy. Oedipus suffers for the sake of Thebes, Orestes for his father, Alcestis for her husband, Prometheus for mankind, Antigone for her brother, Iphigenia for Hellas. Macbeth (after the murders) offers himself, if we take a somewhat unusual point of view, as a sacrifice for Scotland. Perhaps Lear does so for England, for the sake of the unity which he had destroyed. In modern tragedy, Ibsen's Brand takes upon himself the sins of his people in his progress to the Ice-Cave: Becket accepts his death for the sake of the Church, though there is also an element of personal atonement in his actions.

5. The dying hero can also take upon himself, voluntarily or in-voluntarily, the sins of the people. The process may be conscious or unconscious, active or passive. The kings of the Shakespearian history play are loaded at their end with a kind of collective responsibility for the many kinds of evil which have been freed (by whatever agencies) during their reign. Such characters may be shaded in many ways. King John starts with a fatal taint: the Bastard assumes the task of speaking for England, while the King becomes a scapegoat. Richard III represents, in a simplicity that verges on melodrama, the cycle of crime and nemesis; more distantly, the releasing of force with all its repercussions, until the resolution comes in a ritual Dance of Death—the procession of the ghosts being the prologue to the death of the King. Richard II falls in a natural though accelerated curve, and the rays of the whole country's evil, perceived in many facets, converge upon him. At Bolingbroke's coming the slate is wiped clean, of all but the question of the usurper's right, which is a dormant menace until he in turn passes beyond the zenith of his fortunes. But the problem of heredity is always with him, shadowed even at the end of *Richard II*: the rebellion of youth against age, the uneasy retention of power. And the speculations as to power and responsibility attain their clearest and most ironical statement in Henry V's soliloquy on the night before Agincourt.

6. The hero, man, king, or God, is killed in his prime for one or more of several reasons: to avoid the decay or destruction of the community which will follow on his waning powers;[1] to placate, consciously or unconsciously, individual or communal jealousy; to ensure that his soul goes to its dwelling place in the purity that death in his prime, or near it, can give.[2]

7. From his own point of view the hero may have much in common with the Byronic or anti-social type of hero, whose psychological components we have already suggested. He is isolated by his very condition: he sees clearly the possibilities of his powers: he is made, at the last, violently aware of their limitations. Basically, he is liable to the suggestions of the *Todtentrieb*; self-sacrifice, suicide, the last battle against overwhelming odds, present satisfying dramatic solutions to this type of mind. We may suspect that the motives are often highly complex; both the heroic and anti-social qualities may well be associated in the fantasy-world in which he lives, the power which he desires so intensely, and the excesses of deed and word by which he seeks perpetually to reassure himself as to his own stature. Tamburlaine and Mr Eliot's Becket of Canterbury are at opposite poles in their disinterestedness.

8. 'We must therefore recognize two distinct and seemingly opposite features in these ceremonies: on the one hand sorrow for the death, and affection and respect for the dead; on the other hand, fear and hatred of the dead, and rejoicings at his death.'[3]

9. 'It may be suspected that the custom of employing a divine man or animal is much more widely diffused than appears from the examples cited . . . Thus the killing of a god may sometimes come to be confounded with the execution of a criminal.'[4]

10. 'So many broken lines seemingly (converge) towards the Cross on Calvary . . .'[5]

§ *iii*

Myth displays the working of unconscious complexes; aggressiveness between parents and children, sexual jealousy, the desire for a magical shortening of the normal roads to an objective. The King

---

[1] The slaying, in fact or wish, of the Dictator-Tyrant, is of interest: from Agamemnon to Mussolini. The effigies, burnt or mutilated in various Italian villages on the news of the latter's death, seemed to effect a peculiar release of tensions.

[2] Frazer, *The Dying God*, p. 10.

[3] *Ibid.*, p. 264.

[4] Frazer, *The Scapegoat*, p. 227.

[5] *Ibid.*, p. 414.

stands for the father. The virility of the father-hero-king, his jealousy of his possible supplanter, his assumption of peculiar powers through an unnatural or divine birth, are all part of the pattern. The danger to the new-born hero-child, the intervention of miraculous agencies to nurture it after it has been exposed to die, are familiar incidents.

These considerations offer interesting parallels with ritual practices. The hero-God suffers and is slain; because he has outlived the cycle of his reign, because the power which he wields has passed the bounds of moderation and what is desirable for the health of the State, because there are associated with him the complex feelings of hatred, fear, respect for his powers whether physical or magical, and a lingering terror that, at the last, he may produce a magical revival of power and revenge himself on the wolf-pack that is closing about him. Thus it comes about that his death suggests something both of relief and of safety. Prospero's action in destroying his magical equipment is significant.

It is therefore clear that a double tide is running in the spectator of the tragic pattern. He is aware consciously of a definite set of social and political values. The king or hero is the saviour of the State. Conscious projection, even identification, towards him is a normal feeling, encouraged by tradition and upbringing. Illness or danger affecting him has an instant depressive effect, which modern democratic values have failed to eliminate. The 'ambitious' types of projection, towards power, great place, wealth, dignity of bearing, are all sanctioned by society, and are probably not amenable to 'rational' evaluation.

Thus arises the perpetual paradox of the spectator's identification with the tragic hero, the transference to him of individual and collective responsibility, the vicarious satisfaction in perceiving the fulfilment of the cyclic law of power that waxes and wanes, and the satisfaction of complex and contradictory impulses at his death. These satisfactions are achieved in a state of intense excitement: which is both expressed by, and arises from, the poetic statement.

'It is especially at times when barriers of personal repression are removed and images of "cosmic" character are arising freely, that the fantasy figure may appear of some great prophet who tends to assume control of the personality.' [1]

The results of this identification, and the tragic experience arising from it, have been formulated by Miss Bodkin in what seems to me to be the most suggestive account yet written of the tragic balance or

[1] Bodkin, *Archetypal Patterns*, p. 18.

release. It will be seen that the view has some kinship with that of Richards's.

The experience of tragic drama both gives in the figure of the hero an objective form to the self of imaginative aspiration, or to the power-craving, and also, through the hero's death, satisfies the counter-movement of feeling toward the surrender of personal claims and the merging of the ego within a greater power—the 'community consciousness'.

Thus the archetypal pattern corresponding to tragedy may be said to be a certain organization of the tendencies of assertion and self-submission. The self which is asserted is magnified by that same collective force to which finally submission is made; and from the tension of the two impulses and their reaction upon each other, under the conditions of poetic exaltation, the distinctive tragic attitude and emotion appears to arise.[1]

The removal of these personal repressions, the breaking down of the barriers, can be seen in that kind of rhetoric which expresses and releases the histrionic element in humanity; which can perhaps be described as a projection of personality above itself by language that consciously aligns the speaker with noble or heroic conduct in the past or future; some element of this conduct attaching itself to him by the magic of words. In rising to these heights he is at once asserting his stature as the hero and as the victim. Sophocles, Shakespeare, Racine and Yeats provide examples. On a more recent scale we can see its operation in O'Neill's *Mourning Becomes Elektra*.

The second current is unconscious to a greater or less degree. Again it is probably double in character. The fantasies of which we have spoken approve his death, rejoice in a fulfilment of the cyclic law; at the same time they shrink from the disruption of the family or cosmic pattern which that death involves.

It seems likely that we must ascribe to these ambivalences the so-called immorality of tragedy. The tragic response is, in fact, a continuous process of oscillation between desires whose poles are positive and negative, both in the conscious and unconscious. For that reason we must recognize the perpetual inconsistencies in it. A quotation from Yeats throws some light on the matter:

> The character, whose fortune we have been called in to see, or the personality of the writer, must keep our sympathy, and whether it be farce or tragedy, we must laugh and weep with him and call down blessings on his head. The character who delights us may commit murder like Macbeth, or fly the battle for his sweetheart as did Antony, or betray his country like

[1] *Ibid.*, p. 23.

Coriolanus, and yet we will rejoice in every happiness that comes to him and sorrow at his death as if it were our own. It is no use telling us that the murderer and the betrayer do not deserve our sympathy . . . Complain of us if you will, but it will be useless, for before the curtain falls, a thousand ages, grown conscious in our sympathies, will have cried *Absolvo Te* . . . We understand the verdict and not the law; and yet there is some law, some code, some judgment. If the poet's hand had slipped, if Antony had railed at Cleopatra in the tower, if Coriolanus had abated that high pride of his in the presence of death, we might have gone away muttering the Ten Commandments.[1]

§ *iv*

The boundary-line between ritual and ceremony is not easy to discern. Donne speaks of 'Ritual and ceremonial things which . . . are the subsidies of religion.' We shall do no violence if we use ritual in the sense of an ordered ceremonial, which has or has had in the past a frame of reference to a religious or numinous view of human living, and which can be traced back to such a concept, if the memory can be revived. On such a basis, processions, pageants, dances, feasts, can be retraced to their beginnings, and seen as the outcome of the human desire to impose a rhythm or pattern upon a sequence of events so as to present in them a significance which is, remotely or immediately, allegorical in kind; and, above all, perspicuous because of their pattern. We may remember *Hero and Leander*:

> Thus she appear'd, and sharply did reprove
> Leander's bluntness in his violent love;
> Told him how poor was substance without rites,
> Like bills unsign'd; desires without delights;
> Like meats unseason'd; like rank corn that grows
> On cottages, and none or reaps or sows;
> Not being with civil forms confirm'd and bounded,
> For human dignities and comforts founded;
> But loose and secret all their glories hide;
> Fear fills the chamber, Darkness decks the bride.[2]

Fergusson in his analysis of Hamlet finds civil or military or religious ritual in various parts of the play, serving to gather together the threads of the plot and to remind us of the 'traditional social values'.[3] Such scenes are: the changing of the Guard, Claudius's First Court, the blend of ritual and entertainment in Hamlet's Play; Ophelia's madness ('a

[1] *Plays and Controversies*, pp. 103–4.
[2] *Third Sestiad.*
[3] *The Idea of a Theatre*, pp. 113 ff.

mock ritual, a mixture of false and lewd marriage, and false and savage funeral'); Ophelia's funeral 'a maimed rite, but a real death'; the duel between Hamlet and Laertes with 'every element in it false or mistaken: a mockery of invocation'.

If it is construed in this way, 'ritual' covers a wide area. We may perhaps divide it up into two groups; ritual which in drama refers to or recalls directly a civil and religious ceremonial within the knowledge of the audience, and ritual which is oblique to their knowledge,[1] evidenced in image or symbol only. To the first group belong all processions, dances, law trials, marriages, funerals. The second group is far more obscure. We may suggest tentatively that the following represent buried or unconscious ritual:

1. The slaying (or its equivalent) of the King. The actors may be partly conscious of a special significance in this, as in *Julius Caesar*:

> Let's carve him as a dish fit for the gods,
> Not hew him as a carcase fit for hounds.

2. The encounter with the numinous: the hero who goes to challenge or consult oracle or ghost, often in the symbolic Cave.
3. The Virgin as Helper, Mediator, the Triple Goddess, Mother.
4. The appearance of the magical Child.[2]
5. Seasonal imagery, particularly that which is connected with re-birth.
6. Incidents or imagery involving mythological type-contests, such as the epic of the one against the many, the contest with dragon, serpent or other monster,
7. which often involve the idea of the Secret Helper.
8. Purification and humbling.
9. Apotheosis and resurrection.

As images that may be connected with these we have those clusters connected with sun, moon and stars; the horse in its metamorphoses, including the centaur; ritual beheading and the Singing Head;[3] the sword and its cognate images; fertility images, and their innumerable analogies with the human situation; the sea as a life and death image; the tree; the Cave and the Desert.

---

[1] How much is, in fact, oblique to our conscious awareness is apparent, say, from A. W. Watts's *Myth and Ritual in Christianity*.
[2] Jung and Kerényi, *op. cit.*, Ch. I.
[3] Cf. the wide incidence of the Jael-Holofernes-John the Baptist themes in painting.

§ *v*

Now the 'release', which I use in preference to *catharsis*, seems to be the point at which the tragic theory of I. A. Richards converges upon the philosophy of Jung. For Richards the peculiar poise of the tragic experience 'arises out of the relation between the two sets of impulses. Pity and Terror'.[1] The result is a 'balanced poise, stable through its power of inclusion, not through the force of its exclusions'.[2] But this is a general characteristic of all artistic experiences of the highest value, the balance or equilibrium of the response. 'The equilibrium of opposed impulses, which we suspect to be the ground-plan of the most valuable aesthetic responses, brings into play *far more of our personality* than is possible in experiences of a more defined emotion.' [3]

Richards's hierarchy of appetencies, which seemed at one stage to have opened the way to a theory of value, has now revealed its incompleteness, perhaps because of his view—at that time—of a value-range dominated by utilitarian concepts. But the phrase that I have italicized, *far more of our personality*, is capable of much expansion, and such expansion does not run counter to Richards's own views. In some sense the experience of tragedy is a microcosm of being, the experience, at a greater or less distance, of fear, suffering, loneliness, pity. Spiritual maladies, of the kind to which Aristotle expressly refers, are in their essence conflicts of the subliminal. From another point of view, such conflicts are the single most important factor in denying the integration of personality, the power of progression. Tragedy presents an ordered ritual experience. Its myth, infinite in the forms that it may take, is continuously re-created in the poetic statement.

Our approach in the theatre is one of great complexity. It seems certain that we see and recognize evil as akin to that latent in ourselves; and it is too naïve a view to hold, with Gosson or Collier, that its manifestations are merely *exempla* for or against wrongdoing. Conscious attitudes are probably compounded of moral superiority (because it is make-believe), a partial recognition of his kinship, but they are intellectually offset because they are under our control. Unconscious attitudes are a matter of speculation, and we must work by analogy. They belong to that realm of artistic creation that Jung called the *visionary*, and his account of it is so important that it must be quoted at length.

---

[1] *Principles of Literary Criticism*, p. 247.   [2] *Ibid.*, p. 248.
[3] *Ibid.*, p. 251.

The experience that furnishes the material for artistic expression is no longer familiar. It is a strange something that derives its existence from the hinterland of man's mind—that suggests the abyss of time separating us from pre-human ages, or evokes a super-human world of contrasting light and darkness . . . The value and force of the experience are given by its enormity. It arises from timeless depths; it is foreign and cold, many-sided, demonic and grotesque . . . The disturbing vision of monstrous and meaningless happenings that in every way exceed the grasp of human feeling and comprehension makes quite other demands upon the powers of the artist than do the experiences of the foreground of life . . . But the primordial experiences rend from top to bottom the curtain upon which is painted the vision of an ordered world, and allow a glimpse into the unfathomed abyss of what has not yet become.[1]

We have then, I suggest, in the tragic experience

the perception of an order, imposed by the dramatist upon an experience which is bounded in time and space as an action, and as an action involves the ambivalent attitudes of recognition, participation in, and conscious rejection of major moral values, but which is unlimited in time and space by reason of
its ritual values
its ability to imply the existence of *orders* of various kinds
its power, through its imagery in general and through the archetypes in particular, to convert subliminal forces into active agents for the integration of personality.

§ *vi*

It would be foolish to suggest either that all dramatic imagery is related to archetypal images, or that their effect is always towards a specific psychological relief. All we dare say is this:

1. A very considerable degree of verification of these images as outcrops of the hidden reefs of the unconscious has been obtained through psychiatric analysis and interpretation. The archetypes are not on trial; their effect, on which we can only speculate subjectively, is.
2. If drama, employing as it does a method of communication which presupposes a peculiarly intense state of emotional reaction *in a collective field of influence*, is found to embody such archetypes, part of their emotional effect may be reasonably attributed to the

[1] *Modern Man in Search of a Soul*, pp. 180–1. The hint of the Aristotelian 'Poetry is a more philosophical and a higher thing than history' is of interest.

release of unconscious tensions relevant to the situations which that drama imitates.

3. The selection of the archetypes to which we respond is not, *a priori*, a matter of our conscious choice. We may again refer to Jung:

> In reality we can never legitimately cut loose from our archetypal foundations unless we are prepared to pay the price of a neurosis, any more than we can rid ourselves of our body and its organs without committing suicide. If we cannot deny the archetypes or otherwise neutralize them, we are confronted, at every new stage in the differentiation of consciousness to which civilization attains, with the task of finding a new *interpretation* appropriate to this stage, in order to connect the life of the past that still exists in us with the life of the present, that threatens to slip away from it.[1]

And if indeed those myths, and their expression through archetypal images, might affect us in this way, we have, in this sense of release, both a partial explanation of the classic catharsis, a link with religious origins, and some explanation through 'those masterful images' of the exaltation that tragedy gives.

[1] *Introduction to a Science of Mythology*, pp. 105–6.

CHAPTER 9

'Let Mans Soule be a Spheare'

Let mans Soule be a Spheare, and then, in this,
The intelligence that moves, devotion is,
And as the other Spheares, by being growne
Subject to forraigne motions, lose their owne,
And being by others hurried every day,
Scarce in a yeare their naturall forme obey:
Pleasure or business, so, our Soules admit
For their first mover, and are whirl'd by it.[1]

DONNE

All tragedy, so I would be inclined to state it, is a broad and deep account of the life of the individual, and, at least by inference, his fellows, in which neither man's problems, nor his ability to cope with them is belittled.[2]

ERIC BENTLEY

§ i

IN an earlier chapter we considered some of the possible meanings that might be given to the Aristotelian *hamartia*, or tragic flaw. In carrying a stage further our speculations as to the psychology of the tragic protagonists, Donne's great image is of some service; not only because it is traditionally—whether in the form of sphere or of circle— a way of regarding the soul, but because it appears to embody certain archetypal qualities which poets have used to the full. Instances from Dante, Shakespeare, Donne, Yeats, come readily to mind. It is an image which has many explicatory uses; as for example the armouring or hardening of the sphere, through received experience, in its endeavours to attain security.

If, for the sake of simplicity, we consider at first the circle rather than the sphere as an emblem of personality, we can suggest that there are two primary forces working upon it, in opposite directions; these will be the positive and active, and the negative or self-destructive elements respectively. Each force produces tensions in that portion of being on which it operates; the one struggling upwards to attain a position of superiority, spiritual or material, and therefore of safety, the other dragging downwards through the sense of inferiority. We can, if we

[1] *Goodfriday, 1613, Riding Westward.*
[2] *The Playwright as Thinker,* p. 55.

wish, elaborate the figure further to suggest the element of schizophrenia. In general, human nature can be seen in terms of an alterna-
tion or oscillation between these psychic polarities; whatever the terms
(such as Self and Anti-Self, Man and Mask, Spectre and Emanation)
we may use to express them.

The destructive impulse or sense of inferiority can be symbolized by
a portion which is missing—bitten out, as it were, from the lower
portion of the circle—and so fostering the sense of inferiority. This is,
in fact, the *hamartia* (in one sense at least), the joint in the armour.
Opposing this, in the upper half of the circle, we may suppose a bubble
or blister, the psychic compensation for the flaw which is often a
deliberately-assumed contradictory aspect of personality. (The arrogance of the basically shy, self-reassurance by rhetoric or histrionics,
are convenient examples.) To the extent that it is assumed rather than
an intrinsic aspect of personality this bubble or blister is liable to sudden
pricking, deflation. But between the compensation and its corresponding defect a kind of oscillating movement takes place, complicated by a
torsional effect of the two primary forces upon the whole. If the plain
circle is then expanded imaginatively to a sphere, with corresponding
complexities, the image will perhaps serve our purpose. As in Donne's
poem, the psyche is 'subject to forraigne motions', that is, to external
circumstances; it may lose its sense of purpose, its 'naturall forme'
through its own internal conflicts, of which Donne's 'Pleasure or business' are secondary manifestations.

The *Philoctetes* of Sophocles offers an almost perfect example of the
individual conflict in this respect. Here Philoctetes is conscious of his
supreme power through his bow, itself an ancient and mysterious
symbol.[1] He suffers from a double *hamartia*, part physical and part
spiritual: the offensive festering wound, and his grievance at his com-
rades' desertion. (This last is purged by Herakles, who tells him to go
and fight at Troy.) It is true that the interest centres mainly in the
character of his Neoptolemus, and his vacillation, who finally over-
comes the deceitful intrigue of Odysseus, and the supreme temptation
to be false to his loyalty. The play also shows the complex response to
suffering, reiterated throughout by the Chorus and Philoctetes' own
complaints; intense physical pain that has no release in death, and in
which the stench of the putrefying wound forces upon Philoctetes his
terrible isolation on Lemnos. The ending is factitious, for Troy must
fall, and therefore Herakles intervenes; but the archetype of the aged

---

[1] Compare also Ishmael, the outcast, who 'dwelt in the wilderness'.

hero with his power and his weakness,[1] and the play's justification of loyalty in human relationships, remain significant.

The hero's characteristic quality is power, the ability to do for others what they would, but could not; or to *know* what others cannot know, to answer the riddles for them. In this situation he is liable, as man, to a number of catastrophic flaws.

He may, in putting forth what is essentially a spiritual effort, become the victim of his bodily weakness or desire; such as lust, sleeplessness, and various psychotic states.

He may be tempted either to an excess of power beyond his capacity, or he may ascribe his actions to his own capabilities—the act of *hubris*.

He may, while relying on some *mystique* of personality, or magical formula, share or communicate that knowledge so that it is no longer private, and hence no longer potent.

He may fail to continue to communicate his characteristic 'vision' to those whom he leads, and on whom his loyalty depends; and hence his position declines.

At this stage it is of interest to consider a description of the genesis of the hero in terms as stated by a psychologist:

> The initial stage of personal infantilism presents the picture of an 'abandoned' or 'misunderstood' and unjustly treated child with overweening pretensions. The epiphany of the hero (the second identification) shows itself in a corresponding inflation: the colossal pretension grows into a conviction that one is something extraordinary, or else the impossibility of the pretension ever being fulfilled only proves one's own inferiority, which is favourable to the role of the heroic sufferer (a negative inflation). In spite of their contrariety, both forms are identical, because unconscious compensatory inferiority tallies with conscious megalomania, and unconscious megalomania with conscious inferiority (you never get one without the other). Once the reef of the second identification has been successfully circumnavigated, conscious processes can be cleanly separated from the unconscious, and the latter observed objectively. This leads to the possibility of an accommodation with the unconscious, and thus to a possible synthesis of the conscious and unconscious elements of knowledge and action. This in turn leads to a shifting of the centre of personality from the ego to the self.[2]

[1] We may refer to this archetypal situation in modern dress: the dream of a young man who knew himself to be shut up in a stockade or zareba, armed with a rifle and ammunition, and surrounded by savages armed with spears and shields. He knew he could keep them at a distance with his magical weapon, but that ultimately he would be overwhelmed by sheer numbers. The reference was to the young man's engagement, of which his parents, and society in general, disapproved: the rifle, his superior intelligence as a defence against the masses.

[2] Jung and Kerényi, *op. cit.*, pp. 137–8.

Now it would be idle to speculate on the childhood of the tragic hero, though the Byronic semi-autobiographical character fits accurately with this diagnostic interpretation. But it is clear that the traditional tragic hero is on every count liable to precisely this kind of psychological inflation, and the oscillation of which I have spoken. It is merely another statement of the corrupting influence of power; its megalomaniac aspects are perhaps both cause and effect, inseparably intertwined in recent history. Further, the tragic hero, caught in the net of circumstances, is never given an opportunity of reaching an accommodation with the subconscious; the familiar and normal process of the non-heroic type.

If we consider again the image of the sphere it will be apparent that only a limited number of the negative elements are brought into play in the tragic situation. It is probably fair to say, with Aristotle, that the good qualities must outweigh any single flaw. We have already dealt with the question of 'height' or 'eminence', but the hero must at all events have a large 'reserve' of positive qualities, since the dramatist must at some stage release or re-establish a preponderant amount of sympathy for him. The stage at which such sympathy is evoked will vary with each play. For *King Lear* it starts with the Heath Scene, and reaches its peak in his speech to Cordelia as they both depart to prison. For *Macbeth* we begin with full sympathy, lose it, regain it through the full poetry of his speech at his wife's death, and then either lose it or substitute for it a half-reluctant admiration at the sheer ferocity, courage and power to accept life on an active and superficial plane. Othello loses it when he grows hysterical, and recaptures it for a moment in the histrionics of his dying speech.[1] Both Antony and Cleopatra drown all other emotions in the death-splendour; as does Coriolanus, for whom our feelings are probably more divided than they would have been for a Jacobean audience.

§ ii

All characters show this oscillation between weakness and strength, though it differs both in kind and in degree. The clearest example is Othello. Whatever we take to be his *hamartia*, it is clear that to a contemporary audience he was, in essence, a character study of The Jealous Man, as well as of a southern race with peculiar emotional characteristics. As such he is doubtful of his own power to dominate and hold

[1] The effects of such histrionics probably differ a good deal on, say, a Jacobean audience, and a modern one, and have repelled certain modern critics.

a woman of a foreign race, in a city notorious for its loose morals, in surroundings which, if not actually bewildering, are at least to be regarded with the suspicion proper to a noble African. As the jealous man, he is a little doubtful even as to his wooing; in which he has to be assisted by Cassio. He tells of it at length to refute the charge of witchcraft; and it is worth while noting that his courtship follows Sir Philip Sidney's prescription:

> Loving in truth, and fain in verse my love to show,
> That She, dear She! might take some pleasure of my pain;
> Pleasure might cause her read, reading might make her know,
> Knowledge might pity win, and pity grace obtain.[1]

At the same time, Othello's account of his miraculous travels, hardships, adventures, suggests a self-created and cherished myth; a most powerful instrument in producing a temporary stabilization, but in the long run dangerous to mental equilibrium because it will fail to respond to circumstances which lie outside those included in such a myth. Throughout the play he is perpetually clutching at any means of reassurance, any pretext which will hold him from the *hysterica passio* to which he eventually succumbs. All his soldiership, his past deeds, his service to the State, hang in the one balance, so that, consciously, he can rehearse his role of the violent yet self-governed man, who makes a deliberate use of his own breaking-point as an authoritative threat:

> Now, by heaven,
> My blood begins my safer guides to rule,
> And passion, having my best judgement collied,
> Assays to lead the way. If I once stir,
> Or do but lift this arm, the best of you
> Shall sink in my rebuke.[2]

At the end, he seeks reassurance in three ways: by recalling his past glory, which is unassailable; by setting out that past in magnificent rhetoric, which is, to all heroic types, the method of reassurance in the present; and finally by his dramatic suicide. His last few lines exemplify all three:

> And say, besides, that in Aleppo once,
> Where a malignant and a turban'd Turk
> Beat a Venetian and traduc'd the state,
> I took by the throat the circumcised dog,
> And smote him, thus.[3]

---

[1] *Astrophel and Stella*, I. [2] II. iii. 202. [3] V. ii. 351.

8

Perhaps the memory of that episode is wrenched, histrionically, into the dying speech; but it is just such a moment as is needed to give the man of action a memory of a time when his own self-reliance has triumphed, and to afford a dramatic setting for the final stab, the compulsive suicide which is at once a re-assurance and an escape.

§ *iii*

It is not necessary that the flaw should be simple, or wholly in the consciousness of the hero. It would be in keeping with what the Elizabethans would have called decorum, and what we should call psychological truth, if there should be, together with certain symptoms of overt insecurity, a residuum of the *hamartia* which is inexplicable to conscious thought.[1] Perhaps something of this kind lies at the base of all speculation as to Hamlet's character. He may well be the victim of a so-called Oedipus complex, as set forth in the Freud–Beaumont–Jones theories; and this still remains the most satisfactory account of the reason for the sexual outbursts. But whether this is the *sole* inhibitory cause may be doubted. On the evidence of the soliloquies there is the typical oscillation between the two poles, of action and of self-contempt for refusing the challenge to action. The quotations are too well known to bear repetition. But many critics have noticed the assumption of a power in action, a self-reassurance through rhetoric, usually (as such a mood demands) [2] of the 'exsufflicate' type:

> What is he whose grief
> Bears such an emphasis? whose phrase of sorrow
> Conjures the wandering stars and makes them stand
> Like wonder-wounded hearers? this is I,
> Hamlet the Dane.[3]

And commentators have long been aware of the change in Hamlet's tone and bearing after the active episode of the pirate ship, the calm violence of the murder of Polonius; which allow the play to run rapidly down the smooth slope of the Fifth Act. Hamlet's own *hamartia*, I suggest, remains insoluble in its *total* content; we can if we wish cancel the whole argument by withdrawing ourselves outside the play,[4] but this

---

[1] In other terminology we may think of Jung's account of the complexes. 'They are "vulnerable points" which we do not like to remember and still less to be reminded of by others, but which frequently come back to mind unbidden and in the most unwelcome fashion. They always contain memories, wishes, fears, duties, needs or views, with which we have never really come to terms.' *Modern Man in Search of a Soul*, p. 91.
[2] Consider the Marlovian rhetoric in this respect.   [3] v. i. 262.
[4] As in 'Q's' solution: if Hamlet had not delayed there would have been no play.

procedure, though legitimate, leaves the tragic pattern incomplete. What is clear is that Hamlet's is a character of indecision in one particular direction; that the factors producing the indecision are complex, but not wholly accidental in terms of birth, environment, love, incest, or what you will; but sufficiently basic in human nature to afford a strong 'recognitional' response to successive generations of audience and scholars, and thereby to fulfil one of the prime conditions of tragedy.

§ iv

Coriolanus affords perhaps the simplest instance of both the joint-in-the-armour and the oscillation between the poles of inferiority and superiority; an oscillation which is illustrated graphically in action as well as in words. At the root of his characterization lies an elementary psychological problem which is symbolized in the whole story. We may put it thus; the individual who is yet immature in some particular respect will tend to rely on the family (usually the wife or mother), or tribe or nation, while at the same time rebelling against the limitations which such an association places on the individual. In other words, the Roman system of suffrage for the Consulship is precisely calculated to bring out the worst in Coriolanus, who has neither the sense of humour nor the 'patience', in the Shakespearian sense, to rationalize the situation; to perceive, as Mark Antony does, the rules for the rhetorical handling of democracy.[1] Every lesson learnt in the discipline of war, every move of the politicians, confirms him in his immature desire for the quick results of actions. Iago knew the other side:

> How poor are they that have not patience!
> What wound did ever heal but by degrees?
> Thou know'st we work by wit and not by witchcraft,
> And wit depends on dilatory time.[2]

Each time he attempts to compromise he withdraws to nurse his injured pride; perpetually he seeks reassurance in hyperbole; in rhetoric as 'exsufflicate' as that of Hamlet or Othello:

> Let them pull all about mine ears; present me
> Death on the wheel, or at wild horses' heels;
> Or pile ten hills on the Tarpeian rock,

---

[1] The end of every war tends to bring great soldiers into quasi-political roles: with interesting results.
[2] *Oth.*, II. iii. 367.

That the precipitation might down stretch
Below the beam of sight; yet will I still
Be thus to them.[1]

After he has joined the Volscians (and in his defection the scene among
the serving men is exquisitely timed to parody, as it were, the preceding
scenes in Rome), Aufidius comes most nearly to a complete analysis of
his character. The speech is such a memorable epitome of the tragic
hero that it deserves some detailed comment:

First he was
A noble servant to them; but he could not
Carry his honours even; whether 'twas pride,
Which out of daily fortune ever taints
The happy man; whether defect of judgement,
To fail in the disposing of those chances
Which he was lord of; or whether nature
Not to be other than one thing, not moving
From the casque to the cushion, but commanding peace
Even with the same austerity and garb
As he controll'd the war; but one of these,
As he hath spices of them all, not all,
For I dare so far free him, made him fear'd,
So hated, and so banish'd: but he has a merit,
To choke it in the utterance.[2]

Aufidius, it seems, is conscious of a highly complex *hamartia*, and is not
prepared to commit himself as to which aspects he should stress.
Coriolanus could not retain his balance under conditions of success in
war; it may have been pride, which to an Elizabethan was familiar as
a Deadly Sin. He may have been stupid, or unlucky, in not turning
favourable circumstances to account ('There is a tide in the affairs of
men'); or he may have been in error in thinking he could give orders,
impose his will, on a democracy. Yet there is the invariable re-balancing
of the indictment—

but he has a merit
To choke it in the utterance.

which recalls the more famous

a rarer spirit never
Did steer humanity; but you, gods, will give us
Some faults to make us men.[3]

---

[1] III. ii. 1.   [2] IV. vii. 35.   [3] *A. & C.*, V. i. 31.

§ v

Romeo and Juliet exemplifies the incomplete sphere: partly because of Romeo's own immaturity, partly because of the excessive domination of the stars, partly because the essential responsibility for the conflict is transferred to the rival houses of Montagu and Capulet. The flaw in Romeo is a malady rather than a defect of character; it is merely one aspect of the love-energy which the mechanism of the plot combines alternately to forward and to frustrate. The weaknesses are those of adolescence: but they are completely overshadowed by his sickness and by the pace of events. Indeed, it may be doubted whether any of the great tragic love stories readily admits this immediate schizophrenia, unless the hero is confronted, as in Racine and Corneille, with delicately opposed forces in which love is balanced by an artificially buttressed honour or patriotism. An equally simple play, Marlowe's *Dr Faustus*, shows a *hamartia* so obvious, so heavily underlined in his soliloquies and in the externalized symbolism of the Good and Bad Angels, as to afford no great interest in the psychological subtleties of character.

§ vi

The tragic hero in religious drama shows something of the same oscillation within the sphere of personality. The movement can be seen clearly in Job's violent and penitential abasement, his unrestrained despair when confronted with his tragic chorus; the solution in the final act of faith which has for its epitome the words

Shall mortal man be more just than his Maker?

Of the Christian tragedy it is less easy to write.

It is clear that there is the same consciousness of power, the quiet certainty of a mission; there is, so far as can be judged, the recognition of weakness proper to His guise of Man, the prayer that the Cup might pass, the desperate cry from the Cross. Later dramatists have sought to enlarge the dramatic scope by introducing a more balanced statement of the conflicting claims against Christ. This will serve as an example:

Christ (to Judas) You were beside me every day, and saw
The dead raised up and blind men given their sight,
And all that I have said and taught you have known,
Yet doubt that I am God.

Judas	I have not doubted; I knew it from the first moment that I saw you; I had no need of miracles to prove it.
Christ	And yet you have betrayed me.
Judas	. I have betrayed you Because you seemed all-powerful.
Christ	My Father Even now, if I were but to whisper it, Would break the world in His miraculous fury To set me free.
Judas	And is there not one man In the wide world that is not in your power?
Christ	My Father put all men into my hands.
Judas	That was the very thought that drove me wild. I could not bear to think you had but to whistle And I must do; but after that I thought, 'Whatever man betrays Him will be free'; And life grew bearable again. And now Is there a secret left I do not know, Knowing that if a man betrays a God He is the stronger of the two? [1]

Here we have in a very simple form, though coloured by Yeats's peculiar conceptions of theology, a statement of the basic conflict.

§ vii

Modern tragedy, with its questioning of traditional values and its lack of a philosophical framework within which human personality may be profitably considered, exemplifies an interest in the internal stresses of the sphere and a Swift-like readiness to puncture the bubble or blister of the compensation. Sometimes in its anxiety to explore the interior it loses sight of the traditional resources and limitations of the theatre for which it is designed; sometimes, as in the ritual masks and music of the Nōh drama, it appears to retreat completely from character analysis in search of a totally different effect. The Ibsen hero shows the oscillation between weakness and strength, decision and indecision: in both contrasting with the ruthlessness and single-mindedness of the women characters; and these, indeed, show (as I shall suggest in a later chapter) the typical oscillation between femininity and steadfastness. Against them the men appear swollen with idealism, or with a curious sacrificial obsession. In Shaw the manipulations of the dramatist

[1] W. B. Yeats, *Calvary.*

are far more conscious, the iconoclasm more sharply-edged, conceived in the brain; more apparent, perhaps, in a near-tragedy such as *Candida* than in *St Joan* or *The Doctor's Dilemma*. Against both we can set the rigid, carefully tinctured figures of the French Classical drama, whose predetermined poles of conflict remain rigid throughout each play, and force our interests on to other aspects.

§ *viii*

Perhaps *hubris* itself, the sin of pride, is only one aspect of this compensation for the *hamartia*; for, being grafted on to human personality, or rather an excrescence upon it, it is not only a source of insolence, of failure in decorum and ceremonial, a challenge to the gods, but a peculiarly inviting target for the thunderbolt or the 'little pin' of human injustice or malice. The commonest form of *hubris* is the boast, the challenge, that cannot be made good; the vanity that demands praise because it is self-distrustful; the very extravagance of language, its oaths and hyperbole, the *hysterica passio* of control that breaks down from insecurity—all these are symptomatic of its emptiness.

In a wider context, *hubris* can be seen as the term which connects tragedy most readily with Christian ethics. To commit that sin it is not essential that we should challenge the gods, or 'set black streamers in the firmament', or blaspheme them, or commit some error of ritual, or omit some sacrifice. Its opposing term is humility: in turn to be defined as that sense of man's place in his environment which, arising out of all the judgement and knowledge that his perceptions allow him to master, results in an ultimate consciousness of his own powers and his resolution not to transgress them. The commonest result of transgression is obsessional neurosis, the product of *hubris*, usually attaching to the desire for power, reputation or affection [1] beyond the proper limits of the human situation. We are, perhaps, over-prone to consider *hubris* as a gesture, the outward action of insolence; and fail to notice the inevitable distortions of judgements when translated into action (for action is necessary to heal the wounded psyche) which lie at the heart of the transgressor, and which shade so readily into madness.

When *hubris* is punished the victor-victim usually, but not always, attains some consciousness of the nature of his sin. Both he and the spectators are aware of his atonement, but any overt repentance—which

---

[1] The desire to be 'loved', in the most general terms, is perhaps more powerful than is usually apparent. Setting aside the *King Lear* archetype (and its social implications), this desire has strange ramifications and is closely linked to violence when it is frustrated. The conduct of occupation troops during war is worthy of study from this angle.

appears proper to the unmixed villain only—will alienate our sympathy. Why this should be so is not easy to explain. In some degree repentance is an act of self-accusation; and of all such states of mind it is the one in which the individual finds it most difficult to be utterly certain of his own sincerity. Any hesitation here will break the hero's claim upon us.

§ *ix*

In our consideration of the *hamartia* and its complexities we must, I believe, resist the temptation to seek any inclusive formula. There are many reasons. In the foreshortening, the funnelling-down as it were of the material into the dramatic form, an element of the irrational will intrude. That in turn will be offset by the richer and more complex perceptions of character made possible by the 'imitation' of the hero in the theatre; the number of contacts with his fellow-protagonists, and the swiftness with which they alternate; the tone and tensions of the language; the 'minute particulars' of the elements of the production that set the multiple actions in shadow or relief. But we must beware of violating the utmost mystery of personality. A philosopher has put the matter concisely for our purpose:

> You can study a man scientifically to just the extent that you can grasp and systematize his thing like characteristics, which form an ontological substructure of every one of us; but the man in his wholeness, which is to say in his distinctively human character, eludes every network of rational concepts that is thrown out to cover him.[1]

And again,

> A person's total relation to his world is neither simple nor mono-logical. Partly he stands over against his world, confronted and confronting; partly he finds himself immersed in it, continuous with it, more or less identified with it.[2]

And if we remember that such complexities are inherent in real life, we shall be content to allow, in any criticism (or in a production of the play so good that it is in itself a criticism) the right of the great character to emerge in successive ages in its Protean forms.

[1] Philip Wheelwright, *The Sewanee Review*, Winter, 1953, p. 57.
[2] *Ibid.*, p. 60.

CHAPTER 10

'The Woman's Part'

Sure I did heare a woman shriek: list, ha!
The Duchess of Malfi [1]

For there's no motion
That tends to vice in man but I affirm
It is the woman's part . . .
Cymbeline [2]

Any man has to, needs to, wants to
Once in a lifetime, do a girl in.
Sweeney Agonistes

§ *i*

IN the Huntington Art Gallery at Pasadena there is the famous picture of Mrs Siddons as The Tragic Muse. The painting suggests strength and inexorable will, coupled with a romantic melancholy; behind her, on either side, mysterious figures display the poison and the knife. We may suspect that this conception of tragic womanhood has a long ancestry: Clytemnestra, Medea, Lady Macbeth, Cleopatra, Athalie. These are images of superhuman power achieved through a concentrated passion, or of regal fortitude, like Iphigeneia; in self-sacrifice or in passive suffering. They go forward, through history, to Racine, Shelley, Ibsen, Strindberg, Chekhov, Shaw; Hedda Gabler, Ellida of *The Lady from the Sea*, and St Joan are perhaps the most memorable. Behind or beside them stand a host of lesser women, whose suffering is usually passive in character: their role partly one of contrast, partly to arouse a series of masculine emotions:

Das Unbeschreibliche,
Hier ists getan:
Das Ewig-Weibliche
Zieht uns hinan.[3]

If we set aside the Active Heroine and the Saint, tragic womanhood seems in general to be approached and appraised in a

---

[1] II. iii.   [2] II. v. 20.   [3] *Faust.*

predominantly elegiac mood. Tennyson's *Dream of Fair Women* sets the tone:

> Those far-renowned brides of ancient song
> Peopled the hollow dark, like burning stars,
> And I heard sounds of insult, shame, and wrong
> And trumpets blown for wars.

For woman in tragedy may be either the heart's victim or its torturer; her sufferings, while they are simpler than those of man, find expression more easily on the stage. We may attempt to classify some of the components of the emotional responses found in tragedy.

1. A conscious or unconscious alignment with the Mother-Virgin group of images, with the ancillary suggestions of purity, comfort, safety, pardon.
2. A yielding on the part of man to the paradox of domination under such conditions; reconciled by the sexual appeal, which may sometimes assume a mask of weakness to attain its ends.
3. A desire—perhaps largely unconscious—for sexual revenge by the male, finding its expression in abuse and cruelty; which may well be rationalized on some pretext or other.
4. A pity for the spiritual and material fate of woman because of her biological conditions. This pity is the purer because it has an aspect of mystery, being incapable of being realized or stated by the masculine mind, and as such, jealously guarded by feminine ritual. This element of mystery may on occasion be an important dramatic resource.
5. An aspect of woman in her supra-natural powers—witchcraft, prophecy, the power of the curse; or even of some more than ordinary sensibility which causes man to credit her with mysterious powers.[1]
6. The increasing interest, throughout dramatic history, in the psychology of woman; in proportion to her material and spiritual emancipation. And this appears to have a correlation in the attempt to thrust her back, as it were, into her primordial functions, and falling back on irony or cynicism when she denies them.

---

[1] e.g. her connection with moon-imagery. The virgin-prophetess is a constant in mythology.

§ *ii*

There are, perhaps, two main ways in which women are brought to suffer. First, the sheer physical conditions of their being; secondly, the biological fact that, while they desire domination by men, this domination may lead to slavery. In this fact lies the seed of eternal conflict. Their characteristic virtue is adaptability, which is the price of their survival in marriage; and the singleness of purpose in their lives removes all hope of sublimation or transference when the death of the lover, or his desertion, follows. Euripides' plea in the mouth of Medea stands as the most eloquent of all time:

> Of all creatures that have life and reason we women are the most unhappy. For, first, by payment of much wealth we must needs purchase a husband, a master of our persons . . . And herein lies a fearful peril: will he be base or good? For the wife is disgraced by divorce, yet to refuse marriage is impossible. Then, when a woman has come to live with a strange character and strange ways of life, she must needs have second-sight (for her past experience tells her nothing) if she is to know how to deal with her husband. If, then, we solve this riddle, and the spouse who dwells with us proves not a brutal yoke-fellow, our life is to be envied; otherwise, death were best. When a man is wearied of his home, he walks abroad and relieves his spirit of its distaste in the society of some friend or companion; but we are forced to look to one person only. And they say of us that we pass within the house a life un-threatened by any peril, whereas they engage in the toil of war. Fools! for I had rather go into the line of spears three times than once to bear a child.[1]

For Medea, in her outburst against masculine complacency, is the first of a long line of protestant heroines; in whom the rapid reversal of the 'womanly' emotions may lead to a virulent bitterness of purpose, the conversion of milk or manna into gall. To these (we think of Clytemnestra, Antigone, Lady Macbeth, Hedda Gabler, St Joan) the dramatist's attitude is always complicated in terms of the social back-ground; the accusations of 'unwomanliness' dealt with in the Shavian Prefaces and in Shaw's critiques of Ibsen may be contrasted with the denial of 'nature' in Lady Macbeth, or (initially) in Cordelia.[2] Perhaps it is only in the Protean change of Shakespeare's Cleopatra that the balance is held with emotional exactness, the triple-turned whore set against the lass unparalleled, the mistress transformed to the wife, the harlot to a queen. St Joan might in theory have presented Shaw with

---

[1] Quoted (in part) from Gilbert Norwood, *Euripides and Shaw*, p. 36.
[2] This 'nature' aspect, filial affection and duty is the more strongly emphasized by the male's perception of his daughter as a subsitute for, or reincarnation of, the wife.

the perfection of Virgin mother, saint, leader and victor-victim; but she becomes the affectionately-manipulated puppet of Shaw's peculiarly outrageous historical sense.

The sacrificial aspect, from Iphigeneia onwards, is of some interest; woman may become, one suspects, the scape-goat, her sacrifice rationalized in other terms. The blind fury of the biological urge, whether fulfilled or distorted into the channels of crime, intrigue, or ambition, is usually a source of admiration and embarrassment to men; from Macbeth's awed

> Bring forth men-children only;
> For thy undaunted metal should compose
> Nothing but males.[1]

to Nora Helmer's cry in *A Doll's House*

> *Helmer*: But no man would sacrifice his honour for one he loves.
> *Nora*: It is a thing hundreds of thousands of women have done.

And this sacrificial function may be self-generated, born out of a half-understood desire for atonement or redemption; we think of Hedwig of *The Wild Duck* or the death of Celia in *The Cocktail Party*.

The atonement or redemption may well be the outcome of woman's training, her ability to identify herself with men's interests, so that she may further them:

> Upon such sacrifices, my Cordelia,
> The Gods themselves throw incense.

§ *iii*

Greek drama is full of 'women who wept'; the Trojan Women, Medea, Deianeira, Iphigeneia, Antigone, Cassandra, Polyxene, Hecuba. The scale of emotion runs from the sense of a terrible collective wrong, woman's fierce energy for evil and intrigue under the stimulus of unmixed emotion, the madness of Cassandra (in some sense the proto-type of Ophelia), their confrontation with the alternatives of chastity or death. Above all there is the sense, often ruthless common sense, of women as they assess and suffer the futility and childishness of war. They confront, in a unity of ageless passion, the actions that wreck the sacrifices of bearing and nurture for pride, or greed, power, or revenge: Hecuba's lament as she prepares the body of Astyanax for burial has the quality of Maurya's lament over her dead son in *Riders*

[1] I. vii. 72.

to the Sea. In some strange manner the nakedness of the babe is as the nakedness of the dead, whether in comedy (as the Nurse in the *Choephoroë*) or in the lament for the eternal exclusion from fulfilment. There is the unswerving loyalty of Antigone, impatient with the technical details of ritual, utterly single-minded in her disobedience to Creon, insolent even in her stubbornness; but spreading outwards around her this progressive circle of sympathy that ultimately overthrows the King. Deianeira's slaying of her husband by the robe steeped in the centaur's blood has a double irony: that Hercules should be slain by a woman, that Deianeira, for all her modesty and sweetness of temperament, should, with the best intentions, be the agent of this typically feminine intrigue and deceit.

Euripides' Electra suggests the Lady Macbeth type, and is perhaps an example of woman's inconstancy of mind: alternating between the arrogance over her triumph over the dead Aegisthus, and repentance for the evil as 'nature' returns, like a recoiling wave, to overwhelm her. Woman is 'the gleaming snare'; she is the victim of the irrational, or of the mysterious workings of Aphrodite or of Dionysus. The Nurse in the *Hippolytus* sums up the woman's part as seen by Euripides:

> And so, dear daughter, cease this black despair,
> Cease from this pride of heart—*for pride it is*
> *To think you can be stronger than the Gods.*
> Have the courage of your passion. For a God
> Hath willed it so. *And since your soul is sick,*
> *Deal wisely with the sickness.*
> There are, for such things, magic words and charms
> And we will find some sovereign remedy.
> *Ay, truly men would be hard put to it,*
> *Without us women to find out a way.*[1]

It seems as if these types of tragic womanhood, burdened with the curses of Eve and of St Paul, pass through with little alteration into Elizabethan and Jacobean literature. In tragedy we think most readily of the great queens, and of the women victims; on the one hand there are the complex studies of dignified nobility, as in Vittoria Corombona and the Duchess of Malfi, the victims of intrigue and torment, yet carrying in themselves their own eternal flaw:

> *Cardinall*   Curs'd creature!
> Unequal nature, to place women's hearts
> So far upon the left side!

[1] *Hippolytus*, 472 (transl. F. L. Lucas).

Ferdinand   Foolish men,
             That ere will trust their honour in a bark,
             Made of so slight, weak bull-rush, as is woman
             Apt every minute to sink it! [1]

That woman should, by her frailty, have power to damn a lineage by
bastardy; that she should be able to be overpowered, with astounding
rapidity (her desires tangled) by the rhetoric of the wooer, that she
should be capable of the utmost ruthlessness in intrigue—these characteristics persist. In old age she may be the witch-prophetess, with the
terrible power of the curse. Yet she remains the emblem of transfiguring beauty, man's eternal image of the mother-lover-saint, the thing
'ensky'd and sainted': but not, with three exceptions, in the tragic
vision. Shakespeare's greatest and most vital women belong, save for
Juliet and Cordelia and Cleopatra, to comedy: perhaps because in
tragedy they are never wholly free from the levity of Eve or the
weakness of Lilith. Volumnia and Virgilia of *Coriolanus* are deliberately
at two poles. Virgilia as 'my gracious silence', Volumnia the warrior-
woman, the embodiment of Rome's undaunted mettle, yet with a
certain shrewd unscrupulousness in politics that shows her feminine
realism. The twisted tragedy of *Troilus and Cressida* contains a caricature of the faithless woman who can yet—momentarily—rise to heights
of supreme tenderness:

             Prince Troilus, I have loved you night and day
             For many weary months.[2]

and whose famous betrayal scene still bears quotation for the woman's
part:

             Troilus, farewell! one eye yet looks on thee,
             But with my heart the other eye doth see.
             Ah! poor our sex; this fault in us I find,
             The error of our eye directs our mind.
             What error leads must err. O! then conclude
             Minds sway'd by eyes are full of turpitude.
                                                   (*Exit*)
Thersites   A proof of strength she could not publish more,
             Unless she said, 'My mind is now turn'd whore.'
Ulysses   All's done, my lord.
Troilus   It is.[3]

---

[1] *Duchess of Malfi*, II. v.   [2] III. ii. 114.   [3] V. ii. 104.

Against this we may set the vision of D. H. Lawrence, in a poem which is itself a microcosm of tragic antinomies:

> I had dreamed of love, oh love, I had dreamed of love,
> And the veil of the temple rent at the kiss on kiss,
> And God revealed through the sweat and the heat of love,
> And God abroad and alight on us everywhere,
> Everywhere men and women alight with God,
> My body glad as the bell of a flower
> And hers a flowerbell swinging
> In a breeze of knowledge . . .
>
> But shall I touch hands with death in killing that other
> The enemy, my brother?
> Shall I offer to him my brotherly body to kill,
> Be bridegroom or best man, as the case turns out?
>
> The odds are even, and he will have it so.
> It may be I shall give the bride
> And the marriage shall be my brother's—it may be so.
> I walk the earth intact hereafterwards;
> The crime full-expiate, the Erinnyes sunk
> Like blood into the earth again; we walk the earth
> Unchallenged, intact, unabridged, henceforth a host
> Cleansed and in concord from the bed of death.

§ iv

Many generations of critics have praised Racine's portraiture of women. His characters are displayed in certain essences or concentrations of emotion that (given the assumptions regarding his theatre) become, as it were, touchstones for all time. In *Britannicus* there is a fresh and vivid portrait of two young lovers, who become the pawns for intriguers; Princess Junie is a type of the fresh and innocent heroine. But in general the studies are of older women, obsessed by something for which love, lust, passion, are all inadequate terms; a kind of obsessive absorption in the beloved, heightened to a terrifying extent by every kind of material frustration, till it ends in catastrophe. Phèdre's thirst for Hippolyte, checked until it is beyond bearing by her own sense of shame, is only to be explained by the visitation of an angry goddess; nothing less will account for the *fureur*. So Hermione's love for Pyrrhus, Roxane for Bajazet. In Roxane, indeed, we have the compressed antinomies of love and hatred, desire of love and desire for the peculiar cruelty that is the correlative of rejected love.[1] Queen Esther (whether or not she is a portrait of Mme de Maintenon) has, like Agrippine of *Britannicus,* the dark and fierce qualities of the sorceress-woman, of whom Medea is perhaps the prototype.

Racine observes these women, caught in the fatal net, from a distance; but his genius is to allow them to speak for themselves. 'Love is a disease'; but instead of the whip or the madhouse we see the wave-moments of the fever, the irrational fancies, the swift rationalizations as despair succeeds hope. When the mercury is at its highest a word that leads to a murder seems to promise relief; phantasy and deed and disavowal succeed each other. Always behind them, their last and supreme weapon, is their rhetoric, their infinite capacity for twisting the wrong cause the right way, their rapid canalizations of reason into the irrelevant. But this rhetoric never fails their dignity. They remember that they are queens, that they are public figures, that the expression of pain, rage, venom, can be achieved with dignity in the drive and surge of the tirade, or in the short broken phrases, of the Alexandrine.

It is a conception of love which is, by its very concentration, alien to our experience to-day. The century before Racine had inherited the medieval tradition; in which, though love might indeed be fatal, its game was played under conventions that admitted various subterfuges for the satisfaction of desire. A century later the same relief was possible, with its preludes of sentimental eroticism that merit Dr Johnson's stricture, however strangely it sounds in the *Preface to Shakespeare*: 'But love is only one of many passions; and as it has no great influence upon the sum of life, it has little operation in the dramas of a poet, who caught his ideas from the living world, and exhibited only what he saw before him.'

Few would agree with Johnson's generalization, or its application. Perhaps the truth, as regards neo-Classic drama, is that 'love' in whatever degree or disguise, can serve best, among all possible human emotions, to focus human irrationality and fallibility in their most uncompromising forms; and therefore lends itself most readily to a simple dramatic system of tensions.

---

[1] Consider the *Salome* theme in general, for woman's cruelty, and the extension of it in the Singing Head theme. Allori's picture of Judith and Holofernes, in which the severed head is a self-portrait, and Judith and her mother portraits of his mistress and her mother, is a classic example.

CRISTOFANO ALLORI: THE SEVERED HEAD

Judith with the head of Holofernes

It is said that the younger woman is a portrait of Allori's mistress, the older
her mother; and that the head is a self-portrait of the painter himself

§ v

The plays of Brieux have not justified, in time, the startling claims that Shaw made on his behalf.[1] The handling of the woman's part seems to contain, historically, two components. The first is constant, the physical conditions of women, and their psychological conditions in so far as these depend on the physical. The second varies from age to age: and is a function of woman's place in each civilization: social, political and economic. If the drama that is concerned in the main with women fails to achieve a balance between what is constant and what is relevant only to a particular period of history, *and* if the dramatist does not succeed in universalizing the temporary and local element, the play may rapidly become 'dated'. This recessive tendency is still apparent in our revaluations of Ibsen, and will probably continue until the background of his characters has become part of history. It seems that time has already taken its revenge upon Brieux.

The reasons are fairly clear. The French *petit bourgeois* setting of his characters is too familiar (in one sense) to be interesting, and too remote in another. The bargaining that accompanies the 'arranged marriage' is peculiar to the Latin countries, and the whole economic position of women and their employment has been changed by the two wars. Much of the consequence, and some of the horror, of venereal disease has been removed from our consciousness, and birth control provides alternatives to separation, or abstinence: whether of mistress or of wife. These facts have changed the material situation: much of the thesis of the first version of *Maternity* (for example) now sounds empty and false. It remains to consider what elements are constant, and how Brieux presents them.

The Three Daughters of Monsieur Dupont will serve as an example. M. Dupont has a small printing business. His daughter Angèle has been driven from home, because of an illegitimate child, some fifteen years previously. The second, Caroline, is weak, sentimental and intensely religious. The third, Julie, is married off, after much bargaining between the parents, to Antonin Mairaut; she does not love him, but she passionately wants a child. This intrigue is complicated by the existence of an uncle of the bridegroom's, who is believed to be both wealthy and influential. He turns out to be neither. An aunt dies in India, leaving legacies to Angèle and Caroline: this forces Angèle to revisit her home, and their father is anxious to obtain some of their

[1] 'After the death of Ibsen, Brieux confronted Europe as the most important dramatist west of Russia.' (Preface to the Translated Plays, p. ix.)

9

money for his printing business. But Caroline secretly gives half her legacy to one Courthezon, an elderly man with whom she has fallen in love. She discovers that he has been living with a mistress for the past twelve years, and has two illegitimate children. The houses of cards collapse. Julie proposes to leave her husband, and like Angèle, to make her own living. But Angèle disillusions her:

> You think women—women like me—are happy because you see us laugh. But to laugh is our trade. We are paid for that. And I swear to you often we would ask nothing better than to sit and cry. And you talk of *choosing*! You poor child. Do you suppose we women *choose*? Oh, if you could but know how one comes to loathe the whole world, to be wicked, *wicked*! They despise us so. We have no friends, no pity, no justice. We are robbed, exploited. I tell you all this anyhow, just as it comes, but you understand, don't you? And once you start downhill you can't stop. That is our life, the life of women like me. That is the slough in which I have struggled ten years. No, no, Julie! No, little sister. I implore you don't do as I did. It is too horrible, too abject, too degrading.
>
> *Julie.* Poor Angèle.
>
> *Angèle.* You understand, don't you?
>
> *Julie.* Yes.
>
> *Angèle (rising).* I must go. Goodbye. I dare not look either of you in the face again now that you know everything, now that I remember what I once was. I knew you could never have anything more to do with me. But I felt such a craving to be loved that I half fancied you, at least, Caroline— I see I was wrong. Well, goodbye. I am going away. Forgive me, both of you, for what I have done. Goodbye. (*She turns to the door.*)
>
> *Caroline.* Angèle. (*A pause. Angèle turns at the door.*) I pity you with all my heart. (*Another pause.*) May I kiss you? (*Angèle throws herself into her arms.*)
>
> *Angèle.* Caroline! My kind, good Caroline!
>
> > *The three sisters embrace with tears.*
> > *Dupont, Antonin and Mairaut come in.*
>
> *Antonin (pushed forward by his father. To Julie).* My dear wife, I have come to ask you to forgive me.
>
> *Julie.* It is I who ask *you* to forgive *me*. I was full of romantic ideas. I thought marriage something quite different from what it is. Now that I understand I will be reasonable. One must make allowances. I will make some—to myself.
>
> *Dupont.* That's right.
>
> *Antonin.* That's right. You can't imagine how glad I am that you understand me at last. It seems to me that from to-day our marriage really begins.
>
> *Julie.* Perhaps.

Antonin. To celebrate our reconciliation I will give a grand dinner. I will invite the Puchelets, the Rambourgs, Lignol——

Julie (sadly and with meaning). Exactly—Lignol.[1]

Dupont. Ah, my children, everything comes right when once you make up your mind to be like the rest of the world.

Julie (slowly). Yes: like the rest of the world. I dreamed of something better. But it seems it was impossible.[2]

I have quoted this at length to show something of Brieux's method: Julie's return to the marriage she loathes, to the man who refuses to give her a child, because of the pressure from her parents, and because there is no alternative in her world. The careful understatement of the prose must be allowed for in translation, the hints of sentimentality discounted because of what Brieux has built up previously in the play. It is the realist ending, which sacrifices a dramatic rhythm to the conventions of realism, the ending that Shaw thought would replace the traditional technique:

> Not only is the tradition of the catastrophe unsuitable to modern studies of life: the tradition of an ending, happy or the reverse, is equally unworkable. The moment the dramatist gives up accidents and catastrophes, and takes 'slices of life' as his material, he finds himself committed to plays that have no endings. The curtain no longer comes down on a hero slain or married: *it comes down when the audience has seen enough of the life presented to it to draw the moral*, and must either leave the theatre or miss its last train.[3]

Now we may credit Brieux with a great deal more artistic integrity than Shaw suggests. There is sufficient interest in characterization throughout each play to keep the thesis in a reasonable balance: and the progressive recognitions, particularly in *Damaged Goods*, are competently managed. The tone is grey and neutral, like a Hardy poem. It is a type of tragedy that has no recourse to symbolism,[4] no exaltation, and which has no system of references in history, no sense of the continuity of woman's problem. It has not, as Shaw pointed out, Ibsen's gift of being 'to the last fascinating and full of a strange moving beauty'.[5] Only once or twice does a lyric sense break through Brieux's prose; and it is therefore of interest to consider another dramatist whose sole concern is with the woman's part, and whose method is primarily poetic.

[1] Lignol is Julie's would-be lover.   [2] Act IV.
[3] Preface to Brieux, p. xvii.
[4] Except, perhaps, the wall that protects the house given as part of Julie's dowry, and which gives way before a flood.
[5] Preface to Brieux, p. xv.

§ *vi*

Three plays of García Lorca—all that are as yet available in English translation [1]—offer some unusual material for reflection on the woman's part, for all three are concerned with women's tragedy. *Blood Wedding* is a variant of the Young Lochinvar story: the Bride elopes on her wedding day with her former lover, the pair are tracked down, by a man-hunt of the neighbourhood, in the forest in which they have taken refuge; the two men, lover and bridegroom, kill each other with knives. At the end the lover's wife, the bride and the bridegroom's mother are left to lament among their neighbours; it is a scene curiously suggestive of the ending of *Riders to the Sea*.

But no such summary of the plot is helpful. The play is built up skilfully with the utmost economy of speech. As in a Greek drama there is a previous history of crime: one of the Felix family has killed the bridegroom's mother, and it is Leonardo Felix, a younger brother, who carries off the Bride. The dialogue is mainly in single clipped sentences; much use is made of song throughout. It is difficult to judge of the imagery in translation, but the dominants are clear; the cradle song of Leonardo's wife concerning the black horse, for it is Leonardo's horse that carries the lovers away; the Bride lives in a Cave-house; the lovers take refuge in a forest, and are there hunted to their death. And while they are thus hunted three Woodcutters become a chorus to the tragedy they foresee: their dialogue shifts into a scene with the Moon and a Beggar Woman, a figure completely covered by a green cloth—who does not appear in the cast. A fragment of the verse will give some idea of Lorca's method:

> *Beggar Woman.* The moon's going away, just when they're near.
> They won't get past here. The river's whisper
> and the whispering tree trunks will muffle
> the torn flight of their shrieks.
> It has to be here, and soon. I'm worn out.
> The coffins are ready, and white sheets
> wait on the floor of the bedroom
> for heavy bodies with torn throats.[2]
> Let not one bird awake, let the breeze,
> gathering their moans in her skirt,
> fly with them over black tree tops

---

[1] *Three Tragedies of Federica García Lorca*, transl. James Graham-Luján and R. L. O'Connell. *New Directions*, 1947.
[2] The repetition of *torn* suggests the hound-deer aspect of the man-hunt.

or bury them in soft mud.
>   (*Impatiently*)
>   Oh, that moon! That moon!
>   (*The Moon appears. The intense blue light returns.*)

Moon.	They're coming. One band through the ravine and the other along the river. I'm going to light up the boulders. What do you need?
Beggar Woman.	Nothing.
Moon.	The wind blows hard now, with a double edge.[1]
Beggar Woman.	Light up the waistcoat and open the buttons; the knives will know the path after that.
Moon.	But let them be a long time a-dying. So the blood will slide its delicate hissing between my fingers. Look how my ashen valleys already are waking in longing for this fountain of shuddering gushes![2]

At the end the emotions are exquisitely and ironically balanced. Here is the dialogue as the bodies are brought in, borne shoulder-high:

Mother.	It's the same thing Always the cross, the cross.
Woman.	Sweet nails, cross adored, sweet name of Christ our Lord.
Bride.	May the cross protect both the quick and the dead.
Mother.	Neighbours: with a knife with a little knife, on their appointed day, between two and three, these two men killed each other for love. With a knife, with a tiny knife that barely fits the hand, But that slides in clean through the astonished flesh and stops at the place where trembles, enmeshed, the dark root of a scream.
Bride.	And this is a knife, a tiny knife that barely fits the hand;

[1] iii. 1. The knife-motif has been apparent from the opening scene, in which the Bridegroom's mother laments her murdered men.
[2] III. i.

> fish without scales, without river,
> so that on that appointed day, between two and three,
> with this knife,
> two men are left stiff,
> with their lips turning yellow.

Mother. And it barely fits the hand
> But it slides in clean
> through the astonished flesh
> and stops there, at the place
> where trembles, enmeshed
> the dark root of a scream.[1]

Even in translation, the restraint, the curious liturgical repetitions, convey the frozen quality of woman's grief; and make this one of the most remarkable endings in modern tragedy.

Lorca's play *The House of Bernarda Alba* is in his own words 'a drama about women in a village of Spain'. Furthermore 'these Three Acts are intended as a photographic document'. (They are, very definitely, not.) The characters are the five daughters of Bernarda, whose ages run from thirty-nine to twenty; Bernarda herself ('the domineering old tyrant' as her maid calls her); Bernarda's old mother, aged eighty, who is insane, and is kept locked up but who escapes at intervals to punctuate the action; two women friends of the family; and a chorus, two hundred strong, of women in mourning.

The plot is simple, but impossible to summarize briefly. Bernarda's husband has just died. The eldest daughter, Augustias, is half-engaged to one Pepe el Romano, a man of twenty-five. Even during the funeral service the women are watching the men. At night Pepe comes to the windows of the house for his courting; part of the time he gives to Augustias, but actually is in love with the youngest sister, Adela. But Augustias has inherited the larger portion of her father's money. The curtain of the first Act falls on the appearance of the mad grandmother who has dressed herself and run away from the servant:

Maria Josefa. I ran away because I want to marry—I want to get married to a beautiful manly man from the shore of the sea. Because here the men run from women.

Bernarda. Hush, hush, Mother!

Maria Josefa. No, no—I won't hush. I don't want to see these single women, longing for marriage, turning their hearts to dust; and I want to go to my home town. Bernarda, I want a man to get married to and be happy with!

Bernarda. Lock her up! [2]

[1] III. ii.   [2] Act I.

The plot develops: Poncia, the 'friend of the family', tells the girls how she managed her husband:

> Then he acted very decently. Instead of getting some other idea, he went to raising birds, until he died. You aren't married but its good for you to know, anyway, that two weeks after the wedding a man gives up the bed for the table, then the table for the tavern, and the woman who doesn't like it can just rot, weeping in a corner.

Amelia. You liked it.

Poncia. I learned how to handle him!

Martirio. Is it true you sometimes hit him?

Poncia. Yes, and once I almost poked out one of his eyes!

Magdalena. All women ought to be like that!

Poncia. I'm one of your mother's school. One time I don't know what he said to me, and then I killed all his birds—with the pestle!

(*They laugh.*)

Magdalena. Adela, child, don't miss this! [1]

Martirio steals Augustias' portrait of her betrothed, Pedro; she too is in love with him. But it is Adela who is finally seduced by Pedro; Bernarda drives him from the house. Adela hangs herself. The scene of the catastrophe is worth quoting. The knocking of a hammer is heard. La Poncia goes to investigate.

> Don't go in!
>
> *Bernarda.* No, not I! Pepe, you're running now, alive, in the darkness, under the trees, but another day you'll fall. Cut her down! My daughter died a virgin. Take her to another room and dress her as though she were a virgin. No one will say anything about this! She died a virgin. Tell them so at dawn, the bells will ring twice.
>
> *Martirio.* A thousand times happy she, who had him.
>
> *Bernarda.* And I want no weeping. Death must be looked at face to face. Silence!
>
> (*To one daughter.*)
>
> Be still, I said!
>
> (*To another daughter.*)
>
> Tears when you're alone! We'll drown ourselves in a sea of mourning. She, the youngest daughter of Bernarda Alba, died a virgin. Did you hear me? Silence, silence, I said. Silence! [2]

And the full terror of the scene is brought out as we remember an earlier knocking on the wall:

> (*A heavy blow is heard against the walls.*)
>
> . . . What's that?

[1] Act II. [2] Act III.

Bernarda. The stallion. He's locked in the stall and he kicks against the wall of the house.

(*Shouting.*)

Tether him and take him out in the yard!

(*In a lower voice.*)

He must be too hot.

Prudencia. Are you going to put the new mares to him?

Bernarda. At daybreak.

Prudencia. You've known how to increase your stock.

Bernarda. By dint of money and struggling.[1]

The bare laconic dialogue of the play, the intensity of hatred generated among the women, the sparse but effective symbolism, make the play worth consideration. The old devices are used, but with a freshness that suggests that continuous power of vitality is archetypal; the village harlot, the knocking outside, the appearance of the mad grandmother with her devastating comments on the theme, the lip-service and religious hypocrisy; all these are used as a poet uses them.

§ vii

So the woman's part, of which the greatest will always be the love of man or of children, or even of both, must always bulk large among the material of tragedy. As we confront it, the cry we hear most often is that of negation or despair; sometimes the attribution of responsibility to the crossing stars, sometimes to the institution of marriage, occasionally to the responsibility of the individual. We remember Hippolytus' cry in Euripides' play:

> O God, why hast Thou made this gleaming snare,
> Woman, to dog us on the happy earth?

and Phaidra's

> Sad, sad and evil starred
> Is woman's state
> What shelter now is left or guard?
> What spell to loose the iron knot of fate? [2]

and Julie's outcry in *The Three Daughters*:

... You understand now. You can never again imagine the tears I shed are tears of love. They are tears of remorse and misery. I hate you after your kisses. Our love is a duel in which I am worsted because what is best in me turns traitor. I blush at your victories because you could never have gained

[1] Act III.   [2] Transl. Gilbert Murray.

them without the help of what is base in me, without the baseness you know how to excite.[1] It is not I who yield. It is the animal in me. It is all that is vile. I hate you for the crime of our loveless marriage, the crime you force me to share. I admit you are not the only guilty one, you are not the only one worthy of contempt. But I have had enough of it.[2]

or this fragment of dialogue from *The House of Bernarda Alba*:

Poncia. . . . Years ago another one of those women came here, and I myself gave my eldest son money so he could go. Men need things like that.
Adela. Everything's forgiven *them*.
Amelia. To be born a woman's the worst possible punishment.
Magdalena. Even our eyes aren't our own.
                              (*A distant song is heard, coming nearer*)
Poncia. There they are. They have a beautiful song.
Amelia. They're going out to reap now.
Chorus.   The reapers have set out
                              Looking for ripe wheat;
                              They'll carry off the hearts
                              Of any girls they meet.

   (*Tambourines and carrañacas are heard. Pause. They all listen in the silence cut by the sun*.) [3]

Or Strindberg's pathological insight in *Lady Julie*, who has seduced her father's valet:

Jean. . . . You hate men, Lady Julie?
Julie. Yes, for the most part. But sometimes—when weakness comes—oh, the shame of it!
Jean. You hate me too?
Julie. Beyond words! I should like to have you killed like a wild beast.
Jean. Just as one shoots a mad dog. Is that what you mean?
Julie. Yes, just that!
Jean. But now there's nothing here to shoot with—and no dog! What are we to do then?
Julie. Travel!
Jean. And plague each other to death? [4]

[1] Cf. Yeats's:
                    I am in love
                    And that is my shame.
                    What hurts the soul
                    My soul adores,
                    No better than a beast
                    Upon all fours.   *The Lady's First Song*
[2] Act III.
[3] *Loc. cit*., pp. 320-1.   [4] *Plays*, 1930, Vol. II, p. 217.

What is the place of all this in the tragic conflict and resolution? The violence and ruthlessness of the biological urge, unfulfilled because convention or economics forbids it, lead to destruction. Its interest for the interactions of character upon character appear to be limited, since the seminal urge is sealed, as it were, in the very fabric of woman's being, and is not susceptible of a quick fulfilment and forgetting:

> Thou hast committed
> Fornication: but that was in a far country,
> And besides, the wench is dead.

We are brought by our response to such suffering a stage on the tragic road, but not to the frontiers of the human spirit. But it is not easy to see just *why*. If 'the lineaments of satisfied desire' are against the nature of things, is any sublimation possible? We have abandoned Blake's vision, as well as that of D. H. Lawrence. Is the tragic resolution best seen in women whose vision transcends the sense of their own human dilemma? Was this easier when such speech could be set in the mouth of Cleopatra, or Richard II's Queen, or the Duchess of Malfi?

It may be, indeed, that the woman's part is, for the reasons I have suggested earlier in this chapter, to be the supreme evoker of pity; to offset the heroic mood in man; to bring us to question (as Ibsen and Brieux did) man's humanity; to repeat the question

> Is there any cause in nature that makes these hard hearts?

But the true woman's part, in high tragedy, is beyond all doubt to mirror the perfection of selfless love; springing from the quality of womanhood; that quality which Dante unravelled and wove into the *Convivio*. I do not find it in completeness except in one character: that of Cordelia upon whose sacrifice the gods throw incense. She is the pattern of the love that delivers from evil, she alone has the power to suffer all extremity without yielding to pain. In her is the earthly forgiveness of sin, charity made perfect: reflected in Lear's lyric utterance

> No, no, no, no! Come, let's away to prison

and manifested in the multiple emotions of joy, tenderness, the largesse of the spirit, the essential gentleness of Cordelia. In other women of other great tragedies, the spirit shines through the blood momentarily; as a whole it is intermittent, incomplete, made impure by the pathetic or the sensual. Only in *Faust* can we find something parallel; the mother and lover in a momentary perfection. But in those moments Shakespeare's vision remains:

> Sorrow would be a rarity most belov'd,
> If all could so become it.

The 'Minute Particulars'

For what but eye and ear silence the mind
With the minute particulars of mankind?
YEATS [1]

In the presence of wax figures we have all felt a peculiar uneasiness. This springs from the ambiguous impression they make on us, which prevents our adopting a definite attitude towards them. When we feel them as human beings they mock us; and if we see them as fictions they seem to quiver in irritation. There is no way of reducing them to mere objects. Looking at them we are confused with the suspicion that it is they who are looking at us, and we end up by feeling a loathing towards this kind of superior corpse. The wax figure is pure melodrama. [2]

ORTEGA

§ i

INNUMERABLE critics have commented on the 'richness' of the texture of Chaucer or Shakespeare, and (from a very different angle) on that of Milton. We remember the strange and casual irrelevancies in Chaucer that somehow illuminate character; the moistness and newness of the Wife of Bath's boots, the inconsequential humour in the description of the Cooke:

> But greet harm was it, as it thoughte me,
> That on his shine a mormal hadde he;
> For blankmangere, that made he with the beste.

We remember too the conversation in Justice Shallow's orchard, two old men talking of their dead friends, and of the price of bullocks and ewes; Lear's madness evoking his memories—the review of troops—the challenge—the flying of the hawk; the incredible and inconsequential puns of Antony or Lady Macbeth; the fatuities of Pandarus' comments to Cressida on the procession of knights. The 'minute particulars' are not stream-images [3] or symbols, though we sometimes try to perceive them as such. They are rather the most delicate and sensitive perceptions of a rounding quality in humanity, a shading and contrasting of personality. We may suspect they are in fact significant

[1] *The Double Vision of Michael Robartes.*
[2] Ortega: *cit.* Wheelwright, *The Burning Fountain*, pp. 84–5.
[3] Cf. p. 135 *infra.*

lines left to emerge from character that has been conceived in the round and far more fully; and then, as it were, erased with a happy selectivity. Nor are they of the nature of comic relief, though they may have in Shakespeare a delicate humour of their own. Sometimes a memory may be thrown up, integrated, with a kind of metaphysical wit in its context; as when Hamlet whirls an imaginary lure about his head to make the Ghost stoop to it:

Hillo! ho, ho, boy! Come, bird, come!

It was perhaps the abundance of richly-stored memories, a common bond in the countryside between dramatist and audience, that made this rounding abundance possible. It is in part the extreme objectivity of the modern dramatist that makes it comparatively rare to-day. The tradition of the *tendenz-drama*, the well-made tightly-knit play whose every phrase must tell, is also against it; attention is concentrated, by stage directions or even by preliminary instructions to the producer, on 'significant' details that will earn an obvious place in the dramatic whole; and this may be at the cost of the apparently irrelevant richness and inconsequentiality in the delineation of character—idiosyncrasies is too strong a word for what I have in mind—which contribute to the essential humanity of the tragic characters. The most dramatic failures in this respect are the procession of personages, with their strange historical trajectories, in Hardy's *Dynasts*, the otiose characters with which Ibsen deliberately crowded his canvas in *Emperor and Galilean*, or the ponderous manipulation of historical character in modern tragedy in accordance with the demands of 'research'.[1]

§ *ii*

Character in drama has many facets. The quality of energy, that 'eternal delight', is quickly perceptible on the stage or in the study, but is never easy to define. 'You cannot give a body to something that moves beyond the senses, unless your words are as subtle, as complex, as full of mysterious life, as the body of a flower or of a woman.' [2] Character, at its greatest, moves beyond the senses. Its quality derives from a certain pregnancy and individuality of phrase, 'it talks itself into life'; the first being its creator's response to the economy of the

---

[1] We may instance Drinkwater's *Abraham Lincoln*; and the vast amount of money, time and labour expended by 'researchers' for Hollywood's historical subjects. This type of detail too often swathes the characters in 'approved' detail of dress and character, and masks them from any semblance of humanity.

[2] Yeats, *Essays*, p. 201.

play, the second a matter of portraying its characteristic habit of thought and the establishment of relationships within the orbit of that thought. The qualities of 'charm' and 'versatility' are brought out by its response to the apparently trivial or irrelevant moments of its experience; and the great dramatist can—without a laboured over-loading of imagery—make these moments contribute simultaneously to the rounding of the character and to the significance of the larger aspects of the action.

The quality of extension in tragedy is in part dependent on the felicity with which the minor characters are drawn. Unless they are in some way made both credible and living the main characters lack reflected light and a certain warmth. In any play that carries a multi-plicity of them there cannot be adequate drawing; and the flash of inspiration that brings a character to life, as it does Osric in *Hamlet* or the drunken Lepidus in *Antony and Cleopatra*, requires a special genius. Webster is full of selected detail that sometimes leaves us with a sense of hopelessly overdone violence; but which at its best, backs up char-acter unerringly with its explosive image-making. In neo-classic drama in general the care for correctness, the emphasis on the platitudinous heroic, seem to eliminate any rounding off by the irrational-significant. Once moral character is isolated and focused to illuminate passion, the figures are burdened with a peculiar rhetorical stiffness superimposed from without by their creator. 'They came to hear a certain number of lines recited with just gesture and elegant modulation.'[1]

English Romantic tragedy is at once too serious in a minor sense, too consciously poetic in its own neo-Shakespearian style, to allow its characters to grow: Keats's *Otho the Great* is now unreadable, and Byron's *Manfred* little better; Browning's *Luria*, with its complex plot and heavy language, wholly lifeless. (It is curious that Browning, who could use the minute particulars with such effect in the dramatic mono-logues, seemed incapable of embodying them in tragedy proper; it is as if his eyes were focused on the need for a strange stiff discipline of the dialogue for the stage that inhibited creativity.) It is not till the end of the nineteenth century that we get this significant detail building up again, and here the most interesting statement is Strindberg's:

> I have avoided the mathematically symmetrical construction of French dialogue and let people's brains work irregularly, as they do in actual life, where no topic of conversation is drained to the dregs, but one brain receives haphazard from the other a cog to engage with. Consequently, my dialogue

[1] Johnson, *Preface to Shakespeare*.

too wanders about, providing itself in the earlier scenes with material which is afterwards worked up, admitted, repeated, developed and built up, like the theme in a musical composition.[1]

The danger of Strindberg's method is over-emphasis on this thematic haphazard quality of speech, so that the dialogue becomes contrived; the Count's boots that Jean is cleaning, Julie's handkerchief, her pet dog that runs after the lodgekeeper's dog,[2] take on by the emphasis of repetition the nature of symbols. The 'particulars' must be kept in a delicate balance, lest they oppress the tragedy and rob it of vitality. The background incidents of such a play as Maeterlinck's L'Intruse are too heavily contrived to subserve the tragic effect. We may remember the artificial concatenation of them; the carpenter sawing, the gardener sharpening his scythe, the nightingales that stop singing and the lamp that dies for want of oil, the glass door that is open, and that cannot be shut because something invisible has blocked it. The marked and precise imagery of Les Aveugles, the gradations of darkness, the blind girl who can only smell the flowers while the others can only smell the earth, suggests a recondite and literary approach to the poet's characteristic attempts to approach the Unexpressed. Les Sept Princesses, with its imagery which reads like a case-book of dream interpretation, is the reductio ad absurdum of his method; Pélléas and Mélisande, with its more cogent action, its shadow of desire, and its momentarily effective symbolism, is more satisfying. But his revolt against 'pathetic' and 'heroic' tragedy, his attempt to communicate his own particular world, lead him to his own interpretation of the minute and troubling particulars. The 'inner communication' which he seeks is to be attained by the unspoken:

> There must be something other than the dialogue which by external standards is necessary. It is really only those words which at first seem useless that mean anything in a play. They contain the soul of the play. Alongside the inevitable dialogue there is nearly always a second dialogue which appears superfluous. Watch carefully, and you will realize that this is the only dialogue to which the soul is attentive, for only there do we speak with it. You will also find that it is the texture and range of this unnecessary dialogue which finally determine the quality of the play and its significance.[3]

The attempt to communicate by devices other than dialogue, the silences of Galsworthy and of O'Neill, presuppose an excited and collaborating audience, wrought to such a pitch of attention that

---

[1] Preface to Lady Julie.   [2] Cf. the coupled dogs in Hogarth's Marriage à la Mode.
[3] Le Trésor des Humbles, pp. 173-4.

silence, detail, light, the accessories of costume and staging, are allowed to do their work. This thread of attention is easily broken, particularly in quasi-naturalistic tragedy, and the spoken word remains the most potent device for building emotional tension. It is possible that the growing subtlety of cinema technique, and the gradual education of the audience in response to them, may ultimately increase the tragic dramatist's resources.

Yet it is perhaps in Ibsen that the minute particulars can still be studied with most profit, because of the perfection of their integration with the general design. There will always be differences of opinion both as to their interpretation and their centrality. We may remember the white shawl that Mrs Solness wears that suggests a shroud; Wehrle the photographer in *The Wild Duck* reproducing stereotyped senti- ments that are the commonplaces of those who see superficialities only; the 'burning' motifs in *Ghosts*. That they sometimes appear intrusive, or too contrived, is partly because we hear or read them in the strange idiom of translation. It is of their essence that, like the images, they should stimulate the imagination without setting limits to the shores on which the ripples end: that the language in which they are expressed should have the peculiar pregnancy of phrase that throws its double light: backward upon the characters, and forward, however faintly, into the nature of the tragedy itself.

The element of the pathetic in tragic communication can be con- sidered as among the minute particulars. It appears to deal with a type of response that is valuable as sensitizing certain accessible but super- ficial layers of emotion. As such, it may be thought to have two objects: the establishment of a rapid, pitiful relationship with day to day or 'domestic' experience, and the establishment of sympathetic links with the physical side of pity as perceived in day to day aspects of living. The pathetic is always delicately balanced on the knife-edge between what is effective and acceptable, and what may be thought sentimental, and this again depends mainly on the setting and 'timing' of its use. At its best, we may think of it as important in preparing the way for deeper emotions, perhaps even existing in its own right to release initial clusters of emotions that must be cleared away before the full response can take place. The sense of place, childhood and its happiness (and all accessories to childhood), the Nurse, faith or its lack in servants, pets or animals, all enter in. The Duchess of Malfi's

> Farewell, Cariola!
> I pray thee, look thou giv'st my little boy

Some syrup for his cold, and let the girl
Say her prayers ere she sleep.—Now what you please:
What death? [1]

may be remembered beside Shakespeare's children, and the dead child's
clothes that Brand denies to its mother. Ophelia's ballads have relevant
pathos in their context; Antony's discourse over the dead Caesar
touches deliberately the springs of the pathetic past:

> You all do know this mantle: I remember
> The first time ever Caesar put it on;
> 'Twas on a summer evening, in his tent,
> The day he overcame the Nervii.
> Look! in this place ran Cassius' dagger through . . .[2]

We may consider, side by side, two laments, each seeking to establish
the sense of sorrow through the pity of the mother-son relationship.

> *Mrs. Tancred.* Me home is gone, now; he was me only child, an' to think
> that he was lyin' for a whole night stretched out on the side of a lonely
> counthry lane, with his head, his darlin' head, that I ofen kissed an'
> fondled, half-hidden in the wather of a runnin' brook. An' I'm told that
> he was the leadther of the ambush where me nex' door neighbour, Mrs.
> Mannin', lost her Free State soldier son. An' now here's the two of us oul'
> women, standin' one on each side of a scales o' sorra, balanced be the
> bodies of our two dead darlin' sons.[3]

O'Casey's speech, both in rhythm and in idiom (I do not think that
the last image is of the common language) has a false ring, even in its
relation to the particular character: and the pathetic is used with something less than tact. Contrast the following from Synge:

> *Maurya.* There was Sheamus and his father, and his own father again, were
> lost in a dark night, and not a stick or sign was seen of them when the
> sun went up. There was Patch after that was drowned out of a curagh
> that turned over, I was sitting here with Bartley, and he a baby lying on
> my two knees, and I seen two women, and three women, and four women
> coming in, and they crossing themselves and not saying a word. . . .[4]

'And he a baby on my two knees.' The tragedy of the spirit is balanced
against the tragedy of the body, to remind us, whether in a mood of
morbidity, cynicism or tenderness, of those antinomies. This is one
function of the Nurse in tragedy, that half-irrelevant character who

[1] IV. ii. 206 .   [2] III. ii. 170.
[3] *Juno and the Paycock*, Act II.   [4] *Riders to the Sea.*
10

draws a rich abundance from her double contact with the physical, and with the wonder of personality emerging in growth. So the Nurse in *Romeo and Juliet* with her coarseness, vitality, and vulgar love of suspense is an essential counterweight to a romantic dream of love that might easily have become vapid or over-ethereal. For the Nurse, as that character in the *Choephoroë* of Aeschylus points out, is the essential link in the human chain of being, the crude and constant remembrancer of man in his utmost extremity of flesh, whether in infancy or in old age:

> Though You can fashion everything
> From nothing every day, and teach
> The morning stars to sing,
> You have lacked articulate speech
> To tell Your simplest want, and known,
> Wailing upon a woman's knee,
> All of that worst ignominy
> Of flesh and bone.[1]

So the Nurse's jesting at Juliet's marriage bears retrospectively a terrible irony when she is deserted by both mother and Nurse, as in that strange dialogue when Juliet suddenly puts on womanhood; immediately after the Nurse has betrayed her by praising Paris:

Juliet. Speakest thou this from thy heart?
Nurse.   And from my soul too;
          Or else beshrew them both.
          (*The slight hint of garrulity contrasting with Juliet's sharp staccato words.*)
Juliet.   Amen!
Nurse.   What !
Juliet. Well, thou hast comforted me marvellous much.
          Go in, and tell my lady I am gone . . .[2]

The Nurse or the old servant, deference and familiarity and maybe bawdry too, serves as 'the weather-beaten conduit of many kings' reigns'. Such a character enforces a new perspective, a sense of time and of the body, a healthy corrective to over-much conflict of the spirit, and an extended perception of the ironical through the difference of planes. And the ironic possibilities of the Nurse-child relationship (have we not lost much by eliminating servants from tragedy?) are considerable. Antigone in Anouilh's play has been out to bury her brother. She knows that her action will be discovered.

---

[1] Yeats, *A Prayer for my Son.*   [2] III. v. 228.

Nurse. . . . But your Uncle Creon will hear of this! That, I promise you.
Antigone (*a little wearily*). Yes, Creon will hear of this.
Nurse. And we'll hear what he has to say when he finds out that you go
wandering alone o' nights. Not to mention Haemon. For the girl's
engaged! Going to be married! Going to be married, and she hops out of
bed at four in the morning *to meet somebody else in a field.*[1] Do you know
what I ought to do to you? Take you over my knee the way I used to do
when you were little.
Antigone. Please, Nurse, I want to be alone.[2]

And a little later; for the pathetic itself, though incapable of resolution,
is valuable as a lyric interlude.

Nurse (*very tenderly*). Where is your pain?
Antigone. Nowhere, Nanny dear. But you must keep me warm and safe, the
way you used to do when I was little. Nanny! Stronger than all fever,
stronger than any nightmare, stronger than the shadow of the cupboard
that used to snarl at me and turn into a dragon on the bedroom wall.
Stronger than the thousand insects gnawing and nibbling in the silence of
the night. Stronger than the night itself, with the weird hooting of the
nightbirds that frightened me even when I couldn't hear them. Nanny,
stronger than death, give me your hand, Nanny, as if I were ill in bed
and you sitting beside me.[3]

Something of the same function is fulfilled by the bawdy in tragedy,
with additional complexities. This may arise from the by-passing of the
subconscious censor in time of great stress, extremities of physical pain;
in this last lies the supreme genius of Edgar's acting of a madman, or
the pathos of Ophelia's ballads. Or it may show itself with a kind of
bitter ferocity that betrays, maybe, the sadism of the speaker, as often
in Webster. The by-play in *Antony and Cleopatra* between Charmian,
Iras, Alexas and the soothsayer is to have its ironic echoes later in the
play (as in the jest on the figs); but brings out the human gaiety and
love of innuendo of the two handmaidens, and lends some colour to
Heine's picture of the witty brilliant court against the background of
the eternal Pyramids: 'Wie witzig ist Gott!'
   A censorship now forbids the Rabelaisian, driving the dramatist to
innuendo: which in its turn has to be so brain-contrived as to rob it of
vitality. We may, for instance, speculate with profit as to how an
Elizabethan would have handled the following piece of dialogue
from O'Neill's *Mourning Becomes Elektra.* The General has just died,

---

[1] Her brother Polyneices, who is lying unburied outside the city.
[2] p. 15.   [3] pp. 22–3.

poisoned by his wife; the doctor, who has attributed the death to angina, is discussing it with Borden:

> *Blake.* I'll tell you a secret, Josiah—strictly between you and me.
> *Borden (sensing something from his manner—eagerly).* Of course. What is it, Joe?
> *Blake.* I haven't asked Christine Mannon any embarrassing questions, but I have a strong suspicion it was love killed Ezra!
> *Borden.* Love?
> *Blake.* That's what! Leastways, love made angina kill him, if you take my meaning. She's a damned handsome woman and he'd been away a long time. Only natural between man and wife—but not the treatment I'd recommend for angina. He should have known better, but—well—he was human.
> *Borden (with a salacious smirk).* Can't say as I blame him! She's handsome! I don't like her and never did, but I can imagine worse ways of dying! (*They both chuckle.*) Well, let's catch up with the folks.[1]

The madman may bring many offerings to the tragic tomb: mainly because he is an ambivalent figure of horror, and (among the unsophisticated) of veneration; because his licence of speech may extend to comment, prophecy, irony, bawdry, or truth. Like the Fool, he is afflicted and beloved of God. The song in *The Duchess of Malfi* sung by a madman 'to a dismal tune', is poor stuff, but the dialogue that follows upon the entry of Bosola is memorable:

> 1. Mad-man (*Astrologer*). Dooms-day not come yet? I'll draw it nearer by a perspective, or make a glass, that shall set all the world on fire upon an instant: I cannot sleep, my pillow is stuffed with a litter of porcupines.
> 2. Mad-man (*Lawyer*). Hell is a mere glass-house, when the devils are continually blowing up women's souls on hollow irons, and the fire never goes out.
> 3. Mad-man (*Priest*). I will lie with every woman in my parish the tenth night: I will tithe them over like hay-cocks . . .[2]

But the madman, because of his segregation, is now an impossible figure on the stage, unless the scene is laid in the most primitive communities. Gerd in Ibsen's *Brand*, and the old grandmother in Lorca, are among the few examples in modern tragedy. In the close community of the ship in *Moby Dick*, Pipe and Ahab are linked by a common madness; and just as the dogs bark at King Lear, and horse, hound and hawk desert the dying knight in *The Twa Corbies*, so the

---

[1] *Plays* (Cape, 1929), p. 119.   [2] IV. ii.

school of fish leave their escort doomed vessel to follow another ship
homeward bound.

The minute particulars are not essential to all tragedy; but they can
be of great power in the troubling of the mind to further receptiveness.
From one point of view they are important indications of the dramatist's sense of unity over the whole range of his material; his sympathy
with the extremities of mankind, and his realization that, in Richards's
words, 'Tragedy is perhaps the most general, all-accepting, all-ordering experience known.'

CHAPTER 12

'Those Masterful Images . . .'

Those masterful images, because complete
Grew in pure mind, but out of what began?
YEATS [1]

Imagery is the urgent means by which experience holds our attention. . . .
Images are not still lifes to be hung on walls. They are visions of the history
of the race and of life and death.　　STEPHEN SPENDER [2]

One of the benefits of tradition is that it allows the subconscious safely
to take the upper hand.　　THEODORE SPENCER [3]

§ i

IN the last thirty years the nature, function and system of references of
the poetic image have been handled by many eminent writers: in particular Miss Bodkin, Miss Spurgeon, Miss Tuve, W. H. Clemen, Wilson Knight, Cecil Day Lewis, William Empson, E. A. Armstrong.
Much of their work, in its turn, owes a debt to such varied sources as
The Golden Bough, Jane Harrison's *Themis*, and the writings of Freud,
Jung and Jones. Any attempt to carry speculation a stage further must
start by acknowledging its debt to them; and in particular to Miss
Bodkin's *Archetypal Patterns in Poetry*.

There are special dangers in such a study. Interpretations have an
unduly large subjective element, and conclusions do not lend themselves readily to verification. The deductions made by the amateur in
psychological or anthropological studies tend to a licence of conjecture
from which the professional is usually free. At the same time the moral
and philosophical implications of the tragic dramatist's imagery are of
such importance that, if the propositions with which I have been concerned are tenable, the image remains the single most important device
for communicating the essential complexity and depth of the tragic
experience. The task will not be any easier because of the need to deal,
not only with individual images (themselves compounded of variables
in time, space and human experience) but with groups of images, used
in conjunction with other communicatory devices, to produce a final

[1] *The Circus Animals' Desertion.*　　[2] *The Destructive Element*, p. 280.
[3] *Death and Elizabethan Tragedy*, p. 209.

134

response of which the permutations of the possible components might well seem infinite, and any selected response too personal or too arbitrary. Fortunately it is possible to check our investigations by taking note of the apparent recurrence—whatever their superficial modifications—of the images in the history of thought; by some contextual limitation in the poetic statement; and by the technical factors implicit in the dramatic structure.

For the purpose of this essay I propose to accept as read the more obvious image-classifications which have already been sufficiently emphasized: sometimes, we may think, to a degree which causes us to lose sight of the wider implications of the play. It is sufficiently clear, for example, that the storm in *Lear* has a symbolic value as indicative of cosmic disorder; that blood and darkness are dominants in *Macbeth*; that the wild duck—whatever the meanings that commentators may have attached to that not wholly satisfactory symbol—was intended to lie at the heart of Ibsen's play; that the statues of Artemis and Aphrodite show forth the dichotomy of the *Hippolytus*. We shall have occasion to mention these 'dominants'; but I am more concerned with the investigation of the 'intermittent' or 'accessory' images in the tragic structure. I therefore suggest three divisions of the image:

1. The Dominants:[1] that is, one or more images that, by specific statement or inference, provide a framework or theme for the play; and in terms of which part or all of the dramatic statement is made. These will be of varying degrees of subtlety. Such are the Ice-Cavern in *Brand*, the Mill-Race in *Rosmersholm*, the Tower in *The Master-Builder*.

2. 'Stream' images: that is, a sequence or cluster of images which work through repetition, absolute or incremental, and thereby establish and reinforce their meaning in the body of the play. Such images may serve to communicate various forms of irony and ambiguity.

   How far we are entitled to bring to the interpretation of such images our knowledge of previous usages established by the dramatist in work outside the given play is a matter of some difficulty.[2]

3. 'Intermittent' images, establishing their validity through their context; usually unconscious in their origin; with functions—in

---

[1] This usage corresponds, I think, to Empson's use of 'master symbol': cf. *The Structure of Complex Words*, p. 176.
[2] This question arises in the interpretation of Yeats, and perhaps of Eliot and Hardy.

addition to the excitement of sensibility proper to all such—of showing the impact of the relevant-irrelevant upon the design of the play.

Any or all of these may be used to reflect, illuminate or extend the dramatist's purpose. In all of them we shall keep in mind the ambivalence of many, perhaps all of these images; and this ambivalence will frequently be perceived as one symptom of the tragic balance. The 'stream-images' appear to serve three functions. They emphasize the time-scale of the dramatic action. They draw attention to the 'purposive' quality in the structure of the play. And I suggest that, under certain circumstances, they set up a secondary or inductive current in the whole dynamic of the tragic statement.

§ ii

At this point it is convenient to consider the verse in Yeats's poem that immediately precedes the heading of this chapter:

> And when the Fool and Blind Man stole the bread
> Cuchulain fought the ungovernable sea;
> Heart-mysteries there, and yet when all is said
> It was the dream itself enchanted me:
> *Character isolated by a deed*
> *To engross the present and dominate memory* . . .

Here are three images which exemplify the modification of traditional material to the purpose of the tragic poet. All three refer primarily [1] to the play *On Baile's Strand*. It is obvious that the myth of Cuchulain, with its powerful epic elements, had a multiple symbolic value for Yeats [2] as having been equated, in various ways, with his own personal mythologem, and as being the last of the 'Celtic' images that appeared to have stood the test of time. They will serve for the moment to suggest something of the mechanism of an archetypal image.

Cuchulain stands for the hero, begotten mysteriously by a hawk [3] out of a woman. He is typical of a score of such magical births. He has conquered, and loved, a fierce warrior woman: he does not know that she has borne him a son. He rebels against the High King, Conchubar, refusing to take the oath of loyalty to him. Unknowing, he fights with,

---

[1] Since they occur also in *The Death of Cuchulain*.
[2]   'Who thought Cuchulain till it seemed
                    He stood where they had stood?'
[3] We need not stress the hawk-dove antinomy here, but the reader will be conscious of the dove-symbolism in many pictures of the Annunciation.

and kills his son: after the Sohrab and Rustum pattern. The anagnorisis comes too late. Cuchulain rushes out to fight the sea, and dies in the waves.

The multiple pattern is sufficiently clear: magical birth, the conquest and subjugation of woman, the slaying of the son, the death in conflict with the sea: standing for the One against the Many, or man against nature, or sex, or the life-matrix: the whole representing a many-sided conflict whose only possible resolution is death. But the pattern is even more complicated than this: for Cuchulain is wearing a cloak woven from the sea-foam; itself apparently a sexual image of some complexity.[1]

The Fool and the Blind Man are the two subsidiary images; part traditional, part formed to constitute the two poles of the play:

> *Second Woman.* Who would have thought that one so great as he
>   Should meet his end at this unnoted sword!
> *First Woman.* Life drifts between a fool and a blind man
>   To the end, and nobody can know his end.
> *Second Woman.* Come, look upon the quenching of this greatness.[2]

The Fool is the empty man; to whom the knowledge of ultimates, or of God, is in some sort given. The Blind Man is powerless without his eyes, which he borrows from the Fool: but it is his knowledge that reveals to Cuchulain that he has killed his son. (The type of the blind seer is a very ancient one.) Both are aspects of natural man (consider Caliban's 'I must eat my dinner'). Both punctuate the action of the play. They supply the commentary on the final reported scene, but from two different angles; for the Fool is aware of the mystery of what he has seen. The passage is worth quoting in full:

> *Blind Man.* Come here, Fool!
> *Fool.* The waves have mastered him.
> *Blind Man.* Come here!
> *Fool.* The waves have mastered him.
> *Blind Man.* Come here, I say.
> *Fool (coming towards him, but looking backwards towards the door).*
>   What is it?
> *Blind Man.* There will be nobody in the houses. Come this way; come
>   quickly!
>   The ovens will be full. We will put our hands into the ovens.[3]

---

[1] Consider the pictorial representations of the birth of Venus.
[2] *Collected Plays*, p. 271.   [3] *Ibid.*, p. 278.

§ *iii*

We may see both the dominant and stream-images in the *Oresteia* of Aeschylus. The originating crime, begetting its accumulation of evil, is 'Thyestes' banquet of his children's flesh'. The trilogy is primarily concerned with the parent-child relationship, analysed in the ingenious debate in the *Eumenides*. Yet through it runs the train of images from eating: devouring, bloodsucking, biting; Clytemnestra describes herself as 'a dog watching over a house'; the Furies are 'my mother's angry dogs'. The apophthegm *homo homini lupus* is older in folk-lore than the Eumenides, and it is still possible to evoke the terror of the pursuit. Miss Bodkin, indeed, suggests a Furies Archetype,[1] the energy of passion fixed in an evil relationship but capable of transformation into a good one. Both the wolf and the horse, their terror abundantly verified in dream-psychology, are common in this context. Macbeth's vision of the sightless couriers of the air (and Blake's intensification of it), Ibsen's White Horses of *Rosmersholm*, and man's perennial attempt to express compound attitudes in the centaur or the unicorn, will serve as examples. The wolf-dog imagery has many facets; man's desired control of brute creation, and his partial failure; the pursuit in the dark; fidelity, subservience and treachery; a kind of snobbishness in the rejection by the dog, as in *King Lear*:

> The little dogs and all,
> Tray, Blanch, and Sweet-heart, see, they bark at me.

Empson [2] has pointed out with the utmost ingenuity the multiple and conflicting imagery of the word *dog* in *Timon of Athens*, and shows how opposing feelings can exist simultaneously. At the same time it is probably wise to remember, in the quest for ambiguities, the traditional usages, as in the Hindu or Homeric or Biblical scale of insults and threats. The presupposition of a State in a condition of conflict or disunion gives rise naturally to a train of disease imagery: whether in Sophocles' *Antigone*, or in *Hamlet*, or in so much of Ibsen,[3] and the idea of the commonwealth as a body is too common to require Menenius' laboured parable in *Coriolanus*. The love-death antinomy, as one of the originating tragic situations, carries with it its own appropriate images; bed-tomb, death the ravisher or bridegroom, form a natural sequence in the delineations of unsatisfied desire. The images

---

[1] *The Quest for Salvation.*   [2] *The Structure of Complex Words*, p. 177.
[3] Cf. the common (and partly justified) accusation of Ibsen's obsession with concealed disease.

spread out their delicate tentacles into the past, maintaining (at their best) a delicate and deliberate balance between enrichment of meaning and sheer decoration. So in the passage from *Romeo and Juliet*:

> Death, that hath suck'd the honey of thy breath,
> Hath had no power yet upon thy beauty:
> Thou art not conquer'd; beauty's ensign yet
> Is crimson in thy lips and in thy cheeks,
> And death's pale flag is not advancèd there.

It is easy to expand our exegesis of such a passage, without reference to what we may take to be the far more generalized impact of it upon the audience in a theatre. We can, for instance, point to the death-bee-sting cluster from the Lesson for the Burial of the Dead, without immediately admitting the honey-sexual pleasure or potency-wisdom group.[1] We may or may not connect the sexual kiss in connection with the leave-taking of the dying, remembering Donne's

> Soe, soe, breake off this last lamenting kisse,
> Which sucks two soules, and vapors Both away . . .

or the *power*, the accented word, as having its sinister implications of rape, imprisonment, corruption. It is legitimate to perceive, in the battle imagery of the next three lines, a normal prothalamic approach, to point to the ante-sign of the royal passionate colour; without necessarily remembering the line in the Song of Solomon

> . . . Terrible as an army with banners.

The image of the coldness, advancing from feet to head, may draw simultaneously on memories of the deaths of Socrates and of Falstaff.

We must, I believe, hold to an intermediate position in the interpretation of the images, keeping in mind traditional usage, the requirements of the stage, the difficulty of communicating 'the minute particulars', and the increasing gap between the reader and the audience; the latter reacting at high speed and at widely-differing levels, the former bringing to interpretation the equipment and presuppositions of the literary mind. Certain images suggest themselves naturally in a given context, and may, by repetition or by emphasis, acquire the character of symbols. The uncurtained windows in a lighted room (Maeterlinck and Eliot), Hedda Gabler's pistols, the Silver Tassie as the chalice in O'Casey's play of that name, are all obvious devices.

[1] Cf. '. . . Honey of generation has betrayed': and honey in the story of Samson. Cf. also Kranach's *Venus* in the Borghese.

The animal imagery in *Lear*, musical imagery in *Othello*, disease in *Hamlet*, are no more than evidence of high competence in a well-established poetic tradition, in which just such a range of simile and metaphor is part of the poetic equipment and heritage. It is possible that we may be led to dangerously subjective interpretations by pressing them to conclusions (whether archetypal or Freudian) without full and prior consideration of their simpler connotations. And if such images appear irrational or arbitrary, it is worth while to examine them in order to ascertain what personal memories or associations may have set up in the poet's mind such image-clusters or groups.[1]

§ *iv*

A striking analysis of the Romantic Image is given by W. H. Auden in *The Enchafed Flood*: much of which is concerned with a ship symbol, leading to a most illuminating analysis of *Moby Dick*. There is some analogy, in the choice of the ship setting for a tragedy, with the qualities of the tragic structure itself:

> A constant aesthetic problem for the writer is how to reconcile his desire to include everything, not to leave anything important out, with his desire for an aesthetic whole, that there shall be no irrelevances and loose ends. The picture has to be both complete and framed. The more society becomes differentiated through division of labour, the more it becomes atomized through urbanization and through greater ease of communication, the harder it becomes for the artist to find a satisfactory solution.[2]

The image clusters of drama are infinite in their character, inter-relation, and potential interaction. It is misleading to give anything approaching equivalent meanings: the suggestions in brackets are no more than indications of some of the apparent significances in dramatic imagery.

Sun (fire, father, power, fertility, harshness)
Moon (mother, change, gentleness, chastity)
Storm (all types of conflict)
Ship (security and jeopardy; co-operation and order; passage from life to death)
Fog and Mist (confusion of the spirit, loss of objective)
Birds (soul; ominous; cf. the carrion birds; pride for hawks and eagles)
The Dragon and his kindred (the supreme Enemy, the swallower of the Sun; the evil haunter of springs and wells; the deceiver of the young and helpless)

[1] Cf. E. A. Armstrong, *Shakespeare's Imagination.*   [2] p. 62.

Beasts (man less soul: cf. *Lear* vs. *When We Dead Awaken*; Blake's Nebu-
chadnezzar)
All Sea-Beasts (power uncontrollable by man; the saviour or helper of man;
that which issues from the depths and returns to them)
Sea (life and death-giver: sleep or restlessness; the eternal engulfment of man
and his creations)
River (the crossing to death; the time-flow; mergence into the sea)
Horse (power, terror, justice of the skies: combination of its noblest qualities
with man—combined in the centaur)
The tree (mystery of growth; magnificence and strength; microcosm of
seasonal cycles; helplessness before man's power)
The garden (order; man's power vs. nature's wildness)
The stone (death, insensibility, the sealer of the past)
The candle and lamp (vitality, fertility, sexual union, destruction of life)
The cave (refuge, rebirth, security, prison)
All weapons (essentially a confirmation and extension of individual power,
often phallic)

As examples of some of these mysterious effects we might quote,
arbitrarily, the following:

> . . . the odds is gone,
> And there is nothing left remarkable.
> Beneath the visiting moon.[1]

The Stranger in Ibsen's *The Lady from the Sea.*
  The conclusion of the making of the supreme harpoon for theWhite
Whale:

> This done, pole, iron, and rope—like the Three Fates—remained inseparable,
> and Ahab moodily stalked away with the weapon; the sound of his ivory leg
> and the sound of the hickory pole, both hollowly ringing along every plank.
> But ere he entered his cabin a light, unnatural, half-bantering yet most
> piteous laugh was heard. Oh, Pip! thy wretched laugh, thy idle but un-
> resting eye; all thy strange mummeries not unmeaningly blended with the
> black tragedy of the melancholy ship, and mocked it! [2]

(Spear-harpoon; the substitute limb made out of ivory of the sea-
beast; the archetypal Fool—the *black* ship.)

> Death deserves only your scorn. He lets the immense net fall, mows men
> down at random, grotesque, appalling, vast . . . But whoever has seen how
> you ride the storm, finger the trigger of a machine gun or the helm of a
> ship, make the most of everything and adroitly down your foe, knows that
> the valour of a man is a very different thing. Poor death . . . clumsy fool.[3]

[1] *A. & C.*, IV. xiii. 66.   [2] *Moby Dick*, Ch. CXII.   [3] Anouilh, *Eurydice*, pp. 145-6.

§ v

The power of the pregnant image, its resonances and overtones, can
be readily seen by contrast with 'flattened', and ineffective imagery,
whatever the cause of its failure. Perhaps these come most often into the
'frigid' category of 'Longinus'; they lack vitality because they are both
too 'literary', too obvious, too single-moulded in their purpose. We
may quote from Hardy's *Dynasts*:

> the enormous tale
> Of your campaign, like Aaron's serpent-rod,
> Has swallowed up the smaller of its kind.[1]

or

> Till dangerous ones drew near and daily sowed
> Those choking tares within your fecund brain.[2]

When Hardy speaks of the accoutrements of cavalry flashing in the
sun 'like a school of mackerel' we are conscious not only of the inept-
ness of the image but also of its inelasticity; as contrasted, say, with
Vernon's description of the rebel army before Shrewsbury:

> All furnish'd, all in arms,
> All plum'd like estridges that wing the wind,
> Baited like eagles having lately bath'd . . .[3]

For it is not only the flatness of conception but the rhythm that marks
the effective image: we may contrast this from Arnold's *Merope*:

> He would not let his savage chiefs alight,
> A cloud of vultures on this vigorous race;
> Ravin a little while in spoil and blood,
> Then gorg'd and helpless be assail'd and slain.[4]

with a passage where the tension is admittedly low:

> For once the eagle England being in prey,
> To her unguarded nest the weasel Scot
> Comes sneaking and so sucks her princely eggs,
> Playing the mouse in absence of the cat,
> To tear and havoc more than she can eat.[5]

It is true to say that the rhythm of the setting of a given image will
be a fair indication of its vitality, its kinetic energy. Where we have to

---

[1] p. 254.   [2] p. 201.   [3] *I Henry IV*, IV. i. 98.
[4] l. 295.   [5] *Henry V*, I. ii. 169.

deal with translation we suffer correspondingly, and must grope for the total meaning: or accept the looseness of the 'poetic' translation.[1]

§ *vi*

But when we speak of the 'rhythm' of the image-setting, or of the total rhythm of a play, we are dealing with a subject for which no critical terminology exists,[2] and of which no satisfactory analysis or explanation can be given.

Macbeth's

She should have died hereafter . . .

or Cleopatra's

Give me my robe, put on my crown . . .

can be discussed only tentatively as regards their imagery and its relationship to the rest of the play. The rhythm of the play itself is built up by the dramatist's intuitive skill in checking or accelerating the pulse of a general movement, by balancing the release of forces from the past to impinge upon developing action in the present and future. The rhythmic setting of the images is a reflection of the pressure behind the poetic statement, and it may be suspected that the lyric impulse may generate and order the images in such a way as to transcend, modify, or even appear to deny the previously-communicated qualities of a character. This is one explanation of the endlessly divergent interpretations of character. The critic selects one particular aspect to be 'stressed', often in pursuance of an *a priori* conception, and interprets imagistic elaborations in terms of this; and he does so the more easily because of the essential indefiniteness inherent in the images. In such states of exaltation or intensity the creative imagination draws more freely upon the vast reserves of the subconscious, moves more easily between them and the conscious stored memories. These last may be related either to the dramatist's personal experiences and habits of association, *or with the imaginatively conceived memories of the characters themselves*; for I believe that the creative identification of a great dramatist with his characters is of such an order as to permit of this. It is thus that we may account for the recurrent link-images in

[1] Consider the controversies aroused by, e.g., Gilbert Murray's translations of Euripides, or Yeats's of *Oedipus Tyrannus*. On the other hand, much of Lorca's imagery seems to 'come through'.

[2] A similar difficulty is apparent in attempts to use prosodic analysis for purposes of applied criticism.

Shakespeare; the image-clusters [1]—which usually appear on a lower level of poetic statement—representing the more personal experiences of the poet himself. Perhaps at the last we can say no more of this rhythmic setting in tragedy than we can of any great poetry; that its insufficiency is patent in second-rate work, and that the intuitive perception of the organic quality of rhythm and image is the only measurement.

§ vii

The 'masterful images', then, perform a number of complex functions as components of the dramatic structure. The use of one or more dominant images may provide a complete framework for the Idea, a framework whose joints may be tightened or loosened as the dramatist desires. When the dominant acquires or arrogates to itself multiple meanings, either at different levels of perception or by different applications to different parts of the play, it may become a symbol. As such it may become 'penumbral' or extensible, its significance deliberately set out of focus to correspond with the limitations of human perception. If it appears to be related to a recurrent human situation it may be called archetypal, the only test being the recurrence of that image in the history of poetry, combined with its continual power to radiate new meanings, since the inner tensions that it represents are both constant and not susceptible to analysis. The Fool in his various manifestations [2] is perhaps the most mysterious and interesting example, the source of wisdom, the evoker of pity and terror, the afflicted and blessed of God, whose speech reveals essential antinomies, oscillating between laughter and fear, and who is in certain ways peculiarly fitted to become the poet's mouthpiece.[3]

The 'stream-images' grow naturally out of the poetic, partly through a conscious selection of language appropriate to the theme, partly because of effective and serial associations [4] that take place in the act of composition. They are to some extent 'self-begetting', in Yeats's phrase; their groupings about a single referent may, through an attack from different angles, build up in the time-scheme of the play an effect which resembles that of the dominant.

[1] I am indebted here to E. A. Armstrong, *Shakespeare's Imagination*, and in particular to Ch. XIX.
[2] Cf. Enid Welsford, *The Fool*.
[3] If it is true that the neurotic and the poet both react symbolically, the character of a neurotic as depicted by a poet raises some interesting questions. James Joyce uses the word Drauma (= drama + trauma). Cf. F. J. Hoffman, *Freudianism and the Literary Mind*.
[4] Used in Armstrong's sense: *op. cit.*, p. 175.

The 'intermittent' image, one that does not rely on repetition or some combination through association grouping, has a function of sudden illumination. If it is arbitrary, or appears extrinsic to the total statement, it can upset the tragic balance all too readily. At its most successful it offers the most memorable of all compressions:

> . . . and it is great
> To do that thing that ends all other deeds,
> That shackles accident, and bolts up change,
> That sleeps, and palates never more the dug,
> The beggar's nurse and Caesar's.[1]

or the Duchess of Malfi's famous:

> What would it pleasure me, to have my throat cut
> With diamonds? or to be smothered
> With cassia? or to be shot to death with pearls?
> I know death hath ten thousand several doors
> For men to take their exits; and 'tis found
> They go on such strange geometrical hinges
> You may open them both ways—Any way, for heaven sake,
> So I were out of your whispering.[2]

The images of a tragedy serve many purposes. They may tighten and cross-link its structure, emphasize and differentiate character, illuminate a situation. Above all, they assist in building the tragic perspective. Through them the play is perceived or distanced in time, related to past present and future in the historical scene, united to a specific poetic tradition. By their recurrence, our 'recognition' of them, they may link us to similar images, themselves pregnant of meaning in the past. Since the image at its best exists in virtue of its capacity to express what it itself contains, and is not expressible in other terms, its indeterminate quality or capacity for extension may assist the poetry of the play in its 'super-aesthetic function' 'in giving concrete unity and shape to "prospective ethos"—ideals dawning in the moral consciousness of the community'.[3] And Hinks's phrase is illuminating for all dramatic characterization:

> But when we look into our minds and try to explain to ourselves why we behave as we do, symbolic expressions become at once inevitable and inadequate. We are conscious of a unity, yet no single symbol is sufficient to render it.[4]

---

[1] *A. & C.* v. ii. 4. [2] IV. ii. 219.
[3] Maud Bodkin, *The Quest for Salvation* (Oxford, 1941), p. 4: quoting Hartmann's *Ethics*.
[4] Roger Hinks, *Myth and Allegory in Ancient Art* (London, 1939), p. 95.

CHAPTER 13

Towards a Shakespearian Synthesis

§ i

THE critical history of Shakespearian Tragedy affords what is, perhaps, the classic instance of the perpetual shifting and development of the values attached in successive ages to an organic form. That it contains in itself qualities which produce this constant radiation of light, permitting the refraction and diffraction of the waves by such critical apparatus as is current from time to time, is a commonplace of literary critical history. The twentieth-century interpretation will tend to be less objective than Dryden's or Johnson's, more so than Lamb's or Carlyle's. Every shade of opinion can be seen in this living complexity.

Two comparatively recent formulations may be selected for a starting point, those of Croce and A. C. Bradley. Consider first the sentences of Croce:

> Shakespeare shows himself clearly to be outside . . . every religious, or rather every transcendental and theological conception . . . He knows no other than the vigorous passionate life upon earth, divided between joy and sorrow, with around and above it the shadow of a mystery.[1]

Here is a flat denial of any conscious view of the tragic world, an assumption of an equilibrium which appears to exclude intuitive content other than 'the shadow of a mystery'.

And in another sentence:

> The poet . . . is beyond being on the side of one or the other. He receives them all in himself, not that he may feel them all, and pour tears of blood around them, but that he may make of them his unique world, the Shakespearian world, which is the world of undecided conflicts.[2]

> The sky becomes dark after the devastating hurricane, honourable men occupy the thrones from which the wicked have fallen, the conquerors pity and praise the conquered. But the desolation of faith betrayed, of goodness trampled upon, of innocent creatures destroyed, of noble hearts broken,

[1] *Ariosto, Shakespeare and Corneille*, p. 154.   [2] *Ibid.*, p. 144.

remains. The God that should pacify hearts is invoked, His presence may even be felt, but He never appears.[1]

Here are explicit statements of 'negative capability', of tragic equilibrium, enclosed in a sense of destructive waste. There appears to be no resolution in any implicit or explicit morality; and Croce seems to deny the possibility of a positive synthesis.

> Nor is there anything to be built upon in those rare passages where it may seem that the poet breaks the coherence and aesthetic level of his work, in order to lay stress upon some real or practical feeling of his own.[2]

It may be noted that the general suggestion is that of a balanced stoicism. Beside these quotations we may consider Bradley; remembering that his position is largely conditioned by his re-statement of the Hegelian position, and by his emphasis on character as the significant source of action.

> We remain confronted with the inexplicable fact, or the no less inexplicable appearance, of a world travailing for perfection, but bringing to birth, together with glorious good, an evil which it is able to overcome only by torture and self waste. And this fact or appearance is tragedy.[3]

For the moment it is enough to remark that Bradley, as opposed to Croce, appears to envisage the conquest of evil by good, but does not offer any consideration of the Christian position on the problem of evil, or any aesthetic considerations that might offer some alternative to Croce's stoicism. More recently we have a frank denial of Shakespeare's philosophical *Anschauung*: 'in his work [is] no system, exposed or half-exposed, of what may rightly be called a philosophy'.[4]

Against this we may set a recent pronouncement by Fluchère, who finds both an intuitive knowledge of man's strength and weakness which is, in effect, the prelude to higher things. Of *Antony and Cleopatra* he writes:

> The heavy covering of lead that weighed down the universe is lifted, the horror of death dispelled, the triumph of evil is no longer the only reward promised to human passions, revolt no longer the only possible attitude against indifferent or cruel gods. Shakespeare's tragic experience has gone full circle, and the first reconciliation takes place in a brilliant world, loud with the clash of arms, traversed by grandiose political ambitions but made poetic by an immortal love. Man this time accepts his condition, measures his

---

[1] *Ibid.*, p. 144.   [2] *Ibid.*, p. 131.   [3] *Shakespearian Tragedy*, p. 39.
[4] D. G. James, *The Dream of Learning*, p. 2.

weaknesses without disgust, but knows his grandeur also. The impossible task of being oneself no longer ends in failure because the true spirituality of man, which so many storms had obscured, ends by coming to light.

This does not mean that evil has been finally laid low, or that the serpent will no longer dare show his head, but it does mean that he is no longer assured of being always the only victor . . . But we are still in a tragic universe where revelation is possible and complete only in the supreme test of abandoning a finite for a infinite world. It is reassuring that the passage should be made with the sense of eternity. But this is perhaps only the first step towards a new and even more exalting vision of life. In what are called 'the last plays' of Shakespeare it is this new final and reassuring vision that is given us.[1]

Tentative though this is, we have progressed a good way from the Crocean world; and the regeneration themes of the last plays, the wrenching back of *A Winter's Tale* from tragedy to pastoral 'great' comedy, appear to have won general acceptance. But Fluchère is cautious: 'Perhaps' this is only a first step towards the new vision: and as much has been said, though in different language, in the past.

§ ii

An examination of the divergent views on Shakespearian tragedy reveals a series of interpretations and explanations; few of them without some aspect of the truth as successive ages see it. At one end of the scale it is a historical phenomenon, the supremely fortunate though fortuitous meeting of a number of traditional currents. It is a form which owes something to medieval drama, both to Miracle and Morality; something (though decreasingly so of late) to the Greek ethics or to the Senecan stoicism; something to the Chronicle Plays; something to the medieval taste for the *Gesta Illustrorum Virorum*; all of these elements fused in the crucible of personality, and shaped and exsufflicated to meet the entertainment demands of a restless, cruel, emotional, superstitious and patriotic age. At the root of its 'philosophy' (if it may be called so) is the medieval conception of tragedy; mutability, the fall of Princes, the turning of the wheel. The quotations from the *Monk's Tale* are familiar enough; less often quoted is Chaucer's passage on Mutabilitie:

> This wrecched worldes transmutacioun,
> As wele or wo, now povre and now honour,
> With-outen ordre or wys discrecioun
> Governed is by Fortunes errour;

[1] Henri Fluchère, *Shakespeare*, pp. 263–4.

But natheless, the lak of hir favour
Ne may not don me singen, though I dye:
'*Iay tout perdu mon temps et mon labour:*'
For fynally, Fortune, I thee defye!

Yit is me left the light of my resoun,
To knowen frend fro fo in thy mirour.
So much hath yit thy whirling up and doun
Y-taught me for to knowen in an hour
But trewely, no force of thy reddour
To him that over him-self has the maystrye!
My suffisaunce shal be my socour:
For fynally, Fortune, I thee defye! [1]

Spenser propounds a not entirely satisfactory solution on Platonic lines:

I well consider all that ye have said;
And find that all things steadfastness do hate
And changèd be; yet being rightly weigh'd,
They are not changèd from their first estate;
But by their change their being do dilate;
And turning to themselves at length again,
Do work their own perfection so by fate:
Then over them Change doth not rule and reign
But they reign over Change, and do their states maintain.[2]

Shakespearian tragedy certainly inherited such traditions; but its very vitality is due to the divided outlook of the age, the uncertainty as to what, and how much, the new philosophy might call in doubt. At its best it could place under tribute the noblest that the High Renaissance had brought of both Hebraism and Hellenism, to combine them, for the only and last time, as Michaelangelo did, perhaps, in the Sistine Chapel. At its worst it could plumb the depths of sadism, sensationalism, bawdry, and delight in childish gambolling among the new lush verdure of words.

Another age sees in this tragedy a moral wisdom of the highest order, though its appearance may be intermittent, and itself distorted from time to time by a vulgarity which is ascribed to the author, or to its age, or to both. Yet another praises a divine power of insight, an organic creativity from which nothing is to be excluded or rejected. Another concentrates on the psychological subtleties of character, seeking to find the clue to the nature of the whole organism in their

---

[1] *Balades de visage sanz peinture: Le Pleintif countre Fortune.*
[2] *F.Q.*; Mutabilitie, VII, 58.

interactive responsibilities. Another may stress, and even idolatrize, the psychological significance of the complex images, their part in the poetic interpretation and evaluation of each play, and the implicit connections between them; projecting the images (as some think) beyond any legitimate interpretation, but claiming the irrefutable right to say: 'This is what it means to me.'

§ *iii*

At the outset we may admit that the original formulae for Shake-spearian tragedies are 'impure'; as containing elements which are fortuitous, designed to appeal to and at various levels of consciousness, and only reconcilable by a certain effort of the imagination, or at certain speeds and by certain emphases of production. The traces of the heterogeneous can be seen in all plays, but perhaps most strikingly in *Romeo and Juliet* or in *A Winter's Tale*, though critical opinion differs periodically as to the degree to which characters such as the Nurse are to be considered as integral with the tragic stream. The Porter in *Macbeth* and the Fool in *Lear* are standard instances; and no doubt the modern consciousness would go further than de Quincey or Lamb in the subjective interpretation of their values. (The symbolism of the Fool and the Blind Man in the tragic pattern will be discussed later.) Indeed, much of the controversy over the value of comic relief seems to hinge on the power to perceive the comedy in its counterpointing functions, and this in turn demands a full understanding of what the reader or spectator takes to be the dominant rhythms of each play. These conditions will in themselves vary according to the method of study, the additions or detractions given by remembered productions, and by personal preconceptions. For example, the interpretations of *Antony and Cleopatra* in terms of the tragic emotion have been vitiated either by considerations of morals, or by a narrow view of dramatic technique; that of *Hamlet* or *Macbeth* by a reluctance to accept the supernatural machinery even on symbolic terms.

The dominant consideration would seem to be this: how far can we subordinate all such preconceptions to (*a*) our perception of the play as a structural rhythmic entity and (*b*) our response to its poetry and its symbolism? In short, we are probably committed, in the Shakespearian synthesis, to the individual consideration of a highly complex system; of which the components will vary according to political, social and personal settings in the study, and which are subject to startling modifications in production. This intricacy can be suggested more readily if we consider a play of, say, Racine's, as a system of forces in a plane surface; Shakespearian tragedy might be denoted by such a system in three, or possibly four dimensions. In the third dimension, the solid-geometry characteristic given by the depth of the Shakespearian synthesis is equated with the counterpointed values of the plot; the fourth dimension is suggested by the elusive quality of the imagery and symbolism.

§ *iv*

But it would, I think, be wrong to approach Shakespeare without a vivid appreciation of the Shakespearian interest in character, its projection into action, and the judgement of both character and action by time. Shakespeare's very progress through the historical plays and their immense implications, to the tragic form in which the manipulation of material was easier, suggests that, ultimately, the problem was that of recognizing, explicitly or intuitively, the pattern from a standpoint which, however dispassionately studied, must possess important psychological and political links with events of his own day. If history were to be seen, intermittently and amid the confusion of conquests, in terms of a plan (which might, in moments of still higher exaltation, shadow forth a high mystery), then its importance lay not only in the *exempla* of Plutarch but in the conflicting personalities of *Henry VIII*. And behind such interest there was the whole Hebraic tradition, its mutations and characters; made vivid by minute particulars, coloured by the magnanimity or the eccentricity of individual leaders.

It seems probable that, if we are honest with ourselves, there are two courses open to us.

1. To attempt to perceive the Shakespearian synthesis, initially, in its historical proportions; and having done that to allow for variation and deviation to the extent that seems necessary to make it comprehensible and significant. (The *order* of doing this is important.)

2. To jettison any serious attempt to achieve a historical perspective, and to assume the right to interpret the plays in accordance with a strictly individual and subjective viewpoint, which may or may not assume a licence to disregard the historical perspective.

(*a*) Contemporary sensibility which is devoid of exact knowledge of Shakespeare's place in the development of the British Drama, the physical and legal conditions of his stage, his acting company, his audience, and persons and events of his time, may easily lead to reading back into

Shakespeare intentions, references, ideas and purposes which are monstrous, where they are not ludicrous.[1]

(b) To analyse the sequence of events, the 'causes' linking dramatic motive to action and action to result in time, is a blunder instinctive to the human intellect.[2]

(c) We should not look for verisimilitude to life, but rather see each play as an expanded metaphor.[3]

(d) The tragedies of Shakespeare's maturity, from *Macbeth* onward, are characterized by a consistent progress towards the development of dramatic symbolism. This symbolism, which derives originally from an extension of the scope and purpose of the poetic image in the dramatic scheme, implies logically a new conception of plot.[4]

The three last pronouncements are of some interest. As regards Wilson Knight's view, it is enough to say that it is meaningless unless we attach some specific and unusual meaning to the inverted commas that surround 'causes'. A 'cause' does not, in any normal sense, *link* an action to its result; a state B *is* the outcome of an action A. Nor does a motive become linked to an action by a 'cause'. What does happen in drama, as Brunetière saw, is that the springs of action are volitional and arise directly out of the Elizabethan preoccupation with ethical problems; it is primarily, a question of moral responsibility which is seen at its simplest in *Dr Faustus*, at its most complex in *Hamlet*, and at its most naïve in, say, *The White Devil*. By the act of willing a character initiates a train of events. Whatever justifications we may adduce, in time past or time present, in supposed neurosis or environment, are subsidiary to this central fact. Upon this train impinge subsidiary trains of events, originating in others' wills, sometimes brought into collision by what appears to be accident, but which may, in proportion to the playwright's skill in unifying his subject, be perceived either as an acceleration in time, or as some manifestation, however dim and arbitrary, of the First Cause. The original train, modified or distorted, arrives at a result which we call, for dramatic purposes, the end.[5]

Now it is not clear how each of the tragedies is to be seen as 'an expanded metaphor', or what results are gained in a consideration from

[1] W. S. Knickerbocker, *The Sewanee Review*, XLVII, January 1939.
[2] G. Wilson Knight, *The Imperial Theme*.
[3] *Ibid.*
[4] D. A. Traversi, *Scrutiny*, October 1952.
[5] See, in general, Arthur Sewell's *Character and Society in Shakespeare*.

this angle only. All dramatic imagery is reinforced by repetition; that repetition is thematic, arising out of the intrinsic nature of the subject. *Macbeth* from its whole setting demands poetic statement in terms of night, darkness, blood, and the traditional vocabulary for such themes; *Lear* employs, and repeats with variations, animal imagery,[1] comparisons and similitudes that originate from the Bible, Elizabethan proverb lore, the normal images of 'the common passionate speech of the people'. Generation, ingratitude, and treachery are at the centre of Lear's world; its emblems are copulation or seed-time, the animal worlds that have particular relations with man—serpent, dog, wolf, bear. Cataclysmic events in nature have always been related by man to the human situation, and his sense of guilt and terror at the numinous; they predict hardship, poverty, war or death. Against this compound background of beast and storm a king is purified by suffering, a combination with precedents enough in religion and history. But in the foreground of Shakespeare's world there is, always, this failure of the *will* to act with *judgement*. In the last analysis there is character, the garment of the will; but, since it is not within the power of the dramatist to show the antecedent complexities of character formation,[2] he is concerned with no more than a minimal selection of these. His concern is with the will, the right of choice; without attempting to show what lies outside this energy, except to speculate on how the will may be modified by a curse, or fate, or some cause in nature that makes these hard hearts.

If we consider a Shakespearian tragedy as 'an expanded metaphor' we are, instead of elevating the function of the poverty, in danger of losing much of the effect of the play as a complex organism. If, in Traversi's words, our emphasis upon the 'expanded metaphor' 'leads logically to a new conception of plot' we must, I think, question what that new conception is. Does the plot now become merely a framework for the dramatic poetry, or rather for a particular aspect of that poetic 'content'? Are the ethical problems, the roots of will and choice in character, merged in a larger unity to which we are given no clue save our total 'poetic response' to the play? And if that is so, are we committed to a new subjective aestheticism in which the image becomes

---

[1] This seems more spontaneous and closer to common speech than many critics appear to suggest. I have heard the storm-dog image used by a peasant in the west of Ireland.

[2] The *exemplum ad absurdum* of this is Mrs. Cowden Clark's *The Girlhood of Shakespeare's Heroines*. The *jeu d'esprit* of L. C. Knights' *How many Children had Lady Macbeth* is of course no more than a caricature of the Neo-Bradleians: it is difficult to see how it can be taken seriously as an attack on Bradley himself.

paramount; even though it is, in essence as in fact, a device for communicating intense passion in speech? It is repeated because that passion
is at the core of the play; it is dominant, or composed of dominants,
because the poet has selected just those kinds of statement as appropriate
to his theme.

We can now examine one or two of the tragedies with these points
in mind.

§ v

Of all the plays it seems generally agreed that *King Lear* presents
the most complicated pattern, at once the most profound, intimate,
and 'public' of the great tragedies. We may distinguish a number of
strands in the fabric after the following fashion.

1. It is a play of Wrath in Old Age; a psychological study, on
   traditional lines, of petulance, choler, and the decayed judgements
   of senility.[1]
2. It is a play of mis-timed action, associated with this type; Lear's
   refusal to organize efficiently the matter of his abdication;
   Cornelia's obduracy when confronted with what must have been,
   to her, a known psychological condition.[2]
3. It is a play of Nature, and of the nature of Nature; of the
   existence and limitations of filial affection and compassion in
   Edmund, Edgar, Goneril, Regan, Cordelia, wolves, bears, dogs.
4. It is a play of convulsion, the distemper of the heavens echoing
   the distemper of man, and his state; a breach of the cosmic order.
5. It is a play of expiation; not only by Lear but by Gloucester,
   Edmund, and perhaps Cordelia.
6. It is a play of political forces, combining to achieve a somewhat
   timid reversal of the situation.[3]
7. On a symbolic level, there are perhaps five dominant images
   that appear to be archetypal.

   (1) Man *vs.* Beast.
   (2) The Blind Man ⎫
   (3) The Fool   ⎬ as components of Man.

---

[1] Cf. Lily Campbell, *Shakespeare's Tragic Heroes.*
[2] Consider the various attempts to account for the apparent inadequacy of the Abdication Scene.
[3] We need not agree with Miss Winstanley in finding a political key to the whole play
(Lear and the Coligny Murders) or with those who find Cordelia's *hamartia* (in the Greek
manner) in the unlawful invasion of Britain with alien forces.

(4) The stripping of the king to his nakedness (cf. The Emperor's Clothes).

(5) The Fighting of the Storm (or of the Sea).[1]

All these strands are woven into the pattern; and harmonized or counterpointed by Shakespeare's perpetual concern with the Nature of the King. (The immediacy of that subject to an Elizabethan can be readily understood.) One pole of that nature is his kingship, the other his childishness; between these two the personality of the Hero oscillates in time and space. Miss Bodkin has pointed out the ambivalence of the father-child relationship: the father is both the loved protector and the obstructive tyrant, the child both the loving support of old age, and the ruthless usurper.[2] The devices might easily have become sentimentalized; with Shakespeare it is always, or nearly always, redeemed by a strong dignity of control, as evidenced by the extreme simplicity of language, or by its contrived inadequacy in hysteria. There is precedent enough: Andromache causing the cauldron to be heated for Hector's bath against his return from battle. 'She little dreamed that he lay far away from all baths now, dead at the hands of Achilles': Hector, tamer of horses, dragged by horses round the walls of his own city. So, too, the anchor in reality provided by Orestes' Nurse in the *Choephoroë* of Aeschylus, and common to all such figures who emphasize the extremities of the human by the remembered pathos and comedy of the physical. So Juliet's cry

> O God! O Nurse!

Charmian's remembrance of her attiring of her mistress:

> Your crown's awry:
> I'll mend it, and then play.

Nora's cry in *Riders to the Sea*:

> And isn't it a pitiful thing when there is nothing left of a man who was a great rower and fisher but a bit of an old shirt and a plain stocking?

Between the poles of the heroic and the homely, king and beast, the play oscillates on its violent sea. At its centre the Fool and the Blinded Man stand beside the King: one in danger of whipping for speaking his wisdom, the other blinded for a night's pleasure, both now wiser than the King. Over all is the sense of power that has been borrowed, and which has released evil, and must work itself out in convulsion.

---

[1] As Xerxes, or Cuchulain.   [2] *Archetypal Patterns*, pp. 15, 16.

§ *vi*

How much these strange minor figures do in fact contribute to the total tragic effect is impossible to define. They grow half-consciously : they cannot be interpreted rationally. It is in the nature of all archetypal figures that they should be indeterminate, expansive, in their significance; that they should be called into full activity in the pattern and rhythm of each play. They are accessories, but indispensable once tragedy begins to be thought of as multi-dimensional in character. Little has been made, for instance, of the child-symbol in *Macbeth*; the dream child that Lady Macbeth denies, the Bleeding Child of the supernatural vision, the naked new-born child that is Pity, the murdered children of Macduff. For the child is life-in-death; it is the symbol of man's yearning for resurrection.[1] It is the ultimate focal point of all pity, love, and hate; since it carries in itself its mysterious heritage from the past in its own unique framework of simplicity.

§ *vii*

The intricacies of the pattern are less apparent in *Antony and Cleopatra*, where the system of tensions appears to be, at first sight, laid out upon a single plane. The overt moral principle embodied in Rome conquers ignominiously, cheated by death after the high Roman fashion. Like all, or nearly all the tragedies, it is a play of mis-timing, of forces loosed irrationally at critical moments by a strumpet's kiss, of a battle-ground chosen by mere sentiment, of strongly-marked periodic oscillations of intention. (Consider the balance of the scenes between Alexandria and Rome.) There is little suffering of the kind that is in *King Lear*, little endurance or patience. Twice catastrophe appears to admit of redemption. In the background we are aware of two forces; the *Pax Romana* which exacts the Augustan lip-service to morality: and the strange phenomenon of luck (so familiar to any soldier) that is symbolized partly in the two daimons, partly in the musical desertion of the god Hercules. Again the poles of normality determine the bearings of hero and heroine; Enobarbus throws his cap into the air after the drinking-party where the third part of the world is carried drunk to bed, Cleopatra returns to womanhood before she can become a queen in

[1] Cf. Kerényi, *The Primordia Child in Primordial Times* (*Introduction to a Science of Mythology, loc. cit.*).

THE IMAGE OF PITY

'For he saw that life liv'd upon death:
The Ox in the slaughter-house moans,
The Dog at the wintry door;
And he wept and he call'd it Pity,
And his tears flowed down on the winds'

BLAKE

death (consider Desdemona's Willow Song, Ophelia's snatches of bawdry):

> No more; but e'en a woman, and commanded
> By such poor passion as the maid that milks
> And does the meanest chares.[1]

§ viii

Of *Hamlet*, too much has been written; it is doubtful whether the woods of psychological criticism will ever be completely cleared of the undergrowth again. At the risk of over-simplification we may try to disentangle some of the threads:

1. It is a play of revenge, and as such comprehensible to us only with a strong effort of the imagination. To an Elizabethan it was an activity of a quasi-sacred character, a rough but otherwise unattainable justice.

2. The revenge theme is enforced, repeatedly, by the Ghost itself a phenomenon of horror; the disruptive past impinging upon the present, as surely as in an Ibsen tragedy. Again, it is only by an imaginative effort that we can recover the emotion of the *unnaturalness* of the situation, the resurrection of actions that should have been statute-barred; the perpetual fact of the past being stored against our ruin.

3. Both the idea of revenge, and the idea of the ghost, thrive on the natural hostility between the King and his stepson, admirable though the former's tact may be.

4. The loosing of evil is the more terrible because of the uncertainty of that evil—its possible diabolical character—and because moral and psychological law appears to support its claims.

5. Woman's desire is seen as the first and second causes: and is in imagination refracted from the Queen to Ophelia and back again till both are sacrificed.

6. The Ghost, *plus* the idea of infidelity in the world of the court, from bed to arras, emphasize the total distortion of the world. 'Change or insecurity, seen without reference to some stable principle, becomes terrible and sensational.' [2]

7. Against these is set the Renaissance world, with its ideal of the prince, governed by reason, master of all excellencies, yet as man allowed the licences proper to his position in the hierarchy.

---

[1] IV. xiii. 73.   [2] Howard Baker, *Induction to Tragedy*, p. 206.

8. 'In *Hamlet* there is not fatalism, but good Christian doctrine, somewhat coloured by Neo-Stoicism.' [1]

The 'linkage' to our own world (for we need not distance ourselves unduly, or to the point at which it might seem 'an artistic failure') perhaps includes some or all of the following:

1. The common experience of hostility to the father-substitute.[2]
2. Frustration through a new set of circumstances that debar the individual from power.
3. Sexual frustration turning to bitterness through the Ophelia-Gertrude situation.
4. The fear and irritation caused when intense intellectual and critical activity confronts a stupid but solidified social front.
5. The oscillating moods, between depression and excited exultation, which grow from such a mind in its attempt to penetrate the known false appearances of things.
6. The tensions set up in the mind when complicated and obscure situations have to be solved through action *under pressure of time*.[3]
7. The prevalence of the type of the 'malcontent', admirably summed up by Stoll: 'His meditations on the processes and transformations of life and death, as in the grave-yard, his indecency with women, his doggerel and snatches of old ballads allusively and derisively used, his jeering, mimicry, and gibberish, his abrupt enigmas, his quick and gruesome misinterpretations of the words of others—these have, of course, nothing necessarily to do with the "humour" of the physiologists.' [4]
8. The view of Hamlet himself as a 'hero' in the mythological sense: the call to the adventure of revenge, the series of 'tricks' in the plots against him, Ophelia's betrayal, the players' arrival, the pirate ship: the appeasement of the ghost, his own apotheosis.

§ *ix*

As Hamlet is the most complex form of the Shakespearian synthesis, so the Historical plays afford the most convenient examples of tragic

---

[1] v. C. F. Johnson, *Shakespeare Quarterly*, July 1952, pp. 187 ff.

[2] We need not agree fully with the Freud–Beaumont–Ernst Jones theories; but F. L. Lucas has shown convincingly the prevalence of the son–mother–stepfather conflict.

[3] We tend, perhaps, to lose sight of the accelerating factors that force Hamlet into action, though critics have repeatedly noted the sense of relief after the episode with the pirate ship. And such a relief when thought is translated into action by circumstances is a commonplace of psychological case-histories.

[4] E. E. Stoll, *Hamlet the Man*, p. 5 (English Assoc. Pamphlet No. 91).

simplicity. It is because of their simplicity that we have not, perhaps, paid sufficient attention to the tragic qualities of, say, the *Henry VI* cycle, *Richard II* and *III*, and possibly *King John*. For the historical tragedy had to the Elizabethans a continuous and pressing relevance to their own affairs. So long as the great nobles grew unhindered the fear of rebellion was constant. The holder of the crown, his powers and obligations, were still a subject of debate, and were to remain so for another century; whether the King was, in fact, a 'histrionic young tyrant' or

The Deputy elected by the Lord.

One thing was certain: that the fall of the monarch led to the fall or at least the confusion of the State; the broken hierarchy might be symbolized by the Garden at Langley, presaged by signs in the heavens. And in his elevation the King's sin surrounded him, Fury-like, to wake to the pursuit when Richard III's sleep could no longer restore that ferocious energy, or when Henry IV woke to find his son trying on the crown. The plays show the working of Nemesis, single or complex,[1] in obedience to a simple morality that is plainly Christian, yet which retains traces of the medieval Wheel. In the trajectories of Princes, whatever the duration and height, there is a profound sense of a pattern in life which is related (at opposite ends of the scale) to the path of the Hero-God and to the rise, maturity and decay of the common man.

Of these tragedies there are two main groups of spectators, the women and the common people. The women move a little apart, sometimes to rail, sometimes to loose the terrible weapon of the curse (one of the many emotional agents that a modern audience is unable to assess) but most often to weep. At times they shed a strange glow upon the main characters, as does Richard II's Queen:

... thou most beauteous inn,
Why should hard-favour'd grief be lodged in thee,
When triumph is become an alehouse guest? [2]

The Histories are of special interest as tragic *exempla* showing the elements of Shakespeare's mature tragedy which they lack within a chronicle framework, the tradition of the chronicle play with a serious

---

[1] R. G. Moulton's analysis of the plot of *Richard III* has become a classic. (*Shakespeare as a Dramatic Artist.*)
[2] v. i. 13.

theme and a strong interfusion of the morality. Figures such as Henry VI and Richard III are conventional in their clear-cut representation of their absolute good and evil, products of the traditional philosophy of kingship overlaid upon Holinshed and More. *Richard III* is the perfect example of fear and admiration in a simple blended response; the gaiety, intellectual energy, and cynical rejection of all morality suggest that an audience is prepared to respond liberally to heroic villainy to just the point at which crime becomes unrelated to the political objective. This point is the murder of the princes in the Tower. Nor is there enough evidence to suggest an internal conflict of the kind that arouses sympathy in *Macbeth*, and which invites that sympathy by an awareness of metaphysical issues beyond the action of the play. Only *Richard II* presents a complex study of perennial interest; that is, the relationship of the *act* to the *word*, and how the sheer conditioning to kingship (for Richard had been on the throne since the age of ten, and could never forget that dramatic moment in which his appearance and an impulsive, perfectly-timed word dispelled rebellion) leads to this inextricable confusion between the emotion, the word, the act. The tendrils of the imagery intertwine, luxuriate, in antithesis and in puns, these last the sign that the word has taken charge of the intelligence. In this there is a shadow of Hamlet; the need to unpack the heart causes the whole character to oscillate dangerously on the pivot of 'brave and glorious words', that may so easily decline into self-pity.

For self-pity, perhaps the commonest of the vices that link the spectator to the tragedy, is seen, in a greater or less degree, in the majority of tragic heroes. There are, no doubt, purely dramatic considerations that determine why it should be so. The last speech from the scaffold is an enduring tradition, and the spectator will always be curious as to such messages. They are the necessary epilogue before the page is turned and the new men take over. There is the immemorial tradition of reverence for the dying hero-god, though the other protagonists may have been the agents of his death; his death is a ritual becoming, a benediction handed on. And he demands this last office from the spectators, the chorus of lesser men.

> What would the hero of tragedy do without these weeping, appreciating and revering spectators? This necessity of pity from the lesser men who keep the law for the greater men who break it out of an inner necessity is the symbol of an unresolved conflict in the heart of Greek tragedy. It does not know where the real centre of life lies, whether in its law or in its vitality.

Therefore the weak law-abiders must honour the strong law-breakers, lest the latter seem dishonourable.[1]

It is in *Henry IV* and *Henry V* that the concept of kingship broadens out, though into more shallow and winding channels of related intention than the tragic effect can tolerate. But the King, besides being, by implication,[2] the ideal aristocrat, temperate, wise, governed and governing by reason, is now asserting his own humanity; the questioning of kingly ceremony, the critical assessment of father by son, the attempt to probe the mind of the subject, the weariness of responsibility, the final torment of sleep withheld. To forge this link between the audience and an idea of a patriotic, vigorous monarch, who was master at once of the book of the people and of the rhetoric of politics and war, was a supreme effort to solidify that slowly disintegrating concept. Perhaps the problems of the contemporary situation were too close for consistency of character and concentration of dramatic effect.

§ *x*

We are then confronted in Shakespeare's tragedy with a world in which his conception of the form, its genesis and its consequences, turns steadily inwards, increasing in complexity, probing the mystery of the individual, and perhaps recoiling at the last (if *Timon* be indeed the last of the tragedies) before his own inability to go deeper without paying a Swiftian penalty. Perhaps the two last abstracts are the problem of disloyalty (in three degrees) in *Coriolanus*, and the problem of ingratitude, itself a form of un-nature, in *Timon*. Within this framework we may suggest certain general propositions.

1. His ideal world is one of order. Evil, whatever its genesis, has for its immediate result a distortion of that order.
2. His tragedy follows, adheres to, traditional values in the medieval tradition. They are Christian in so far as the two coincide, or even converge.
3. It is concerned with characters 'to whom it is proper to do honour': whether through birthright or achievement.
4. Only through such characters can the *exempla* be made plain, since
   (a) it is through their stature that their doings have a large significance,

<hr/>

[1] Reinhold Niebuhr, *Beyond Tragedy*, p. 165.
[2] e.g. *I. H. IV*. II. ii. 126.

    (b) the mirror or contrast work which gives depth can only be shown in lower, not higher planes,

    (c) evil generated in them can be perceived more clearly in contrast with their nobility, yet in more intense and intricate conflict with their proper virtues.

5. The evil generated in the Shakespearian world is directly the consequence of *sin*: readily perceived in terms of the traditional theology of the age.

6. In sin 'there is an element which we may call "unripeness"; man's attempt to pluck flower or fruit before its season, to forestall the natural maturity of man, woman or event. Once we attempt to overleap the time-process, disaster follows: for it is implicit in time that, once scorned, he takes revenge by appearing to distort all human planning by a series of "just-too-late" events.' [1]

7. As with all evil its self-propagation, its immeasurable and unpredictable resurrection from past to present, its apparent arbitrariness in operation, is imaged mirror on mirror. But this is no reason to deny Shakespeare a background of morality, or to call his world one of undecided conflicts, or to perceive in it a sheer division of the ethical substance.

The emergence of evil through personality into action is the theme of tragedy. How and under what stimulus it emerges, its immensely complicated reactions upon the individual soul, its rapid and violent infection of the most remote and improbable lives is not to be argued in the metaphysics of the tragic writer. In the exaltation and resolution of death, in the intermediate confrontings of the mystery, the dramatist is under no more obligation than the poet. He can do no more than convey to us, even 'for one throb of the artery', the conviction of a unity and a pattern. We may remember Melville's words:

> . . . those deep faraway things in him; those occasional flashings-forth of the intuitive Truth in him; those short, quick probings at the very axis of reality;—these are the things that make Shakespeare, Shakespeare.[2]

---

[1] Cf. L. A. G. Strong, *The Sacred River*, especially Ch. IV. Impatience with time may become a neurotic obsession: hence the repeated injunctions to the effect that 'Ripeness is all'; and the long penalties, even in comedy, for hasty action.

[2] W. E. Sedgwick, *Herman Melville*, p. 85.

CHAPTER 14

The Marble Altar

There is no 'mystery' in Racine—that is to say, there are no metaphysical speculations in him, no suggestions of the transcendental, no hints as to the ultimate nature of reality and the constitution of the world . . . The more we examine Racine, the more clearly we shall discern in him another kind of mystery . . . the mystery of the mind of man . . . Look where we will, we shall find among his pages the traces of an inward mystery and the obscure infinities of the heart.

LYTTON STRACHEY [1]

§ i

'THE marble altar of Racine'; the phrase is from an essay by F. L. Lucas. In French Classical Tragedy we are confronted with a world which is, in many ways, unique. The plays are constructed with an architectural symmetry, and possess something of the serenity of a landscape by Claude, where column and architrave, erect or in ruins, convey a mood at once exalted, and sorrowful, and serene. In the Preface to *Bérénice* Racine himself spoke of 'the experience of majestic sadness in which the whole pleasure of tragedy resides'.

It is a tragic world bounded by many conventions; the neo-Classic rules impose their selective intensity of a moment, and offer no challenge to the transcendental world. It is a tragic theatre which is highly-wrought, based on a consummate rhetorical tradition in which the sheer virtuosity of verse composition acquires, seemingly without effort, a peculiar spontaneity of its own. It is an art judged by its civilized qualities, its 'finesses', delicate and strong, rooted in a world where reason and rule, though always ready to be transcended by genius, are themselves unquestioned. It cannot make use of the lyric, though lyrical functions are perceptible in the impetus and exaltation of many of the set speeches. It sets out to be universal and therefore must not employ the material of contemporary history. Arnold's 'great actions', brought into focus and made significant through distance, time and their quasi-sanctity as universals, form the groundwork of tragedy. The great mutations of the world are set against backgrounds that also are like the landscapes of Claude; luminous with Italian light,

[1] *Books and Characters*, p. 16.

grave and dignified with vast monumental architecture. The scene is almost invariably the terrace of a palace; the characters cross and re-cross the world on their related travels, while the centre of rule and of policy remains. Like Poussin, the dramatists draw their attitudes to life and death from the Greco-Roman scene. Their values are in part determined by the heroic world, since their empire and their peace had been built on foreign wars under Louis XIII and Louis XIV: and this marched well enough with the Homeric scale of conflict, the nobility, passion and dignity of man. In death the underworld or the darkness of a pagan ending symbolizes well enough (without challenging the Church) the uneasiness, stoicism, pathos, that they had learned from Bossuet's *Oraisons Funèbres*. And because this tragic art is above all 'serious' in Arnold's sense, it admits no relief, no grotesque, no fantasy. Its sense of the numinous is poised, as it were, on a delicate pivot between the classical and Christian worlds, its virtues regulated in accordance with what those worlds might, to a reasonable man, be thought to possess in common.

The system of tensions demands, often, a diamond-shaped figure with four protagonists, two men and two women, of differing stature, with their counsellors or confidants about them; Dryden imposed a similar pattern in his re-writing of *Antony and Cleopatra*. Such a system is seen at its clearest in *Andromaque*, initially cyclic in character, with the catastrophe cutting, as it were, across the diameter of the circle. Oreste is in love with Hermione, who is in love with Pyrrhus, who is in love with Andromaque, who is faithful to the memory of her dead husband, Hector; but she, with her son Astyanax, is in the power of Pyrrhus. But Hermione is the affianced of Pyrrhus, and state policy requires that he should marry her. Oreste, as an official envoy, is under orders to arrange the marriage, and this in turn cuts athwart his own love for Hermione. The tensions snap when Pyrrhus is murdered by Oreste, at Hermione's instigation: and, having persuaded her love to this murder, she then turns against him.

In *Bérénice* the pattern is even simpler—'tragedy wrought to its uttermost'. Antiochus is in love with Bérénice, who is in love with Titus, and he with her; Antiochus and Titus are united by their friendship. Titus is about to be crowned Emperor of Rome; he would then naturally marry Bérénice were it not that the Roman Senate may forbid the marriage of their emperor to a foreign queen. They do forbid it, and the tragic setting, now sharply triangular in structure, is complete.

It is a world that has its existence under the shadow of a literal invocation of Aristotle,[1] supported by a rigid conception of aristocracy and by the conventions which that aristocracy had built for self-justification. In the society which Racine transposes to a Greek or Roman or Old Testament setting, the privileges of birth are all-important. When they are compared with the subsidiary figures the princes and princesses show a sensibility, delicacy of mind and speed of perception that diminishes steadily as we descend the social scale. They are conscious of themselves, and of their actions, as *exempla* in the stream of history; just as Shakespeare's Roman world speaks proudly to posterity.

> Adieu, servons nous tous d'example à l'univers.

There are other qualities that we must consider. Because Racine is under the double constraint of the Unities and of plots that have their strong framework in the past, the net is tightly drawn about the characters; the circle is already narrowing when the play begins, though it is not until the catastrophe that the characters realize that the last possible hole for escape is blocked. Racine even apologizes for his departure from the plot of Euripides in relation to the character of Phèdre:

> J'ai même pris soin de la rendre un peu moins odieuse qu'elle n'est dans les tragédies des anciens, où elle se résout d'elle-même à accuser Hippolyte. J'ai cru que la calomnie avait quelque chose de trop bas et de trop noir pour la mettre dans la bouche d'une princesse qui a d'ailleurs des sentiments si nobles et si vertueux. *Cette bassesse m'a paru plus convenable à une nourrice, qui pouvait avoir des inclinations plus serviles,* et qui néanmoins n'entreprend cette fausse accusation que pour sauver la vie et l'honneur de sa maîtresse. Phèdre n'y donne les mains que parcequ'elle est dans une agitation d'esprit qui la met hors d'elle-même; et elle vient un moment après dans le dessein de justifier l'innocence et de déclarer la verité.[2]

This extract has several points of interest. The great protagonists, in whatever net of evil they are entangled, have these sentiments 'si nobles et si vertueux'. Phèdre's horror, that allows her to lean for a moment on the accusation of the Nurse, is perceived as a momentary thing.

In the background is the eternal dualism; the position of the Reason confronted with emotion; honour, duty, friendship, policy, set against Venus and her prey. In the curiously neutral world of Racine's creation, which is neither Roman nor Greek nor French, this sensual urge,

---

[1] Cf. the first Preface to *Andromaque*.   [2] Preface to *Phèdre*.

heightened to the utmost nobility by the stride of the rhythm and the clarity of the language, dominates the characters. It is at once a curse, a punishment for an unknown sin, and a disease. It ebbs and flows by the moon, and Racine as a trained observer marks its course with almost unfailing insight. Andromaque, Roxane, Clytemnestra, Phèdre, are all victims:

> Je reconnus Vénus et ses feux redoutables
> D'un sang qu'elle poursuit tourmentes inevitables...

So again in the Preface:

> En effet, Phèdre n'est ni tout à fait coupable, ni tout à fait innocente: elle est engagée, par sa destinée et par la colère des dieux, dans une passion illégitime, dont elle a horreur toute la première...

Racine, as a pupil of Port-Royal, is said to have held the doctrine of predestination, fitting well enough with Euripides' perception of the insensate wrath of a goddess. But adds to Phèdre torments by jealousy, making Hippolyte in love with Aricie, the gentle timid girl; one of several such who are confronted with mature women, clear-sighted yet in the grasp of these terrible passions, which they know yet do not understand. Théramène, typical of many virtuous confidants, is the *punctum indifferens* of the play.

The situation of these characters is exacerbated through the conditions of their lives. They are public figures; their love or marriage has political consequences. Against the pomp of the courts this wild irrational impulse, this joyless yet obsessive desire, lights up both itself and the reason and ceremony that oppose it. In their conduct two dominant emotions are called into play in Racine's audience: the potential *tendresse* of woman,[1] the ceremony and *virtus* of man, the peculiar dignified relationship to the confidants who are so vital to the pace and rhythm of the play. The men move between their Roman thoughts, an elegiac sadness at their own position, and perhaps a certain bewilderment before the subtlety and swiftly-changing moods of their women.

Love, friendship, duty; but it would be wrong to suppose that these are the only boundaries of Racine's world. *Britannicus* is a play of intrigue, mother against son, a study of villainy and poison: Agrippina has poisoned her second husband so that Nero shall become Emperor. She realizes when it is too late that Nero will not remain her puppet,

---

[1] Which, as an aspect of the Life-Force, is so readily converted into other forms of energy.

and allies herself with Britannicus. Between the three stands the
Princess Junie, desired by Britannicus and Nero: again the diamond-
shaped structure of two women and two men, with the two counsellors, Burrhus and Narcisse, who (like the Good and Bad Angels
in *Dr Faustus*) serve to make clear the oscillations in Nero's mind.
Innocence and youth is confronted by a kind of tigress-woman; a
character which, perhaps more than any of Racine's characters, lives
throughout endless dramatic incarnations; her own recognition and
reversal is one of the most dramatic moments of the play:

> *Agrippina.* Ah! ciel! de mes soupçons qu'elle était l'injustice!
> Je condamnais Burrhus pour écouter Narcisse!
> Burrhus, avez-vous vu quels regards furieux
> Néron en me quittant m'a laissés pour adieux?
> C'en est fait, le cruel n'a plus rien qui l'arrête;
> Le coup qu'on m'a prédit va tomber sur ma tête.
> Il vous accablera vous même à votre tour.
> *Burrhus.* Ah, madame! pour moi j'ai vécu trop d'un jour.[1]

§ ii

But it is the verse that is the special glory of Racine, the instrument
by which he can isolate, clarify, focus the distinctive tragic emotion.
The French Alexandrine is unlike any other metre; it is at once formal
and flexible, ritualistic and rhetorical. Caesura and rhyme give the
thing said the credibility, the finality of achievement that is so cleanly-
cut that no alternative is possible but to believe it true. When it is
merely used for exposition it can roll along with scarcely a hint of its
own severe discipline; it can be broken (yet with the components still
fitting perfectly) into staccato dialogue; and it can carry, in Racine's
hands, the extremity of passion. Hermione's outburst against Oreste,
when she learns that he has murdered Pyrrhus at her instigation, is
well known: but will serve to illustrate something of the range of the
medium:

> *Oreste.* ...Vous seule avez poussé les coups...
> *Hermione.*   Tais-toi, perfide,
> Et n'impute qu'à toi ton lâche parricide.
> Va faire chez les Grecs admirer ta fureur,
> Va: je la désavoue, et tu me fais horreur.
> Barbare , qu'as tu fait! Avec quelle furie
> As-tu tranché le cours d'une si belle vie!

[1] V,7.

> Avez-vous pu, cruels, l'immoler aujourd'hui,
> Sans que tout votre sang se soulevât pour lui!
> Mais parle: de son sort qui t'a rendu l'arbitre?
> Pourquoi l'assassiner? Qu'a-t-il fait? A quel titre?
> Qui te l'a dit?

Oreste.   O Dieux! Quoi! ne m'avez-vous pas
> Vous-même, ici, tantôt, ordonné son trépas?

Hermione.   Ah! fallait-il en croire une amante insensée?
> Ne devais tu pas lire au fond de ma pensée?
> Et ne voyais-tu pas, dans mes emportements,
> Que ma cœur démentait ma bouche à tous moments? . . .[1]

At the opening of the scene Oreste has announced his deed: it is a species of sacrifice on the altar; a worthy deed and one that will win the woman whom he worships.

> Pyrrhus rend à l'autel son infidèle vie.[2]

And now in his bewilderment he is faced with Hermione's rage, and the superbly evasive turnings of the feminine mind. The tirade overwhelms him: the words as they lock into place in the rhymes, or fall so easily into their stride in the rhythm, seem to gather and convey a vicious compact load of meaning: *parricide, tranché, immoler, l'arbitre.* It is a common technique of woman in anger, this defence by attack, with dull-witted man helpless before it. Then, convicted, she falls back on a second line: Oreste should have known her thoughts; she should have been left to carry out her own revenge; he has brought to her presence the very misfortunes that are his curse. And as the rapid-fire of words goes on there comes the half-truth that lies behind all this rationalization:

> Il m'aimerait peut-être...

By now, in her mind, Oreste has become a monster. And, in a sense it is true. In the soliloquy which follows on Hermione's exit he realizes that he has violated reason:

> ...Je suis, si je l'en crois, un traître, un assassin.
> Est-ce que Pyrrhus qui meurt? et suis-je Oreste enfin?
> Quoi! *j'étouffe en mon cœur la raison qui m'éclaire;*
> J'assine à regret un roi que je révère;
> Je viole en un jour les droits de souverains,
> Ceux des ambassadeurs, et tous ceux des humains...[3]

---

[1] *Andromaque*, V, 3.   [2] *Ibid.*   [3] *Ibid.*, V, 4.

Reason has been violated; all rationalizations are torn away. And it is all done so easily through a rhetoric that does not rely on the blaze of imagery but upon its own close-packed sinewy strength.

The *Iliad* and the *Aeneid* lie close behind this verse. To such audiences the classical tradition of education provided a close link with the dramatists; and unlimited opportunities for evoking that momentous past. Sometimes it is done simply, almost with a word:

> Favorables périls! Espérance inutile!
> N'as-tu pas vu sa gloire, *et le trouble d'Achille?* [1]

> Un voile d'amitié vous trompe l'un et l'autre,
> Et mon amour devint le confident du vôtre .
> Mais toujours quelque espoir flattait mes déplaisirs:
> *Rome, Vespasien traversaient vos soupirs...* [2]

And when we see the plays against the tapestry of history, the whole conception of *la gloire* falls into place. The Roman thoughts do not strike these characters; they are always with them.

§ iii

The values suggested by Racine's work are, from the point of view of this study, more difficult to determine. It is probable that he himself would regard the tragedies as didactic in character:

> Ce que je puis assurer, c'est que je n'en ai point fait où la vertu soit plus mise en jour que dans celle-ci; les moindres fautes y sont sévèrement punies; la seule pensée du crime y est regardée avec autant d'horreur que le crime même; les faiblesses de l'amour y passent pour de vraies faiblesses; les passions n'y sont présentées aux yeux que pour montrer tout le désordre dont elles sont cause; et le vice y est peint partout avec des couleurs qui en fait connaître et haïr la difformité. *C'est là proprement le but que tout homme qui travaille pour le public doit se proposer*; et c'est ce que les premiers poètes tragiques avaient en vue sur toute chose. Leur théâtre était une école où la vertu n'était pas moins bien enseignée que dans les écoles des philosophes. [3]

We may, no doubt, discount some part of the apology for Phèdre as a concession to the contemporary attacks on the theatre; yet it represents fairly the standard neo-Classic view. It would be impossible to justify it in any more profound system. We must therefore endeavour to stand away from the vast canvas of the plays.

Our main interest lies in the concept of reason in perpetual and

[1] *Iphigénie*, IV, 1.   [2] *Bérénice*, I, 4.
[3] Preface to *Phèdre*. Compare the tone of Sidney's *Apologie*.

varied collision with that human emotion called (for convenience) love. The sharpness of the conflict, the assumption by dramatist and audience that, ultimately, the power and rightness of reason was un-questioned and unquestionable, belongs to a static society whose hierarchical and moral values were for the moment solidified: whatever aberrations, social and moral, might appear in practical life.[1] Such a society is well fitted to approve a tragedy which is idealized, concen-trated, the mirror of its own highest aspirations perceived in alignment with a Cartesian world of reason, with the Roman and Greek Fates, and with a Jansenist sense of predestination. It sees itself, in some measure, as the civilized pupil at the feet of classical history and myth; translating that situation into a kind of neutral, remote world yet one that, like the innumerable steel engravings of its artists, represented for it a special kind of reality.

That reality is unquestioned, unchanging. Its characters are doubly predestined; once by the fable, once or more by the ancient dramatists who have imposed form upon it. Within that framework the char-acters are free, not to attempt a breach in the net of destiny; but to watch the movements of their own minds, to follow and to express the alternations of love, hope, anger, frustration, despair. At the roots are a theoretical Reason that, untrammelled, can provide the answer to the riddle; and a human nature, also constant in its broad characteristics as perceived in history, but confronting its destiny with a range of emotions proper to its station and tradition.

The negative aspects are clear. The lower-level characters (there are no 'low' ones) are puppets, their sensibilities modulated to the brilliance of the main protagonists. There is little or no imagery, little that pro-vides extension or depth of meaning; there is no reconciliation, only suffering, stoicism or death. The pagan characters adhere rigidly to their proprieties: Christianity never intrudes into Racine's world. And it is a strangely joyless one; there is only a peculiar kind of exaltation, that is largely aesthetic in character, at this superb ordering, insight, and sheer concentration of passion.

It would not be true to say that this is a tragedy of ideas, though the plots are distilled to this fine essence; for character is—within the given limits—differentiated and full. But it does stand for this dichotomy perceived in a manner whose links with reality are of the mind; trans-lated with difficulty into common experience; breaking easily into the

---

[1] e.g. the endless scandals, themselves microcosmic examples of human irrationality, at the Court of Louis XIV.

ridiculous or sentimental if we do not hold closely to its conventions, and to the whole concept of baroque tragedy.

In the last resort it is valuable that the human mind should be directed repeatedly to the elemental qualities of its moral law, even though these should be set forth in the name of 'reason'. It is valuable that the irrationality of love (even though the characters who languish and die for it seem now unduly sentimental) should be presented in its nakedness as the origin of crime, frustration, and despair; for it may bring us to a recognition, because of the very absorption of the characters in that passion, and their half-disavowal of responsibility, of our own vice of attributing it to heredity, environment (which are no more than symbols of the insensate fury of the gods), rather than to ourselves. In this tragedy the ideas that lie at its core are drawn from the Hebrew, Greek and Roman thought; components of Christianity, but not Christian; since it does not know in full the depths of humility and compassion or reconciliation. For we can perceive in Racine's plays this clarified and ordered statement—however limited—of the elemental human situation: the evil that I would not, that I do; the good that I would, that I do not. And neither the tirades, nor those stiff figures in brocaded robes, nor the heavy atmosphere of court and drawing-room, can cloak the power of this knowledge.

CHAPTER 15

A Note on Ibsen

... How far is the scheme of Ibsen's drama, the design as apart from the execution of it, compatible with the highest ends at which tragedy can aim? Are not his details overloaded, his themes depressing, his characters too persistently lacking in the nobler, the more heroic qualities without which our sympathies remain cold?

C. E. VAUGHAN [1]

His greatness lies in the fact that, denied the elevated themes of theomachies and dynastic struggles, the stature of heroes and princes, and the language of poets, he yet continues by means minute yet evocative to suggest in drama, beneath the familiar prosaicness of modern life, the perpetual mystery of human personality in its struggle with necessity.

J R. NORTHAM [2]

§ i

THE turmoil of indignation that greeted Ibsen's plays, particularly *A Doll's House* and *Ghosts*, has long since died down; partly because the New Woman of Shavianism is no longer a controversial figure, partly because inherited disease has been recognized as an open and most serious problem, and partly because he has ceased to be regarded as the exponent of any particular iconoclasms or as a propagandist for a new morality. Time has set him clearly in perspective against a political and social background, and recognized him as the inheritor of certain philosophical ideas, in particular those of Kierkegaard and Schopenhauer.[3] We are now aware of 'Scandinavianism' and the threats to Norwegian nationalism which were such burning questions in the middle of the nineteenth century; a sense of bitterness and frustration at national ineffectiveness, corruption and muddle-headedness; a fairy-romanticism that had been born of Norwegian ballad and folklore; and a strong personal sense of guilt and bitterness, relieved initially by the temperament and equipment of a considerable poetic talent,[4] and later by a mordant sense of humour. His Norway is the scene of a violent conflict between liberal idealism and a regressive conservatism,

---

[1] *Types of Tragic Drama*, pp. 269–70.
[2] *Ibsen's Dramatic Technique*, p. 220.
[3] See, in general, B. W. Downs, *Ibsen: the Intellectual Background*.
[4] See, in particular, the chapter on The Poet in Dr M. C. Bradbrook's *Ibsen*.

accentuated by a relatively classless society; and of a conflict between the teachings of the orthodox church and the coldly-rising flood of nineteenth-century criticism: both conditioned by a fear on the part of established authority of opinions in almost every sphere of national activity that might be termed 'subversive'. All in all, the time and place provided a situation of conflict, nationalism and general evolutionary problems that suggests comparisons with Tudor and Stuart England, and with nineteenth-century Ireland. A personal 'heroic' romanticism in his youth, an illegitimate child, a strong sense of personal guilt, and a power to exacerbate popular sentiment, may serve to carry resemblance a stage further. We are now aware of an Ibsen who is far from the sordid realist of earlier artificial portraits, something much greater than 'the clinical analyst at the bedside of society', and a personality far more complex than Shaw's *Quintessence of Ibsenism* would seem to suggest. He is revealed as a technician of great subtlety and distinction, building his effects out of minute attention to detail, yet retaining a broad and tightly-jointed structure; a writer with a strong discipline of his own, made more unyielding by a Calvinistic sense of guilt. We are aware, too, of an impish sense of humour, perhaps best seen in *Love's Comedy* or in his remark to Georg Brandes: 'Now you go home to provoke the Danes, while I stay at home to annoy the Norwegians.' [1] We can afford to contemplate Clement Scott, and the *Daily Telegraph* of the eighties, with a detached amusement.

§ *ii*

Ibsen's world is of the Middle Classes, unrelieved by any contact with workman or noble, and only occasionally concerned with the Saint or Fool. Minor officials, journalists, bankers, writers, sculptors, ineffectual clergymen, local politicians, are the new tragic material; the choruses are drawn from cynics, idealists, and the compact conservative majority or the less compact liberal minority. The earlier plays—*The Feastings at Solhoug* or *Vikings at Helgeland* will serve as examples— suggest that youthful dramatists assume something like a heroic mantle or mask: which is later discarded, but which leaves an emotional impetus that finds expression in a strong sense of the irrational, and at times the supra-natural, in his dramatic world.

Characters of the new tragedy have, in themselves, no *a priori* interest arising from their station in life; the dramatist must re-create an interest both in their past and, through some 'recognitional' bond with the

---

[1] Quoted Downs, *op. cit.*, p. 139.

audience,[1] a sympathy with the intricacies of character. Such characters will not speak poetry, and the resources of rhetoric are usually given to them only to be deflated in the Shavian manner. The burden on the characters is usually separated from the mystery, which is thrown back, as it were, to adumbrations of the supra-natural, the operations of something like Greek Destiny, or the compulsive indeterminacy of symbolism. It is through such devices that Ibsen makes credible the irrational or mystical impulses in human nature, the desire for revenge, atonement, self-sacrifice. The pattern gains its momentum from the spiral or repeating pattern, the interaction of past and present.

An attempt to assess Ibsen's tragedy must take account of his own development, as well as the balance which he maintained by reason of his own implication in the Norwegian social and political scene, and his deliberate reversal of popular deductions as to the 'moral'. *An Enemy of the People, The Wild Duck,* and *Rosmersholm* are, in a sense, conflicting studies of idealism; just as Nora Helmer, 'the woman who left', is balanced by Mrs Alving of *Ghosts,* who stayed to do her duty. It is therefore best to consider those plays which are least dependent on local and contemporary conditions; and first to isolate, as far as possible, Ibsen's apparent 'themes'. These appear to be seven in number:

1. The relationship of man to woman, in love, incest,[2] marriage.
2. The relationship of woman to her social and economic setting.
3. The claims of idealism as a guide to practical living.
4. The nature of Christianity: both absolutely and as an evolutionary philosophy.
5. Individual *vs.* collective crime and punishment; including the problems of heredity.
6. The impact of the non-rational—whether supro-natural or psychological—upon character in action.
7. What is reality?

More than one question is always treated in each play. Tone and setting are usually given by the title: sometimes with subtlety as in *Ghosts* or *John Gabriel Borkman,*[3] sometimes with such emphasis—as in

---

[1] Cf. the endless discussions as to the 'probability' of such characters as Nora Helmer; and 'As for Hedda Gabler, I take her in to dinner twice a week.' In general it seems likely that a considerable amount of 'guilt-identification', more than we are usually prepared to admit, takes place in the theatre.

[2] e.g. *Ghosts, Rosmersholm.*

[3] As suggesting the dual personality of the hero: John Borkman the practical business man, and Gabriel the angelic component.

The Wild Duck—that the recurrence of the symbolism grows wearisome. (It seems, in fact, that the symbol, to be effective, must not be burdened with conscious multiple meanings; and is best left to expand, as it were, in space.) But the 'themes' are, in any scale of values, central to humanity. The problem in evaluating Ibsen as a tragedian might appear to involve an answer to the following questions:

1. Does Ibsen as a tragic artist achieve a balance—as Shaw does not—between the 'theme' and its dramatic presentation?
2. What elements in the plays (bearing in mind Vaughan's quotation at the head of this chapter) serve to replace the traditional requirements, and to give the necessary universality?
3. What value are we to attach to the *total* response to this tragedy in view both of these traditional requirements, and of any new interpretation of such terms as *katharsis* that may be apparent from them?

§ *iii*

At the outset we may notice that *Emperor and Galilean* and *Brand* provide us with examples of the 'great' subjects, emperor and would-be saint, and that Ibsen considered the former his most important play. Both are, from different angles, attacks upon the conventional religious morality of Ibsen's time; in that conflict State interference seemed, in 1872, to be a possibility, and we must perhaps go back to the English debates on Disestablishment to form any conception of the background. Further, the Hegelian theory of thesis, antithesis, and synthesis had impressed itself deeply upon Ibsen's mind. In *Emperor and Galilean* the hero, Prince Julian, reacts violently against the official religion of Constantine, with its corruption and aimless ritual. Christianity has embodied and made decadent the beauty of paganism. Is a new synthesis—not a 'Second Coming'—a possibility? The claims of Emperor and Galilean are irreconcilable:

> Yes, this Jesus Christ is the greatest rebel that ever lived. What was Brutus—what was Cassius compared with him? They murdered only the man Julius Caesar; but he murders all that is called Caesar and Augustus. Is peace conceivable between the Galilean and the Emperor? Is there room for the two of them together upon the earth? For he lives upon the earth, Maximus—the Galilean lives, I say, however thoroughly both Jews and Romans imagined they had killed him; he lives in the rebellious minds of men; he lives in their scorn and defiance of all visible authority . . .[1]

[1] Archer, p. 369.

The dramatic answer is that both Emperor and Galilean shall one day be replaced by 'the right man' (a shadow, perhaps of Nietzsche's Superman): but

> You solve the riddle by a still darker riddle.[1]

Nor does the ghost of Judas Iscariot contribute anything to a solution; the 'empire' will be established by 'the way of freedom', which is 'the way of necessity', by the 'power of willing' 'what man must'.

Emperor and Galilean is an unsatisfactory and uneven play. Its moral as tragedy is that a tragedy of too grandiose a scale is bound to fail; that the machinery—such as the spirit-raising scene—is never more than machinery, for there is no poetry to help us in the willing suspension of disbelief; and that the play shows throughout no understanding of the Christian position. In it the individual is swamped by ideas. Maximus the Mystic is a kind of commentator on the action:

> Your God is a spendthrift God, Galileans! He wears out many souls! Wast thou not then, this time either, the chosen one—thou victim on the altar of necessity? What is it worth to live? All is sport and mockery.—To will is to have to will! [2]

The ratiocination is trite and fragile. There seems to be a sort of Schopenhauer World-Will, not unlike Hardy's; the occasional outbursts of the Dionysiac element are quite unconvincing. Emperor and Galilean is a colossal failure: its theme is entirely un-tragic in the terms in which Ibsen stated it. And we may think that the lack of any core of philosophy commensurate with the subject—for Ibsen was at that stage in search of a faith—are sufficient to account for this.

§ iv

Brand is, by contrast, a far more interesting exercise in tragedy; perhaps because it is vécu, whereas Emperor and Galilean was born of his brain only. It is also the single most important exposition of Kierkegaard's philosophy in dramatic form. For Brand as a play centres on the absolute will of the hero, a will which stops at nothing in its efforts to achieve complete surrender to the will of God. The sheer power of will must subdue man's sinful nature, and that which he perceives to be sinful in others. A contempt for institutional religion, and for the general weakness, the lack of all conviction, in the parish which is a microcosm of Norway, makes this will loom even larger in Brand's

---

[1] Archer, p. 371.   [2] Ibid., p. 479.

own philosophy as the prime necessity. In order to fulfil himself his
mother, child, and wife are in turn sacrificed; but no less than he
sacrifices himself in his own epic attempt at self-conquest.

> Come, then, dullard souls who roam
> This my narrow valley home!
> Man to man, in converse still,
> Trial of our work we make;
> Lies and half-truths fight, and wake
> The young lion of the will! [1]

But the exercise of Brand's will, while it compels admiration, results
in untold misery for mother, wife, parishioners. The only possible
church is the Ice-Church in the mountains, the only possible ending
the avalanche that overwhelms him.

It is not a perfect tragedy, for it is unactable; it is not even a really
great tragic poem. From any Christian standpoint Brand's God is still
a ferocious Jehovah of the Old Testament, demanding not mercy but
sacrifice. In Brand himself there is no humility, no sign of a search for
grace; only a totalitarian religious fanaticism. Those account for its
limiting and limited appeal. Within this range, however, conflicting
emotions are brought into play preparatory to a tragic synthesis; pity
and pathos, as in the Christmas scene with Agnes when Brand forces her
to surrender the dead child's clothes. The counterpointing is skilful;
the opening scene of the lovers Einar and Agneta, with all its joy and
energy, is broken when Agneta decides to follow Brand, and parodied
when Einar becomes, as it were, a parody of Brand himself. But Ibsen
is himself utterly blind to the Christian solution; the antitheses are too
simple. Perhaps this is because there is in the poem so much of Ibsen
himself; social and ecclesiastical propaganda, mainly diverted against
the sin of sloth; the symbolism of the Troll-world for his own dual
personality; and, we may suspect, some discharge of the scorpion's
poison generated by his own family relationships. 'For I had a kind of
imposthume in my brain that I did desire to be unladen of, and could
imagine no fitter evacuation than this.'

Image and symbol, in so far as they can be valued in translation, are
vivid and appropriate up to a point. The comments of the mad girl,
Gerd, her shooting of the mysterious eagle that turns out to be a dove,
have been the object of much criticism. The ice-cavern, the voyage on
the stormy fjord, the avalanche, are sufficiently clear: the hawk I take

[1] *Everyman* Edn., transl. F. E. Garrett, p. 68.

13

to be the Law of the Old Testament that changes, too late, into the
Spirit of the New, for just before Gerd kills it there is a moment when
Brand seems to be on the verge of Christian salvation:

> Frost endures throughout the Law;
> Then the sunlight, then the thaw!
> Till to-day, to be a white
> Tablet where God's hand could write
> Was the only aim I saw;
> From to-day, my life shall change;
> Warmth and richness in its range;
> Breaks the stillborn crust: to-day,
> I can weep, and kneel, and pray! [1]

But it is too late; the avalanche started by Gerd's shooting of the eagle
overwhelms him; and the voice from the avalanche, 'God is Love', is
dramatically effective in a superficial way but fails utterly to round the
poem.

§ v

Both *Ghosts* and *A Doll's House* raise in an interesting manner the
possibility of a modified interpretation of *katharsis*. In *Brand* the
materials for it were available; his mind, in spite of its lyric qualities, was insufficient to compass it, and we may compare the ending with that of *Samson Agonistes* in this respect. In these two plays
there is no attempt to round off the play, by death, resignation, or a
choric synthesis. Both develop guilt-themes, and both project them
into space and time at the fall of the curtain. That this ending has
repeatedly proved a shock to the conventional audience is sufficiently
proved by the notorious 'improved' ending to *A Doll's House*, recalling
Nahum Tate's rewriting of *Lear*, and the refusal of a celebrated actress
to play the part of Nora: 'I would never leave my children'; as well as
the endless speculations on *Ghosts* as to whether Mrs Alving did or
did not give Oswald the poison. Nor is it enough to dismiss these
protests as conventional and dated; it is clear that they have an important bearing on the evolution of the tragic pattern. If dramatic life
is not to be punctuated by dramatic death, if no reconciliation is to be
proposed by any poetic statement, what is the final response?

The effect seems to be the thrusting of the whole responsibility back
upon the audience or reader; the presentation of certain facts, assumptions, attitudes and emotions which are carried forward, incomplete,

[1] Transl. Garrett, p. 221.

outside the theatre. All great tragedy probably produces some degree of psychic unrest,[1] but this is a troubling of deeper spiritual waters; whereas the Ibsen interrogation mark at the stage at which the final curtain falls, is continued mainly as a process of the mind, raising speculations which are cerebral rather than aesthetic. At the same time we must regard this cerebral activity projected outside the limits of the play as incidental even if we do not dismiss it as a futile and otiose response. Within the strict framework of the play, Ghosts is a tragedy, compact and vehement like a Greek play, though it is Hebraic rather than Greek in terms of the Second Commandment; its close circle of crime and retribution leaves us aware of the irrational or the uncomprehended factor in that sequence; the pity and terror accumulate as past certifies present, though the pity, we may think, is less than the terror. And this is, perhaps, because Ibsen's thesis as regards Mrs Alving's conduct is too carefully worked out in terms of social convention. By contrast, the issues and issue of A Doll's House seem more of the surface; the symbolism, or more accurately, the stage devices, suggest no deeper issues. While Ibsen's own opinion of it was high—'he himself called it at first "the modern tragedy", so great and inclusive did it seem in his mind' [2]—we feel that it remains a domestic tragedy that can be readily stressed in production to a comic pattern. In its psychology and motivation it is, perhaps, the most 'dated' of Ibsen's tragedies.

§ vi

Rosmersholm and Hedda Gabler represent for our purposes two aspects of tragedy of great importance. The title of Rosmersholm in its first drafts was White Horses. The White Horse is the symbol of Rosmersholm: it is linked with dead who cling to the house; the Mill-Race that has drowned Beata, the footbridge which Kroll will cross and Rosmer will not; the portraits that recall the dead burden that lies on Rosmer himself; the white shawl that Rebecca wears: all these point the contrast between the darkness that belongs to the dead wife, Beata, and the new hope and life that Rebecca seeks to bring down from the North.

Much of the controversy that surrounds the play becomes redundant if we regard it as the tragedy of Rebecca, defeated by the spirit of Rosmersholm and of the past. Rosmer is too supine to be a hero. But

---

[1] Its symptoms in the audience varying greatly according to temperament and sophistication, the extent to which they say 'Ah, that is I!'

[2] Koht, p. 67.

if we focus our interest on Rebecca, she is, in three ways, the victim struggling in the net; the revelation of her illegitimacy (and hence the incest of her relation with Rosmer); the struggle against her own love; the struggle with the house and its drowned mistress. For the cumulative evil generated by a house is very real,[1] and is a complex of physical surroundings, past thoughts and deeds, and, I think, an attempt to arrest the time-stream; an image to which we can relate the Mill-Race and its victims. The action of clinging to a house and its past, of a failure to realize when the stream of history has passed it by, is a deep-rooted and evil instinct, the more insidious because it is so easily rationalized into a belief in aristocracy, pride of race and birth, and so on. The plays of Chekhov show this craving at its worst.

As Rebecca's tragedy, the emotional impact is great. Rosmer's *accidie*, the second-hand sterile philosophy, the catastrophic impinging of the idealist Brendal in his borrowed clothes, the background of small-town scandal and gossip, are set against Ibsen's northern romanticism which is now adequately controlled. The horse is an archetypal image; its part in the play is the more powerful because it is never artificially related (as the Wild Duck seems to be) by too large or too explicit a number of connections. The position of Rebecca has been criticized, since it is she who induced Beata's suicide; it is possible in view of Beata's mental illness to condone her action in some measure. But the crimes of both Rosmer and Rebecca are confronted squarely by each; the final suicide of both in the Mill-Race has at least the strength of their love—for Rosmer's is now awakened to respond to and confront hers—to justify their expiation. That expiation is whole and satisfying; for Rosmer's earlier and tentative suggestion, so close to that made to Hedwig in *The Wild Duck*, is now submerged in a knowledge of mutual responsibility.

§ *vii*

If, as I think possible, there should be established a genre of satiric tragedy, less profound than true tragedy and yet valuable for its cathartic astringency, *Hedda Gabler* would be the classic example. Hedda is the explosive, masculine, frustrated woman, her vitality in perpetual conflict with her inhibitions; imitating her dead father, the General; taking as her symbols fire and pistols; hating and desiring children, and finding relief in the narration of Lövborg's sexual escapades. All this frustration is consistent with a steadily-developing sadism; expressed

---

[1] e.g. the Mannon house in O'Neill's *Mourning Becomes Elektra*.

in youth in the threat to burn off Thea's hair, in her exhortation to Lövborg to shoot himself, in the final burning of the manuscript. Like *Rosmersholm*, the play is bound to the past; Hedda is the victim of the past, of her father, and of a dying aristocratic tradition, the shreds of gentility to which so many characters in modern tragedy seem to cling. This is at once a psychological compensation, an assumption of privilege, the opportunity for leisure and boredom, the playing with fire or pistols that boredom brings.[1] The satiric element is to be found in the larger and smaller aspects of the design; the progressive revelation of Hedda's character through the interaction of the others, the manner in which her own dramatic gestures recoil perpetually upon her; and the final closing of the circle with her suicide. That death offers no reconciliation, completes no response save that of our own interest in her character and the destruction of all that is empty, histrionic or ineffectual in herself, Lövborg, Thea and Brack. Because of this lack of extension or depth it demands the description of limited or satiric tragedy. Its final justification is our inner knowledge of the falsity of Judge Brack's epilogue:

People don't do such things!

I am inclined to think that *Little Eyolf* is, from a formal point of view, the most perfect of Ibsen's tragedies. It is of a circular structure; the sacrificial death of the child, his lameness that was caused by the momentary sexual abandonment of his parents, demand this atonement. They cannot give that until, in the famous second act, they strip from each other layer upon layer of pretence and selfishness; finding at the end a sad and resigned peace, dedicating their house and lives to unwanted and unloved chlidren. The regeneration through suffering is complete; both Rita and Allmers are changed after each has attempted to retain some last shreds of self-hood, and each wins the grace of pity.

But such a bald account gives no consideration to the considerable and vital depth-images of the play. The Rat-Wife whom Little Eyolf follows to his death is, as Archer suggests, a mysterious and ambivalent character; the image of the gnawing rats (is not this a figure of the conscience of the three protagonists?) whom she lures to the happy safety of death, does not strain our credulity as do the wilder emblems

---

[1] This sense of boredom, emptiness, frustration that occurs so frequently in Ibsen, Chekov, Strindberg and sometimes in O'Neill might be ascribed in part to national conditions, where this sense of race existing in semi-decay provided exactly the right conditions for its growth.

of the White Horses of *Rosmersholm*. The problem of the boundary-line between objective and subjective guilt is faced and ravelled out; as also the problem—so common in Ibsen—of the discrepancy between thinking and living. Allmer's great work, as yet existing only in his brain, is on 'Human Responsibility'; circumstances conspire to reduce the problem to its practical and most terrible elements, with recurrent ironic overtones.[1] The eyes of the drowned child that stare upwards from the sea-bed, the crutch that floats and is rescued, the implications of the Rat-Wife's

> I know one ought never to get tired of doing good to the poor little things that are hated and persecuted so cruelly. But it takes your strength out of you, it does.[2]

—all this serves to build up the pity and fear of the child's death. Because the symbolism of the drowning is never overstressed—unlike the complex and *nachgesucht* interrelations of the Wild Duck—it becomes continuously effective, woven into the threads with precision and tact. *Little Eyolf* achieves a degree of dispassionateness on the part of Ibsen, perhaps because the matter of the play is less autobiographical than usual. And the progressive and deliberate conversion from fantasy to reality under the impulse of grief is one of the most morally important of all tragic themes.

John Gabriel Borkman is also a character of guilt and retribution, and set in a framework that is familiar enough to every reader. The struggle between the two sisters, with their utterly conflicting personalities, for Gunhild's son, and his breaking-away from both, is another aspect of the dead world that, as so often in Ibsen, sucks the vitality of the living. Borkman dies, because he has sold his love of Ella Rentheim; Gunhild is deserted by her son because the 'missionary' ideal, the redemption of his father's name and fortune which she seeks to impose, is too fantastic to be pressed against the claims of living flesh and blood as represented by Mrs Wilton.

It is the depth-imagery that is of special interest. John Gabriel is the son of a miner; he dreams of liberating all the wealth that lives underground: at the end the dream and the reality converge:

Borkman. Can you see the smoke of the great steamships out on the fjord?
Ella Rentheim. No.

---

[1] Consider Allmer's remark early in Act I.
. . . 'You see, I have been such a fool hitherto. All the best that is in you goes into thinking. What you put on paper is worth very little.' Archer, p. 12.
[2] *Ibid.*, p. 20.

Borkman. I can. They come and they go. They weave a network of fellowship all round the world. They shed light and warmth over the souls of men in many thousands of homes. That was what I dreamed of doing.
Ella (softly). And it remained a dream.
Borkman. It remained a dream, yes, And hark, down by the river, dear! The factories are working! My factories! All those that I would have created! Listen! Do you hear them humming? The night shift is on—so they are working night and day. Hark! hark! the wheels are whirling and the bands are flashing—round and round and round. Can't you hear, Ella?
Ella. No.[1]

Now Borkman is a complex image of modern man: who has denied love, committed a crime in his ambition, and seen a Prometheus-vision of himself as the bringer of happiness to man. But he is, over and above this, archetypal in character. Like the Rhine-gold in Wagner, the silver mine in Conrad's *Nostromo*, the hidden treasure of the earth is the supreme attraction and bane of man: the metal denies, torture, kills humanity. Borkman dies as he and Ella climb together (up the winding path) through the wood: 'it was an ice-cold metal hand that gripped him by the heart'.[2] At the end the resolution is complete; the two sisters are alone:

Ella Rentheim (with a painful smile). A dead man and two shadows—that is what the cold has made of us.
Mrs Borkman. Yes, the coldness of heart—And now [3] I think we two may hold out our hands to each other, Ella.
Ella. I think we may, now.
Mrs Borkman. We twin sisters—over him we have both loved.
Ella. We two shadows—over the dead man.

But there are other depth-aspects of the play. The sub-plot that involves the old clerk Foldal and his daughter Frida is not, I think, as extrinsic to the plot as recent critics have suggested.[4] Borkman is made more credible by the fact that Foldal is a poet, has remained his friend, is rejected by him. The brutality and egoism of Borkman, the contrast between the two types of failure, the mirror-effect of the desertion of daughter and son, the pathos and the naïveté of Foldal, add appreciably to the tragic effect. And Mrs Wilton's cynicism in carrying

---

[1] *Ibid.*, pp. 316–17.   [2] *Ibid.*, p. 322.
[3] Notice how Mrs Borkman's character and limitations are suggested by the transition between the two phrases; and Ella's patience in reply.
[4] e.g. Dr Bradbrook in *Ibsen the Norwegian*, p. 140.

away Frida with them on their honeymoon, to become Erhart's mistress, makes all three characters immediately credible:

> *Mrs Borkman (with a malignant smile).* Mrs Wilton, do you think you are acting quite wisely in taking that girl with you?
> *Mrs Wilton (returning the smile, half ironically, half seriously).* Men are so unstable, Mrs Borkman. And women too. When Erhart is done with me— and I with him—then it will be well for us both that he, poor fellow, should have someone to fall back upon.
> *Mrs Borkman.* But you yourself?
> *Mrs Wilton.* Oh, I shall know what to do, I assure you. Good-bye to you all.[1]

John Gabriel Borkman is thus a multiple-level play; of the betrayal of Ella's love by Borkman's search for gold and ambition; of Gunhild's revenge upon him for the stigma that he has brought upon the family name (two kinds of guilt value); of three kinds of possessiveness by women (the two sisters, in different ways, of Erhart, and Mrs Wilton's sensual conquest); the dreamers (Foldal with his forgotten play, in which his family have long ago lost faith, and Borkman with his dreams of 'rehabilitation', of the wealth that he will drag from the earth, and of the happiness it will bring). And each dreamer kills the other's dream. The problem of guilt is sharpened and brought into touch with reality by the Lear-like battle of the twin sisters. Their reconciliation is all the more terrible because Ella has foreknowledge of her own death, and because Gunhild has been stripped of both husband and son. The peace between Capulets and Montagues at the end of *Romeo and Juliet* leaves us unmoved, and perhaps a little exasperated; but here the renewed sacrifice of Ella completes the tragic cycle.

The Master Builder and *When We Dead Awaken* are perhaps best considered as poems of the last phase; the latter is scarcely possible on the stage. *The Master Builder* is the tragedy of the artifex facing, in old age, the claims of youth: and thinking (as so many have done) that young and radiant womanhood i sthe key to rejuvenescence. Hilda's youth and high spirits give Solness just this hope; confirmed by her own repeated sacrifice of herself:

> Can't you make use of me?

and his reply:

> You are that of which I have the sorest need.

Yet both are in love, not with each other, but with an idea; and with

---

[1] Archer, p. 294.

the idea that their union will neutralize the two fears that haunt him: the fear of youth following close on his heels, to take his reputation from him, and the fear of retribution for the evil that he has committed. The fire which he started in the Solness home, and through which he grew successful and wealthy, shattered his wife's life and killed his children. The new house that he builds for Hilda can never be a home.

Solness is perhaps the only one of Ibsen's central characters, except Brand, who is of heroic stature; in the main because he is vigorous (in spite of age and sickness); because his gruff virility is consistently shown in his accent and actions; because he is, for all his sin, a visionary and a poet; because he confronts God, triumphantly, on the tower of the new house, and falls to his death. The play is satisfying in the agencies of retribution, and in the symbolism—the building of churches versus the building of homes—that supports it. Solness's early dream of the ideal fire is a good example of the day-dream rationalization. We can even perceive a pattern in his relations with the three women, like three terms of an equation; Maia, his girl secretary who idolizes him and is spurned; his wife, the murdered woman to whom he is married; and Hilda, who might in his thought have saved him, and who is in fact the agent of retribution.

Like Antony, Solness is a believer in his luck, his 'guardians'; Hilda is to some extent possessed of a troll, and, with the vitality of youth, can change from mood to mood in harmony with his. But such a harmony is only for a moment; youth and age are incompatible; sin must be expiated individually. And just as Rosmer suggests Rebecca's sacrifice, so Hilda suggests, urges, that of Solness. Like *When We Dead Awaken* the play concerns the problem of the artist's integrity, the part played by marriage, love, humanity, in the complicated 'duty' of the artist. But because of the vastness, universality and credible symbolism of the artifacts, *The Master Builder* raises these issues in a manner that is at once more intense and more in contact with reality.

When We Dead Awaken is, as a tragedy, a kind of apocalyptic vision of man's guilt, of woman's love and suffering. Like Borkman, the sculptor Rubek has killed Irene's soul, in the name of art; and in rejecting her he has killed art and life as well. The statue of the Resurrection grows animal heads around it. That again is archetypal; we may think both of *King Lear* and of *The Dog Beneath the Skin*, and of Circe's swine, or those of Gadara. Such symbols fall naturally to the hand of the dramatist who wishes to suggest the dual nature of man; and have sanction enough in dreams. Other symbols are less obtrusive:

Rubek's vision of the stations in which 'there were two railwaymen walking up and down the platform—one with a lantern in his hand—they said things to each other in the night, low, and toneless, and meaningless'.[1]

The Christian system of references is of some interest. Rubek, on his courtship of Maia, has promised her that he would take her 'up to a high mountain and show her all the glory of the world'.

> *Professor Rubek* (*with a slight start*). Did I promise you that, too?
> *Maia.* Me too? Who else, pray?
> *Rubek* (*indifferently*). No, no, I only meant did I promise to show you—?
> *Maia.*—all the glory of the world? Yes, you did. And that glory should be mine, you said.
> *Rubek.* That is a sort of figure of speech that I was in the habit of using once upon a time.
> *Maia.* Only a figure of speech?
> *Rubek.* Yes, a scholarly phrase—the sort of thing I used to say when I wanted to lure the neighbours' children out to play with me, in the woods and on the mountains.[2]

Like the manuscript in *Hedda Gabler*, Rubek's great statue is his 'child'. Like Allmer's in *Little Eyolf* he is the victim of his own 'artistic' self-delusion, the perpetual *hubris* of the writer or artist. The symbolism of the 'revisions' to the Resurrection-Statue is perhaps a little too obvious, as well as being materially impossible; the recession of the figure into the background, the guilt-laden figure of the artist in the foreground, the animalized men and women burgeoning about it.

It is, in one sense, a 'neutral' tragedy: Rubek with his intolerable self-centredness, with his monstrous suggestions of a *ménage à trois*, can never be a tragic hero. Irene is, perhaps, more of the stamp of the tragic heroine, but as a victor-victim; of multiple personality, prepared to take revenge for the ruin of her life, prepared to surrender utterly in her transfiguration as she and Rubek are about to ascend the peak. To her Maia is a clumsy foil, though not without some subtlety of character drawing in her very naïveté and ecstatic horror at the bear-hunter's attractions. The song of her freedom sounds through the roar of the avalanche that carries away Rubek and Irene. It is a *Brand*-like ending, a little mechanical, even to the Sister of Mercy's *Pax Vobiscum*: but the mountains and their symbolism, the Norwegian fjords and mists, the horror of winter, are realities that grow comprehensible with some

---

[1] Archer, p. 334. Consider the vitality, and the profundity, of the symbol.
[2] Archer, pp. 340-1.

residence in Norway. Yet the play is unactable, confused; the texture of its ironies is not handled with Ibsen's usual certainty. Only it represents, for us, the compelling and eternal dilemma of the artist: the exaltation and nemesis of his humanity; his self-assumed prerogative to sacrifice others for the sake of his art; the inevitable discontent, self-distrust, desire to revise, and better, that follow the completed work. 'Life, how or what is it?' Is the artist to deny life that he may live more abundantly, and does not that denial bring its retribution? Perhaps in Yeats's words:

> The intellect of man is forced to choose
> Perfection of the life, or of the work,
> And if it take the second must refuse
> A heavenly mansion, raging in the dark. . .[1]

§ viii

The Ibsen contribution to the 'fact or experience' of tragedy can now be considered. It is, I think, advisable to say first what it is not. All earlier estimates of the 'pallid and joyless' realist, of the 'clinical analyst' or of the 'prudential moralist' are now perceived to be incomplete. As a dramatist he is seen to be, in many ways, the product of a peculiar Zeitgeist. In his work, several streams meet; the heroic nationalism that must be, as always, perceived in terms of energy, courage, the supra-natural that appears to be climatically proper to the North. He is 'thrown upon the filthy modern tide' of apathy, pettiness, *accidie* rather than active corruption, a spiritual failure accentuated by the attempt at national revival. He is, by upbringing and environment and the intellectual pressure of his time, a paradoxical figure in that he inherits a strong sense of guilt,[2] is conscious of a wide break between the aesthetic and the practical, and oscillates between the desire for a clear-cut solution and a quasi-prudential system of morals. When agnosticism is superimposed on an early religious background, we may expect to find the sense of guilt reinforced, seeking for expiation, in later life. And Ibsen, as a practical man of the theatre and a technician of immense resources, had his ear always close to the ground as regards the response to his plays; and assumed a mask as a legendary European figure which gained appreciably through his own inscrutability.

[1] *The Choice.*
[2] Maybe all writers of tragedy possess this sense; or can know it, imaginatively, to the full.

The tragic material is ample in scope, profound—up to a point— in treatment. His interest in character and skill in its delineation is sufficient to guarantee that. It is valid, from the point of view of Christian ethics, in that it appears to progress towards conceptions of personal responsibility, personal guilt, and atonement: though in an imperfect and imprecise manner. It falls short of the greatest tragic art in that any admiration we may possess for the human spirit is always modified, balanced, by the tragi-comic. There is, save Brand, no single potential hero; and Brand fails from the lack of common humanity to balance the fierce and ruthless Kierkegaardian ethic. Nor is Ibsen himself of such poetic stuff as to allow his characters to find resolution or relief or ecstasy in defeat. From one point of view we may perhaps ascribe this to his own carefully-guarded and masked position, from another to the meticulous balance of the plays; or we may see in it failure to think greatly enough to perceive the true nature of man's defeat, and his tragic victory. We may doubt Shaw's statement ' . . . I think Ibsen has proved the right of the drama to take scriptural rank, and his own right to canonical rank as one of the major prophets of the modern Bible.' [1]

[1] *Major Critical Essays*, p. 148.

CHAPTER 16

The Shavian Machine

He understands everything in life except its paradoxes, especially that ultimate paradox that the very things we cannot comprehend are the things we have to take for granted.[1]

G. K. CHESTERTON

§ i

IT is related that Yeats perceived, in a dream or vision, Shaw as a sewing-machine 'that clicked and clicked continually'. There is a pleasantly surrealist quality about such a vision, and we must discount many of Yeast's statements about his friends and enemies; but there is, as often, a germ of the truth here. The two Irishmen, opposed in almost every conceivable aspect of background, upbringing and personality, offer some interesting material for a consideration of Twentieth-century Tragedy. Shaw professed an immense admiration for his own interpretation of the Ibsen tradition; Yeats and Synge, in different ways, rebelled against the 'pallid and joyless realism' that they saw there, although Yeats had a far more sensitive understanding of Ibsen than had Synge. For Ibsen was a poet; Shaw, taking over from those elements of Ibsen's art which best fitted his own optimistic scepticism, could only produce poetry from the teeth outwards; in spite of three notable attempts.[2]

The social and intellectual climate of England in the period 1880 to 1920 was perhaps less fitted to provide favourable conditions for a tragic Anschauung than either the Norway of Ibsen or the Ireland of Yeats and O'Casey. The slowly-broadening freedom, the inanities and inconsistencies of a world that was still sorting out its own 'complexities of mire and blood' offered magnificent material for the socialist satirist, but little or nothing towards a constructive vision based upon conflicting antinomies. The pressures, religious, philosophical or national, were either insufficient to provide a sense of urgency, or obscured in the indefiniteness of objectives suggested by twentieth-century warfare. The vast problems of centralization raised by new

---

[1] *George Bernard Shaw*, p. 192.
[2] In *The Doctor's Dilemma, John Bull's Other Island*, and *St Joan*.

methods of communication, the bewildering impact of 'news' upon the public mind, were beginning to exercise those peculiar powers of induration and confusion which persist to-day. But to Shaw it must have seemed that the only refuge lay in a creative scepticism extended impartially over militarism, feminism, journalism, economics, medicine, big business and political philosophy, and in the Nietzschean romanticism of the Superman.

§ ii

Three only of Shaw's plays deserve consideration as tragedies; *The Doctor's Dilemma*, *Mrs Warren's Profession*, and *St Joan*.

At first sight *The Doctor's Dilemma* affords a striking example of the Hegelian theory of tragedy, the conflict of two balanced and irreconcilable claims, which by their conflict raise important questions of value but which point to a division in the substance of The Good. If circumstances allow the salvation of only one life, which is to be preferred; that of the morally worthless artist or that of the worthy general practitioner? By what scale is the choice to be justified? The stage is set, the victim dies; the famous epilogue is spoken by Ridgeon:

Then I have committed a purely disinterested murder!

The play is well constructed, theoretically effective, with excellent characterization; and yet the tragic failure is complete.

There are, I think, several reasons. *The Doctor's Dilemma* is the supreme example of the multiple-aspect-and-object play whose artistic statement is wholly vitiated by the impurity of its intention and the failure (in spite of signs that Shaw attempted this late in the play) to achieve a true balance within that statement. As usual we must first consider the Preface with its ninety-four pages, in which Shaw tells us specifically what he is attacking: the shortcomings of doctors; the evils of poverty (generally, and specifically as regards doctors); inoculation; vivisection; cruelty; national health; medical training and organization. We must supplement these 'topics', in the Ibsen manner, by ancillary discussions of the shortcomings of journalists, and the place of the artist in the State. The long and unrelieved first act is cumbered with endless medical debate, allowing just enough character to emerge to serve the developing mechanics of the plot, but adding appreciably to the subjects proposed in the Preface: criminal law, cremation, Jewish *vs.* Gentile commercial morality, bourgeois views on marriage, and Christian Science. Behind these is the oscillating attack of the Puritan-Moralist on the artist and his function in society. And because of the very multiplicity of these topics, the play fails utterly to accumulate momentum; the whole of the first act is 'discussion'. The third is concerned with the *anagnorisis* of Dubedat's character as a scoundrel with artistic gifts, and provides further material for the Shavian polemic; for a moment we have some hint of human relationship in the opening between Dubedat and Jennifer, which is not picked up again till the death-scene. In this there are two speeches, admirably designed to illustrate Shaw's idea of the power of the *false word*—his conception of rhetoric—to persuade to *that which is not*. But such an analysis is too simple; Shaw would, I think, like us to be carried away by Dubedat's eloquence, is aware that it is *pastiche*, and by sheer brilliance introduces, as it were, a double falsification. The following piece of dialogue is illuminating, from Dubedat's death-scene:

> *Louis.* I want you to be beautiful. I want people to see in your eyes that you were married to me. The people in Italy used to point at Dante and say 'There goes the man who has been in hell.' I want them to point at you and say 'There goes a woman who has been in heaven.' It has been heaven, darling, hasn't it—sometimes?
>
> *Mrs Dubedat.* Oh yes, yes. Always, always.
>
> *Louis.* If you wear black and cry, people will say 'Look at that miserable woman: her husband made her miserable.'
>
> *Mrs Dubedat.* No, never. You are the light and blessing of my life. I never lived until I knew you.
>
> *Louis (his eyes glistening).* Then you must always wear beautiful dresses and splendid magic jewels. Think of all the wonderful pictures I shall never paint. (*She wins a terrible victory over a sob.*) Well, you must be transfigured with all the beauty of those pictures. Men must get such dreams from seeing you as they could never get from any daubing with paints and brushes. Painters must paint you as they never painted any mortal woman before. There must be a great tradition of beauty, a great atmosphere of wonder and romance. That is what men must always think of when they think of me. That is the sort of immortality I want. You can make that for me, Jennifer. There are lots of things you dont understand that every woman in the street understands; but you can understand that and do it as nobody else can. Promise me that immortality. Promise me you will not make a little hell of crape and crying and undertaker's horrors and withering flowers and all that vulgar rubbish.[1]

Beneath the surface the weakness and sentimentality is apparent;

[1] Act IV.

partly because Shaw has failed to build up sufficient stature for either
of the characters in the earlier part of the play, partly because the
emotional pressure is insufficient to carry conviction. And two re-
dundancies—the allusions to 'the woman in the street' and to funeral
customs—are admirable illustrations of Shaw's failure to achieve unity
of tone.

§ iii

By contrast, *Mrs Warren's Profession* comes very close to a true
tragedy in the Ibsen manner. It is not hard to see why. The theme and
its characters are integral, the psychological insight more subtle than
usual; and because the speech of the characters is wholly in tone with
the playwright's conception of them, it does not jar by any attempt
at the self-consciously poetic. The ending is modulated sufficiently into
the unspoken to leave room for the imagination to work upon the
whole; Shaw's fondness for abruptness and finality has for the moment
been abandoned And while the component themes are drawn from
Shaw's stock-in-trade (poverty, morality, clerical hypocrisy, parent-
child relationships) they are sufficiently absorbed into the idea of the
play not to appear discordant.

In some strange manner, too, the play has links with the great
classical themes; the nature of 'nature' between mother and daughter,
father and son; hypocrisy, and the power of the individual and of
society to rationalize or mask it; perhaps, too, the shadow of incest
in the discovery of the relationship between Vivien and Frank.
Through them the 'society' which Shaw attacks so constantly achieves
a kind of monstrous objectivity of its own. The sentimental artist,
Praed, produces the ironic criticism of conventional values, though he
is a little distorted. There is indeed much truth in Shaw's statement in
the Preface:

> Thus it comes about that the more completely the dramatist is emanci-
> pated from the illusion that men and women are primarily reasonable beings,
> and the more powerfully he insists on the ruthless indifference of their great
> dramatic antagonist, the external world, to their whims and emotions, the
> surer he is to be denounced as blind to the distinction on which his whole
> work is built. Far from ignoring idiosyncrasy, will, passion, impulse, whim,
> as factors in human action, I have placed them so nakedly on the stage that
> the elderly citizen, accustomed to see them clothed with the veil of manu-
> factured logic about duty, and to disguise even his own impulses from him-
> self in this way, finds the picture as unnatural as Carlyle's suggested painting
> of parliament sitting without its clothes.

We can remember with profit *Timon, Lear* and Swift. When this social criticism is successfully merged with the dramatic structure the ironies of speech and situation support the whole, and when Shaw's sense of the theatre allows him to trust his audience to complete the pattern of the unspoken, we have an approach to the only kind of tragedy his genius allowed him to compass, the tragedy of woman.

§ *iv*

St Joan is for our purposes the single most interesting play: not merely because controversy has raged for so long about its value as a tragedy, but because Shaw has in the Preface given us some account of what he conceives to be the essential tragic principles:

> There are no villains in the piece. Crime, like disease, is not interesting: it is something to be done away with by general consent, and that is all about it. It is what men and women do at their best, with good intentions, and what normal men and women find that they must do and will do in spite of their intentions, that really concern us. The rascally bishop and the cruel inquisitor of Mark Twain and Andrew Lang are dull as pickpockets; and they reduce Joan to the level of the even less interesting person whose pocket is picked. I have represented both of them as capable and eloquent exponents of the Church Militant and the Church Litigant, *because only by doing so can I maintain my drama on the level of high tragedy and save it from becoming a mere police court sensation.* A villain in a play can never be anything more than a *diabolus ex machina*, possibly a more exciting expedient than a *deus ex machina*, but both equally mechanical, and therefore interesting only as mechanism.

We are led by this statement to look for a Hegelian balance, like that proposed in *The Doctor's Dilemma*; a balance to 'maintain the play on the level of high tragedy'. This careful manipulation of the scales is predominantly intellectual; and it appears to involve the exclusion of any philosophy of evil [1] in favour of stupidity, ignorance, self-will; and a general blindness to the ultimate outcome of a given action in time. The conflict is, in the most generalized terms, between Genius and Discipline, as Shaw points out in the Preface.

But this intellectual framework, this immense care to present both sides of the conflict and to provide a rational basis for the supranatural,[2] has some interesting effects. Both sets of protagonists are deflated, impartially, by the darts of Shaw's wit; and have scarcely

[1] This is made clear by the irony of Ladvenu's reading of the confession she is required to sign.
[2] Cf. Shaw's care to stress the commonplace aspect of Joan's 'voices'; as well as the commonplace character—from several aspects—of Joan herself.

any breath left to sustain the moments of high tragedy in the trial scene. We have thus an interesting reflection on the whole question of comic relief in modern tragedy; it seems that the humour must be carefully adjusted to the characters without depriving them of the potentiality for rising, momentarily at least, above the memory of their demonstrated weakness. And we are led to the suspicion that Shaw is obsessed with the idea of the 'ordinary', as opposed to the theatrical, representations of his characters, an 'ordinariness' which is itself treated theatrically in order to emphasize it even at the expense of a certain cheapness of wit. In the trial scene the Inquisitor alone retains his full dignity; the Chaplain is over-caricatured, the anti-imperialism handled with far too heavy a touch. It becomes very clear that the central problem of the modern writer of tragedy is to achieve this delicate balance between the ordinary and the theatrical, so that the ordinary is not robbed of its power of exaltation, nor the theatrical degraded to the sentimental. And the wit must, in some manner, be merged into humour, if we are to believe in the capacity of the main protagonists to rise, in the later stages of the play, to the high emotion that will be demanded of them. But most interesting of all is Shaw's attempt to solve the problem of lyric speech at the moment of greatest tension:

> Yes: they told me you were fools (*the word gives great offence*), and that I was not to listen to your fine words nor trust to your charity. You promised me my life, but you lied (*indignant exclamations*). You think that life is nothing but not being stone dead. It is not the bread and water I fear: I can live on bread: when have I asked for more? It is no hardship for me to drink water if the water be clean. Bread has no sorrow for me, and water no affliction. But to shut me from the light of the sky and the sight of the fields and flowers; to chain my feet so that I can never again ride with the soldiers nor climb the hills; to make me breathe foul damp darkness, and keep me from everything that brings me back to the love of God when your wickedness and foolishness tempt me to hate Him: all this is worse than the furnace in the Bible that was heated seven times. I could do without my war horse; I could drag about in a skirt; I could let the banners and the trumpets and the knights and soldiers pass me and leave me behind as they leave the other women, if only I could still hear the wind in the trees, the larks in the sunshine, the young lambs crying through the healthy frost, and the blessed church bells that send my angel voices floating to me on the wind. But without these things I cannot live; and by your wanting to take them away from me I know that your counsel is of the devil, and that mine is of God.[1]

[1] Scene VI.

The rhythms here are an interesting index to the quality of the emotion; having in mind the previous delineation of Joan's character; and the two stage directions in the first two lines show that Shaw could never leave the obvious to the good sense and tact of his readers. We suspect the playwright's integrity because of the lack of rhythmic unity in the passage as a whole, as well as for the occasional clumsiness. ('You think that life is nothing but not being *stone* dead.') The passage that starts 'if only I could hear the wind in the trees' [1] is consciously 'poetic', quite out of keeping both with Joan's character and with the sentences that precede and follow it.

The Epilogues to Shaw's plays, both in *The Doctor's Dilemma* and in *St Joan*, have been the source of endless controversy. They serve several purposes. They stand in part for a negation of the traditional ending, that of the death of the hero. The play and life continue; the extension is, perhaps, designed to tempt us to view them *sub specie aeternitatis*. Any intention of the kind is denied by the irresistible opportunities they offer for a deflation of traditional attitudes, and to hammer home some of the propositions already set in the play. Shaw takes a final critical and ironical look at what has gone before. Death is neither eloquent, nor just, nor mighty, nor yet 'a queer untidy thing'. It is a chemical change through cremation. Ideas live on, modify themselves; illusion and stupidity continue in different forms; and, standing aside, Shaw's world is seen to have some measure of intellectual pity, but not of fear.

But why? Does this mean that Shaw, or Shaw's audience, demand a *Weltanschauung* sufficiently distanced that, like Troilus, they can laugh 'from the holwe of the seventh sphere', at human stupidity? There are grounds for believing that this is so. 'The tragedy of such murders is that they are not committed by murderers' (cf. *The Doctor's Dilemma*). 'They are judicial murders, pious murders; and this contradiction at once brings an element of comedy into the tragedy: the angels may weep at the murder, but the gods laugh at the murderers.' [2]

But to extend the tragedy in time and space in order to perceive the comedy is to remove at a stroke the possibility of a full tragic response. Any tragedy, thus produced in time, is seen, from an altitude, to

---

[1] I do not think it is fantastic to perceive curiously Synge-like rhythms as well as substance in this passage: 'but you'll be hearing the herons crying out over the black lakes, and you'll be hearing the grouse and the owls with them, and the larks and the big thrushes when the days are warm . . . but its fine songs you'll be hearing when the sun goes up, and there'll be no old fellow wheezing, the like of a sick sheep, close to your ear'. (*The Shadow of the Glen.*)

[2] Preface to *St Joan*, p. lvi.

provide its own resolution; as in medieval religious drama. It removes from the audience the need for any individual response or responsibility in the present. There are none of the old misgivings, the crooked questions that lie at the roots of individual experience; and Joan's cry 'How long . . . ?' fades into the commonplaces of history.

§ *v*

Such considerations, themselves negative as regards Shaw's position as a tragic artist, may yet suggest certain thoughts on the nature of tragedy. The tragic artist must present the problems which he handles as intrinsic with the plot, character, and imagery, the whole a colloidal mixture rather than a series of separate globules existing in a kind of surface-tension relationship. There would appear also to be a limit to the number of propositions that form the raw material; it is, for example, apparent that Shaw's 'subjects' are far more numerous, and less relevant to the central theme, than say, those of Ibsen or of Brieux. The sense of a tragic pattern is all-important; if this does not emerge from the interaction of character, the pattern must be brought out by imagery or symbol in the broad poetic statement. That poetic statement cannot be *appliqué*'d, at those points of the play where the dramatist thinks that they are demanded by the theatrical context; it must be, as it were, latent from the very beginning of the play, as much in its Image [1] as in its language. Comic relief, in general, must illuminate, contrast with, or round off this total idea; it must not be designed merely to puncture, deflate or wound *for its own sake*. And finally, the dramatist must achieve a certain measure of identification with his characters and situations; if he stands (even for a moment) outside them to criticize them with his own lips, he has withdrawn from them in just that measure their whole poetic life. Arland Ussher's words are worth quoting in this context:

> The tension we miss in him consists of those wholly un-Shavian ideas—sin, temptation and remorse; or in an older language than the Christian, in fear and pity—those emotions which the adolescent superman-worshipper will always despise—pity for the unalterability of the human lot, fear of the forces which lurk under the most polished social surface. [2]

[1] I use the word in Abercrombie's sense. Cf. *Principles of English Prosody.*
[2] Arland Ussher, *Three Great Irishmen*, p. 58.

CHAPTER 17

The Irish Tragedy

(Synge, Yeats, O'Casey)

They know that Hamlet and Lear are gay;
Gaiety transfiguring all that dread.
Lapis Lazuli

§ i

ON general grounds it is arguable that the first quarter of the twentieth century offered in Ireland a cultural and political background that seemed exceptionally favourable to the growth of tragedy. A high degree of patriotism and nationalist feeling, fostered in the popular poetry of the preceding century, was to be given expression through the Irish Literary Movement. The dramatists could draw on three layers of material, or on various interpenetrations of those layers: the long memories of oppression, and the sporadic epic protests against it, inflated or distilled into a mythology; the newly-revived Celtic legends which could, it was hoped, be used as symbols to fire popular imagination to a new heroism in pursuit of liberty; and a capacity to accept, in varying degrees and conflicts, the possibility of the supranatural. There was a further asset in rhythmical peasant speech, capable both of precision and of lyric flexibility, which appeared to offer a more promising medium than the Elizabethan imitations of the preceding century. The general setting invited parallels, however farfetched, with the great ages of tragic production; even the material of violent or significant action—both before and after the Easter Rising of 1916—was of a character that was well suited (being itself theatrical) to manipulation for the theatre. It was, in fact, a conflict sufficiently small to be perspicuous, sufficiently linked to personalities to rely upon a presentation of character not yet submerged by the larger wars. In the temper of the people we can perceive factors both favourable and hostile to the growth of a great tragedy. Of these the most important is the infinite distance between the popular audiences of Dublin and the playwrights themselves. The latter were, in the main, Anglo-Irish, Protestant, and of a cultural tradition which, whether through Choice or Chance, had sought fulfilment in England, where a more liberal tradition of speculation upon ultimate values might allow such questions to be represented in the theatre. The former were excitable, often curiously informed and as often semi-literate in their preferences, unyielding in their prejudgement of problems of sex, viewing larger philosophical issues under the shadow of a rigid theological system. The memories of the audience were long; they had fed themselves on grievances and phantasies; they were deeply sensitive in the pride which is built upon the past, and a future which sought, often a little artificially, to find roots therein. Yet that history, like the national grievances, was too remote to admit of a resurrection which might produce any significant alignment with the present; there was no classical or Biblical tradition, popularized in pageant, masque and dumb show, to offer common ground. We may doubt whether drama based on Celtic legend could ever approach, in contemporary relevance and significance, that which had established itself on Biblical and classical foundations. A drama based on Celtic sources would be liable to become factitious, in spite of all literary attempts to implant it in the book of the people; and, if it were so implanted, there remained the question whether the language of its representation should be in the English poetic tradition, or in some such variants of the illustrious vulgar as were evolved by Synge and Lady Gregory. Only rarely could a classical theme be re-kindled with profit, as Yeats translated *Oedipus*; though both Celtic and Classic had the advantage of being distanced sufficiently to avoid direct criticism of social or theological kind. The same consideration applied to Biblical subjects; Yeats's *Calvary* and *The Resurrection* could hardly have been approved, even if their implications had been understood, any more than could George Moore's *The Apostle*. The tragic dramatists tended, probably unconsciously, to fall back on themes which were based on the 'reality and joy' of peasant life, itself limited in complexity, hard to universalize, and apt to acquire overtones of a bitter comedy; or to the impact upon their time of political and military violence which three wars brought to their thresholds. In the Ireland of the first half of the twentieth century there was neither creative scepticism to synthesize past and present, nor a social liberalism to present a vision of the future.

§ ii

The tragedy produced in this period in Ireland is best typified in the work of Synge, Yeats, and Sean O'Casey, for there is little other work of note. Of these it seems likely that Synge will remain in our judgement as the outstanding tragedian. He did not, indeed, produce a body of explicit theory; demanding only in the theatre reality—not realism—and joy, and finding new resources in the country-folk:

> In Ireland, for a few years more, we have a popular imagination that is fiery, and magnificent, and tender; so that those of us who wish to write start with a chance that is not given to writers in places where the spring-time of the local life has been forgotten, and the harvest is a memory only, and the straw has been turned into bricks.[1]

But it was Yeats who provided, in his endeavour to shape the Abbey Theatre and by his own development as a playwright, a considerable body of material on the theory of tragedy. It is clear that it owes much to Shakespeare, and that it is in part at least a revolt against Ibsen for his alleged 'realism':

> There is an art of the flood, the art of Titian when his Ariosto and his Bacchus and Ariadne give new images to the dreams of youth,[2] and of Shakespeare when he shows us Hamlet broken away from life by the passionate hesitations of his reverie. And we call this art poetical, because we must bring to it more than our daily mood if we would take our pleasure; and because it delights in picturing the moment of exaltation, of excitement, of dreaming (or of the capacity for it, as in that still face of Ariosto's that is like some vessel soon to be full of wine). And there is an art that we call real, because character can only express itself perfectly in a real world, being that world's creature, and because we understand it best through a delicate discrimination of the senses, which is but entire wakefulness, the daily mood grown cold and crystalline.
>
> We may not find either mood in its purity, but in mainly tragic art one distinguishes devices to exclude or lessen character, to diminish the power of that daily mood, to cheat or blind its too clear perception. If the real world is not altogether rejected it is but touched here and there, and into the places we have left empty we summon rhythm, balance, pattern, images that remind us of vast passions, the vagueness of past times, all the chimeras that haunt the edge of trance . . . so that it is in the supreme moment of tragic art there comes upon one that strange sensation as though the hair of one's head stood up.[3]

It appears, then, that Yeats is considering a tragic drama in which character receives comparatively little emphasis (for he considers that character delineation is more belonging to comedy, or to comic relief

---

[1] Preface to *The Playboy of the Western World*.   [2] Cf. his poem, *The Statues*.
[3] *Plays for an Irish Theatre*, pp. vii–viii. We may recall the frequent repetition of the Job image, no doubt remembering Blake's illustration. Cf. *The Mother of God*.

in tragedy), but which relies on the evocation of a peculiar and characteristic state of mind. Such exaltation is simple in its quality, and is seen in direct alignment with the past, upon which it must often draw. 'All folk literature has indeed a passion whose like is not in modern literature and music and art, except where it has come by some straight or crooked way out of ancient times.' [1]

Yeats developed his own vision of a return to a form which should combine simplicity and intensity. The following passage is of great importance:

> In poetical drama there is, it is held, an antithesis between character and lyric poetry, for lyric poetry—however much it may move you when read out of a book—can, as these critics think, but encumber the action. Yet when we go back a few centuries and enter the great periods of drama, character grows less and sometimes disappears, and there is much lyric feeling, and at times a lyric measure will be wrought into the dialogue, a flowing measure that had well-befitted music, or that more lumbering one of the sonnet. Suddenly it strikes us that character is continuously present in comedy alone, and that there is much tragedy, that of Corneille, that of Racine, that of Greece and Rome, where its place is taken by passions and motives, one person being jealous, another full of love or remorse or pride or anger. In writers of tragi-comedy (and Shakespeare is always a writer of tragi-comedy) there is indeed character, but we notice that it is in the moments of comedy that character is defined, in Hamlet's gaiety, let us say; while amid the great moments, when Timon orders his tomb, when Hamlet cries to Horatio 'absent thee from felicity awhile', when Antony names 'Of many thousand kisses the poor last', all is lyricism, unmixed passion, 'the integrity of fire'. Nor does character ever attain to complete definition in these lamps ready for the taper, no matter how circumstantial and gradual the opening of events, as it does in Falstaff who has no passionate purpose to fulfil, or as it does in Henry the Fifth whose poetry, never touched by lyric heat, is oratorical; nor when the tragic reverie is at its height do we say, 'How well that man is realized, I should know him were I to meet him in the street,' for it is always ourselves that we see upon the stage . . .[2]

Yet, in the initial stages, Yeats saw clearly a vision of the high destinies of drama and of tragedy:

> If Literature is but praise of life, if our writers are not to plead the National Cause, nor insist upon the Ten Commandments, nor upon the glory of their country, what part remains for it, in the common life of the country? It will influence the life of the country immeasurably more, though seemingly less, than have our propagandist poems and stories. It will leave to others the

[1] *Essays*, p. 221.   [2] *Ibid.*, pp. 296–7.

defence of all that can be codified for ready understanding, of whatever is the especial business of sermons, and of leading articles; but it will bring all the ways of men before that ancient tribunal of our sympathies. It will measure all things by the measure not of things visible but of things invisible . . . We will be more interested in heroic man than in heroic actions, and will have a little distrust for everything that can be called good or bad in itself with a very confident heart . . . Could we understand it so well, we will say, if it were not other than human life? We will have a scale of virtues, and value most highly those that approach the indefinable.[1]

The same ideas are re-stated in Yeats's later critical work, though the emphasis on folk-literature gives way to the conception of a stylized drama, a small and select audience, and a greater interest in traditional themes. Tragedy is still both personal and indeterminate:

A poet creates tragedy from his own soul, that soul which is alike in all men. It has not joy, as we understand that word, but ecstasy, which is from the contemplation of things vaster than the individual and imperfectly seen, perhaps, by all those that still live. The masks of tragedy contain neither character nor personal energy. . . .[2] The soul knows its changes of state alone, and I think the motives of tragedy are not related to action but to changes of state.[3]

He appears to have been impatient of the 'pathetic' in tragedy:

I saw Hamlet on Saturday night, except for the chief 'Ophelia' scenes, and missed these (for I had to be in the Abbey) without regret. Their pathos, as they are displayed, has always left me cold. I came back for Hamlet, at the graveside: [4] there my delight always begins anew. I feel in Hamlet, as so often in Shakespeare, that I am in the presence of a soul lingering on the storm-beaten threshold of sanctity. Has not that threshold always been terrible, even crime-haunted? [5]

§ *iii*

The best of Synge's work represents tragedy reduced to its simplest elements, and it may indeed be questioned whether the simplification has not been carried too far. In essence the formula is of man's conflict

[1] *P. & C.*, pp. 112–13.
[2] This passage is related to the Nōh plays. Cf. also *Letters*, ed. Wade, p. 587: 'I shall not be able to use the word joy in my lecture for it would confuse things. I shall have to use the word "ecstasy". Ecstasy includes emotions like those of Synge's *Deirdre* after her lover's death which are the worst of sorrows to the ego.'
[3] *Dramatis Personae*, p. 89.
[4] Again, the 'wisdom of the tomb' to which Yeats returns continually. 'No dark tomb-haunter once . . .' (*A Bronze Head*).
[5] *Dramatis Personae*, p. 140.

with circumstance or environment, in a setting which shows a continuous and poignant awareness of the passing of beauty, the immanence
and inevitability of death. His world is at once mysterious, beautiful,
brutal. It is unified by rhetorical-lyrical statement, drawing freely on a
range of imagery which is either traditional, or from 'the book of the
people', and sometimes a compound of both.

    Riders to the Sea, one of the few effective one-act tragedies in litera-
ture, is of considerable technical interest, particularly in the light of
Synge's solution of the problem of obtaining sufficient momentum
within a single act. He achieves this by simplifying the conflict of
Man vs. *Necessity* into *Man* vs *The Sea*: and the impetus is given by
the setting of the Aran cottage, the new boards for the coffin, the
interpenetration of the world of the living by the world of the dead,
and Maurya's final resignation:

> They're all gone now, and there isn't anything more the sea can do to me . . .

The accessory symbolism is never stressed, but glows and fades again
with the tensions of the action; the dead and the living riders, the
water-spring by which Maurya meets her sons, the bread which she fails
to give the living, and which refreshes the makers of her son's coffin.
The elemental structure of the play is clear; two recognitions (the girl's
identification of their brother's body by its clothing, and the realization
that the body carried in at the door is not Michael, but Bartley) and
this last reversal of the situation: the rider to the sea who seeks to sell
his horses that he may live.

    It is effective because the age-old sense of fatality is communicated
simply and vividly, so that it becomes clear even to those who do not
know the Islands. The symbolism of the red mare and the grey pony,
the ageless and noble terror-image of the horse, communicate its sense
of mystery even without the memory of the Four Riders.[1] It is
punctuated, linked to reality by the everyday life of the Islanders, as
well as by the petulant wisdom of the old. We can perceive the double
value in such a passage as this:

> *Bartley (to Cathleen).* If the west wind holds with the last bit of the moon [2]
>   let you and Nora get up weed enough for another cock for the kelp.[3] It's
>   hard set we'll be from this day with no one in it but one man to work.

   [1] *Revelations* vi. 5.
   [2] The common reader is perhaps aware only of the broad evocative values: the fisher-
man knows that the weather changes with the visiting moon.
   [3] For manuring the stony fields of Aran.

or Maurya's

> I looked up then, and I crying, at the gray pony, and there was Michael
> upon it—with fine clothes on him, and new shoes on his feet.[1]

or the laconic grumbling of the old men who are to make the coffin:

> We have fine white boards herself brought, God help her, thinking
> Michael would be found, and I have a new cake you can eat while you'll
> be working.
> *The Old Man* (*looking at the boards*). Are there nails with them?
> *Cathleen*. There are not, Colum; we didn't think of the nails.
> *Another Man*. It's a great wonder she wouldn't think of the nails, and all the
> coffins she's seen made already.
> *Cathleen*. It's getting old she is, and broken.

The tragic resolution is achieved with ease and tact. Maurya is
beyond lamentation. Her benediction on the souls of her dead is quiet
and gracious, with the natural and familiar dignity of the Irish peasant.
The grave is quiet and deep, and the burials have been accomplished;
paganism and Christianity meet.

By contrast, *Deirdre* is infinitely less effective in spite of its more
conventional form. The legend is relatively remote; more exposition
is necessary; and above all the language, which involves the transposition of Synge's characteristic peasant speech to a traditional heroic
action, is only intermittently successful. The transitions from the lyrical
mood to the language of actuality, with its hint of the 'clay and the
worms', are less happily achieved, and we feel that the original rhythms
have become a little stereotyped. Nor is the attempted alignment, in
image and myth, with the European tradition handled with complete
success. The following passage will suggest both its qualities and defects:

> *Deirdre*. Draw a little back with the squabbling of fools when I am broken up
> with misery . . . I see the flames of Emain starting upward in the dark
> night; and because of me there will be weasels and wild cats crying on a
> lonely wall where there were queens and armies and red gold, the way
> there will be a story told of a ruined city and a raving king and a woman
> will be young for ever . . . I see the trees naked and bare, and the moon
> shining. Little moon, little moon of Alban, it's lonesome you'll be this
> night, and long nights after, and you pacing the woods beyond Glen Laoi,
> looking every place for Deirdre and Naisi, the two lovers who slept so
> sweetly with each other.

---

[1] The Resurrection image, common to many religions.

§ iv

I am inclined to think that *The Playboy of the Western World* has a
very special place in the history of tragedy; for I see it in some sort
as a deliberately distorted tragedy, all the joints wrenched out of place
by a comic vision that Synge imposed upon it, a comic vision in the
manner of Molière. If this is true, we may have the real explanation of
the resentment, distrust and anger aroused by its performance at the
Abbey Theatre in 1907. It is convenient to recall the overt bases of the
popular attack:

1. The play was blasphemous.

    Perhaps this was the inevitable outcome of an Anglo-Irish
    Protestant's attempt to 'imitate' peasant speech, and the
    blasphemies which are ambivalently pious and humorous.[1]

2. It showed Irish womanhood in an unbecoming and indelicate
    light—as pursuing their men, in the manner of Shakespeare or
    Shaw—and described in improper language: such as 'the drift of
    chosen females standing in their shifts itself'.[2]

3. It showed the inhabitants of an Irish village in the West as pre-
    pared to welcome, and to protect, an avowed murderer.

But the very violence and incoherence of the popular attack suggest
that there may be other reasons than these.

Now it has not, I think, been noted that the *Playboy* contains in
itself a number of the formal qualities of traditional tragedy.

The hero possesses, or acquires through the story of his parricide,
a Promethean virtue in his destruction of the 'jealous old tyrant'; who
is, moreover, about to force him into a loathed marriage. The murder
has been accomplished with a heroic strength and precision by 'the
gallant orphan that cleft his father with one blow to the breeches belt';
and a legend of Herculean strength is born.[3] The Playboy has become
a mock-epic figure. His story is received and approved by an audience of
men and women, like a Greek Chorus. The women present him with
the standard heroic situation, the offering of the apple to the virtuous
and virile hero. And Christy confirms the probability of his story by

---

[1] 'Is it killed your father?'—'With the help of God I did, surely, and that the Holy
Immaculate Mother may intercede for his soul.'

[2] It is not quite clear whether the offence was in the shift or in the drift. The latter word,
not wholly familiar to an English audience, is applicable to a small herd of cattle, especially heifers.

[3] Especially if we have seen the tool used, a 'loy': a narrow spade used for digging
potatoes. Cf. Samson and the jaw-bone.

his achievements in the village sports; which come conveniently, like
the funeral games, to convince everyone of his prowess as the slayer
of a tyrant, the supplanter of his father, the inaugurator of a new and
heroic race to be bred upon a publican's daughter:

> It's many would be in dread to bring your like into their house for to end
> them, maybe, with a sudden end; but I'm a decent man of Ireland, and I
> liefer face the grave untimely and I seeing a score of grandsons growing up
> gallant little swearers by the name of God, than go peopling my bedside with
> puny weeds the like of what you'd ,breed, I'm thinking, out of Shaneen
> Keogh.[1] (*He joins their hands.*) A daring fellow is the jewel of the world, and a
> man did split his father's middle with a single clout should have the bravery
> of ten, so may God and Mary and St Patrick bless you, and increase to you
> to this mortal day.

In all these speeches the ironic verbal comedy, so close to peasant speech
and yet so definitely twisted from it, prepare us for the catastrophe:
for the comic resurrection of the slain tyrant father (itself the most
dreaded of dreams), and for the dissolution of the heroism which the
Playboy's rhetorical imagination had built up. The hero vanishes, the
son is reconciled to his father; our interest, in so far as it is tragic, is
transferred to Peegen, with her Didoesque lament:

> O my grief, I've lost him surely. I've lost the only Playboy of the Western
> World.

§ v

We can best examine Yeats's practical contribution to Irish tragedy
in six plays: *The Countess Cathleen, On Baile's Strand, The Player Queen,
Calvary, Purgatory, The Death of Cuchulain.* The selection may seem
curious; but it is designed (within the scope of this essay) to illustrate
the changing positions that he took up. The first three were designed
for, and acted in, the Abbey Theatre: that is, for a normal audience;
the remainder for the small and eclectic audience in which he had come
to believe as a result of the double stimulus of the Nōh plays and his
disappointments at the Abbey.

The Countess Cathleen takes its plot from a French story, its characterization from Yeats's need for projecting something of himself and
his situation into the play, and its resolution, perhaps, from the audience
before which the play was to be presented. The theme of the selling
of souls for gold, of a heroine sacrificing herself for her people, is

---

[1] The reversal of the image from horse-breeding is not, perhaps, always apparent to an
English audience.

straightforward, without a hint of the complex motivation of the
Faust stories that might allow its roots to touch ordinary humanity.
For that reason it is lacking in human interest,[1] its pity and terror held
at a distance to be mirrored in superb flashes of lyricism which are
never wholly assimilated to the action. It has therefore something of
the remoteness of a Victorian verse-drama, and corresponding ineffectiveness as pure tragedy. There is no room for conflict in the
heroine's attitude to death; her choice was inevitable; and there remains
only a lyricism that suggests, faintly, the ending of Shelley's *Cenci*,
overcast with the Celtic pre-Raphaelitism of the 1890's. On analysis
it becomes strangely heterogeneous, with many borrowings:

> Bend down your faces, Oona and Aleel;
> I gaze upon them as the swallow gazes
> Upon the nest under the eave, before
> She wander the loud waters. Do not weep
> Too great a while, for there is many a candle
> On the High Altar though one fall. Aleel;
> Who sang about the dancers of the woods
> That know not the hard burden of the world,
> Having but breath in their kind bodies, farewell!
> And farewell, Oona, you who played with me,
> And bore me in your arms about the house
> When I was but a child and therefore happy,
> Therefore happy, even like those that dance.
> The storm is in my hair and I must go.[2]

And the famous ending, the reception of the Countess's soul at the
hands of the Virgin Mary, has neither the elegiac quality of the
Marlovian ending, nor the resigned fortitude of the Stoic. It is not
quite clear why it should be ineffectual: perhaps it was indeed an
inorganic conclusion in deference to its audience. But whether or not
this is so, the ending did not save the rest of the play from the severity,
and even the savagery, of popular criticism.

The Sohrab and Rustum theme is the centre of *On Baile's Strand*.
It is handled in a manner which, while it owes something to Shakespeare, is original and effective. Like most of Yeats's plays, it is too
short to allow for any development or true interaction of character; we
may argue that the poet neither desired, nor was capable of, these
things, lacking (at this stage of his poetic career) what Aristotle called
a 'happy gift of nature', as well as Keats's 'negative capability'. Instead,

---

[1] Except as we consider it in relation to Maud Gonne and Yeats.   [2] *C.P.*, p. 47.

he has to rely on the poetry to carry through a basic situation in three classical movements, reverse, recognition and catastrophe: a situation which is powerful enough in its own right to retain its significance and its irony; linked in this respect to the prophetic witch-song of the women. That and the Lear-symbolism of the Blind Man and the Fool serve the extension in meaning; nor does the supra-natural intrude beyond the credible. Cuchulain believes that he has no son:

> I think myself most lucky that I leave
> No pallid ghost or mockery of a man
> To drift and mutter in the corridors
> Where I have laughed and sung.[1]

He swears the oath of allegiance to the High King Conchubar; goes out to fight the invader, kills his son, and dies fighting the waves:

> And when the Fool and Blind Man stole the bread
> Cuchulain fought the ungovernable sea.
> Heart's mysteries these; and yet when all is said
> It was the dream itself enchanted me . . .[2]

It is pertinent to inquire the place of these 'heart-mysteries' in the tragic pattern.

The Fool and the Blind Man of the opening are not merely devices for the purpose of exposition, or for their place as symbols of two aspects of personality The Fool is the friend of the Witches who work the final madness upon Cuchulain; the Blind Man has lived in Aoife's country and was blinded 'for putting a curse upon the wind'. And wind and wave are the dominant symbols of the play; so much is clear from the Women's Song; which picks up, too, the theme of *Odi et Amo* at which the Blind Man has hinted in the exposition. And a further depth is given by the hint that this drama is in a sense a repetition of a previous action by Cuchulain's own father.[3] He is offering the young man, his son, gifts of friendship, and shows him his cloak:

> My father gave me this.
> He came to try me, rising up at dawn
> Out of the cold dark of the rich sea.
> He challenged me to battle, but before
> My sword had touched his sword, told me his name,
> Gave me this cloak and vanished. It was woven

---

[1] C.P., p. 256. [2] *The Circus Animals' Desertion.*
[3] Cf. the play *Purgatory*, discussed later. This cyclic or spiral repetition of doom is one of the commoner ways of inducing the sense of the enclosing circles of tragedy.

By women of the Country-under-Wave
Out of the fleeces of the sea. O! tell her
I was afraid, or tell her what you will,
No; tell her that I heard a raven croak
On the north side of the house, and was afraid.[1]

But he kills his son: recognition comes at the mouth of the Blind Man. Cuchulain dies fighting the waves, on which we can place such symbolism as we will; the imagined enemies that confront a man in his obsession, popular hostility towards the poet-hero, life and sex. It is both dolphin-torn and gong-tormented.

Our measure of this play as a tragedy depends on a number of factors: how far we can assume a knowledge of the basic myth and accept it as an archetypal situation, of that tense relationship between father, mother, son; how far we can accept imaginatively the detailed symbolism of, say, the feathers of the hawk; the feathers which are all that the Blind Man leaves to the Fool of the fowl they have stolen; the feathers on which Cuchulain wipes his sword clean from the blood of his son; the counterpointing of death and hunger (remembering Odysseus, and Caliban's 'I must eat my dinner'); the Fool looking backwards at the fighting of the waves before both go to rob the ovens of the great. It is a little strained if we are not prepared to study and to sympathize with Yeats's method. If we do, it becomes, in its kind, good tragedy.

The Player Queen has not, perhaps, received the attention it deserves. Many tragedies have been written about poets.[2] Yeats alone has brought to the play a peculiar mixture of sardonic levity, esoteric symbolism, and a passionate pleading for the place of the Poet in society. It is unique among tragedies in that it is compounded of ritual elements (the play within a play), stylized figures, a series of complex allusions—unicorn, witchcraft, the mysterious Old Man who brays like a donkey when the King's dynasty changes, the Rabelaisian flood of erudition in the mouth of the drunken poet Septimus, the Queen's saintly and futile devotion to Saint Octema, and Decima's song, that illuminates her whole character and purpose. It is unique among tragedies in that it represents the triumph of pure evil, and the destruction by woman (who takes her sexual revenge upon him), and by society, of the inspired poet. It is difficult to read and more difficult to

---

[1] *C.P.*, p. 268.
[2] Perhaps the most famous, and to modern readers the most ridiculous, example is de Vigny's *Chatterton*.

act: when both difficulties are overcome the play acquires a strange and sinister life of its own.

I think we could argue that *The Words Upon the Window-Pane* is the only example of a modern tragedy that employs the supernatural, not as an accessory, but as the centre of the plot. Again the scale is tiny, the characterization negligible. It is born out of political considerations, as Yeats tells us in the Preface; and this accounts in some measure for its power, since there is always the intense pressure of the personality of the dead. 'In Swift's day men of intellect reached the height of their power, the greatest position they ever attained in society and the State . . .' That the dead should re-enact their passionate scene is the centre of *The Dreaming of the Bones* and of *Purgatory*; and in Swift's voices, and in Stella's, there is something that is neither temporal nor personal, but the shadow of an epic destruction of a whole race and its values: charged with a peculiar vehemence by the dramatist's sense that past and present were converging in Irish history. 'No character on the stage spoke my thoughts'; and perhaps it is because of this that this play, and *Calvary*, acquire on the stage a peculiar life of their own; which in the study lies dormant under the stiff flattened prose. If we can suspend initially our disbelief, the play reveals a counterpointed rhythm of a special kind (perhaps we glimpse something of the kind in Richard III), where death and life speak from a medium's mouth, and 'all about us there seems to start up a precise inexplicable teeming life'.

Purgatory is of particular interest as a tragedy; not only as having received Mr Eliot's eulogy for the quality of its verse, but because, with Synge's *Riders to the Sea*, it affords the best example in the language of the compressed or 'miniature' tragedy. Further, its narrative component is larger than we are accustomed to consider possible; yet it retains sufficient action for its own dramatic purposes. It suffers, perhaps, from the disadvantage that we must accept Yeats's theory that past actions are re-created by the dead in time; once this is granted, the tragedy fulfils all the classical demands upon it, in spite of the very large element of narrative in the composition.

We are concerned with a dialogue between an Old Man and a boy, his son: they are watching the ruin of a great house, which has suddenly become a blaze of light. It is the wedding anniversary of the Old Man's mother; who had married a drunken groom, and died in childbirth. As they watch, a window lights up, showing a young girl standing at it; the bride is waiting for the return of her man, half-drunk

15

from the public-house. The Old Man has killed his own father: he is watching his parents' bridal night being re-enacted in the ruined house. He can hear the horse-hoofs on the avenue as the bridegroom returns. His son, who can hear nothing, thinks he is mad. It is important to quote at length in order to give some idea of the quality of the verse:

> *Old Man.* It's louder now because he rides
> Upon a gravelled avenue
> All grass to-day. The hoof-beat stops,
> He has gone to the other side of the house,
> Gone to the stable, put the horse up.
> She has gone down to open the door.
> This night she is no better than her man
> And does not mind that he is half-drunk,
> She is mad about him. They mount the stairs.
> She brings him into her own chamber.
> And that is the marriage-chamber now.
> The window is dimly lit again.
>
> Do not let him touch you! It is not true
> That drunken men cannot beget,
> And if he touch he must beget
> And you must bear his murderer,
> Deaf! Both deaf! If I should throw
> A stick or a stone they would not hear;
> And that's a proof my wits are out.
> But there's a problem; she must live
> Through everything in exact detail
> Driven to it by remorse, and yet
> Can she renew the sexual act
> And find no pleasure in it, and if not,
> If pleasure and remorse must both be there
> Which is the greater?
> I lack schooling
> Go fetch Tertullian; he and I
> Will ravel all that problem out
> Whilst those two lie upon the mattress
> Begetting me.[1]

At the end of the play the Old Man has killed his son, with the same knife with which he had killed his father—in the hope that his action

[1] *C.P.*, pp. 685–6.

will stop this train of dreams, terminate this terrible doom to re-enact the crime. But it is useless; the sound of the horse-hoofs returns:

> Her mind cannot hold up that dream.
> Twice a murderer and all for nothing,
> And she must animate that night
> Not once but many times!
>   O God,
> Release my mother's soul from its dream!
> Mankind can do no more. Appease
> The misery of the living and the remorse of the dead.[1]

The tragedy is enhanced by the ancillary images throughout the play; themselves fortified by Yeats's usage elsewhere, by their part in his personal mythology, but even more by their archetypal character. There is the ruined, or the burning house; 'the shadow of a cloud that falls upon it'; the bare tree, stripped of leaves by the thunderbolt; the knife that killed now used for a dinner; the ever-mysterious sound of the horse-hoofs that move, as always, through the human mind with their message of foreboding and terror.

The Death of Cuchulain is interesting because it shows, in a small compass, the final reduction to its essence of the Nōh type of play, Yeats's final embodiment of the theme of sexual revenge and of the Severed Head, a drawing together of personages from the heroic legend, and a counterpointing by ferocious comedy and song. In the Old Man's Prologue there is the last statement of Yeats's desire for an intimate and understanding audience, and of that ambivalent theme of hatred and love, its tragedy and tragi-comedy; the place of the ritual of the dance to state or resolve conflict. 'I could have got such a dancer once, but she has gone; the tragi-comedian dancer, the tragic dancer, upon same neck love and loathing, life and death.'

The plot is simple: Cuchulain is set between three women, Emer his wife, Eithne Ingula his mistress (who brings a message from his wife), and Aoife, the Scottish Queen upon whom he had begotten the son he had killed on Baile's Strand. But as he talks with Eithne, the Morrigu, the crow-headed war-goddess, appears: by that he knows that he is about to die. Aoife, the mother of his son, appears, and binds him to the stump of a tree by her veil. He is killed by the Blind Man who has heard that there is a price of twelve pennies upon Cuchulain's head: with the knife that he keeps sharp 'because it cuts my dinner'.

[1] *Ibid.*, p. 689.

The ending, given the acceptance of its strange mood, is effective. Following the dance of the Morrigu about Cuchulain's head, the stage darkens slowly: there follows 'the music of some Irish Fair of our day', with three ragged musicians with pipe and drum. The song they sing starts with bawdry, the harlot's song to the beggar-man; and we may speculate (but give no answer) as to why bawdry may often have, as it were, a chemical affinity with moments of high tragedy. The second verse slides into the Easter Rising, Yeats's identification of himself with Cuchulain, that heroic mask; passes to the statue, which the action of the play has shadowed forth: Cuchulain bound to the stump of a tree, dying, with the crow perched, watching him, beside.[1] And in this song, though we perceive them only with labour, the symbols crowd together: birds that are souls, the harlot and virgin, hero and beggar, the Blind Man who brings death, the horse from the sea, the delicate veil of woman's power.

§ vi

The work of O'Casey includes the only examples of merit in the genre of realistic tragedy produced in the Irish Theatre. They are, perhaps, unique in being the product of a native but strictly limited genius responding to the actuality of a limited and perspicuous war, in an environment (that of the Dublin tenements) with which he was familiar; but condemned to work without having had any literary training, or aware of any steadying tradition. The speech of that environment, well enough adapted for comedy, was by its nature of insufficient resource to become an instrument for the higher moments of tragedy. It is a crude and violent theatre, highly competent in its handling of situation and in its understanding of comic relief; so much so indeed, that the Dublin audiences appeared to have concentrated their interest upon the 'recognition' and approval of its comic types. It is possible that such an attitude was to some extent a defence mechanism against the rawness of their recent memories of the 'Troubles' and the Civil War.

The first, and most famous of the plays, is *Juno and the Paycock*. It has a strong photographic element: the background of the tenements is accurately portrayed, and the tone of the opening is skilfully counter-pointed between the comic, the vulgar and the tragic. It is made clear that this is in some sense a continuation of the Easter Rising, not an

---

[1] The symbolism here is familiar: the best known example being, perhaps, Mantegna's *Agony in the Garden*.

isolated episode. The neurotic son, Johnny, with all his pitifulness, is a 'heroic' victim:

> *Mrs Boyle.* I don't know what's goin' to be done with him. The bullet he got in the hip in Easter Week was bad enough, but the bomb that shatthered his arm in the fight in O'Connell Street put the finishin' touch on him. I knew he was makin' a fool of himself. God knows I went down on me bended knees to him not to go agen the Free State.
>
> *Mary (her daughter).* He stuck to his principles, an', no matther how you may argue, Ma, a principle's a principle.

And this is parodied, in the Shakespearian manner, by the 'principles' of Johnny's drunken and worthless father. The tragedy of war and of self-delusion is brought home swiftly, and given depth, by the false news of the legacy and Mary's love affair with Bentham, that collapse together before Johnny is taken out to be shot by the Irregulars for having betrayed his comrade. And if the prose at its moments of tension sounds sentimental and forced, we may note that such sentimentality is entirely in key with those who speak it. There is a shadow of Synge's rhythms, the West of Ireland vulgarized by the East:

> *Mrs Boyle.* . . . Maybe I didn't feel sorry enough for Mrs Tancred when her poor son was found as Johnny's been found now—because he was a Die-Hard! Ah, why didn't I remember that then he wasn't a Die-Hard or a Stater, but only a poor dead son! It's well I remember all that she said—an' it's my turn to say it now: What was the pain I suffered, Johnny, bringin' you into the world to carry you to your cradle to the pains I'll suffer carryin' you out o' the world to bring you to your grave! Mother o' God, Mother o' God, have pity on us all! Blessed Virgin, where were you when me darlin' son was riddled with bullets, when me darlin' son was riddled with bullets? Sacred Heart o' Jesus, take away our hearts o' stone, and give us hearts o' flesh! Take away this murdherin' hate, an' give us Thine own eternal love! [1]

The first world war is the background of *The Silver Tassie*, its waste of spirit and body. Its realism is crude and violent, but is interesting for the scene in France set against the background of a ruined monastery: in the foreground a soldier lashed to the wheel of a gun, undergoing field punishment, and reflecting the figure on the crucifix. The scene opens with an invocation to the gun in position against the monastery, and continues with an intonation of the Ezekiel dry-bones passage, in

---

[1] Contrast this with the dignity of Maurya in *Riders to the Sea.*

reverse. The invocation to the gun gives some idea of O'Casey's methods, and of the limitations of his verse:

> *Corporal* (*singing*). Hail cool-hardened tower of steel emboss'd
> With the fever'd, figment thoughts of man;
> Guardian of our love and hate and fear,
> Speak for us to the inner ear of God!
> *Soldiers.* We believe in God and we believe in thee.
> *Corporal.* Dreams of line, of colour and of form;
> Dreams of music dead forever now;
> Dreams in bronze and dreams in stone have gone
> To make thee delicate and strong to kill.
> *Soldiers.* We believe in God and we believe in thee . . .
> *Corporal.* Remember our women, sad-hearted, proud-fac'd,
> Who've given the substance of their womb for shadows;
> Their shrivel'd empty breasts war-tinselled
> For patient gifts of graves to thee.

The Shadow of a Gunman which also deals with the theme of the Irish 'Troubles' is realistic in treatment, but without the skill in plot or the freshness of *Juno and the Paycock*. *The Plough and the Stars* has the same background, but is more cogently constructed. It is clear that O'Casey is a writer of limited experience and still more limited negative capability, with a certain rough skill in counterpoint. The moral values are clear; 'patriotism is not enough', the deadly power in Ireland of the dream embodied in rhetoric; the inchoate character of popular 'war' emotions; the suffering of the women for the arrogance and stupidity and vanity of their men. It fails to become great or moving tragedy because it possesses no inner core, because it seeks to achieve depth by mere counterpointing of emotions, and because the speech cannot encompass the emotions which it seeks to express. There is a deliberate forcing of O'Casey's characters into a language which is admirable for low comedy, provided the actors can achieve its peculiar intonations, but which has no flexibility to cope with pity and fear. And perhaps the lesson is that tragedy based on such history must either be of vast scale (perhaps of the nature of trilogies) so that a wider pattern may be discerned in it; or else embody some system of references or projection, to give it universality. For the mood of those times has been caught better in the short story or in the lyric:

> Now days are dragon-ridden, the nightmare
> Rides upon sleep: a drunken soldiery

Can leave the mother, murdered at her door,
To crawl in her own blood, and go scot-free;
The night can sweat with terror as before
We pieced our thought into philosophy,
And planned to bring the world under a rule,
Who are but weasels fighting in a hole.[1]

§ *vii*

It will be seen that I have called this chapter 'The Irish Tragedy' with a double intention: for we can perceive, in the workings of the form, so many reflections of historical and social conditions. There is the bending of a national will to an effort, comparable to that of the ages of Aeschylus, Calderon, or Shakespeare; an attempt to throw off, once and for all, the dead weight of the Shakespearian form; the prospect at least of a popular imagination that might have proved itself fiery and magnificent and tender; a dramatic theory that had at least a vision; and place in the stream of history that offered ample material on which a tragic theatre might be based. For its chosen poet it had one of the two great figures of the first half of the twentieth century. It is therefore instructive to reflect upon its failure.

There are, I think, two main reasons for this. The quarry of peasant experience and corresponding speech was a small one, and could not be worked for long. The experiences were limited and profound, of the nature of those that Wordsworth wished to find in the North. But while they knew sorrow and exaltation, there was little complexity to match their century; and indeed the peasant quality became rapidly stereotyped and exploited in the lesser followers of the Synge technique.

There is also the disparity between playwrights and audiences: their philosophy and tradition. Before an audience can be moved in tragedy it must share with the tragedian a sympathy born, not necessarily of a common religion, but a common agreement as to the kinds of qualities that go to make men great. Provided that the rigidity of a religious framework does not obscure, or criticize with an unbalanced destructiveness, this common thought, it becomes possible for the dramatist to communicate and to move. But before he can communicate fully he must share with the audience some common stock of imagery; or at least have their trust and sympathy to such an extent that he can impose upon them his own.

These conditions were not fulfilled in Ireland; perhaps because its

---

[1] Yeats, *Nineteen Hundred and Nineteen*.

traditions of revolt and liberty were spun too tenuously on words, but more probably because of the lack of any true community of thought between its poets and its people. Its tragedy was seldom if ever free to question the ultimates in the only manner by which a synthesis could be presented. A suspension of disbelief in the supra-natural might only be excited cautiously, and within that narrow circle of literature that might be considered respectable (because of its antiquity) by the Roman Catholic Church. The gulf that opened between Protestant men of letters and Abbey audiences was enough to ensure that the line between acceptance and corrosively vulgar comment was always precarious, and ceased to be so only when those who were capable of leading, but who had not led, were extinguished. The tragedy of Ireland offers interesting parallels with its history.

CHAPTER 18

Mr Eliot's Compromise

I said to my soul, be still, and wait without hope
For hope would be hope for the wrong thing; wait without love
For love would be love of the wrong thing; there is yet faith
But the faith and the love and the hope are all in the waiting.
East Coker III

All things fall and are built again,
And those that build them again are gay.
YEATS: *Lapis Lazuli*

§ *i*

ON general grounds it would seem that no writer of our time showed greater promise of producing the supreme examples of twentieth-century Tragedy. The equipment of a great poet, of a carefully-poised and conscientious critic of literature, awareness of the European tradition, and a strong religious sense; these would seem to complete the resources of a writer in a warlike, various and tragical age. He has, in his criticism, told us more of his attitude, ideas, and technical experiments than any writer in history. No one since Arnold has been a more courageous protagonist for 'our most important and fundamental beliefs'.[1] He has put into practice, and defended, the technique of the 'poetic prose' dramatist; his pronouncement is so important that extracts must be quoted:

> For I start with the assumption that if poetry is merely a decoration, an added embellishment, if it merely gives people of literary tastes the pleasure of listening to poetry at the same time that they are witnessing a play, then it is superfluous. It must justify itself dramatically, and not merely be fine poetry shaped into a dramatic form. From this it follows that no play should be written in verse for which prose is *dramatically* adequate. And from this it follows, again, that the audience, its attention held by the dramatic action, its emotions stirred by the situation between the characters, should be too intent upon the play to be wholly conscious of the medium.[2]

The argument here should be noted carefully. 'If the poetry is merely a decoration an added embellishment . . . then the audience . . . should

---

[1] *Faith that Illuminates*, 1935.   [2] *Poetry and Drama*, pp. 11–12.

be too intent upon the play to be wholly conscious of the medium.'
And Mr Eliot develops this further:

> To-day, however, because of the handicap under which verse drama
> suffers, I believe that prose should be used very sparingly indeed; that we
> should aim at a form of verse in which everything can be said that has to be
> said; and that when we find some situation which is intractable in verse, it is
> merely that our form of verse is inelastic. And if there prove to be scenes
> which we cannot put in verse, we must either develop our verse, or avoid
> having to introduce such scenes. For we have to accustom our audiences to
> verse to the point at which they will cease to be conscious of it; and to
> introduce prose dialogue, would only be to distract their attention from the
> play itself to the medium of its expression. But if our verse is to have so wide
> a range that it can say anything that has to be said, it follows that it will not
> be 'poetry' all the time. It will only be 'poetry' when the dramatic situation
> has reached such a point of intensity that poetry becomes the natural utter-
> ance, because then it is the only language in which the emotions can be
> expressed at all.[1]

There are other critical dicta that must be taken into consideration
before we can obtain an idea of Mr Eliot's position. The weakness of
Elizabethan drama is plainly due to the lack of a convention. 'What is
fundamentally objectionable is that in the Elizabethan drama there is
no firm principle of what is to be postulated as a convention and what
is not': [2] his own search for 'conventions', and the peculiar synthesis
which he makes, for instance, of the Chorus and of Ritual, are apparent
in his dramatic experiments. Most important of all, there appears to
be a separation (which is apparent even when we allow for his own
complaint 'of having to use the same words for different things')
between 'thought' and 'thought used for dramatic ends'. Hence the
attack on the dramatic poet as thinker:

> In truth neither Shakespeare nor Dante did any *real thinking*—that was not
> their job; and the relative value of the thought current at their time,
> *the material enforced upon each to use as the vehicle of feeling, his* is of no
> importance [3]

And again:

> Mr Lewis, and other champions of Shakespeare as a great philosopher, have
> a great deal to say about Shakespeare's power of thought, but they fail to

---

[1] *Poetry and Drama*, pp. 14–15.   [2] *Four Elizabethan Dramatists*, p. 17.
[3] *The Stoicism of Seneca*, p. 48. (My italics.)

show that *he thought to any purpose*; that he had any coherent view of life, *or that he recommended any procedure to follow*.[1]

We have considered something of this problem in a previous chapter; it is sufficient to say that there appears to be a confusion between

1. philosophy as a system; and poetry that is 'philosophical' as a potential component of a system;
2. the duty placed upon the artist to state a coherent view: when in fact his capacity for intensity (by definition intermittent and partial) would seem to preclude such coherence;
3. didacticism which is explicit, and that which is incidental: as involving, consciously or unconsciously, modifications of attitudes.

We may suggest that the gap between thought and emotion is not so wide as Mr Eliot believes: that 'thought' is not capable of abstraction: that thinking is an activity, not an object; and reflect on the position of the Logical Positivist who has evaded the problem of building a systematic philosophy by dedicating his efforts solely to the perfecting of the building tools before he starts to contemplate the site or the materials. Erich Heller [2] has put the matter lucidly:

> To define 'thinking' in such a way that the activity which Shakespeare pursued in composing the speeches of Hamlet, or Ulysses, or Lear has to be dismissed as 'non-thought', is to let thinking fall into the rationalist trap from which it is likely to emerge a cripple, full of animosity against that other deformed creature, mutilated in the same operation: the Romantic emotion. If thought, stripped of imaginative feeling, and emotion, stripped of imaginative thought, become the dominant modes of thinking and feeling, the outcome is the 'Leid-stadt', that insufferable city of sorrows, or the Waste Land, in which the spirits of Nietzsche, as well as Rilke, as well as Mr Eliot feel ill at ease. Paradoxically enough, it is precisely this neat separation between thought and feeling which has forced, on the one hand, upon modern philosophy 'the Absurd' as one of its principal themes; and on the other hand, upon modern poetry a degree of *intellectual* complexity.

I now wish to isolate certain passages from Mr Eliot's writings which seem to me to bear upon the interpretation and evaluation of his dramatic work as tragedies.

[1] *Ibid.*, p. 46. The italics are mine. We may quote Erich Heller's comment: '. . . For the assumption underlying his essay is that the thinker is interested in the *truth* of thought, but the poet merely in its fitting expression.' *The Disinherited Mind*, p. 123.
[2] *The Disinherited Mind: Rilke and Nietzsche*, p. 121.

1. . . . even the humblest Christian layman can and must live what, in the modern world, is comparatively an ascetic life.[1]

2. But when I speak of the family, I have in mind a bond which embraces . . . a piety towards the dead, however obscure, and a solicitude for the unborn, however remote.[2]

3. We need to recover the sense of religious fear, so that it may be overcome by religious hope.[3]

4. What I should hope might be achieved, by a generation of dramatists having the benefit of our experience, is that the audience should find, at the moment of awareness that it is hearing poetry, that it is saying to itself: '*I* could talk in poetry too!' Then we should not be transported into an artificial world; on the contrary, our own sordid, dreary daily world would be suddenly illuminated and transfigured.[4]

5.   Because one has only learnt to get the better of words
       For the thing one no longer has to say, or the way in which
       One is no longer disposed to say it.[5]

6. I was talking in abstractions: and you answered in abstractions.
   I have a private puzzle.[6]

With these quotations in mind, together with the whole of the explanatory apologetic of *Poetry and Drama*, we can attempt some examination of the plays.

§ ii

Mr Eliot's statements on *Murder in the Cathedral* are unusually frank. 'I had the advantage, for a beginner' (the implications of this are interesting), 'of an occasion which called for a subject generally admitted to be suitable for verse.' He had also before him, though this is not stated, the lesson of Tennyson's *Becket*, the inconsistencies in Becket's character which the conception of a personal *hamartia* involved, as well as the cumbrous love interest and equally cumbrous verse. Other advantages were the period costume, the 'serious' audience, the religious occasion. A deliberate avoidance of Elizabethan verse and rhythms ('The rhythm of regular blank verse has become too remote from the movement of modern speech') was balanced by 'some use of alliteration, and occasional unexpected rhyme', which helped to

---

[1] *Thoughts after Lambeth.*   [2] *Notes towards the Definition of Culture.*
[3] *The Idea of a Christian Society.*   [4] *Poetry and Drama*, p. 27.
[5] *East Coker.*
[6] *The Family Reunion*, p. 92. Until a definitive biography is written, the nature of Mr Eliot's 'private puzzle' is not a subject for speculation.

distinguish the versification from that of the nineteenth century. But the problem was solved only for *Murder in the Cathedral*.

The success of the play is unquestioned. 'A man comes home, foreseeing that he will be killed, and he is killed.' . . . 'I wanted to concentrate on death and martyrdom.' [1] The extreme formal compression of the play, the selection of the action at its point of ripeness and of Becket's maturity, gives the intensity and seriousness that the subject demands. The conflict is that between the values of the world and of the spirit: as seen by the Chorus of the Women of Canterbury, the Four Tempters, the Four Knights, and focused in Becket's own choice. And his leading temptation is one of the Christian forms of *hubris*, pride in one's own humility:

> The last temptation is the greatest treason:
> To do the right deed for the wrong reason.

Given its limits as ritual setting, versification, intention, Mr Eliot has succeeded in his purpose of a complete integration of the dramatic rhythm with the verse. But this very ritualism, this insistence on the Word, seems to suggest a use of it (which is even more apparent in the subsequent plays) to hypnotize, even to numb, the understanding; rather than to fire it to life. The verse has the obsessive swelling effect of a Vedic chant, in which the words, opposing each other in the paradoxes proper to ritual of a certain kind, and hence perhaps too vast for the tragic scale, overwhelm us with a kind of grey cloud:

> They know and do not know, what it is to act or suffer.
> They know and do not know, that acting is suffering
> And suffering is action. Neither does the actor suffer
> Nor the patient act. But both are fixed
> In an eternal action, an eternal patience
> To which all must consent that it may be willed
> And which all must suffer that they may will it,
> That the pattern may subsist, for the pattern is the action
> And the suffering, that the wheel may turn and still
> Be forever still.

We could deduce, even if we did not know it from other sources, Mr Eliot's intense interest in the Upanishads. The subtlety and close texture of the verse (the subtle play on *patient-patience*, *still-still*) are self-evident: but it is worth while to pause for a moment to consider what Eliot is saying through his mouthpiece Becket.

[1] These, and the quotations immediately preceding, are from *Poetry and Drama*, p. 25.

In one sense the speech is an expansion, as Eliot understands it, of Dante's *In la sua voluntade è nostra pace*. The intellectual movement is perhaps, as a circular structure of opposing diameters; humanity has knowledge and not-knowledge; action and suffering are identified, and self-exclusive. Both are part of a vast design, like Hardy's Immanent will, but through suffering they create that will. Humanity is tied to a vast pattern, like the Buddhist wheel: in part passive, in part active, in its turning. It is submission in suffering, submission in willing suffering which is part of the eternal design.

Now it would appear that such a doctrine is theologically questionable. Any circular structure suggests Determinism; man's strength and glory is not merely in submission to the Divine Will, but in the self-conquest, and in the sense of exaltation that it brings. Nor is the wheel the Christian symbol to-day; we think of the medieval wheels of fortune, of the *De Casibus*, as obsolete conceptions. Nor is a doctrine of semi-passive suffering more than a part of the truth. But in this attitude we shall, I think, find at least a partial explanation of the plays. It is not of any particular interest to accept Mr Eliot's statement that *The Cocktail Party* is a comedy, in the sense that Dante's *Divina Commedia* is a comedy; though to do so would be perhaps to disarm all criticism. The traditional elements of tragedy are too strong: nor is there the wise passiveness and remoteness that might have turned them into 'great' or even 'free' comedy. Perhaps it is 'critical'.[1]

§ *iii*

The Family Reunion is of peculiar interest, since it raises the questions of the possibilities and limitations of the subject-matter as well as the method of Greek drama in a modern setting. We have before us, as touchstone, the varying successes of O'Neill and Anouilh in that technique. Further, Mr Eliot has referred us, somewhat cryptically, to the *Elektra*, just as he has referred to the *Ion* for the background of *The Confidential Clerk*: we may read into such a reference (according to our mood) either an ingenuous alibi for the spectators' inquiries into meaning, or a set of references to the older models, of which the connections are sufficiently variable, and indeterminate, to allow individual interpretation to take its own course; through whatever fogs the plot and diction may generate.

The curse upon the house of Wishwood—the word suggests the confusion and sinister character of the wood, and the desire of its

---

[1] I use these terms in the sense established by Bonamy Dobrée in *Restoration Comedy*.

inhabitants for the past—is the background to the familiar cycle of crime, remorse, expiation: by Harry's symbolic departure from Wishwood and the hint—through his valet, Downing—of his approaching death.[1] The Furies who pursue him to Wishwood appear twice at the window (the stage direction, *The Furies appear*, gives an unfortunate latitude to producers); but even in the more vivid description of the verse they are curiously indeterminate, half-way between ghosts and ideas. So in the Chorus

> I am afraid of all that has happened, and of all that is to come;
> Of the things that come to sit at the door, as if they had been there always.
> And the past is about to happen, and the future was long since settled,
> And the wings of the future darken the past, the beak and claws have
>   desecrated
> History.[2]

This sense of hereditary guilt, indeterminate, choking, appears in *The Waste Land*; and indeed *The Family Reunion* is full of echoes of the earlier poem. There is, for example, the sinister quality of the seasons, the cruelty of the spring, the impression of the sordidness and monotony of life. It is not clear whether Harry's crime of murdering his wife by pushing her off the deck of a liner is real or subjective: the text suggests the latter interpretation, and that the murder is symbolic:

> *Harry.* . . . Perhaps my life has only been a dream
>   Dreamt through me by the minds of others. Perhaps
>   I only dreamt I pushed her.
> *Agatha.*   So I had supposed. What of it?
>   What we have written is not a story of detection,
>   Of crime and punishment, but of sin and expiation.
>   It is possible that you have not known what sin
>   You shall expiate, or whose, or why. It is certain
>   That the knowledge of it must precede the expiation.
>   It is possible that sin may strain and struggle
>   In its dark instinctive birth, to come to consciousness
>   And so find expurgation. It is possible
>   You are the consciousness of your unhappy family,
>   Its bird sent flying through the purgatorial flame.
>   Indeed it is possible.[3]

---

[1] *F.R.*, p. 129. John Peter has suggested that only in relation to Amy's death can the play be called a tragedy. I should contest this view. Harry goes out as if to death.

[2] *Ibid.*, p. 69.   [3] *Ibid.*, p. 104–5.

Now this dialogue raises important issues. We admit the fact of original sin, our knowledge of it as redeemable by grace. We admit also the possibility of collective or cumulative guilt, in families or nations. It is also clear that an individual act may focus or precipitate retribution for that guilt. But here the moral situation is dependent on two uncertainties, which are carefully maintained throughout the play: Harry's father had plotted to kill his mother, and was prevented by Harry's Aunt Agatha. When this is revealed by her, both Harry and she express their relief. For, as Agatha says:

> The burden's yours, now, yours
> The burden of all the family. And I am a little frightened.[1]

Now if the murder was committed by Harry it is reasonable that such an action should be the trigger which has released the load of guilt, and which results in his departure: with a hint of the abnormality of his journey. (It is not unlike that of Celia in *The Cocktail Party*, except that Harry will not be a missionary.) But if the murder is subjective only, then the sin and its expiation become dramatically confused, perhaps even monstrous in their implications. Mr Eliot wishes, justifiably, to convey the mysterious quality of evil: its many mirrors in the many minds of his character. The language in its meticulous flatness, its careful juxtapositions, its veiled velleities, its echoes from previous poems, creates a nebulous swirling of communication: proper to the tone and texture of *The Waste Land* or of *The Magi*, but, in its cumulative impact, unsuited to the theatre. A few quotations will serve:

> You do not know
> The noxious smell untraceable in the drains,
> Inaccessible to the plumbers, that has its hour of the night;
> you do not know
> The unspoken voice of sorrow in the ancient bedroom
> At three o'clock in the morning. I am not speaking
> Of my own experience, but trying to give you
> Comparisons in the more familiar medium . . .[2]

> It seems a necessary move
> In an unnecessary action,
> Not for the good that it will do
> But that nothing may be left undone
> On the margin of the impossible.[3]

---

[1] *F.R.*, p. 106.   [2] *Ibid.*, p. 29.   [3] *Ibid.*, p. 34.

But perhaps the final and most serious objection to *The Family Reunion*, as to *The Cocktail Party*, is the manipulation of determinism in a drama which appears, by intention, to be Christian as to its background, and which uses that background for its snatches of ritual. Agatha is the priestess-sybil of *The Family Reunion*, with a humble assistant in Mary. Their function appears to be psycho-therapeutic; to induce Harry to reveal himself to himself, to accept the Recognition through the appearance of the Furies; as the curious trinity of Reilly, Julia and Alex determine the destinies of the other characters in *The Cocktail Party*. Agatha speaks for the deterministic view, in accents which suggest the oracular priggishness of Reilly:

> I mean painful, because everything is irrevocable,
> Because the past is irremediable,
> Because the future can only be built
> Upon the real past. . . .[1]

So does the Chorus at the end of Part II, Scene I:

> There is no avoiding these things
> And we know nothing of exorcism
> And whether in Argos or in England
> There are certain inflexible laws
> Unalterable, in the nature of music.
> There is nothing at all to be done about it,
> There is nothing to do about anything.[2]

'There is nothing to do about anything': yet 'the awful evacuation cleanses'. The play raises in an acute form the possibility of a distinction between the 'great' 'serious' play and tragedy proper. I have considered it in this latter category, perhaps unjustly, for Mr Eliot has not claimed it as a tragedy: since it seems to me to embody, in structure and dramatic device, so many of the traditional elements of the form. It is possible that the missing element is the sense of exaltation which is communicated under the pressure of defeat or death, that which Yeats called 'joy' or 'ecstasy'. We are aware of a submission to destiny which has somehow become alloyed with a pagan view, yet again lacking the eagerness and vividness of the Greek world. Man has become strangely dwarfed by thinking that he is so.

§ *iv*

The Cocktail Party presents an even more difficult problem. We must consider it (however hesitantly) as a tragedy; because of its ritual

[1] *Ibid.*, p. 17.   [2] *Ibid.*, p. 97.

16

elements, its atonement for guilt, the sacrificial death of Celia, and its religious framework. Superficially, the pattern is clear and symmetrical: Edward's wife, Lavinia, has left him. He has believed himself in love with Celia Copleston; Lavinia has had, unknown to him, Peter Quilpe for a lover. Edward, Lavinia and Celia come into the magnetic field of the three mysterious manipulators of the play: Sir Harry Harcourt-Reilly, the physician and psychiatrist, Julia the comic elderly aunt of the early part of the play, and Alexander MacColgie Gibbs. As a result, Celia is sent on a journey and is crucified on an ant-heap by savages:

> She paid the highest price
> In suffering. That is part of the design.[1]

Edward and Lavinia are in some measure reconciled in a common responsibility of guilt for Celia's death.

The play, for all the comedy that occurs most ingeniously and spasmodically, is deliberately flattened in tone; and confused, again no doubt deliberately, as to the issues raised. (The rhythms of the first two scenes of Act I are very different from those of the remainder of the play; at first they are vigorous, alive, full of music, but later lengthen and become thin and dead. It is possible that the play was built upon an earlier draft.) Edward's chance conversation with Reilly, at that stage the Unidentified Guest at the party, reveals the latter's omniscience. He knows that Edward is only indulging in

> the luxury
> Of an intimate disclosure to a stranger.

But the disclosure

> Is to invite the unexpected, release a new force,
> Or let the genie out of the bottle.
> It is to start a train of events
> Beyond your control.[2]

It is a startling example of a powerful spring liberated by an apparently inadequate trigger: unless we suppose a quasi-divine role for Harcourt-Reilly. And though Mr Eliot has told us that some of his critics

> who were at first disturbed by the eccentric behaviour of my Unknown Guest, and his apparently intemperate habit and tendency to burst into song, have found some consolation after I have called their attention to the behaviour of Heracles in Euripides' play.[3]

[1] p. 163.   [2] p. 24.   [3] *Poetry and Drama*, p. 31. The play is the *Alcestis*.

But this does not really solve the moral issues raised by Reilly and his associates. He has foreknowledge,[1] complete assurance; except, for a moment, when confronted by Julia's

> Henry, you simply do not understand

and the apparent power to impose on others one of the standard psychiatric remedies—the departure, the new environment. They foresee Celia's suffering. She has departed with a pontifical blessing: yet, says Reilly,

> And when I say to one like her
> 'Work out your salvation with diligence', I do not understand
> What I myself am saying.[2]

Reilly, Julia and Alex are apparently metamorphosed in The Guardians, and the gap between their characters as they are shown in Act I, and subsequently, is not easily explained or bridged. If, as seems to me probable, Mr Eliot wished to show, in the play as a whole, the system of tensions between the world of the spirit and that of modern society, and used these figures to resolve that tension, the attempt (though not without precedent in Anglo-Catholic literature) seems to me to be unsuccessful.

Granted that suffering is 'permanent, obscure and dark', granted that the burden of the mystery lies heavily on all his characters, is it in the nature of tragedy, to express these complexities, not by the exaltation of poetic statement, but in poetry so meticulously balanced, in statements that oppose paradox to paradox and leave, as it were, a resultant to emerge, if all goes well, at the discretion of the reader? And if the central character of The Cocktail Party is really indebted to Heracles, we may be pardoned for considering the play a strange witches' cauldron indeed. Reilly, Julia and Alex with their ritual, and their air of priest-like assurance in the final act, are difficult to justify except as manipulators, and have no interest, as characters, outside that role. We seem to be in a world where all the values are grey, where flesh and blood perish by a strangely cruel indirect narration, and where the planes of value merge into each other. Perhaps this is summed up in Julia's words:

> Everyone makes a choice, of one kind or another,
> And then must take the consequences. Celia chose
> A way of which the consequence was crucifixion;

---

[1] The psycho-analyst was equated with the Deity, in an article in a critical journal, many years before the publication of The Cocktail Party.

[2] p. 131.

> Peter Quilpe chose a way that takes him to Boltwell;
> And now the consequence of the Chamberlaynes' choice
> Is a cocktail party. They must be ready for it.
> Their guests may be arriving at any moment.
>
> (Alex *leaves the room*.)
> *Reilly.* Julia, you are right. It is also right
> That the Chamberlaynes should now be giving a party.[1]

Celia, the tragic heroine, has neither the stature nor the interest for such a role. She alone is virtuous, a symbolic figure whose praises after she is gone seem to decrease both her own personality, and perhaps that of those who utter these praises.

§ *v*

We conclude, then, that Mr Eliot, in spite of all his superb technical resources, his unique position as the only great poet of this century who has been concerned simultaneously with Culture and Christianity, has not achieved (and would probably say he has not attempted) great tragedy. If, as the latest evidence suggests, he regards comedy as a more suitable medium for serious thought, it is unlikely that he will progress further on tragic lines. But *Murder in the Cathedral* must be considered, within its range and intention, a great tragic play; and it is pertinent to consider, in wider terms, why the other two plays fail in the tragic mode; remembering the constituent elements, the 'philosophy' of them, Mr Eliot's most strict integrity regarding his own theories of poetic statement, and their traditional ritual framework of confession (or revelation, or Recognition), atonement, and perhaps absolution. An attempt to find what factor or factors may be lacking will therefore be of importance in the investigation of modern tragedy.

Our first criticism would, I think, be that the two plays in question are not completely conceived as character in action, revealing themselves and developing what they do as a single organic conception, and this is perhaps because the plays, because of their debt to Greek sources, tend to be synthetic. The rhythm of the plays, a quality so rightly stressed by Mr Eliot, suggests that there is in fact a double rhythm: one of the changes in key of the verse, as between narrative, 'character', and choric; and one of a rhythm of structure. Both suggest that they have been imposed externally, and after repeated revisions.

[1] p. 165.

One is tempted to say that Mr Eliot is primarily concerned with problems of 'states of mind', with the somewhat pessimistic approach that these states of mind are, above all, beyond the reach of language, however precisely this may, in intention, be planned. We have almost a reversal of the Aristotelian dictum: 'For life consists in action, and its end is a mode of action, not a quality.' There appears to be an attempt to separate the *quality* from the *action*. And this may be because of two reasons: the conception of quality is, to Mr Eliot, capable of separation from the action, because action is, itself, both unimportant and incapable of precise statement:

> All I could hope to make you understand
> Is only events; not what has happened.[1]

And definition of what is beyond definition is left to emerge from a series of linguistic paradoxes or oppositions, with a triple value: they may allow the emergence of the 'star' of meaning, they evoke an atmosphere of a quasi-liturgical type, and they leave the reader and audience free to select their own interpretations. The dramatist is thereby absolved from responsibility; he has not committed himself; the play means to each one what he finds in it. And this half-truth of interpretation renders the next step, that of deciding the 'philosophy' communicated, still more difficult.

The religious framework of the two plays appears to be, intentionally, a little narrow, ambiguous, perhaps confused. In *The Cocktail Party* Reilly enjoins his patients to work out their salvation with diligence. His power is that of a priest—but Julia appears to be above him in this strange hierarchy. The ritual of the libation that concludes Act II, the words for the kindling of the hearth and for those who go upon a journey suggest a magical incantation [2] rather than a Christian prayer; Peter Quilpe 'has not yet come to where the words are valid', and 'Others, perhaps, will speak them.' Celia's right of choice is no choice at all: for Reilly, in his role of prophet-priest, has foreseen her death. And the logic of his description of the sequence of events, once he has had his sudden intuition that she is 'under sentence of death', suggests a curious perversion of reasoning.[3]

---

[1] *F.R.*, I. i. Has not Eliot a kind of defeatism about words; a striving for certain nuances, yet feeling a certain satisfaction, and safety, in their inadequacy?

[2] A debt to Conan Doyle's *The Musgrave Ritual* in *Murder in the Cathedral* has already been noted. I do not know the source, if any, here.

[3] *C.P.*, pp. 162–3.

And yet Reilly's final sanctimoniousness suggests the physician rather than the priest:

> If we were all judged according to the consequences
> Of all our words and deeds, beyond the intention
> And beyond our limited understanding
> Of ourselves and others, we should all be condemned.[1]

For Reilly asserts that Celia Coplestone's martyrdom among savages was triumphant:

> As for Miss Coplestone, because you think her death was waste
> You blame yourselves, and because you blame yourselves
> You think her life was wasted. It was triumphant.
> But I am no more responsible for the triumph—
> And just as responsible for the death as you are.[2]

It was 'triumphant': but I find no suggestion of triumph or exaltation, or of faith, in the carefully toneless verse that adheres so carefully to Mr Eliot's intention: 'The audience may be saying "I could talk in poetry too!" ' but might well add—'if, indeed, this is poetry'. And he continues: 'Then we should not be transported into an artificial world; on the contrary, our own sordid dreary world would suddenly become illuminated and transfigured.' [3]

Fair enough: but there seems little enough either of illumination or transfiguration; only (here and in *The Family Reunion*), the tantalizing half-heard clues to states of mind so complicated or so imprecise that the language, attempting with its precision to match that impreciseness, appears to lose touch with the very objects of dramatic presentation.

In the foreground of Mr Eliot's world are figures whose lives move in a mist of ill-defined guilt, progressing through recognition toward atonement, of which the first stages are discipline and suffering. Their guilt, it is true, is, in the traditional manner, ill proportioned to their apparent deserts, in so far as these are explained to us; but neither is perceived and stated and confronted, at or before their departure. They are in the grasp of destiny, of a psychotherapist, or of a curse; they move strangely across the stage, wrapped in cocoons of their own subtleties, inclined to self-pity and the ruminations of the *moyen intellectuel*. And because of what we may think an obsession with suffering we begin to

---

[1] *C.P.*, p. 164. More simply, 'Use every man after his deserts, and who should escape whipping?'
[2] *Ibid.*   [3] *Poetry and Drama.*

believe that it is, perhaps, the only virtue. In the background there are the vague apparitions of the historical-supernatural: the symbolism of desert, mountain, labyrinth, quicksand, Minotaur terrors for the travellers, the Eumenides which are neither ghosts nor hunters nor conscience nor the curse on the house, but a *pot pourri* of all four: moved in obedience by the playwright to image the Christian pilgrimage, the Calvinist sense of guilt; yet without the pity or terror or exaltation of the Calvinist vision. That is, perhaps, because the protagonists have no clear vision of themselves: Mr Eliot's 'recognitions' seem only a preliminary step towards self-knowledge: which is to be completed by the pilgrimage.

In the middle ground are the figures who are, again, manipulated in accordance with the keen perception of the satiric and pitiful and bored mediocrity whose diagnosis was Mr Eliot's peculiar contribution in his earlier poetry. 'Öd' und leer das Meer'; the spring is cruel; the world of the clubman, the bore, the society woman, are unerringly betrayed. If, as in *The Family Reunion*, they speak in chorus, the effects are self-conscious and grotesque; on the modern stage the chorus effects are, perhaps, only possible for the singing voice (as Yeats used them) or when the setting gives credibility (as in *Murder in the Cathedral*) to the ritual chant. If Mr Eliot's formal experiments have proved anything it may be that they have shown us the impossibility of concerted speech by 'everyday' characters without the formal addition of song; that the problem of dramatic speech has not been formally solved; that plays must be conceived in terms of characters in action. At the root of the problem may be Mr Eliot's own presuppositions:

> What we have to do is to bring poetry into the world in which the audience lives and to which it returns when it leaves the theatre; not to transport the audience into some imaginary world totally unlike its own, an unreal world in which poetry is tolerated.

On this dictum we may ask, without answering them as yet, four questions:

1. Is poetry in tragedy only 'tolerated in an unreal world'?
2. Is the tragic world of Ibsen and Anouilh 'so totally unlike its own'?
3. Is not the work of the dramatist the enlargement of the human vision, the reconciliation of its own sense of guilt with that vision?
4. Were not Synge, and Yeats after him, right to demand of tragedy 'reality and joy'?

Perhaps his position can be summed up, and the last question answered at least in part, by a final quotation:

> For it is ultimately the function of art, in imposing a credible order upon ordinary reality, and thereby exciting some perception of an order *in* reality, to bring us to a condition of serenity, stillness and reconciliation; and then leave us, as Virgil did Dante, to proceed towards a region where that guide can avail us no longer.[1]

[1] *Poetry and Drama*, p. 35.

CHAPTER 19

The Transmigration of the Greek

(Sartre, Cocteau, Camus, Anouilh)

Ended so?
Nowise!—began again; for heroes rest
Dropping shield's oval o'er the entire man;
And he who thus took Contemplation's prize,
Turned stade-point but to face Activity
Out of all shadowy hands extending help
For life's decline pledged to youth's enterprise,
Whatever renovation flatter age . . .[1]

BROWNING

§ i

THE shadowy hands of the Greek dramatists have long been stretched out over European literature. We can suggest many reasons for the dominance of Greek fable or drama in human imagination. Ages that regarded classical reading as fundamental to a common education, who paid lip-service at least to Aristotle and his commentators, would turn—mainly through the more accessible Latin—to the Greek originals. Their value was unquestioned; whether as *exempla* of morality (however interpreted) or of the fate of legendary personages. In Racine both are significant; with such transposition into his own peculiar Roman-French atmosphere as the form and pressure of his time demanded. Goethe's *Iphigenie*, Grillparzer's *Sappho*, exploit the immense emotional possibilities of the fable; Arnold's *Empedocles upon Etna* is no more than a stiff, almost lifeless artefact to justify his own theories.

The twentieth-century revival of interest in Greek myth and fable seems more complex. Part, no doubt, is due to the psychological recognition of the archetypes, and the nomenclature of certain of them from the Greek: Oedipus, Elektra, Orestes, and the Furies archetypes, these last linked to the recurrent image of the Hound. The fables thus acquire a new validity in themselves; and can be re-clothed effectively on what is basically the same skeleton. And the Trojan War, with its

[1] *Aristophanes' Apology.*

233

related actions, has a mysterious vitality as an enduring symbol in relation to our present century:

> The Trojan War was really an attempt to destroy a whole civilization. The attempt succeeded.
> Homer always calls Troy 'Holy Ilion'. This was the original sin of the Greeks, and filled them with remorse. By their remorse they, the execution-ers, were found worthy to inherit something of the inspiration of their victims.[1]

But this is only a partial explanation. If such a re-clothing takes place, with a partial re-articulation of the bones, a new field is opened for the exercise of wit, the perception of metaphysical similarities or dis-cordances, and endless over-and-undertones of irony. Out of such parallelisms, close or remote, the dramatist can invite his audience to find 'meaning' which is usually a synthesis of factors which are, to a great extent, set in opposition or paradox. At the same time he can, if he sees fit, disarm criticism by denying his apparent intention as regards some particular synthesis. He can provide a critical edge, at various planes, by explicit or implicit comparisons between the two ages; the past whose bones he has discovered, the present where breath is upon them.

But perhaps the matter is more complex than this. The experience of two wars has given the ghosts of Greek drama sacrificial blood to drink; conquest, occupation, resistance, have helped further to make them opaque. The clear-cut form, the symmetrical structure, the progressive and even mechanical revelations, have their own specific appeal. More than this, perhaps, the dramatists have perceived an opportunity for a distancing of perspective, a curious philosophical amalgam in which Paganism and Christianity are perceived, abstractedly, in alternate opposition or synthesis; and in the successive removal of layer after layer of the unknown elements of the situation, a microcosm of the discipline towards self-knowledge.

There are certain disadvantages in the method. The dramatist must be close enough to his original to allow similitudes or dissimilitudes to be perceived; and he must postulate an audience as sophisticated and eclectic as Yeats demanded for his final plays, or as Mr Eliot implies by his references to the *Alcestis* and *Ion* as shedding light on his mean-ing. At the same time the 'modern dress' must be carefully imagined, for it can easily become ridiculous. Yet if the dramatist succeeds, he has

---

[1] Simone Weil, *Waiting on God*, p. 168.

at his disposal elements that lend themselves to effects of great delicacy and profundity; as well as a ready-made device for universalizing the significance of his dramatic statement. That device is twofold. Enough of the myth or plot of the original probably lingers in the memory of a middle-class audience to give it still some measure of life; and if the archetypal situations are indeed basic in our own minds, the conditions are favourable. If the dramatist becomes either too familiar or too remote, his similitudes too heterogeneous or *nachgesucht*, his failure will be catastrophic.

But in the French versions which we are now considering the popularity of the Greek fable would appear to rest on more profound reasons. Sartre, writing of the younger generation of French dramatists, gives an interesting picture:

> What is universal, to their way of thinking, is not *nature* but the situation in which *man* finds himself; that is, not the sum total of his psychological traits but the limits which enclose him on all sides . . . A man who is free within the circle of his own situations, who chooses, whether he wishes to or not, for everyone else when he chooses for himself—that is the subject matter of our plays. As a successor to the theatre of characters we want to have a theatre of situation; our aim is to explore all the situations that are most common to human experience, those which occur at least once in the majority of lives. The people in our plays will be distinct from one another—not as a coward is from a miser, or a miser from a brave man, but rather as actions are divergent or clashing, as right may conflict with right. In this it may well be said that we derive from the Corneillean tradition.[1]

Now behind this view of the theatre is existentialism: which asserts that existence precedes essence. 'L'homme n'est rien d'autre que ce qu'il fait.' If existence precedes essence, then situation precedes character. Situation demands of man that he should choose, having a freedom that is perceived within the framework of a deterministic system. By his choice, or by a succession of choices, the facets of his character are in turn illuminated as the crystal revolves on pivots.

For our purpose we may note some of the historical debts of existentialism: to Kierkegaard's treatment of anguish, sin and liberty, in his view of Christianity, and his rejection of all forms of the finite. 'He who chooses despair, chooses himself in his eternal value';[2] to the phenomenology of Husserl in contrast to the traditional German idealism; to the partial acceptance of Cartesianism. His peculiar

---

[1] *Theatre Arts*, June 1946, pp. 325–6.
[2] P. J. R. Dempsey, *The Psychology of Sartre*, p. 22.

conception of *le néant* or nothingness, applies not only to man, but to eternal reality. Man, who is ever conscious of this nothingness, is subject to fear (that which is directed to the object) and anxiety (which arises from reflection on the relationship of the individual to the object). Love demands 'the alienated liberty of the beloved'; the lover asks that the beloved, without

> seeking originally to be loved, should have a contemplative affective in-tuition of the lover, as the objective limit of her liberty, as the ground of transcendence, as the totality of being, as the supreme value. Only thus will the lover be in *security* in the consciousness of his beloved.[1]

But this view of love is subject to perpetual defeat (*les échecs*); from which the lover may endeavour to escape by sadism, masochism, inversion.

Human liberty is co-extensive with human existence. To be is to act; not to act is to cease to be.[2] We attempt to fill up *le néant* in our-selves by drawing upon the goodness of the world. In order to act we are subject to definite conditions which include

1. The variety of the courses open.
2. The evaluation of the good, subdivisible into:
   (*a*) motives: the state of things at the moment, as they present themselves to consciousness.
   (*b*) 'mobiles', that group of passions, emotions, desires, which impel towards an act.
   (*c*) intentions.
   (*d*) ends.

Sartre appears to reach a position that is neither indifferentism nor determinism. There is always an anterior motive for his decisions; man is either utterly free or utterly a slave.

One other concept may be noted in this bare outline; that of *mauvaise foi*. This is the lie that conceals the truth from the individual himself. It implies essentially a unified consciousness in the individual; for which the ultimate responsibility remains with the individual, and is not to be attributed to the unconscious as such.

§ *ii*

It may appear at first something of a paradox that Existentialism should have emerged from the primitive adventure of the French

---

[1] P. J. R. Dempsey, *op. cit.*, p. 43. This point comes out in Anouilh's *Eurydice*.
[2] *Ibid.*, p. 46.

Resistance Movement. It is as if the fall of France, Pétain's surrender, the stark facts of the occupation, and the working of something like a cyclic doom, produced the sensation of a complicated and mysterious collective guilt. That failure extended through a chain of responsibilities which was so long and so twisted that its impact upon the individual was perceived as an oppressive and mysterious cloud rather than as a clear-cut issue. We may suspect that the issues were, and are, further obscured by the French multi-party system, with its Protean changes of loyalty and its capacity for giving absolution from responsibility. The helplessness of a peasantry confronted with armoured divisions is of a peculiarly degraded kind; yet the initial compromise with an occupying force is easy, and the enemy may be, as he often was, *très correct*. Life might (as many pointed out) prove easier under the enemy than under the liberators.[1] Against an initial despair, a confrontation with the mechanical and mechanized fact, the individual reasserted himself, merging gradually into small groups. The individual mood, since it could not be brought to the point of heroism in immediate action, and had no predictable ending in time, is more easily sustained by the courage of protracted pessimism than by the commoner warlike virtues. At the same time the nature of the net is everywhere felt in increasing constrictions, as countermeasures to the resistance are put into effect. The fear of torture and imprisonment are ever-present. This fear can best be prevented from inhibiting action by a kind of perverse acceptance of pain and despair, an intensified and deliberate inspection of the physical horror of life as well as of war, and an assertion of the ultimate freedom of the individual in all that seems left to him, his right of choice.

Sartre's *Les Mouches* is a play of guilt, responsibility and violence superimposed on the skeleton of the *Oresteia*. Argos is afflicted with a plague of flies, the symbol of the city's guilt, a retribution for their passive complicity in the murder of Clytemnestra.

> . . . So the people here held their tongues; they looked forward to seeing, for once, a violent death. They still kept silent when they saw their King entering by the city gates. And when Clytemnestra stretched forth her graceful arms, fragrant and white as lilies, they still said nothing. Yet at that moment a word, a single word, might have sufficed. But no one said it; each was gloating in imagination over the picture of a huge corpse with a shattered face.[2]

---

[1] 'Never were we freer than under the German occupation.' (Sartre, *Lettres Françaises*.)
[2] *The Flies*, p. 12 (transl. Gilbert).

Notice the emphasis on a dramatic purpose in the city, the possibility of averting disaster by a single gesture, the sensuality of contrast between beauty and blood. This guilt leads to a hysteria of confession:

> The Queen is indulging in our national pastime; the game of public confession. Here, everyone cries his sins on the housetops. . . . But the folk of Argos are getting a little tired of these amusements; everyone knows his neighbours' sins by heart.[1]

Such a vision of guilt-hysteria is not an uncommon phenomenon in a disintegrating society, and is of a piece with the sadistic and masochistic elements that Sartre perceives. Argos is obsessed with its relationship to the dead; and at their Festival, where they issue forth from their cave at the bidding of the High Priest, the cry of the crowd is 'Forgive us for living when you are dead!' It is a parody of the death-attitudes of high tragedy:

> Have mercy! Tokens of you are ever with us, we see your faces everywhere we turn. We wear mourning unceasingly, and weep for you from dawn till dusk, from dusk till dawn. But somehow, try as we may, your memory dwindles and slips through our fingers; daily it grows dimmer and we know ourselves the guiltier. Yes, you are leaving us, ebbing away like life-blood from a wound. And yet, know you well—if this can mollify your bitter hatred—that you, our dear departed, have laid waste our lives.[2]

Elektra alone refuses to acknowledge their existence, and dances, sacrilegiously, a gay ritual dance: for an instant the people have a glimpse of what happiness might mean. But the essence of the play, and of Sartre's neo-stoicism, is in the following dialogue:

> *Orestes.* The people of Argos are my folk. I must open their eyes.
> *Zeus.* Poor people! Your gift to them will be a sad one; of loneliness and shame. You will tear from their eyes the veils I had laid on them, and they will see their lives as they are, foul and futile, a barren doom.
> *Orestes.* Why, since it is their lot, should I deny them the despair I have in me?
> *Zeus.* What will they make of it?
> *Orestes.* What they choose. They're free; *and human life begins on the far side of despair.*
> (*A short silence.*) [3]

In Sartre's world there is a curious strain of brutality which is at once the result of, and the justification for, despair. Character appears to be determined by events, and the protagonists are confronted by a simplified system of conflicting claims, each of which demands a sacrifice.

[1] *The Flies*, p. 32.   [2] *Ibid.*, p. 44.   [3] *Ibid.*, p. 97.

Zeus is both mocker and the mocked, and out of it emerges a kind of neo-stoicism which has a certain fierce nobility. It is without pity or charity; its ironic laughter has no extension in time or space. It seems to me likely that this is due to Sartre's attempt to divorce thought from action. *Huis Clos* is a drama which takes place when the net has finally closed in on the protagonists. They have taken their decisions, and there is no return. They are thus doomed to a struggle against the inevitable, and each character is imprisoned in the hell of his own making.

§ *iii*

A critic has said, I think with justice, that M. Anouilh 'alone among modern playwrights is able to wear the tragic mask with ease'. His plays fall readily into groups.

The *Antigone* follows Sophocles closely as regards the plot: except that Polyneices and his brother are revealed, not as heroes asserting their claims against the tyrannical Creon, but as bullies and scoundrels for whom Antigone's sacrifice is, in Creon's eyes, completely unjustified. Antigone is the rebel, the heroine of the resistance; who, driven into a corner by the sheer reason of the course, asserts her right to refuse to accept a compromise, and to die. In accordance with existentialist thought the word 'right' is used to mean the action which results from any choice which is made in absolute freedom:

> I spit on your happiness! I spit on your idea of life—that life must go on, come what may. You are all like dogs that lick everything they smell. You with your promise of a humdrum happiness—provided a person doesn't ask too much of life. I want everything of life, I do; and I want it now! I want it total, complete, otherwise I reject it! I will *not* be moderate. I will *not* be satisfied with the bit of cake you offer me if I promise to be a good little girl. I want to be sure of everything this very day; sure that everything will be beautiful as when I was a little girl. If not, I want to die!
>
> *Creon.* Scream on, daughter of Oedipus! Scream on, in your father's own voice!
>
> *Antigone.* In my father's own voice, yes! We are of the tribe that asks questions, and we ask them to the bitter end. Until no tiniest chance of hope remains to be strangled by our hands. We are of the tribe that hates your filthy hope, your docile, female hope; hope, your whore——[1]

Even in such a brief extract, and in translation,[2] we can see how

---

[1] pp. 58–9.
[2] Though the only available translation is excellent in every way.

Anouilh has found an appropriate modern idiom, full of virility, and flexible: we can see, too, his use of the Greek fable for its ironic values. What follows immediately, is also worth quoting; for its psychological insight, and for the tragedy of defeat:

> Creon (*grasps her by the arms*). Shut up! If you could see how ugly you are, shrieking those words!
> Antigone. Yes, I am ugly! Father was ugly, too. (Creon *releases her arms, turns and moves away. Stands with his back to* Antigone.) But Father became beautiful. And do you know when? (*She follows him to behind the table.*) At the very end. When all his questions had been answered. When he could no longer doubt that he *had* killed his own father; that he *had* gone to bed with his own mother.[1] When all hope was gone, stamped out like a beetle. When it was absolutely certain that nothing, nothing, could save him. Then he was at peace; then he could smile, almost; then he became beautiful . . .

Anouilh is not an existentialist, though we may see traces of the idea of resistance and of the closely-drawn net of circumstances of this theatre. His tragedies are meticulously balanced; there is usually the omniscient commentator, the Chorus who is in part the playwright in *Antigone*; M. Henri with his mysterious pity and wisdom in *Eurydice*. In this play we see Anouilh's division of human beings into two types; the gross, the contented, the sensual, who live like oxen in a stall: and those who are rebels, idealists, yet who find in their idealism a kind of reconciliation.

The setting of the railway station buffet, the theatrical company, the sordidness of the love-making of both the children's parents, set the tone for a peculiar kind of symbolical realism. The third-rate actors, who can make love only in the clichés of their memorized stage parts, are made credible by their character, accent, the minute particulars of their behaviour.

Against it all Orpheus' love is sudden, terrifying in its innocence:

> . . . Now everything's changed, for I know you. It's amazing. Suddenly everything becomes amazing all round us. Look . . . how beautiful the Cashier is, with her great bosom resting delicately on the marble counter. And the waiter! Look at the waiter! Those long, flat feet in button boots, that distinguished bald head, and that air of nobility, real nobility. It is an amazing evening, this! It had to be. . . .[2]

[1] Koestler in *The Invisible Writing* speaks of his own experience in prison: of the peace which comes when the crime is *known*, and the punishment is anticipated. 'The neurotic type of anxiety in the irrational anticipation of an unknown punishment for an unknown crime.'   [2] p. 94.

The story of their flight together from their parents, the suicide of Eurydice's lover beneath the train, the blackmail levied on her by the actor who has had her for a mistress, moves easily to the first recognition, Eurydice's knowledge that it is too hard for her to sustain herself as Orpheus sees her. In one sense it is the projection of all stories of young love beyond marriage, a subject essentially tragic in its first phase. In the theatre it usually ceases there, since its reconciliation through suffering is not readily adapted to the possible scale of time. In the calm that succeeds passion the doubts come, as to Orpheus and Eurydice on their marriage-bed in the sordid inn.

> . . . Maybe the bride-bed brings despair,
> For each an imagined image brings
> And finds a real image there . . .[1]

It is Dulac, Eurydice's lover, who is the agent of the first recognition:

> What's she like, your Eurydice? Have you to drag her out of bed in the morning? Have you to go and snatch the thrillers away from her, and the cigarettes? For that matter, have you ever seen her a single instant without a fag in the corner of her mouth, like any little guttersnipe? And her stockings? Can she find them when she gets up? Come on, be frank. Own up— her chemise was stuck on top of the wardrobe, her slippers in the bathtub, her hat under the armchair, and her handbag God knows where. It's the seventh I've bought her already.[2]

To which Orpheus can only answer dully: 'It is not true.' But the gap between the ideal and the real is too great.

Eurydice leaves Orpheus, leaving a letter:

> . . . Darling, I am going away. Ever since yesterday I have felt afraid, and even when I was sleeping you heard me say: 'It is hard.' I seemed so beautiful in your eyes, darling. Morally beautiful, I mean, for I know quite well you never found me much to look at. In your eyes I was so strong, so pure, so completely yours . . . I couldn't ever quite have lived up to it.[3]

She is killed in a bus accident.

The Fourth Act is an epilogue; full of irony and wisdom; the dialogue spoken between Orpheus' Father, Orpheus and the mysterious M. Henri. Orpheus is given his choice; he can regain Eurydice by dying.

Orpheus. No. I don't want to die. I hate death.

M. Henri (gently). You are unjust. Why hate it? Death is beautiful. Only death offers love its true climate. You heard your father speaking about

---

[1] Yeats, *Solomon and the Witch.*   [2] p. 139.   [3] pp. 166-7.

17

life just now. Grotesque, wasn't it, lamentable? Well, that was life. That
buffoonery, that futile melodrama, is life . . . yes, that heaviness, that play-
acting, is truly it. So go there inside and walk with your little Eurydice.
You will meet her again at the exit, in her frock all pawed and soiled; and
you, strange as you are, will find her again. If you find her, if you find
yourself, it is a Eurydice immaculate I am offering you, a Eurydice of the
genuine features that life would never have given you. Do you want her? [1]

The work of Camus is mainly of interest for two tragedies, *Caligula*
and *Le Malentendu*. The first may be regarded as a study in the tragedy
arising from man's attempt to live wholly in accord with the rational.
Circumstance or destiny becomes a ruthless hostile force, to be met
and crushed with equal violence and cruelty; it is immoral, and can
only be countered by immorality, actively planned. We have thus
what I take to be the only character study in tragedy of a character
whose integrity is complete, whose actions are pure: but who falls
because he is not prepared to compromise with the irrational. *Le
Malentendu* has at its centre the image of Sisyphus: 'Il faut imaginer
Sisyphe heureux.' Again man is confronted with a rigid destiny, complex and inexorable, against which his own hopes and fears become
ludicrous. The mere fact of existence has in its very essence the seeds
of man's incessant struggle, not with his fellows, but against this
perpetual frustration and despair.

§ *iv*

At the root of most of this tragedy it seems that there is one moral
question which determines its whole character. Man is placed in a
setting where he is brought inevitably into conflict with one of two
forces; the jealous mocking tyrannical god who is a relic of obsolete
religious conceptions, but who lives on, enjoying his own kind of
malicious pleasure: or a more abstract rigid deterministic system,
against which man must struggle, but can hope to obtain no more than
a perverted masochistic pleasure in his own futile suffering. Zeus of
Les Mouches is the tyrant of *Prometheus Unbound*, but without his
dignity or his setting in time. Human fear is sweet to him:

> . . . et le peur, la mauvaise conscience, ont une fumet delectable pour les
> narines des Dieux.

It seems as if character is determined neither by heredity nor environment, but is moulded by the tremendous pressure of events.

[1] p. 184.

This is a tragedy of confused and evolutionary values, informed by a strong fear for humanity. It sees at work an immense capricious cruelty. It is perpetually on the defensive, for the highest values it can transmit are irony, satire, stoicism. Except in Anouilh, whose tragic vision is continually illuminated by pity, little of positive integration or release seems to emerge. It is a tragedy of the most profound interest for the contemporary European situation, the record of a mood which has swept clean that chamber of the human mind, and as yet has set nothing in its place.

CHAPTER 20

Tragedy and the State

A state is called the coldest of all cold monsters. Coldly lieth it also; and this lie creepeth from its mouth: 'I, the state, am the people.'
It is a lie! Creators were they who created peoples, and hung a faith and a love over them: thus they served life.

NIETZSCHE [1]

The Stakhanov movement must play an outstanding rôle in the overthrow of religion. It signifies a mighty increase in the power of man, who is conquering nature and breaking down all previously imposed standards. If the scholars of the bourgeois world maintain that there are limits beyond which man's perception and man's struggle cannot go, that there are matters which a limited intelligence will not perceive, it is evident that under the proletarian deliverance from religion the creation of conscious workers in a classless society can, with the aid of the latest technical acquisitions, proceed to tasks which man, fettered by religion, would never have dared to face. In a socialist society everything is free from narrow limits. Man can learn everything and conquer everything. There is no bulwark which bolshevists cannot take by storm.[2]

Man is insecure and involved in natural contingency; he seeks to overcome his insecurity by a will-to-power which over reaches the limitations of a finite mind; but he pretends that he is not limited. He assumes that he can gradually transcend finite limitations until his mind becomes identical with universal mind. All of his intellectual and cultural pursuits, therefore, become infected with the sin of pride.[3]

REINHOLD NIEBUHR

§ i

FROM the beginnings tragedy has concerned itself with considerations that may be called, broadly, political. *The Seven Against Thebes*, the *Antigone*, *Oedipus Rex*, *Prometheus Bound* and *Unbound*; *The Dynasts*; and Ibsen's tragi-comedy *An Enemy of the People*; Schiller criticizes social oppression in *Die Räuber* and *Kabale und Liebe*. In the latter play the whole setting is one of prejudice and corruption, against which the 'good' characters struggle in vain. Lessing's *Emilia Galotti* is an attack on absolute monarchy, the primeval tyrant, whose victims are guiltless; and we may see much of the drama of the Sturm und Drang period in terms of the growth of humanitarian liberalism against an authoritarian rationalism. There is a whole multitude of pseudo-historical

---

[1] *Zarathustra*, I. xi.
[2] *Bulletin of the League of Fighting Godless: cit.* Niebuhr, *Beyond Tragedy*, pp. 37–8.
[3] *The Nature and Destiny of Man*, Vol. I, pp. 190–1.

plays. The reasons are obvious. One pole of the established type of conflict is often formed of a kind of stalactite of petrified law, custom, usage, which is in itself challenged and broken by a new order. An older variant may be personified in a tyrant-figure, man or god; the opposing force has in it elements of heroic rebellion, or of the struggle of the Fox against the Lion, or of an epic or despairing martyrdom. The balance in this conflict may be weighted in accordance with the dramatist's vision. He may hint, as Aeschylus does, at a mysterious ultimate power containing both the progressive and regressive elements; or perceive, as I believe Shakespeare does, a vast but ragged principle of retribution that runs through the cycles of English history.

The State may be regarded as the perfect abstract protagonist in tragedy. It can include among its claims the most powerful stimulatory virtues: honour, patriotism, piety, love of tradition, loyalty; it can call on the hidden *todtentrieb* for its mystical defence through blood.[1] In time of war its claims on truth are absolute in proportion to the strength of its censorship; it cannot afford to cry, with Shaw, 'God must be fair to your enemies too—don't forget that.' Under such conditions it develops a degree of absolutism for just so long as certain conditions can be fulfilled. The justification of its historical objective must hold some hope of amelioration in the future, some moral or material series of five-year plans, or more distant beneficent revolutions. It must smother or depress criticism as that hope recedes. It must retain sufficient hold on the emotional attitudes of its subjects to impose sacrifices upon them, with the sullen consent if not the will of the masses.

The conflict with the State, in these circumstances, can only be one of rebellion: Schiller's *Die Räuber*, Wordsworth's *The Borderers*. Unless the forces of the State can be focused in a single figure, or at most two or three, the clash becomes muffled in clouds of abstraction. The emergence of the tyrant and the tyrannicide are therefore parts of the normal pattern: the Generals' Plot against Hitler is no different in principle from Bolingbroke's deposition of Richard II, though an Elizabethan would have paled before the sadistic fury of Hitler's revenge; and innumerable parallels can be found over the same matter of divided loyalties to the hero who may be, whether in fact or imagination, upon the downward curve of his trajectory of success.

[1] This was exploited with the greatest skill in the German marching songs of both wars.

The whole question has been sharpened and brought to the forefront by modern ideological politics. There are perhaps two main aspects. The individually-led rebellion against the State has ceased to be a practical proposition. In the first place, communications are now such that no single assassination can alter the course of modern government (although the immediate consequences may be difficult to trammel up), as that of Caesar altered the Roman world and its peace. In the second, modern warfare is such that, lacking international assistance in armaments, rebellion on a national scale, say on the *Wilhelm Tell* model, is impossible. Machine guns, aircraft and high explosives have smothered it; men can no longer go out with swords and staves as against a robber.

At the same time internationalism, in the form of dialectical materialism, has precipitated the conflicts of State versus individual. The crop of actual and potential 'traitors' to either side has grown enormously, though not, perhaps, disproportionately to the mechanisms and agencies involved. Motivations for 'treachery' range, as far as one can judge, through the normal scale found in the literature of the past: idealism, vanity, self-pity, revenge, and the various semi-neurotic conditions that involve men in some kind of apocalyptic vision. We may find, in pressing the analysis, elements of *schadenfreude*, of sadism and of masochism, as well as those of the purest disinterestedness. In the philosophy of dialectical materialism there is a formal structure which appears at first sight to possess an essentially tragic bias. Its reading of history is triadic. Thesis is followed by antithesis and is then resolved into synthesis through the dynamism of internal conflict; a process which we may suppose to include evil and self-waste as well as the ultimate apocalyptic vision. We might, then, expect that Marxism would by now have produced, whether directly or as a by-product, great tragedy. The personal conflicts described in prose [1] suggest that ample emotional material is available, and that its roots lie deep in the subtleties of individual neurosis.

It would, perhaps, appear as a tragedy of 'liberation'. Its morals would be 'realistic' following the Nietzscheans, Neo-Machiavellianists, Syndicalists and Freudians. 'Sin' as such would not be an innovation but the survival or 'misuse of habits and tendencies that were incidental to an earlier stage of development . . .' [2] Its morality would therefore be relativist in relation to a higher end, that of the Revolution. It would

---

[1] As, for example, in Whittaker Chamber's *Witness*, or Koestler's *The Invisible Writing*.
[2] Thelen, *op. cit.*, p. 15: quoting Tennant.

probably follow Rousseau's naïve theory that the harmony of nature can be restored by compounding the individual will into a general will, and this might become a central theme. As the second quotation at the head of this essay suggests, it will focus mass emotional energy by battle-imagery. Our only guide to its probable language is the rhetoric of the totalitarian State, for considerations of censorship will restrict the tragic writer to the conventions employed for political ends. We should expect the language to reflect and embody the rigidity of predetermined attitudes, a specific denial of individuality, and a violent simplification of moral problems. It would afford—again in terms of the quotation from *The League of the Fighting Godless*—the supreme example of the *hubris* of man.

That such tragedy has not yet been written, whereas ideological tragedy, under broadly similar conditions, did emerge at the time of the French Revolution, is mainly due to the technical difficulties of focusing such conflicts down to dramatic proportions, of rendering them 'perspicuous' in the Aristotelian sense. The State cannot be personified into a series of abstractions, as in *Everyman*, or even to the extent that Hauptmann succeeds in objectifying authority in *The Weavers*. No individual is now capable of being perceived as an adequate symbol for it; nor can he embody such collective responsibility as could be expressed in terms of the stage, except, perhaps, when he is working in a unit of the smallest kind. (The central character of the hero in the minute Greek city state has already been pointed out.) And even if a long and ingeniously directed propaganda has endowed him with pseudo-mythological qualities, and sought to confirm his significance in the 'Father' role, such assumed qualities can neither be stated in terms of action nor analysed in histrionic conflict.[1] Such a hero is too remote, too statuesque; he cannot be seen in the light of 'the minute particulars of mankind', nor can he be depicted (except in the final stage of his fall) as having been given such faults as make us men.[2]

But beyond and above the complexity of the modern State lies the central assumption of dialectical materialism: that 'the essence of man is no abstraction inherent in each separate individual. In its reality it is the ensemble (aggregate) of social relations'.[3] The power of the

---

[1] The statement may be tested by the imaginative use of the biographical data for any recent dictator, as compared with that provided by Plutarch or Holinshed.

[2] The censorship imposed on the private lives of dictators, and the rumours that precede their fall, are of interest here.

[3] Marx and Engels, *German Ideology*, p. 198. (Thelen, *cit.* p. 37.)

individual is denied; as also his right to self-determination, since life is interpreted, not as the product of ideas, but of economic circumstances. It is a conception that goes far beyond the type of conflict perceived by Toller or Hauptmann, where divergent and responsible man emerged even though he was a component of a collective whole. Thus, while it might be reasonable to expect that tragedies will be written concerning conflicts which will necessarily accumulate on the periphery of such ideological situations, we shall not expect the central conflicts to be susceptible of tragic statement.

§ ii

There remains, however, the larger and less definite question of the collective responsibility of the State in the tragedy of war, and the place of individual responsibility, within that setting, in relation to the matter of tragic guilt. It is a problem presented in an acute form, but not satisfactorily solved or resolved, by the Nuremberg Trials. That problem was presented by the first World War, perceived initially against a philosophical background of liberal optimism, and subsequently against a drop-scene of bitter and bewildered pessimism. Its temper is best assessed by a consideration of the war poetry in the period 1916–18. It was followed by a confusion of values based on a sense of the temporary quality of evil; much on the lines suggested by Herbert Spencer:

> All imperfection is unfitness to the condition of existence. This unfitness must consist either in having a faculty or faculties in excess; or in having a faculty or faculties deficient; or in both. . . . Finally all excess and all deficiency must disappear; that is, all unfitness must disappear; that is, all imperfection must disappear. Thus the ultimate development of the ideal man is logically certain.[1]

Against this we may set the curious mental oscillations apparent as an immediate consequence of the first World War, which was to end all wars. Civilization appeared to have turned on a hinge. The conflict between good and evil receded in the brilliant light that psychology and anthropology seemed to have shed. Massacres and disasters caused only temporary ripples on the conscience of civilized man, and the evasion of responsibility, the refusal to read the signs, is a striking feature of the Thirties. A passage from a writer of distinction sums up something of the spirit of ennui that succeeded the post-war optimism. It was written in 1926.

[1] *Social Statics*, Ch. II. 'The Evanescence of Evil'.

And meanwhile the critical, scientific part of the human mind, all that was anathema to Blake, has grown like the genie of an Arabian tale. Amid the veering perplexities of our age Science alone sweeps on with its strange purposeful blindness, it knows not whither, except that it is assuredly to fresh conquests: and childish scientists perfect for our childish society with childish indiscrimination toys to amuse it, or to murder. We are enabled to hear voices saying across the Atlantic things not worth hearing across a room; and to buzz round the globe like flies round a chandelier, without knowing any better what on earth to do when we arrive, than the jaded Roman noble who had flogged his horses in a whirl of dust across the Campagna from Rome to Tiber, and from Tiber back to Rome . . . And yet Science is at least alive, while Philosophy mopes and religion mutters. This in itself need not matter so much to Poetry; but it does matter to Poetry, to all our creative literature, that the thinking section of society has largely lost its scale of values and is thence in danger of ceasing to have any values at all.[1]

We may, indeed, discern some similarities with an earlier period of liberal and rational optimism:

In the spiritual climate of the eighteenth and the beginning of the nineteenth centuries the terror of a man's exposure to the need for ultimate moral or religious decisions could not be creatively grasped, either on the level of Greek tragedy or on that of undiluted Christianity, or indeed on the level of that unique encounter of both which took place in Elizabethan drama.[2]

There was thus much ground for the deterministic pessimism of Spengler, and the dissolution of values was the more insidious because of two factors in our thought: the unthinkable horror of future warfare, and the general misjudging of the rate of change in society:

And so what threatens civilization is not war itself or the destruction of war, but the changing conceptions of life values entailed by certain types of political doctrines. These doctrines directly impinge upon man's ordinary natural privileges of living and subordinate themselves to the needs of national killing.[3]

It is unnecessary to develop the confused expressions of the period between the wars except as they affect the tragic response. So far as the Zeitgeist found a possible vehicle in the tragic form, it became either satirical, or violent, or sought a passive re-interpretation of the problem

---

[1] F. L. Lucas, *Authors Dead and Living*, pp. 279–80. See also, for the period 1938–9, the same writer's *Journal Under the Terror*.
[2] Erich Heller, *The Disinherited Mind*, p. 41.
[3] Lin Yutang, *The End of Living is Living Itself*.

of evil in subjects of a religious nature; viewing them as if evil and destruction were incidental rather than inevitable in a mechanistic world. At the same time it was clear that Fascist principles, in varying degrees, offered some attraction for the poets and thinkers; [1] perhaps as presenting a clear-cut and pseudo-heroic solution which exalted the Hero in a new guise, without needing to summon either the energy or the intelligence to analyse his deficiencies. Only for Yeats the Irish Rising of 1916, and its aftermath in The Troubles, swung slowly into some sort of tragic perspective,[2] though darkened with prophecy as to the coming European catastrophe.[3] The Spanish Civil War might indeed be thought small enough in scope, sufficiently clear in its ideologies, and artistically distanced in time and space, to produce great tragedy; with a few exceptions,[4] neither its poets nor its novelists could free themselves from personal conflicts to achieve a satisfying work of art.

We may pause to reflect on the consequences of wars as they affect the tragic impulse. Among the most serious are, perhaps, an induration of the faculty of Pity, since some such protective hardening is necessary for the mere living under the mass impact of horror. And in any event Pity in modern war must be short lived, for the State may demand and enforce the iniquity of oblivion by its propaganda, for the sake of trade or of political regroupings. A prolonged or repeated impact deadens other virtues,[5] or exhausts their potency.[6] At the same time the sense of individual responsibility diminishes through the sheer mechanical conditions of a nation at modern war. In its complexity the individual is once again diminished in stature by the demands of the State; he knows that obedience to its precepts is the price of his survival.

Both to the Marxist and to the Christian the moral problem was re-presented in an acute form. The Marxist theory of history, while accepting an economic interpretation of the Fall, believed that man's main weakness lay in his corruption by the class struggle. To him the human struggle was not essentially tragic; its mystery was explicable

---

[1] 'I suspect that in our loathing for totalitarianism, there is infused a good deal of admiration for its efficiency.' T. S. Eliot, The Idea of a Christian Society, 1939.
[2] Easter 1916.   [3] The Second Coming.
[4] One being, perhaps, Hemingway's For Whom the Bell Tolls.
[5] Consider, for example, the very different reaction of London to the bombings of the autumn of 1940, and to those of the spring of 1941.
[6] 'I have supp'd full with horrors.' We may remember the progressive attempts of Jacobean tragedy to produce some kind of response through language and situations of increasing violence.

BLAKE: FAMINE

in ecological terms. He approved, at least implicitly, the statement of
John Stuart Mill:

> All the grand sources . . . of human suffering are in a great degree, many
> of them almost entirely, conquerable by human care and effort.[1]

The class conflict would rise to a climax through a catastrophe, and
thereby purge itself of evil. Afterwards it would move, without
catastrophe, towards a final state of perfection. And whatever economic
interpretations were imposed upon the fact of war, the fact contained
an inexplicable residue which appeared to be Nietzschean rather than
Marxist in character.

To the Christian the recurrent catastrophe presented an insoluble
problem, which has been expressed concisely by Reinhold Niebuhr:

> . . . the generation of a worse evil out of the ostensible elimination of a
> previous one proves that the question of historical evil had not been con-
> sidered profoundly enough.[2]

And Niebuhr, in the same pamphlet, laid down the condition under
which such historical processes might be perceived: anticipating in
some degree the work of Butterfield [3] ten years later:

> The religion of an individual or a generation is the ultimate principle of
> meaning by which men live. It is not a set of conclusions which they deduce
> from the observation of the facts of human life and existence, but the principle
> of interpretation which they use in interpreting the facts, and in trying to
> make them 'mean something', that is, comprehending them as a total unity.[4]

§ *iii*

The circle returns to the problem of Tragic Man in his relation to the
State. For material reasons he cannot offer effective resistance to its
claims upon him unless and until he becomes single-minded in his
adherence to an 'ultimate principle of meaning' within himself. It does
not seem likely that such a principle is to be recovered through classical
or scientific humanism. However strongly man may assert his faith
in these naïve approaches, or in the 'social sciences' upon which so
many hopes have been built, he is confronted both with the sheer
multiplicity of the collective experience, and of the residual fact of
evil which is not explicable in collective terms.

---

[1] *Utilitarianism*, Everyman Edn., p. 14.
[2] *Europe's Catastrophe and the Christian Faith* (1940), p. 12.
[3] In *Christianity and History*.   [4] *Europe's Catastrophe* . . . , p. 8.

The by-products of *accidie* and its allied vices in contemplating such problems are sufficiently well known:

> The world of the bored and especially the world of the frightened—the world of decadence—needs an *ersatz* type of spiritual adventure for the titillation of its inner life; and even more than that it needs 'spiritual revolutions' in order to avoid real ones and to side-track demands for social change.[1]

It is, perhaps, just such a lack of balance between thought and action —the balance that all great tragedy consciously or unconsciously preserves—that lies behind Existentialism. It is one of the curious ironies of history that the 'philosophy' owes its being, in large measure, to the French Resistance Movement. But its influence should not be underestimated, since many of its attitudes both derive from, and support, the peculiar political, strategical and economic conditions in which France finds herself. Albert Schweitzer has directed our attention to the cognate but larger issue:

> In modern European thought there is being enacted a tragedy, in that by a slow but irresistible process the bonds originally existing between world- and life-affirmation and the ethical are becoming slack and are finally being severed. The result that we are coming to is that European humanity is being guided to a will-to-progress that has become mainly external and has lost its bearings.
>
> World- and life-affirmation can produce of itself only a partial and imperfect civilization. Only if it becomes inward and ethical can the will-to-progress which results from it possess the insight to distinguish the valuable from the less valuable, and strive after a civilization which does not consist only in achievements of knowledge and power, but before all else will make men, both individually and collectively, more spiritual and more ethical.[2]

There remains the question of collective guilt of the State and its members for, during, and after a war; and here the metaphysical problem is sharpened by the facts of history. From the simplest point of view, guilt for the outbreak of war can be seen as focused upwards from the people to its oligarchy, and, in the last resort, to the leader of the group that takes the decision.[3] The Tyrant-King is responsible; as Henry V argues his own responsibility before Agincourt. The common soldier or the common people have no choice but to give a faint assent.

---

[1] Roger Garaudy, *Literature of the Graveyard*, p. 25.
[2] *My Life and Thought*, p. 181.
[3] But the spreading of guilt-responsibility among a committee or similar group raises special problems.

They are told that the safety, even the continued life of the State, demands it. An important writer on tragedy [1] argued in 1916 that the war was an abnormal impulse of the irrational in face of man's destiny as it was in process of emergence from the future. All such progress was inevitably accompanied by suffering and sacrifice. Man's ascent must be accompanied by the strange and gruesome shape of war. The irrational is unleashed;[2] the nation must deny its cultural heritage and rush into that hell. Its values are negative, a splitting of the ethical substance that is an outcome of the national struggle to live. Positive values might emerge out of a new life springing from the suffering; a life justified, and secured, by the safety of the State.

Writing after the war Volkelt denied specifically the possibility of collective guilt of a people, but postulated a collective guilt for all the warring nations of the West. (It is of interest to note that after neither was there any conception of responsibility among the conquered peoples; only a sense of grievance for their sufferings, and often a petulant complaint at the slowness of their rehabilitation by the victors. This fact constitutes the central problem—apart from the post-war quarrels of allies—of the indecisiveness, which seems likely to be emphasized in future, of all modern war.) Volkelt finds in this universal guilt responsibility for the tragedy of war. In the last resort its cause is to be sought in the dualism of human motive, in the dualism of the world and of the Absolute. In the very nature of the Absolute there is an intrinsic negative quality, which leads mankind through the excesses of the irrational if they are to reach the highest good.

Yet here is an insoluble dilemma. Without free-will there can be no question of guilt, for guilt is rooted in the very concept of free-will. Nations, says Volkelt, are driven perpetually to this irrational by the dialectic implicit in the world itself.

It seems unlikely that such a view is entirely acceptable in the philosophy of tragedy. To see in the world order the essential dualism is to resign oneself to a Nietzschean self-destructive pessimism. It is the easiest way out of the tragic dilemma of the State, and perhaps the only immediately available answer short of a Christian postulate. For I doubt whether any nation can avoid the imputation of collective guilt in the mere fact of waging war. The individual does, and can, evade responsibility by pleading obedience to higher orders, and by

---

[1] Volkelt, *op. cit.*, pp. 445 et seq.
[2] Compare Yeats's *The Second Coming*, the advent of the 'rough beast'. But the images of hounds unleashed, or of a hawk cast off, are also enlightening.

submerging primary ethical values by an appeal, often transitory in character, to the virtues of patriotism and loyalty. These in turn may be presented as absolute alternatives to annihilation. Yet there must ultimately be some individual in whom responsibility for the issue of the orders must rest, and there must be an individual duty to disobey such orders, even at the cost of one's own life, when the moral order is violated. It is true that the protest may come at differing points; and that in war the point of protest will always be lower in the moral scale than in peace. Volkelt and Niebuhr are both right in finding, as the basis of the situation, a collective rejection of Christian values: but the responsibility, the surrender of judgement of the individual is the tragic *schwerpunkt*.

For the problem of Tragedy and the State is no more than the problem of collective man, awakened to a new consciousness, seeking desperately to adjust himself to his environment. In that setting his dominant obsession is fear:

> We were afraid, and fear has left its mark upon us. Afraid of dying, afraid of dying as individuals, afraid of dying as a nation, afraid of dying as a universe. And the shadow of that fear still lies on us; we are haunted by a terrible dread, explicable but unjustifiable, and dangerous for what may be the results. We believe that, if our civilization were to die, it would be the end of all civilization. We forget that our own death, however tragic, can mean no more than the dawn of a day we shall not see.[1]

Such a view, however morally creditable, is not likely to win more than an intellectual assent, for the fear can never be submerged entirely because of its roots in the irrational and supra-rational. It is perhaps in this refusal to acknowledge and harness these forces that the main weakness of dialectical materialism lies. The naïveté of its claims can be summed up with admirable clarity (in so far as they affect our present problem) by two quotations:

> A synthesis of the contradictions of bourgeois economy having come into being, these contradictions [capitalism *vs.* the exploited proletariat] are now revealed nakedly as truth and error. Bourgeois philosophy now becomes sterile dualism, and it is proletarian philosophy or Marxism which is dialectic. But because it is the task of the proletariat, arising from the mode of their generation, to solve the problems of human relations and of the gulf between knowing and being, Marxism is more than a philosophy, it is a sociology. It

[1] Pierre Bertaux. *The Intellectual and Action.* (*Reflections on Our Age*, ed. Hardman, p. 45.)

is a theory of the concrete society in which philosophy, and other forms of ideology are generated.[1]

The human mind and its environment are locked in an inexorable determinism:

> To rise beyond Hegel's idealistic synthesis, one must see that the mind in its turn is determined by social relations, that knowing is a mutually determining relation between subject and object, that freedom is not accident but the consciousness of necessity. One must see that if freedom for a man in society is the attainment of individual desires, it involves conscious co-operation with others to obtain them, and that this conscious co-operation will itself transform a man's desires. To see this is to cease to be a bourgeois, and to cease to tolerate bourgeois economy. One is already a communist revolutionary.[2]

The Marxist is thus committed to a tragic struggle in a world in which mind is dependent upon environment, and in which desires are modified by the act of satisfying them. Even though thought and will may be private and personal, they become social as soon as they are formulated into a public system of thought.[3]

In this struggle the operative object is the fulfilment of desire: desire conceived on a materialist basis, but subject to modification by environment and by the social contract reached among the proletariat in the course of their warfare, and as a result of their co-operation. We have thus a promise of a kind of mass tragedy, of the material will seeking to achieve its satisfaction through the annihilation of its opponents, whose term *bourgeois* carries a heavy emotive charge. The Marxist is driven to his war by an avowed series of attitudes as striking as those of any Elizabethan 'Malcontent', and expressed in terms hardly less rhetorical:

> To have become a dialectical materialist is to have been subject to exploitation, want, war, anxiety, insecurity; to have had one's barest human needs denied or one's loved ones tormented or killed in the name of bourgeois liberty, and to have found that one's 'free-will' alone can do nothing at all, because one is more bound and crippled in bourgeois economy than a prisoner in a dungeon—and to have found that in this condition the only thing that can secure alleviation is co-operation with one's fellow-men in the same dungeon, the world's exploited proletariat.[4]

There are echoes here.

[1] Christopher Caudwell, *Studies in a Dying Culture*, p. 255.
[2] *Ibid.*   [3] *Ibid.*, pp. 247 et seq.
[4] *Ibid., op. cit.*, p. 256.

Guildenstern. Prison, my lord!

Hamlet. Denmark's a prison.

Rosencrantz. Then is the world one.

Hamlet. A goodly one; in which there are many confines, wards, and dungeons, Denmark being one o' the worst.

Rosencrantz. We think not so, my lord.

Hamlet. Why, then, 'tis none to you; for there is nothing either good or bad, but thinking makes it so: to me it is a prison.

Rosencrantz. Why then, your ambition makes it one: 'tis too narrow for your mind.[1]

The protagonists in the tragic revolution of the world will thus be groups dominated by self-interest: their philosophies respectively some form of Idealism on the part of the 'bourgeois' world *vs*. the Marxist's dialectical materialism. Man as an individual is submerged in a collective mass, actuated by self-interest of the least interesting types: concerned only to defend his property, or to establish himself in a position of impregnable security as to his material life. The individual with his complexities of mire and blood is flattened and compressed to a hypothetical mass mind. It is a conflict of terror, but a kind of flattened exhausted terror, in which the fate of the individual has neither extension nor significance, only a wild self-preservation in which all kind of moral codes are broken without remorse.[2] It will not be a tragedy that will offer any view of the world, precisely because it can never be distanced from the individual nor mirrored in his sympathy with others. It cannot appeal to history or to ritual; it can only look forward to the arid Utopia of a collective self-interest, in obedience to the values imposed on the individual from without.

[1] II. ii. 244.
[2] 'There is no terror and no pity in [Spengler's] acceptance of Destiny, but merely a conscious decision for the false values; and this is the classical decision of sin and wickedness.' Erich Heller, *The Disinherited Mind*, p. 152.

CHAPTER 21

Death in Tragedy

and it is great
To do that thing that ends all other deeds,
Which shackles accidents, and bolts up change,
Which sleeps, and never palates more the dug,
The beggar's nurse, and Caesar's.
Antony and Cleopatra [1]

—Only the dead can be forgiven,
But when I think of that my tongue's a stone.
YEATS [2]

Go, knock at the gates of the tombs and ask the dead to come back to life;
they will shake their heads with a gesture of refusal.
SCHOPENHAUER

§ *i*

IN most of the tragedies of the world's literature it is assumed that death is a natural termination of the tragic fact or experience. The Greek drama assumed, at least in its less pessimistic moments, that it was the supreme misfortune, to which man came, prematurely, through his error or frailty. In other drama it is rare to find 'misfortune' in the formal pattern of tragedy without its conclusion in death. Of all experiences death has the highest emotional potential; though I shall argue later that, of all the social references of tragedy, it is the one that has changed most strikingly within the past forty years. We must consider the conditions of this emotional stimulus, and its historical modifications.

In the first place death is the most satisfactory terminal point from the point of view of the tragic pattern. The circuit closes; the dramatist will emphasize, to a greater or lesser extent, the turning of the new page, the affirmation of new values, the revolution of the wheel. Such new values are often certified, as it were, by recalling the heroic qualities of the dead, in whom evil has been expiated. This celebration is now largely a social convention, probably of steadily-diminishing significance. We have forgotten the origins of such gestures in the placating of the ghost.

[1] v. ii. 4.   [2] *A Dialogue of Self and Soul.*

But it is clear that the emotions attaching to death in tragedy are highly complex. It may be convenient to divide them into two groups, though I believe that the two ultimately merge.

Anthropology tells us [1] that the death of the king or hero has a perpetual ritual significance, conscious or unconscious, with two main aspects or values. He dies because there is concentrated upon him, as symbol, the necessities of the Birth and Resurrection cycle of the year. He dies, often, in his prime, because his virtues (courage, strength and so forth) must not be impaired by old age; perhaps because of the belief that the souls of those who die in battle are purer than those who die of disease.[2] The violence of the death has probably a number of functions from the emotive point of view; blood still cries from the ground in a fashion that does not (except after long hardening through usage) lend itself to rational contemplation, and it seems likely that some dark satisfaction co-exists side by side with the horror.

But he is also the scapegoat, to whom the sins of his people, or of some of the audience, are transferred.[3] We remember the example of the criminals made king for a day, only to suffer death for this very reason: and the act of the Crucifixion may be perceived as a triple ritual sacrifice.[4] The rapid spread of Christianity in the Mediterranean Basin has been attributed to its origin in such common rituals and its symbolic perpetuation of them.

Civilized man appears to swing the balance towards the theme of sorrow and loss rather than fear. There is a certain decorum in the eulogy of the dead, in tragedy as in civilized life. We are quieted by a death so noble: we praise the victims: the funeral procession, whatever its dramatic necessity on the Elizabethan stage, remains a powerful emotional device: enhanced by the symbolism, crude but not always fully perceived, of the torch-bearers who accompany the bier.[5] The coffin, variously used, can either be a noble symbol [6] or a mere morbid fixation as with Donne; one of Webster's characters, considering a pie, thinks of the fowls as 'coffin'd in bak'd meats'. The remembrance of the hero's virtues is in part, no doubt, an ancient ritual to avert evil or placate the ghost, in part a desire to comfort the bereaved; but good

---

[1] The classic expositions are perhaps in *The Dying King* and *The Scapegoat* of *The Golden Bough*.

[2] The belief is perhaps more common still than might be supposed. Consider Wilfred Owen's *Into Battle*.

[3] See Chapter 8.   [4] *The Scapegoat*.

[5] The ending of *Coriolanus* may become particularly effective by this device.

[6] We may instance the symbolism of Roman Catholicism in the funeral service; and the experience, now uncommon, of keeping watch over a coffin through the night.

DELACROIX: OPHELIA'S GRAVE

may be spoken the more easily when there is an acute sense of relief. 'Only the dead can be forgiven.'

These two antinomies of grief and rejoicing exist simultaneously, in anthropology and (however disguised) in man's consciousness to-day. It is part of the tragic pattern that this latter emotion, in itself mixed unequally, should not become apparent in speech or action. The ritual must be observed. It is an aspect of our debt to the dead before the wheel revolves again. And the attitude is so delicate that it can be destroyed by a false step on the part of the dramatist. To a modern audience Caesar's glance at the bodies of Antony and Cleopatra

> If they had swallow'd poison 'twould appear
> By external swelling.[1]

—seems to us full of bathos, however in keeping with the keen-eyed efficiency of Caesar: yet it is doubtful whether a Jacobean would have checked at it. But when Shaw, in the Epilogue to *St Joan*, makes Joan say:

> Woe unto me when all men praise me! I bid you remember that I am a saint, and that saints can work miracles. And now tell me: shall I rise from the dead, and come back to you a living woman?

—he has shattered into fragments the whole tragic ritual. This is of course done deliberately, in keeping with the Hegelian presuppositions contained in the play and its Preface. In *Ghosts*, the emotional effect of the living death of Oswald set against the symbolism of the rising sun (in itself counterparted by the burning of the hospital in Captain Alving's foundation) is sufficient to render unnecessary further torments of destruction.

It is a commonplace of our thought that the changes of emphasis in Christian dogma never modified the moral and physical fear of death. The logic of the medieval Church, but not the emotion of its people, made a tragic dualism impossible. So far as may be judged from the funeral monuments, the Graeco-Roman civilization contemplated death with a distilled purity of loss, and the dignity proper to both tongues. The gloom of Hades, the hunger and thirst of the ghost, the vigorous joy in life in the present, were sufficiently simple explanations, and there is no need to explore the manifold versions and visions of the Underworld. But with the Renaissance, the Reformation with its immense oscillating tides, and the New Philosophy, the macabre side

[1] v. ii. 392.

of the Church's teaching found a soil even more fertile than that of
the fourteenth century with its emphasis on the suffering Christ,[1]
the Stigmata, the ever-recurrent motif of the skull, juxtaposed with the
hermit, saint, or marriage ceremony.[2] These continue long into the
seventeenth century, till they are replaced by the nobler symbolism of
the urn and the flame; and their dramatic handling in Elizabethan and
Jacobean drama reveals not only the differing tact of the dramatists
but also the emotional backgrounds of their audiences.

Now the current of death-imagery, oscillating as it does between
Christianity and paganism, can be traced with reasonable clarity be-
tween the fifteenth and nineteenth centuries. Our anthology pieces
would probably include Dunbar's *Lament for the Makaris*, Bishop King's
Exequy, Nathaniel Wanley's *The Skull*, Blair's *Grave*, extracts from
the Gothick romances, Poe's decadent romanticism, and *In Memoriam*.
Such an anthology would be fittingly illustrated from Dürer, Holbein,
Domenico Feti (and a host of contemporaries), Hogarth, Blake, Fuseli,
Landseer, Richard Hughes, and Watts. But we should find in all these,
and in the selection of elegies to fill the intermediate points, a fairly
consistent pattern in the attitudes displayed:

1. A strong faith, real or apparent, in the 'good end', or the holy
   death.
2. A perception of the grave as a meeting place of lover and beloved;
   whether or not such a meeting had a strictly orthodox religious
   background.
3. A fear of judgement, following closely the changes in dogmatic
   theology, the sectarian differences, and the succession of religious
   revivals.
4. A strong and complex tradition of *les pompes funèbres*: in which
   pity, awe, pride, and grief are blended in various proportions.

   Equally, the lack of such—the unknown or foreign grave,[3] the
   'pathetick' funeral,[4] the animal in its fidelity [5]—are powerful
   emotional stimulants.

---

[1] I accept, in broad outline, the best account I know: in Theodore Spencer's *Death and Elizabethan Tragedy*.
[2] I have in mind Lucas de Heere's painting in the Dulwich Gallery, itself a superb commentary on the psychological connections, direct and oblique, between Love and Death.
[3] Macaulay's *A Jacobite's Epitaph* is a good example.
[4] As in Hogarth's *Harlot's Funeral*.
[5] We may consider, at opposite poles, Landseer's *The Old Shepherd's Chief Mourner* and Hardy's poem *Who is that digging on my grave?*

§ ii

It is, I think, possible to date the change in attitude at about 1915–16: in relation to the losses at Gallipoli, Ypres, the Somme. (It will be remembered that a corresponding change from exultation to cynicism is apparent in the poetry of the First War.) Death, being multiple and remote, becomes from the family point of view a little unreal: and by the time the war cemeteries can be visited the edge of grief is gone.[1] Death in battle is a 'queer untidy thing',[2] intensified in that quality by the demands of static warfare. For the same reason a new *macabre* appears to grow up and become accepted as a natural safety-valve against the pressure of physical horror, so that we get something which appears to be exactly opposite to that of Jacobean drama, where horror is often invoked as a direct and fortuitous stimulant, made from the teeth outward. The kissing of a poisoned skull is revolting to the verge of the ridiculous: the ritual of a certain company in the front line in 1917 by which each man shook the hand of a dead body built into the revetments as they came in on relief is far nearer the Shakespearian *macabre*, used legitimately to express and to relieve through laughter an unendurable tension.

In the period following the end of the war the change in tradition seems to have become permanent, except for the ceremony required for the great. The increasing acceptance of cremation,[3] the speed of the motor hearse, considerations of expense, are all contributory factors, particularly among the upper classes. Among less civilized peoples or even less civilized social ranks, the tradition of the *pompes funèbres* with their nominal Christian ritual partially distorted in the direction of either a frank paganism or a benevolently neutral pseudo-religiosity, still persists.[4] And there is some ground for arguing that a new senti-mentality both unbalanced and morbid, that has grown up towards the animal kingdom, is a typical emotional compensation for our atrophied power of response to human suffering.

The effect of this on death-attitudes in the tragic experience is of some importance. Our 'recognition' of death has become more

---

[1] Kipling's story *The Gardener* may be recalled.

[2] Synge's words in *Deirdre*; contrast Tennyson's *Home they brought her warrior dead* . . .

[3] It seems likely that cremation itself cuts out, because of its speed, tidiness, and 'finality', some of the traditional, and perhaps healthy, response to the fact of loss.

[4] We may take as examples a funeral at Naples, with its ritual prescribed even to the colour of the hearses; and certain American customs as described, for instance, in the mortician's journals or in Evelyn Waugh's *The Loved One*. By 'benevolently neutral' I mean the non-denominational non-committal arrangements of, say, crematorium chapels.

hurried, even furtive, less of a ritual, without allowance for the period of mourning in which the wheel starts, slowly, to achieve its new momentum. Traditional tragedy still carries its emotional effect unimpaired; the tact with which Shakespeare manages his elegiac *epodi* can still be perceived. The carrying-in of Bartley's body in *Riders to the Sea* is perceived as repetition of a formal ritual; the emotional effect of Antigone's death in Anouilh's play is reinforced by the double symbolism of the Cave in which she is immured. But in general the effect of the social processes which I have described suggests a decreasing emphasis on death as a terminal point, in overwhelming grief, and the irreparable loss of a central figure. It is perhaps significant that only one great elegy has been written in the twentieth century,[1] and that by the Last Romantic.

Now it may well be that there has been some general gain in all this. We have jettisoned a good deal of sentimentality, and something of the hysteria of grief by which the living nourish their own ego-centric emotions under pretext of mourning, or attempt some shameful compensation for injury or neglect:

> Only the dead can be forgiven;
> But when I think of that my tongue's a stone.

§ iii

At the same time I cannot but think that something has been lost of the force of modern tragedy, unless it can recapture and use for its purposes the fitting and traditional ritual of death. If there is to be any artistic rounding off of that time sequence, I do not see how it can be effective except through this means. For it is not only a terminal point in the aesthetic experience; it is the only ritual that can mirror the complexity of emotions that seek psychological expression at this precise point. We may speculate on some of these emotions that seem to recur: relief from cumulative tensions; a new hope that is made possible by the symbol of the burial of the past; a curiosity as to the departure of the soul upon its progress (and this need not necessarily be morbid); a common feeling that in the presence of death we are, momentarily, 'better', perhaps more open to the numinous; that we are spectators of that in which we must, one day, be the actors; and even that a mysterious wisdom or clarity of vision is the property of the dying, and that those at the death-bed may in some sort share it.

[1] Yeats, *In Memory of Major Robert Gregory.*

This group of emotions may be thought of as receiving a cumulative sanction in time. In Greek tragedy the hero is thought of, to some extent, as having a continued potency in the grave, and may become the subject of a hero-cult. He may prophesy destruction, as does the agèd Oedipus, of the battle to come:

> Upon that day my buried dust that sleeps
> Cold in the grave, shall drink their steaming carnage.[1]

The *mana* of the hero is still powerful; he may be a kind of guardian or talisman of the land, as well as the exemplar of virtue or of *hubris*. In many of the tragic farewells the 'Remember me!' of the ghost is echoed in the elegiac ritual of its close; as if indeed this faint potency of the bloodless ghost is the only immortality which can comfort it. Yet the thought of death, as always, touches the lips with fire; and Juliet's words but follow those of Antigone:

> O tomb, O bridal-chamber, prison-house
> Deep-delved, sure-guarded ever, whither I
> Go gathered to my kin—that multitude
> Persephone hath numbered with her dead!
> Last of them all, of all most miserably,
> I too must follow, half my life unspent.
> And yet I trust to find a welcome there.[2]

From the point of view of the spectator, there is a strong emotional movement in the direction of a complete moral exoneration. The price has been paid, whatever crimes or follies the hero, or any tragic player, has committed. The deed is removed beyond judgement, or at least distanced until the new order has had time to root itself, and the hero's deeds have become part of the historical cycle. The death is perceived as an atonement calling down, and diffusing, something that might be called grace. And at the same time the tradition brings the hero into line with the historical past of all ages, imposing on him a kind of timelessness. The last speeches of *Samson Agonistes* sum up many of these matters:

> *Semichorus.* But he though blind of sight,
> Despis'd and thought extinguish't quite,
> With inward eyes illuminated
> His fiery virtue rous'd
> From under ashes into sudden flame,

---

[1] *Oedipus at Colonos*, l. 620. Transl. F. L. Lucas.
[2] *Antigone*, l. 890. Transl. F. L. Lucas.

> And as an ev'ning Dragon came,
> Assailant on the perched roosts,
> And nests in order rang'd
> Of tame villatic Fowl; but as an Eagle
> His cloudless thunder bolted on thir heads.
> So virtue giv'n up for lost,
> Deprest, and overthrown, as seem'd
> Like that self-begott'n bird
> In the Arabian woods embost,
> That no second knows nor third,
> And lay ere while a Holocaust,
> From out her ashy womb now teem'd
> Revives, reflourishes, then vigorous most
> When most unactive deem'd.
> And though her body die, her fame survives,
> A secular bird of ages lives.

The long decorative excursion on the Phoenix, from one point of view cumbrous and artificial, is designed to provide just this slowing down expansion and re-alignment of Samson's death into a mythology of its own. Manoa continues:

> Come, come, no time for lamentation now,
> Nor much more cause: Samson hath quit himself
> Like Samson, and heroicly hath finish'd
> A life Heroic, on his Enemies
> Fully reveng'd, hath left them years of mourning,
> And lamentation to the sons of Caphtor
> Through all Philistian bounds: to Israel
> Honour hath left, and freedom, let but them
> Find courage to lay hold on this occasion;
> To himself and Father's house eternal fame:
> And which is best and happiest yet, all this
> With God not parted from him, as was fear'd,
> But favouring and assisting to the end.

There follows the famous passage; it is well to recall it together with the succeeding lines:

> Nothing is here for tears, nothing to wail
> Or knock the breast, no weakness, no contempt,
> Dispraise, or blame, nothing but well and fair,
> And what may quiet us in a death so noble.
> Let us go find the body where it lies
> Soak't in his enemies' blood, and from the stream

With lavers pure and cleansing herbs wash off
The clotted gore. I with what speed the while
(Gaza is not in plight to say us nay)
Will send for all my kindred, all my friends
To fetch him hence and solemnly attend
With silent obsequy and funeral train
Home to his Father's house; there will I build him
A Monument, and plant it round with shade
Of Laurel ever green, and branching Palm,
With all his Trophies hung, and Acts enroll'd
In copious Legend, or sweet Lyric Song.

The epic element, the pride of achieved revenge, and the ceremonial of
the obsequies, combine to distance Samson's death, and to place it in
a peculiarly exalted and familiar setting. We may contrast it with the
weakness of Theophilus' dying speech at the end of Massinger's *The
Virgin-Martyr*:

> I am confirmed,
> Confirmed, you blessèd spirits, and make haste
> To take that crown of immortality
> You offer to me. Death! till this blest minute,
> I never thought thee slow-paced; nor could I
> Hasten thee now, for any pain I suffer,
> But that thou keep'st me from a glorious wreath,
> Which through this stormy way I would creep to,
> And, humbly kneeling, with humility wear it.
> Oh! now I feel thee:—blessèd spirits! I come;
> And, witness for me all these wounds and scars,
> I die a soldier in the Christian wars.

It is not merely the pedestrian rhythm and the hackneyed imagery that
makes Massinger so insipid compared—in so far as comparison is
possible—with Milton. In the submission and humility of the hero
there is a kind of betrayal of the tragic ethos. Is it possible that one
element of the death-resolution demands for our satisfaction this
defiance of the gods, this alignment and unification with history, a
kind of epic challenge? The Hero's record is proud and notable:

> —And in the harsh world draw thy breath in pain
> To tell my story.

And he is concerned that he shall win some healing of his wounded
name, some sort of immortality in the celebrations of men, with perhaps the medieval thought of the *exempla* of his story. 'Reputation'

lies close to the surface of the mind of the tragic hero, for it is of his essence, his dramatic dominance beyond the tomb. The last reduction of this characteristic, trembling on the verge of the absurd, may be seen in the *Death of a Salesman*.[1] We might indeed argue that this aspect of the tragic death is in some sort anti-Christian. Humility and the certainty of balances redressed in the next world negative one part at least of that steel-cored pride, the appeal to unregenerate man, that lies at the heart of our sympathy with the hero. He has erred or sinned; the wheel returns; he meets that fate with a pride which is of a peculiar kind: it is the direct and inevitable projection of his undefinable 'greatness'. To give way to fear, or to submerge fear in the certainty of a martyr's crown, are alien to him. Yet, since the tragic appeal is to men like ourselves, this final recognition of this unregenerate component appears necessary to produce the highest exaltation. They 'do not break up their lines to weep', for their virtues are of another quality; nearer to manhood than to godhead, yet creating and communicating a value that may be the complement of Christian humility: 'mine own arm brought salvation unto me; and my fury it upheld me'.[2]

§ *iv*

The elegiac formulation of sorrow, plucking what berries it sees fit to adorn or nourish its verse, has the effect of enlarging, universalizing, stabilizing; both as regards its original quality of sorrow, and its transmutation into the historical past. When no such continuity is proper the death is sudden, violent, a mere episode at the end; though something like an apologia may precede that death, as Ivanov's last speech in Chekhov's play of that name. Perhaps the ending is in some measure conditioned by the social conventions and mechanics of the modern theatre. But if the statement of the tragedy is in the main poetical, the elegiac relief appears to be essential. The Song of Callicles at the end of Arnold's *Empedocles on Etna* is effective: still more so, because of its archetypal significance, the River Image at the end of the tragedy of *Sohrab and Rustum*. As a ritual ending we may quote the end of *The King's Threshold*; showing how the traditional carrying-forth of the body can still be accompanied with superbly effective lyric, and how the old symbols can be given new vitality:

Oldest Pupil.   Take up his body,
            And cry, that driven from the populous door,

[1] Arthur Miller.   [2] *Isaiah*, lxiii. 5.

> He seeks high waters and the mountain birds
> To claim a portion of their solitude.[1]
>> (*They make a litter with cloak and staffs or use one discovered,*
>> *heaped with food, at the opening of the play.*)
> *Youngest Pupil.* And cry that when they took his ancient right
> They took all common sleep; therefore he claims
> The mountain for his mattress and his pillow.

and, in the last movement—

> O silver trumpets, be you lifted up
> And cry to the great race that is to come.
> Long-throated swans upon the waves of time,
> Sing loudly, for beyond the wall of the world
> That race may hear our music and awake.
> *Oldest Pupil* (*motioning the musicians to lower their trumpets*).
> Not what it leaves behind it in the light
> But what it carries with it to the dark
> Exalts the soul; nor song nor trumpet blast
> Can call up races from the worsening world
> To mend the wrong and mar the solitude
> Of the great shade we follow to the tomb.[2]

Or the high speech and the terse commonplace can be blended, as in the ending of Synge's *Deirdre of the Sorrows*; in spite of, or because of, the echoes:

Fergus. Four white bodies are laid down together; four clear lights are quenched in Ireland. (*He throws his sword into the grave.*) There is my sword that could not shield you—my four friends that were the dearest always. The flames of Emain have gone out: Deirdre is dead, and there is none to keen her. That is the fate of Deirdre and the children of Usna, and for this night, Conchubor, our war is ended. (*He goes out.*)

Lavercham. I have a little hut where you can rest, Conchubor; there is a great dew falling.

Conchubor (*with the voice of an old man*). Take me with you. I'm hard set to see the way before me.

Old Woman. This way, Conchubor.

Lavercham (*beside the grave*). Deirdre is dead, and Naisi is dead; and if the oaks and stars could die for sorrow, it's a dark sky and a hard and naked earth we'd have this night in Emain.

It is a central paradox of the tragic experience that this contemplative

---

[1] Compare the bird-images in the passage quoted from *Samson Agonistes*.
[2] *C.P.*, p. 143.

awe, built out of the elegiac mood, can be the final solvent of
all anxiety. Like the Church's great hymn, the *Dies Irae*, it works by
alternations of hope and dread, yet the swan-elegy ends with a sense
of exaltation, conquest, a blend of pride and humility, a sense of the
vastness of the forces of the universe, of man's helplessness and intrinsic
splendour, 'with inward eyes illuminated'. Perhaps the difficulty that
so many have felt in considering a tragic 'philosophy' to-day lies in
the absence of any elegiac modulation of the tragic statement. The
guillotine ending, the pistol-shot on or off stage, the quick curtain at
the height of the emotional pitch, and the hurried exit after inconsequential music, all contribute to an unsatisfactory emotional turbulence. There is no need for the elegiac ending to be 'pure', or a formal
set piece. It can be at its most effective when the minute particulars, the
trivialities that can carry so much, are woven into it. Lear's

> Prithee, undo this button

Creon called to a cabinet meeting at the end of Anouilh's *Antigone*, are
as legitimate in their kind as the Chorus from the *Hippolytus* or from
Samson, or that weeping gaiety that is half-hysteria underlying
Charmian's

> Downy windows, close;
> And golden Phoebus never be beheld
> Of eyes again so royal! Your crown's awry;
> I'll mend it, and then play.[1]

I believe that tragedy must show, and must recover when it has lost,
the traditional attitudes to death: that the great tragic endings are, in
the last analysis, the supreme assertions of a unity, a resolution of
conflict, that can be terminated in no other way: yet paradoxically not
a terminal, but projecting, out of the re-unification which it suggests,
the sense of continuity and re-birth. I do not find this in conflict with
the Christian hope of immortality: rather as of a lesser order, but in
some sense complementary to that doctrine—always excepting the
Crucifixion—and breaking the response to tragedy (when it does) only
by the clumsiness, vulgarity, or poetic ineptitude [2] with which it is
stated. A verse from *The Wreck of the Deutschland* may make this
clearer:

> Ah! there was a heart right!
> There was single eye!

[1] v. ii. 316.
[2] We might instance this from O'Neill's *Strange Interlude*: 'Yes, our lives are merely
strange dark interludes in the electrical display of God the Father.'

Read the unshapeable shock night
And knew the who and the why,
Wording it how but by him that present and past,
Heaven and earth are word of, worded by?—
The Simon Peter of a soul! to the blast
Tarpeian-fast, but a blown beacon of light.

For the tragic resolution in its highest form is aware of immortality in a sense to which many Christians would now assent:

Our 'self', as the container of our whole living system, includes not only all the deposits, and the sum of all that has been lived in the past, but is also the starting-point, the pregnant mother earth, from which all future life will spring; the presentiment of things to come is known to our inner feeling as clearly as is the historical past. The idea of immortality which arises from these psychological fundamentals is quite legitimate.[1]

[1] Jung, *Die Beziehung zwischen dem Ich und dem Unbewussten. Cit.* Victor White, *God and the Unconscious,* p. 261.

CHAPTER 22

Symposium in the Theatre

AT this point it seemed useful, before attempting to gather the threads of this discussion into some pattern, to consider the possibilities of checking our speculations by the practical response of some selected tragic auditors. A number of men, chosen from among different age groups and of widely-differing backgrounds, were invited to set down their response to tragedy; either generally, as to the form, or in relation to a specific work either seen or read. Not all were 'professional' students of literature, nor had they always a background of reading in tragic theory.

Each contributor is denoted by a letter; which is followed by a number giving his age at the time of writing. Where any statement appears to be of special interest in relation to what is said earlier or later in the book, or is supported or contradicted by other contributors, a reference is made in a footnote. The italics are mine.

§ *i*

A. 32. To speak truth, I've been in such a welter of conflicting opinions that I doubted if I could produce a coherent picture of tragedy that was also consistent with what one knew of tragedy. 'A spirit passed before my face: the hair of my flesh stood up . . .' [1]—that doesn't help much except to suggest that one's personal reaction is so instinctive as to make one despair of ever formulating that reaction in intellectual terms.

One thing I have observed which has led me on to other conjectures, namely the absolute isolation of the tragic protagonist. Whatever one thinks of Mrs Alving, Hedda or Rosmer, at one end of the scale, or Shakespearean tragic heroes, or Antigone, Electra and Oedipus at the other, they are all alone . . .

The protagonist makes a journey into tragic reality and this has to be made alone, since neither the experience nor the nature of his perception can be shared by the other characters who are involved. Is it not also true—and illuminating—that the spectator or auditor is also alone with the tragic

---

[1] 'A', as will be observed, has a strong Christian background. His sense of the numinous appears elsewhere.

characters he sees or hears? You will recall Johnson: 'He that peruses Shake-speare looks around alarmed, and starts to find himself alone.' [1] And does not this constitute a fundamental difference between Tragedy, which remains to be defined, and Comedy, which is a social activity?

I take this 'aloneness' to be the essence of Aristotle's *terror*—and to this extent the term seems to me to have a general application to tragedy. One can, I think, journey further on these lines. For instance, the nature of the tragic experience is at first sight, chaotic. Chaos does, in fact, come again; and now, God-like, the tragic hero is forced to re-create order, a new order, out of chaos before he meets his doom. Incidentally, Webster's characters consistently fail to do this,[2] to achieve this equilibrium,[3] which is why I think he fails as a tragedian. The terror of the first part of this cycle is nowhere more poignantly caught than in Lear's determination

O let me not be mad, not mad, sweet heaven

This is his Gethsemane.

To the extent that one is alone with the protagonist in his tragic experience what might (I suggest) issue in spirits less finely touched as self-pity is trans-muted into the nobler emotion of pity directed away from the centre of self towards the tragic hero. This I'm sure does happen if the play, and the performance, is fine enough. (Forgive the personal evidence that Devlin's 'Lear' moved me to quite unashamed tears.)

The difficulty about the nature of the individual, personal tragic experience I take to be this: it is clear that the experience of 'chaos-come-again' is *intensely personal* [4] and that its nature cannot be explicably stated. Thus the dramatist has resort, almost invariably, I think—to symbolism and imagery. Think of the complexity of symbol, the welter of imagery in, for example, Shakespeare and Ibsen, or, for that matter, Yeats. This is the fire through which the tragic hero passes.[5] Its nature is, I think, that of a mystical ex-perience *only truly comprehensible by others with the same order of experience,*[6] yet still capable of utterance at a level of poetry which, while it taxes to the utmost the resources of the auditor, may take him to the very brink of the experience itself.

And resolution is, it seems to me, achieved in utter and lovely simplicity.[7] What is gained is perspective, a new order of a strictly personal kind, a perception, if you will allow it, of the nature of things as they may seem

[1] *Preface to Shakespeare.*   [2] Agreed. But why, exactly?
[3] Probably he is thinking of Ellis-Fermor's essay in *The Frontiers of Drama.*
[4] It may well be that the definition of what constitutes the chaos has grown steadily more personal since Elizabethan times; when there was at least a consensus of opinion as to what constituted *order.*
[5] Perhaps *A* perceives the *interior* conflict as expressible only in these 'images'.
[6] Here he raises a vital problem.
[7] Almost certainly he is thinking of the cadenced-endings of *Lear, Antony and Cleopatra, The Cenci.*

from a distance, denied to those, who, like the tragic hero, are condemned to live among the fever and the fret.

When the tragic storm blows itself out, order is restored. The damaged tissues of life re-knit, and the cycle of normality—'birth, copulation and death' begins again, probably because the necessary sacrifice has been made. (*I think that the essential sterility that prevails during the tragic phase is worth noting.*) That we are regenerate, so to speak, is important to us, the audience, rather than to the tragic hero, since we must somehow be released to return to those levels of existence which we normally inhabit. The tragic hero, of course, has already won his release, and has effectively added to the sum total of human wisdom [1] by bearing witness to an order that is above the chaos which has begun the cycle of destruction. Incidentally, I think it dangerous to identify the chaos with evil—as some do—since on the evidence of *Lear*, to say nothing of others, that is the nature of the cosmos itself.

And we, the audience? Well, Aristotle was right enough, I think, to postulate Pity and Terror (would not 'Dread' be a better word as having specific connotations [2])—Pity transmuted to a universal; terror, or dread, in the face of what is possibly the nearest that many of us are likely to approach to the Godhead.[3] And I wonder whether the statement 'whosoever will lose his life shall find it' has not some bearing on the problem.

This reflects back again on the dramatist, too. Shakespeare has, I feel sure (like Sophocles), experienced the tragic storm and emerged on the other side.

Neither Webster nor Tourneur gives this impression. *And Ibsen never seems to me to emerge from the chaos of his own experience, which is why I think he is almost always his own tragic protagonist, the catharsis never achieved—like D. H. Lawrence in another genre. His experience is never reduced to that releasing order that constitutes a statement of hope and not despair.*[4]

§ *ii*

Against this we may set a more clear-cut and limited response, which lends some support to the 'joyful safety' idea.[5]

B. *23*. After seeing a tragedy I want to seek company of some sort, either in conversation or in writing enthusiastically. None of the subjects mentioned needs necessarily to be connected with the tragic theme. This seems to me a heightened version of the mental stimulus I possess after a game of chess or bridge. Rarely do I feel 'This could have happened to me'—I think this is because although the events may resemble actual life, the conative part of

---

[1] We must, of course, question this, or explain it.

Probably we want a word between Fear and Dread, yet with |strongly religious overtones.

[3] Consider Karl Barth and Otto on this subject.

[4] This is a remark of considerable acuteness, and probably contains the clue, if we could carry the analysis further, to explain the 'inadequate' tragedy.

[5] See p. 14, *ante*.

my sensations is cut off, since I am not an actual participant but a *spectator abstracted from the action and sitting securely in my theatre seat*.[1] Tragedy on the stage never seems to produce in me any sense of the confusion which results from the necessity for immediate action (*though I often feel this after a good and moving sermon*),[2] and thus [3] the resulting emotions are clear but not strong; I can identify myself vicariously with the pity and terror of the action in the knowledge that I can 'unhook' myself when I want to. *The combination of imaginative and actual life produces a loquacity and relieves my mind by compelling me to discuss any subject I can, often flippantly.*[4] I feel this too after many pieces of music and *especially after an opera*, but I rarely want to indulge in tumultuous applause, only to talk. If the subject is the tragedy itself, this is purely coincidental.

C. *22* is brief and definite; for him the tragic experience is a general extension of sensibility. He owes a good deal to Wordsworth.

For myself there are two main reactions that are uppermost in my experience of tragedy.

Primarily I experience a sense of vision, a feeling of harmony within myself extending consciously outwards; a sense of vision that is a frequent reaction to all great art. It is partly, no doubt, a sense of 'thusness'; a note is struck in the mind and the spirit that opens a door, and perhaps it could be merely a mathematical delight in the particularly and triumphantly apt.[5] I think it is more than this. It is not the content of the vision that matters—for me it has no moral, no picture—so much as the capacity that is given to see deeply into the heart of things. Wordsworth's lines have for a long time had a wider content and application for my own experience than the mere description of the effect of nature.

[Here he quotes the 'burthen of the mystery' passage from *Tintern Abbey*.]

It is then a capacity to see deeply that is the content of the tragic vision, a vision not so much of a man but of Man as a species.[6] While its spell lasts, I see deeply and for that brief moment it would be impossible to act or feel merely human.

Secondly there is the delight, mingled with perhaps an element of horror,

---

[1] Consider, in relation to this, the Johnsonian position: 'The truth is, that the spectators are always in their senses, and know from the first act to the last that the stage is only a stage, and the players merely players' (*Pref. to Sh.*).

[2] A confession of some interest. Cf. 'Longinus', 'a marvellous instrument which produces passion, yet leaves us free'.

[3] This is a typical response to any release of tension: but is of some interest in considering the problem of technical 'relief' of various kinds in dramatic structure.

[4] This loquacity is a typical outcome of any release from tension (cf. the normal experience during psychiatric treatment). It is also of some interest in relation to the flood of words loosed by some of the comic-relief characters in Shakespeare.

[5] This looks like a straight response to the formal qualities of tragedy.

[6] Cf. Shelley: 'Man, O not men! a chain of linkèd thought
Of love and might be divided not.'

19

of having our emotions manipulated for us along unfamiliar channels of feeling and experience, though to a goal which we know to be inevitable. Part of us seems to say 'How long, O Lord, how long?' and yet another part of us clutches at feeble hope. Perhaps this time Iago will not succeed, perhaps Lear will not go mad.[1] We know, however, that the goal is fixed; the ritual sacrifice must be made. These words often echo round my mind when I see a tragedy: 'It is expedient that one man should die for the people.' Connected with these words is a sense of necessity, the necessity for a saving death and its inevitability both in the dramatic and the human context. Only in death do the great tragic heroes really gain wisdom and in the adulatory speeches that follow their end, there is a sense that not only is the hero purged but that all around him are purified also.[2] The peaceful ending and the note of sober joy is partly relief, partly a determination to start afresh and rebuild, now that the ruins are cleared away, partly the sense of wisdom that such purification brings.

C. 30. An airman, with a distinguished war record, has set out his thoughts in a violent and staccato fashion, with a wide range of literary reference. He finds that Tragedy has Dante's Three Subjects —Love, War and Death—in common with poetry: substituting 'Conflict' for 'War'.

It is immaterial whether the individual is struggling with men, gods, fatal fears 'or anything else'. Reading, witnessing or being involved in a tragedy has *at its best* [3] a moral effect. It may only be momentary,[4] but it is basically moral.

Bear in mind Mencius' proof that mankind is fundamentally good—or at least potentially good—and, at heart, compassionate.[5] At the best, our faculty for compassion, commiseration, is exercised. 'Music is to the soul what exercise is to the body.' The same with tragedy. *In general I find films more moving than the theatre principally because of the music.*[6] Music by itself is probably just as effective. (Myers—reaction to music—'felt in diaphragm'.) The reactions to tragedy are legion from sadism upwards—should be, ideally, one of partial identification—it is related somewhere to the mystics, conscious both of misery and joy. (Cf. Huxley's 'mystic ground'.) Yeats in the tea shop, and anyone else's experiences. (Cf. W. James, *Varieties of Religious*

---

[1] An interesting description of a process which is familiar at all times of crisis, but which is probably less common in the theatre.

[2] This is truer of Greek and Elizabethan drama than of modern. One reason may be that the minor characters are not separated from the protagonists by such a wide gap, whether of sympathy or mere stage 'distance'.

[3] But he does not define what this 'best' may be.

[4] Compare with the 'flashes of insight' perceived by other contributors.

[5] Consider pp. 14, 78, *ante.* He has been reading I. A. Richards, *Mencius on the Mind.*

[6] Compare B's response to opera, p. 273, *ante.* And does this statement give a clue to the effect of music in the Greek Theatre?

Experience.) Samuel Johnson always knew it was a stage—but not a book. Not surprising when one remembers the style of acting. How would he have fared with, say, Kean, or a good film? He was sensitive to music, and resisted it. Nor could he bear readily the climaxes of Greek tragedies. Starts to find himself alone, etc.[1]

The spectator could get a certain exhilaration that is not far removed from the real-life fractional moment of the same thing at an actual crisis—'Ha ha in the midst of the trumpets,' 'You ——, I'll get you,' in war, games, playing, sailing in storms, rock-climbing: moments of challenge with physical danger (either near or in the background). It is something to do with the 'Individual *vs.* Destiny.' The little man: cf. Chaplin. The pity element *vs.* forces of good and evil. We partly associate ourselves, unknowingly. The unsophisticated completely identify themselves, and shout from the gallery 'I'll save you!' to Desdemona and the village maiden. In some ways it moves the spectator more. The participant is often inspired or 'out of himself',[2] or loses any sense of identity (cf. Keats: 'I am Achilles in the trenches,' etc. but Achilles was probably 'lost' at the time of action [3]—though not before. The nervous tension is probably the same, very nearly, in life or as a spectator.). It has something to do with a feeling of helplessness—when one is actually *in* the fray it all may become mildly comical.[4] . . . Compare this business of loss of identity with real concentration, etc. This is also related to the 'Revolutionary' or the 'Romantic',[5] the stoicism or indomitableness of the 'Classic': the man at the Bridge, or Marathon, or the rearguard action in the Khyber Pass. The life of Service? Hopeless, but not helpless (again more to see than to be). Any tribute to the spirit over the flesh. Does this lead to a realization of spiritual and moral values? There is a connection with 'A.E.'s' dictum over the Dempsey-Tunney fight: 'How can these men earn more money in an hour than any creative artist?' Answer, because deep down we all recognize (1) strength, (2) courage. We all know that ideally we would be strong and courageous, physically and mentally.[6] This is borne out by the literary men and their yearning for action, etc. . . . Back again to 'the one against the many', etc. 'Ah, that is he! that should be me also were I a man.' Recognize that we all desire to face disaster with romantic or classical resistance. The Socratic example onwards. Refusal to bow to a malignant destiny, even though it has to be accepted.

---

[1] This was a point that A made much of. See p. 270, *ante.*   [2] 'Longinus's' *ecstasy.*
[3] Consider

> Know that when all words are said
> And a man is fighting mad,
> Something drops from eyes long blind,
> *He completes his partial mind* . . .
>   YEATS, *Under Ben Bulben.*

[4] Again a familiar aspect of the relief of tension.
[5] Schiller's heroes are good examples.
[6] Hamlet: 'Yet have I in me something dangerous.'

The self-mastery that all the best people have ('not passion's slave', etc.) and which we all recognize when we see it. The 'masterful administration of the unforeseen',[1] perhaps? Even though it may be only a passive acceptance or passive resistance? Stoic acceptance—Marcus Aurelius & Co.—Christian resignation—'in la sua voluntade è nostra pace'. (The great accent is one of the legion of influences at a show. *I doubt if it enters much into real life. Understatement is the thing there.*)[2] Spiritual strength above and through fear into the next stage—suicide out of pride, as opposed to depression. (Antony and Cleopatra.)

What, in general, of pre-natal influence? The conversion of the sea— rhythm, vibration, movement, music—life, light, sound, molecular physics, the ebb and flow—the wheel turning full circle—the pitcher broken at the fountain—man goeth to his long home.[3]

Suffering in tragedy must be sporadic—if we have supped too full of horrors we cease to get any reaction—the struggle becomes slaughter. To see one person, bird, shot is struggle, to a see a thousand is boredom. Nevertheless, the compassion is exercised initially. What about not giving a damn about crashing an aircraft—is this escapism, or boredom, or being beyond pity into stoicism and resignation? All these, perhaps. Mass slaughter could lead to breaking up through hydraulic pressure. A cup can hold no more than its capacity. Under pressure the emotional cup breaks.[4]

The mechanics of fear should be considered. Hesiod's 'learning through suffering' appears to be generally true. Vicarious association with the faults of the hero. The harrowing experience that makes or breaks. (Physical version is the Glasshouse and the soldier.)

Metaphysical symbols—sea, bird. Is the dove of peace a love-symbol? Flight, the faculty denied of man. Dove—spirit—Holy Ghost? Moves at will. Sea-birds resting on the sea. Sense of guilt on killing a bird—Coleridge and T. H. White.[5] The nearest creature to the sun = heavens.[6]

The chastening effect of suffering—see Hesiod. Physical suffering patiently borne, etc. 'Man of sorrows and acquainted with grief'—but man not the master of things. Is there not a reliving of personal experience?—'a little depression is good for us' (Butler). It is essentially the spectator who is moved. Compare 'One impulse from a vernal wood' with one impulse from the Old Vic. boards. The Sermon on the Mount and Paul to the Corinthians are perpetually being re-stated.

[1] Bridges, *The Testament of Beauty.*
[2] But cannot the 'great accent' exist in understatement?
[3] Cf. Chapter 12, 'Those Masterful Images . . .' But pre-natal only in one sense. He is quoting from *Ecclesiastes* xi.
[4] True. But it is hard to determine its capacity for an individual or for a given time. A good example, though I do not think the writer had this in mind, is the dropping of the teacup by the medium at the end of *The Words upon the Window-Pane.* But the image may be the golden bowl, or the pitcher at the fountain, of *Ecclesiastes.*
[5] Probably T. H. W.'s *England have My Bones.*
[6] I do not think he had read Miss Bodkin's *Archetypal Patterns.*

E. 29. The writer is a philosopher, with a classical background.

Why do we get enjoyment from tragic art? I take it that the paradox that seems to be lurking behind the question is connected with the idea of tragedy, especially literary tragedy, as being doleful and dreary. This question is one that is no doubt peculiarly pressing on myself, since I am a hedonist in philosophy, and hold that the only thing ultimately and directly valued for itself is pleasure. This is not the place for a philosophical disquisition, but let me say in brief that most of the apparent paradoxes and absurdities associated with this view seem to me to disappear if one (*a*) takes 'pleasure' in the widest sense, and (*b*) remembers the extraordinary variety in the different things found pleasant by different people; the fact that A takes pleasure from source X may be quite incomprehensible to B, who takes pleasure from the opposite and incompatible source Y.[1]

With regard to the unhappy ending, I am inclined to treat it as a means rather than as an end. It would be generally admitted that such an ending is not a sufficient condition for a good tragedy, or we could put down our Shakespeare and just look at the nearest Police-Court column: is it a necessary condition? The *Oresteia* would generally be counted as a fair example of a tragedy, but it ends with the purging of Orestes' sin on a note of reconciliation rather than gloom. Still there is no doubt that many of the greatest tragedies have this unhappy ending, and the *Oresteia* has plenty of murder and gloom during the course of itself. I should say that the main point of this is to give the play something which may best be described as 'significance'.[2] In a comedy we know that everything is going to turn out right in the long run, at any rate for those characters for whom we have sympathy; consequently we feel that 'it does not much matter' what happens in the meantime; we can sit back and relax. Now this is the one thing tragedy cannot let us do; it is above all concerned with intensity and tenseness of emotion, and whatever enjoyment we get from it must surely be connected with this fact. Hence we must not be allowed to feel that everything is secure. Something must happen which raises in us a high degree of emotion, and it seems also to be necessary that there should be more than one emotion aroused, and that some conflict must take place between them, so that an emotion of intense pleasure, such as may be aroused by a good farce, will be inadequate. It may well be that the unhappy ending may depend on the fact that drama is a tradition; we have seen other dramas before the one we are considering at any given moment, and have learnt something of what to expect. If dramas tended to end happily after a tempestuous course, we should begin to behave towards them as we do towards comedies. If all literature contained only one tragedy, of which each person saw only one performance,

[1] Cf. Aristotle's 'For we are not to expect any and every kind of pleasure from Tragedy, but only that which is proper to it.'
[2] One aspect of 'high seriousness'.

I see no reason why the tragedy should not have a happy ending, provided that for much of its course the audience had good reason to suspect that this might not be so.[1]

. . . I think tragedy should make use of all the responses available, including spectacle, diction, music, atmosphere,[2] according as they may be suitable . . . There seems to be some opposition to this view in many quarters; it is suggested that the modern spectacular productions of Shakespeare take away our appreciation of the 'play itself', whatever that is.

This seems to me rather an actor's complaint, and it was put forward vividly by Godfrey Tearle speaking on television recently, who compared the sunrise in *Romeo and Juliet* to a modern play where a sunrise took place with resplendent scenic effects to the sole accompaniment of: 'Gee, ain't that pretty,' said by a cowboy. Perhaps the diction of modern drama has suffered in that way,[3] but I see no intrinsic reason why this should matter if the effect is made up in spectacle or in some other dramatic category . . . It need hardly be added that those who are responsible for the scenic effects must be competent at their jobs . . . The chief danger is perhaps that the scenic manager will turn the play into a melodrama, *a situation which may perhaps be defined as one in which emotions are depicted on the stage, or suggested through décor and scenery, that are disproportionately greater than those likely to be more than momentarily aroused in the audience, even when the play is given an otherwise good performance.*[4] Melodrama may thus be either the fault of the author (in which case the play 'is' a melodrama) or of the performers,[5] (in which case is 'becomes' one).

A tragedy should undoubtedly avoid being a melodrama in this sense, but there is no logical reason why it should limit the sources from which it draws its effects.[6]

D. 19 is the youngest contributor. Most of his views are traditional but are sufficiently clear to be worth re-stating in his own words:

The philosopher's theories have ever been unsatisfactory. They chose their favourite play or playwright and deduced their theories backwards: no wonder that they disagreed. Thus from Aristotle to Bradley, each spoke only the partial truth, for the philosopher is concerned with the intellect, and a tragedian with the emotions.[7] He also has an ulterior motive, the development of his particular theory of the universe and the disparagement of the

---

[1] If this proposition is accepted, we should perceive *Philoctetes, Troilus and Cressida, Measure for Measure*, and perhaps *The Winter's Tale*, as tragedies.
[2] Cf. Coleridge's insistence on the unity of 'atmosphere' in *Romeo and Juliet*.
[3] We may profitably consider the 'poetic' passages of Mr Fry's plays in this context.
[4] I should define melodrama as that type of play which attempts to produce the emotions appropriate to tragedy on insufficient emotional pretexts: through *inorganic* conceptions of character or plot.
[5] We should probably lay the blame on the producer.
[6] A naïve decision, but a not uncommon one.
[7] Not wholly true, though it is often propounded as a view.

theories of others; he is obliged, to keep up his reputation, always to be saying something new.

It would have been more practical to have decided first what is tragic in human existence; but philosophers were always the most impractical of men. It is quickly proved that every tragedy depends for a great measure of its power on the aptness of its reference to archetypal human situations.

(Now he gives a series of definitions, axioms and propositions.)

1. *Real Life, Reality*
   —something that is seen to the full only on the deathbed.[1]

2. *The Material of Tragedy*

   (a) The 'eternal commonplaces' of Birth, Life and Death, part of the most primitive fertility rites and religious rituals.

   (b) The theme of sin, suffering and punishment, often in a religious sense as the problem of evil. Suffering is the keynote of tragedy, as of life.

   (c) The age-old theme of man, the divine being, contrasted with man, the animal. This sublime paradox is the essence of *King Lear* and lurks behind all Shakespearian tragedy.

   (d) Human blindness to events to come, and the unintended results of actions well-meant. Tragic Error and Accident are permissible in a reasonable degree.[2]

   (e) The sudden realization of truth after blindness. [3]

   (f) One catastrophe causes others in a chain.[4]

   (g) Man is not master of his fate, or captain of his soul. Christian dogma agrees that man is in control of his own will, but his destiny is decided by external accident. Any violent attempt to defy the Oracle of Apollo, or the forecasts in the weekly papers, is sure to fail and bring disaster.

   (h) It is folly to trust to appearances, or to boast. *Hubris* is not merely a fiction.

   (i) Words and events prove ironic in the light of subsequent events.

   (k) Sin is equally potent whether conscious or unconscious. It is the impulse behind nearly all pleasure; its power is cumulative, and it is like damp-rot, or oak-worm.[5] Man's sin arises from the inability of his weak will to overcome the more potent animal instincts within him. It is more than perverseness, it is an inherent rift in human nature. *Every tragedian must face, but must not solve, this problem.*

   (l) Man's greatness is only apparent at rare moments of victory over bodily limitations; only then is he a little lower than the angels.

   (m) Others suffer from the sin of one.[6]

[1] Cf. Chapter 21, 'Death in Tragedy'. [2] See Chapter 2.
[3] This is merely the *anagnorisis*. [4] See Chapter 6.
[5] Perhaps dry-rot and death-watch beetle would be more appropriate symbols.
[6] See Chapter 7, 'The Ethical Problem'.

3. *Pleasure in Tragedy*

(a) The audience's passions are excited and stimulated, not purged. When witnessing evil, the audience's subconscious evil finds expression; an instinctive pleasure is derived from brutality, sadism and lust. Yet audiences prefer suggestion rather than realism, which is too sordid;[1] then they suddenly want the play censored. Sometimes there is a temporary feeling of purification at such an outlet: temporary only.

(b) There is pleasure to be derived from a luxury of sorrow, of language, and of spectacle.

(c) The noblest pleasure of all is exultation at the greatness of the human soul.

4. *The Necessity for some form of Compensation*

Christian ethics demand the reconciliation of man with God, *but such sudden optimism is likely to be unconvincing. The pagan conception of atonement for evil by self-destruction is more satisfactory to demonstrate moral order in the process of re-asserting itself.* The hero must ultimately perceive the truth, or pessimism will be inevitable: Oedipus blinds himself in repentance, and lives. But all such compensations are poor atonements for the destruction already caused. Why produce a spirit-level when the house has fallen? Yet it is the emotional effect of the act of compensation that seems to matter.[2]

5. *What is inadvisable in Tragedy*

(a) Realism. In opera, which is furthest removed from realism, Brunnhilda at the end of *Die Götterdämmerung* is another Cleopatra.

(b) A religious or political axe to grind.

(c) Angels or deep-dyed villains.

(d) Elaborate language for its own sake. (But the heightened language of poetry has many advantages.)

6. *What is unnecessary in Tragedy*

(a) Love as the theme, *though it would be inevitable in this secure age to-day*: secure compared to Euripides' 'Love does not vex the man that begs his bread.' [3]

(b) Death of the hero, provided that there is some 'compensation'. *The death of some of the principal characters is necessary to heighten the catastrophe.*[4]

(c) Suspense of wondering what will happen next. Anticipation, the sense of knowing that it will, is far more powerful.[5]

---

[1] See Chapter 5, 'The Shadow of the Pleasure'.
[2] There is confusion here between the ideas of *atonement* and *compensation*.
[3] Johnson made much the same point in the *Preface to Shakespeare*. ('But love is only one of many passions,' etc.)
[4] But how? As innocent victims, or oblique objects of accumulated sin, or merely as components of a holocaust?
[5] Coleridge made this point of Shakespeare.

7. *Possible in Tragedy*
   (a) Reconciliation with the world which is always inadequate, moving in its inadequacy. 'What's done cannot be undone.'
   (b) Comedy, provided it is subordinate and organic.
   (c) The Chorus . . . Yet the Chorus is certainly not a necessity; he (or they) often come(s) between the audience and the actors, and tends to over-emphasize the element of Fate. And it is never quite clear whether the chorus himself is one of Fate's minions or not.

8. *Conclusion*
   Tragedy is not a code of literary law. It is a response to the eternal problem of evil in life, in a dramatic representation condensed, arranged and intensified. Man is led to commit evil, and evil can never be made good, though good can easily be made evil. In many things man is physically inferior to the animals, and mentally he frequently sinks to their state; only his momentary greatness of soul makes him superior, and it is this which prevents great tragedy from depressing the audience. In one way tragedy demonstrates the futility of evil, implying that continual virtue is necessary for a good life: but at the same time it points out the condemnatory flaw, that man cannot be free from sin for even the shortest period.

CHAPTER 23

The Harvest of Tragedy

The great fault of all ethics hitherto has been that they believed themselves to have to deal only with the relations of man to man. In reality, however, the question is what is his attitude to the world and all life that comes within his reach? A man is ethical only when life, as such, is sacred to him, that of plants and animals as that of his fellowmen, and when he devotes himself helpfully to all life that is in need of help. Only the universal ethic of the feeling of responsibility in an ever-widening sphere for all that lives—only that ethic can be founded in thought. The ethic of the relation of man to man is not something apart by itself: it is only a particular relation which results from the universal one.

ALBERT SCHWEITZER [1]

These tragic visions and perspectives contain a hidden philosophy, for they lend meaning to an otherwise meaningless doom.

KARL JASPERS [2]

§ i

WHITEHEAD'S quotation, from which the title of this book and of this chapter is taken, suggests that tragedy communicates, through suffering, a supreme sense of harmony with the universe. I have been concerned to suggest a view of tragedy which is not, I believe, out of harmony with Christianity, and which has some bearing on the interpretation of political and social problems. Before I attempt to carry the argument a stage further it may be well to summarize the points which I have tried to make.

§ ii

There neither is nor can be any definition of tragedy [3] that is sufficiently wide to cover its variant forms in the history of world literature. The following propositions regarding its nature may, however, command some measure of assent:

1. It is an organization of one or more limited but organically

---

[1] *My Life and Thought*, pp. 158–9.   [2] *Tragedy is Not Enough*, p. 27.
[3] Apart from A. C. Bradley's dicta, I have only read a single recent attempt at formulation:
'Tragedy is the projection of personal and collective values which are potentially or actually put in jeopardy by the course of the dramatic action; while, at the same time, the jeopardy of these values evokes from the spectator a response through his loyalty to the values involved, a response positive in character, yet differing widely in content from age to age and from individual to individual.' Harris ,*The Case for Tragedy*, p. 182.

complete sequences of events in time, refracted for the purpose of stage presentation into an aesthetic unity.

2. It is concerned primarily to depict human conflict, suffering, and apparent defeat.

3. Its basic material is three-fold:

   (a) the nature and properties of the law or laws, whether 'divine', 'natural' or 'human', under which we live.

   (b) the possible or perceived division, contradiction or conflict within such laws; either as between the three groups themselves; or internally, within any one of them.

   (c) the responsibility of individual or collective man when confronted with such a division, contradiction or conflict: whether it be perceived (by the protagonists or audience)

   (i) wholly as a logical consequence of action,
   (ii) partly as a logical consequence of action,
   (iii) as an aspect of the Irrational; including the supra-natural,

   —or in any combination of these.

4. It is concerned with the consequences of thought and action arising out of such conflict.

5. In doing so it shows Past and Present in specific relationships of causation expounded through character in action.

6. Because of the characteristics of the dramatic form, the nature of the laws and their consequences will appear in different aspects to

   (a) the protagonists, at their different levels of responsibility and knowledge.

   (b) the spectators.

7. The spectator or reader will therefore oscillate between evaluation of the tragedy *quâ* spectator and *quâ* protagonist; [1] in accordance both with the response of the individual to specific psychological aspects of characterization, and with the latent 'potential' of each work.

(These considerations explain, and justify, the wide deviations

---

[1] We have therefore the phenomena of the dispassionate ('The spectators are always in their senses . . .'), and various degrees of identification or projection. It seems probable that these attitudes occur alternately, and simultaneously.

in the criticism of tragedy as a generic form, and of its individual examples.)

8. The tragic statement must employ some or all of the methods of poetry, since

(a) its resources for communication are severely limited in time; therefore it must be economical.

(b) its statement regarding the nature of the Laws is penumbral as concerned with propositions which, both because of their complexity and their emotional roots in times past and present, are not susceptible of full and continuous intellectual communication.

(c) a symbolic communication [1] seems best fitted to convey specific kinds of Past-Present relationship, and is the most effective method of imposing the *appearance*, whether temporary or permanent, of unity.

(d) The themes of suffering and apparent defeat involve, at one stage or another, an emotional response which can be communicated only through poetry.

9. Under 'methods of poetry' we shall include all artistic devices which contribute to the unity of the aesthetic statement. These include: music, lighting, scenic effects, the costumes, gestures, positioning of actors.[2]

10. Since the tragic statement may be penumbral in character, it will often be concerned to work through ambivalences in which opposites may be perceived as existing simultaneously and in apparent contradiction.[3]

11. For the same reason it may make use of paradox, to produce a total response which is intuitional rather than logical in character.

12. This total response is of three kinds:

(a) That which is apparently reconciled or completed within the organic structure of the play.[4]

(b) That which is apparently projected outside and beyond the play as a continuing and revitalized problem.[5]

(c) That which is a compound of these two conditions.

---

[1] I include in this all kinds of imagery.
[2] A recent critic of Ibsen, J. R. Northam, has made clear the cumulative poetic significance of the playwright's directions in such matters.
[3] As, for example, the answers to the question 'What rules the world?' in *King Lear*.
[4] As in most Elizabethan/Jacobean tragedy.
[5] As in Euripides, Ibsen, T. S. Eliot.

13. The 'pleasure proper to tragedy' arises from one or more of the following elements: which vary in composition, proportion and intensity with different tragic forms and with different civilizations.

(a) That pleasure which arises from the imposition of aesthetic form upon an Image [1] which would otherwise be inchoate and indeterminate in time and space.[2]

(b) That pleasure which arises from the recognition, or inference, of certain specific aspects of human or suprahuman character, and hence of their appropriate values: perceived as working in accordance with, or contrary to, 'divine', 'natural' or 'human' laws, or some combination of them.

(c) That pleasure which arises from the imagined or sympathetic relation of such values to the spectator or to his friends or enemies.

(d) That pleasure which arises from the release of certain psychological tensions, conscious or unconscious, in the spectator.

(e) That exaltation or ecstasy [3] which arises from a conjunction of these experiences, which are synthesized in a manner appropriate to the poetic statement.

14. Tragedy can and does concern itself with all questions of moral values, both immediate and ultimate. It is 'philosophical', but it does not, and cannot, propose a systematic philosophy. It raises metaphysical issues, but it has no metaphysic of its own. Yet Jaspers is right in calling it a metaphysical art, 'that is to say, an art whose visible creations reveal the underlying reality'.[4]

§ iii

If we are to respond to the tragic experience we need only possess, at the outset, the imaginative capacity to perceive, and to be moved by, the sufferings of others. When this sympathy is aroused we are confronted with the problems of causation of that suffering, and by a greater or lesser measure of projection and identification, we perceive

[1] I use the word as on p. 196.
[2] This includes, of course, the pleasure experienced in perceiving any past-present relationship as two out of the three terms involved.
[3] I use the word in 'Longinus's' sense; without any suggestion of hysteria. There is, perhaps, no exact equivalent for the German Erhebung.
[4] Op. cit., p. 26.

such problems in alignment with our own. In assessing them we are compelled to consider them from a series of viewpoints which may alternate, or come into operation simultaneously from complementary or opposing angles, in so far as we oscillate between the poles of partial identification and the objective dispassionateness of the spectator. Our attitudes are further complicated by considerations such as these: whether the aspects of tragic experience are to be wholly imagined, whether they involve a partial or complete recognition of our own conscious experiences; whether or not certain subliminal aspects of the psyche are activated or released; and whether the problems themselves are capable of extension to a world or cosmic significance. We are made aware of enlargements both of sensibility and responsibility, a responsibility that is—paradoxically—set free by the fact of the dramatic pattern from the limiting processes of stimulus to immediate physical action.

It is beyond all question that the values stated or questioned in the tragic experience are of the utmost moral importance, both individually and collectively. Its moral structure is firmly based on a general ethic, which is perceived as stable in its principles, evolutionary in its application to an evolving world. Alone of all artistic forms tragedy offers no apologies for its incidental didacticism; its source-material in ritual, religion, myth, history, cannot determine otherwise. Its didacticism may be, and often is, multiform, disguised, working by paradox or antithesis, implicit in its images. In the revelation and interaction of character we are confronted continuously with values, whether implicit or explicit, stated or inferred, that are steadily related to a traditional or evolving ethic. And since the Aristotelian analysis is a convenient method of considering the basic values (and their implied opposites) as they appear in tragedy, it is convenient to set them out here.

Courage—which controls rashness and timidity.

Temperance—which controls indulgence and abstinence.

Liberality—which controls giving and receiving.

Magnificence—which incurs and limits great expense.

Magnanimity—which moderates and acquires honour and reputation.

Love of honour—which moderates and orders us as regards the world's honours.

Mansuetude—which moderates our anger and our overmuch impatience with external evils.

Affability—which makes us 'convivial' or companionable with others.

Truthfulness—which prevents us in our talk from pretending to be more or less than we are.

Pleasantness (eutrapelia)—which sets us free to make a proper and easy use of amusement ('sollazia'—solace).

Justice—which constrains us to love and practise directness in all things.[1]

I do not know of any tragedies which do not suggest and develop one or more of the values comprehended here.

§ iv

The Harvest of Tragedy is the freedom and enrichment of the human spirit.

The phrase sounds trite, but it is difficult to put it otherwise. For tragedy, more than any other art form except the epic, must deal with ultimates. It suffers no specific limitations as to whether its exposition shall be direct or oblique, implicit or explicit. It cannot handle the conflicts of the Laws without raising moral issues, from whatever standpoint they are perceived; it fails as a formal work of art if, in its handling of such problems, it evades them or seeks to translate them into other terms. It may not give definitive answers; both final pessimism, and final optimism, contradict the nature of tragedy as an imitation of life. Its peculiar quality is to present the mingled yarn in such a manner that a pattern is perceptible. If that perception is accompanied by exaltation or ecstasy, by a heightening of the senses, by a transcending of the physical impact of suffering, grief, destruction, we are enabled to recognize and to possess, at least momentarily, values that we have grounds for believing to be permanent in their own right.

All writers of, or on, tragedy have recognized its mystery, or quality of infinitude. The quotation from Wordsworth's *Borderers* is hackneyed, perhaps; but no passage sums up this sense so well:

> Action is transitory;—a step, a blow,
> The motion of a muscle—this way or that—
> 'Tis done and in the after-vacancy
> We wonder at ourselves like men betrayed:
> Suffering is permanent, obscure and dark,
> And shares the nature of infinity.[2]

[1] I am indebted here to Charles Williams's recapitulation and explanation in *The Figure of Beatrice*.

[2] Act III.

Comedy, whether 'critical' or 'free',[1] lives in virtue of acceptance of human limitations as a norm of human conduct; it approves and certifies, in its conclusion, the ultimate rationality of man. Tragedy, even when its conclusions appear to be pessimistic, does not accept this limitation. In this apparent wreckage of human aspirations which it perceives there is implicit, not only the possibility of redemption, but the spiritual assertion that man is splendid in his ashes, and can transcend his nature; the nature that Rousseau thought perfectible,[2] and that Freud once thought evil.[3]

The possibility of redemption may be perceived in many forms. If we are to use non-Christian terminology, we are confronted with the essential fact that man's desires exceed his limitations in the universe in which he is set; and that from this evil must spring:

> Ideally men seek to subject their arbitrary and contingent existence under the dominion of absolute reality. But practically they always mix the finite with the eternal and claim for themselves, their nation, their culture, or their class, the centre of existence. This is the root of all imperialism in man and explains why the restricted predatory impulses of the animal world are transmuted into the boundless imperial ambitions of human life.[4]

In tragedy we are presented with the ἀναγνώρισις, the recognition of this: and through its symbol and ritual with the possibility of psychological liberation, consciously or unconsciously, through participation in its emotions. The result is basically a perception of scale or proportion, a rejection of that pride or civic insolence which is so often the preliminary spiritual state preceding evil. Fear, of whatever kind, may be aroused under one of two headings; the neurotic anxiety of the ego-centric, and the wholesome humility of fear before the unknown.

§ v

But if the Christian point of view is accepted (and I have endeavoured to keep in sight what seems to me a steady convergence of the moral and anthropological sciences upon it) I am clear that the history and theory of tragedy is capable of re-interpretation in those

---

[1] Cf. p. 222, note.
[2] There is no such thing as pure 'nature' in man. It is changed by his participation in the activities of spirit.
[3] I refer to the apparent hope in *Civilization and its Discontents* that there is a solution, in the future, of the neurotic conflict from which it seemed that man could not escape.
[4] Reinhold Niebuhr, *An Interpretation of Christian Ethics*, pp. 84–5. Quoted by Thelen, p. 80.

terms; and that it affords a more adequate solution of the tragic problems than can be found elsewhere. A return to the doctrine of Original
Sin—itself postulated, though in non-Christian terms, by Marx and
Freud—affords both an explanation of the tragic flaw, and, in conjunction with the sin of pride, the emergence of evil upon the tragic
world:

> Original sin is then postulated as a defect of the will, or 'bias' in the will,
> which characterizes the will before any act . . . Original sin is to be dis-
> tinguished from actual sin in that it is not an act at all but the presupposition
> of every act.[1]

In the same way the characteristics of sin are to be perceived in
alignment with the 'delusion' of classical philosophy:

> It is this very blindness and self-deception which constitutes the mystery
> of sin. For it is really a mystery. No one, not even the most astute psycho-
> logist, has ever made a perfectly convincing analysis of the comparative
> degrees of ignorance and dishonesty which enter into it.[2]

I am aware that this view of evil is in direct opposition to a number
of liberal philosophies to-day; which would make the sense of guilt
no more than the product of wrongdoing and punishment in childhood: a product that is, of immediate upbringing and environment,
without reference even to the collective unconscious. The evidence of
history and literature appears to contradict it flatly. It seems to me
that the demonstration offered by the more intimate and usually un-
chronicled heroes of war have reinforced abundantly the metaphysical
concept of implicit evil. Tragedy is perhaps the only art form which,
by its handling of myth, myth-in-history, and history perceived (by
poetic extension) as a cosmic process, can bring home to us the judgements of history in their attempt to establish human justice and in their
violation of divine law.

I do not suggest that the recognition of human evil as the 'defeat of
the will' leads to a negative or pessimistic view. Taken in isolation, it
may well be sterile. But just as the Christian cycle of sin, repentance,
atonement, redemption is completed in its operation by the awakening
of pity and the merging of the self-hood of man in love, so the tragic
cycle may be thought of as operating on the human consciousness in
an analogous manner, though at a lower level. Tragic evil becomes
recognizable as the assertion of the will beyond the limits proper to

---

[1] Thelen, *op. cit.*, p. 95.
[2] *The Nature and Destiny of Man*, p. 105. *Cit.* Thelen, p. 85.

the individual's relationship to his fellows and to his God. Both transgressions are manifestations of *hubris,* the failure to recognize the creature in relation to the creator; and its common form is the concept of God as a projection of the Super-Ego, or as identified with that component of personality: from which spring, whether explicitly or otherwise, all theories of the Super-Man. When once such theories are accepted, pity is killed; all other individuals shrivel before the lust of power, which begets hatred.

It is the recognition of this sin, and of its illimitable consequences, which I see as the root of the tree of tragedy, which is in turn one manifestation of the tree of life. For the tragic statement is, in essence, a patterned showing-forth, in a perspicuous form, of an 'action' of this kind. By its rhythmic patterns, in form, incident, music and language, it produces the heightened attention which is the prior condition of response to all statements proper to that species of morality that are not susceptible of intellectual analysis. By its ritual character it can both satisfy our human demands for that aspect of living, and heighten still further the attention which is necessary. By image and symbol, whether archetypal or otherwise, it can bring into play, fulfil, release, important elements of the subliminal consciousness which hinder, (and which, when released, can help most powerfully) the human understanding. By its cyclic ending in death it seals, and prepares for continuing life, the chain of being whose pattern it mirrors; sin, punishment, atonement, the grace of death. Its greatness is to perceive intuitively and to communicate, the making of the individual soul in relation to his environment.

I do not suggest for a moment that tragedy can in any possible manner become a substitute for religion. It is clear that there are worlds beyond tragedy, and that Karl Jaspers' [1] main thesis is irrefutable. I do suggest that it moves on a lower plane but parallel to, the religious experience which selects, as the material for suffering, the examination of the crooked questions, and the origin of the divine spark in man. The awakening of pity seems the first step (because of this induration through successive wars of which I have spoken) to a sense of Christian charity: that of fear,[2] a necessary state of mind to our readiness to consider the idea of the numinous; both together forcing us to confront a series of ethical problems which have their

---

[1] In *Tragedy is Not Enough.*
[2] 'Always it comes about that the beginning of wisdom is a fear.' Miguel da Unamuno, *op. cit.,* p. 107.

solution only in faith. The groundwork of that faith is to be found in the moments of awareness of a unity (itself of widely differing forms but of a single generic significance) which is derived from all great art. That such moments are made possible only by a preparation through ritual, individual self-discipline, and the exaltation of the soul through a combination of certain artistic communications, is a commonplace of religious history.

Those writers, including Ellis-Fermor and Jaspers, who have assumed that Christianity and the tragic sense are incompatible, do so, I think, on the basis that the latter ceases to have any meaning when apprehended against a background of faith, redemption and salvation through grace. Sin and suffering cease to have any significance *sub specie aeternitatis*: they are transcended in man's approach to God, in Whose hands is redemption through perfect love. In Jaspers' words:

> Every one of man's basic experiences ceases to be tragic in a Christian context. Guilt becomes *felix culpa*, the 'happy fault'—the guilt without which no salvation is possible. Judas' betrayal was necessary for Christ's sacrifice and death, the source of salvation for all believers. Christ is the deepest symbol of failure in the world, yet he is in no sense tragic. In his very failure he knows, fulfils, and consummates.[1]

I cannot agree wholly with this view. That guilt should be *felix culpa* is true only in so far as the individual punishment, on earth or (less probably) in Purgatory, is merged in a specific kind of aesthetico-religious distance; and it is of the essence of tragedy that the experience which it communicates should work upwards from the individual to the universe, and not downwards. We can only subscribe to the doctrine of the Fortunate Fall if we are prepared to allow less ambivalence in our own response to tragedy than seems, on the evidence, to be proper. For while the Fortunate Fall may be, in one sense, the symbol of our psychic redemption, its power to move us is developed concurrently with our sympathetic response to suffering, and a divided response at the conclusion of the play. We cannot *know* how the balances of judgement will be loaded. We are aware of something akin to grace when suffering is merged in exalted death; not grace, but a state that is a preparation for its reception, if faith extends so far.

It would be vanity of the most intolerable kind to suggest that the views which I have put forward in this essay can influence us in our interpretation of the human situation. Literary criticism since Arnold

[1] Jaspers, *op. cit.*, p. 40.

may well be thought to have taken too much upon itself, whether in proposing that poetry should be a substitute for religion, or that civilization may be saved by the values proposed by an eclectic critical taste. All that I have been concerned with is to suggest that tragedy, which is still the most important, and probably the most pervasive, of the great literary forms, can be interpreted, increasingly, as of the highest ethical importance; that the hardening of mind and spirit which I have suggested as a consequence of war, demand that we should return to it with a new interest; that anthropology, psychology, and recent religious developments suggest a convergence, though not an identity, of the values implicit in tragedy; that 'release', 'recognition', expiation and grace have ground in common; that of its fruits the greatest is self-knowledge through suffering. Behind it and beyond there lies always that mysterious activity of all literary creation: *Poetry administers to the effect by acting upon the cause.*

Tragedy can question that cause with the full resources of the conscious and unconscious, of the immediate and the traditional, in a medium of the utmost complexity; yet which continues at a number of levels because it, and it alone, can use the traditional resources of dramatic art with a consciousness, however remote, of its ritual beginnings. What has been called 'ecstasy', 'joy', 'exaltation' by writers on tragedy is perhaps (quite simply) that sense of extended and extending wisdom that is in its essence a prelude to a new sense of unity; from which we can get, with Wordsworth

> Authentic tidings of invisible things,
> Of ebb and flow and ever-during power,
> And central peace subsisting at the heart
> Of endless agitation.

It is then that 'the stupid arrogance of thinking ourselves civilized loses its power over us'.[1] This broadening of sensibility is described, in that language of poetry which is, perhaps, best fitted to explain tragedy, in this extract:

Certainly we have here the Tree of Life and that of The Knowledge of Good and Evil which is rooted in our interests, and if we have forgotten their differing virtues it is surely because we have taken delight in a confusion of crossing branches. Tragic art, passionate art, the drowner of dykes,[2] the

[1] Schweitzer, *My Life and Thought.*
[2] This is an allusion to an earlier sentence in the same essay: '. . . tragedy must always be a drowning of the dykes that separate man from man, and it is upon these dykes comedy keeps house'.

confounder of understanding, moves us by setting us to reverie, by alluring us almost to the intensity of trance. The persons upon the stage, let us say, greaten till they are humanity itself. We feel our minds expand convulsively or spread out slowly like some moon-brightened image-crowded sea. That which is before our eyes perpetually vanishes and returns again in the midst of the excitement it creates, and the more enthralling it is, the more do we forget it.[1]

[1] Yeats, *Essays*, pp. 302–3: *The Tragic Theatre.*

Bibliography

Abercrombie, L. *Principles of English Prosody*. London, 1923.

Anderson, R. L. *Elizabethan Psychology and Shakespeare's Plays*. Univ. of Iowa Studies, III, 4. 1927.

Anouilh, Jean. *Antigone* and *Eurydice*, transl. Lewis Galantière and Lothian Small. London, 1951.

Armstong, E. A. *Shakespeare's Imagination*. London, 1946.

Auden, W. H. *The Enchafèd Flood*. London, 1951.

Auerbach, Eric. *Mimesis; dargestellte Wirklichkeit in der abendländischen Literatur*. Bern, 1946.

Baker, Howard. *Induction to Tragedy*. Univ. of Louisiana, 1939.

Bentley, Eric R. *The Playwright as Thinker*. New York, 1946.

Bergson, Henri. *Time and Free Will*, transl. F. L. Pogson. London, 1950.

Bevan, Edwyn R. *Symbolism and Belief* (Gifford Lectures, 1933–4). London, 1938.

Bodkin, Maud. *Archetypal Patterns in Poetry*. Oxford, 1934.

—— *Studies of Type-Images in Poetry, Religion and Philosophy*. Oxford, 1951.

—— *The Quest for Salvation in an Ancient and a Modern Play*. Oxford, 1941.

Bowra, C. M. *The Heritage of Symbolism*. London, 1943.

Bradbrook, M. C. *Ibsen the Norwegian*. London, 1946.

Bradley, A. C. *Shakespearean Tragedy* (2nd Edn.). London, 1905.

—— *Oxford Lectures on Poetry* (2nd Edn.). London, 1909.

Bridgeman, P. W. *The Logic of Modern Physics*. New York, 1946.

Bronowski, J. *The Poet's Defence*. Cambridge, 1939.

Butcher, S. H. *Aristotle's Theory of Poetry and Fine Art* (4th Edn.). London, 1927.

Butterfield, H. *Christianity and History*. London, 1949.

Campbell, J. *The Hero with a Thousand Faces*. New York, 1949.

Campbell, Lewis. *Aeschylus, Sophocles, and Shakespeare*. London, 1904.

Campbell, L. B. *Shakespeare's Tragic Heroes*. Cambridge, 1930.

Caudwell, C. *Illusion and Reality*. London, 1937.

Clark, B. H. *European Theories of the Drama*. New York, 1929.

—— *A Study of the Modern Drama* (Revised Edn.). New York, 1938.

Clemen, W. H. *The Development of Shakespeare's Imagery*. London, 1951.

Coleridge, S. T. *Lectures and Notes on Shakespeare* (New Universal Library Edn.). London, 1908.

Cornford, F. M. *From Religion to Philosophy*. London, 1912.

Cousteau, J. Y. *The Silent World*. London, 1953.

Croce, B. *Ariosto, Shakespeare and Corneille*, transl. Ainslie. London, 1920.

Danby, J. F. *Shakespeare's Doctrine of Nature*. London, 1949.

Dempsey, P. J. R. *The Psychology of Sartre*. Cork Univ. Press, 1950.

Dixon, W. Macneile. *Tragedy* (3rd Edn.). 1929.

—— *The Human Situation* (Gifford Lectures, 1935–7). Arnold, 1937.

Dobrée, B. *Restoration Comedy*. Oxford, 1927.

Downs, B. W. *Ibsen: the Intellectual Background*. Cambridge, 1946.

Eliot, T. S. *Selected Essays* (3rd Enlarged Edn.). London, 1951.
—— *Poetry and Drama*. London, 1951.
Ellis-Fermor, U. M. *The Frontiers of Drama*. London, 1945.
—— *The Irish Dramatic Movement*. London, 1939.
Empson, W. *Seven Types of Ambiguity*. London, 1930.
—— *The Structure of Complex Words*. London, 1951.
Fergusson, Francis. *The Idea of a Theatre*. Princeton, 1949.
Figgis, J. N. *The Will to Freedom*. London, 1917.
Fluchère, H. *William Shakespeare*, transl. Hamilton. London, 1953.
Foerster, Norman. *The Intent of the Critic*, ed. D. A. Stauffer. Princeton, 1941.
Fortescue, Sir John. *A History of the British Army*. London, 1933.
Frazer, J. *The Golden Bough* (3rd Edn.). London, 1911–13.
Freytag, G. *Die Technik des Dramas*. Leipzig, 1890.
Frohock, W. M. *André Malraux and the Tragic Imagination*. Stamford, 1952.
Garaudy, R. *Literature of the Graveyard*. New York, 1948.
García Lorca, F. *Three Tragedies*, transl. Graham-Luján and O'Connell. New York, 1947.
Gorer, G. *The Revolutionary Ideas of the Marquis de Sade*. (Foreword by J. B. S. Haldane.) London, 1954.
Haigh, A. E. *The Tragic Drama of the Greeks*. Oxford, 1896.
Hardman, D. (Ed.) *Reflections on Our Age*. London, 1948.
Harris, Mark. *The Case for Tragedy*. New York, 1932.
Harrison, Jane. *Themis* (2nd Edn., Revised). Cambridge, 1927.
Hebbel, F. *Sämmtliche Werke*. Vienna, 1851–3.
Heller, E. *The Disinherited Mind*. Cambridge, 1952.
Herbert, S. *The Unconscious Mind*. London, 1923.
Hinks, R. *Myth and Allegory in Ancient Art*. Warburg Inst. Studies, 6. London, 1939.
Hoffmann, F. J. *Freudianism and the Literary Mind*. Univ. of Louisiana, 1945.
James, D. G. *The Dream of Learning*. Oxford, 1951.
Jaspers, Karl. *Tragedy is Not Enough*. London, 1953.
Joyce, J. *A Portrait of the Artist as a Young Man* (1952 Edn.). London.
Jung, C. G. *Psychology of the Unconscious*, transl. B. M. Hinkle. London, 1915.
—— *Collected Papers* (2nd Edn.). London, 1917.
—— *Modern Man in Search of a Soul*, transl. Dell and Baynes. London, 1933.
Jung, C. G. and Kerényi, C. *Introduction to a Science of Mythology*, transl. R. F. C. Hull. London, 1951.
Kierkegaard, S. A. *Either/Or*, transl. D. F. and L. M. Swenson and Lowrie. London, 1944.
—— *Stages on Life's Way*, transl. Lowrie. London, 1940.
—— *The Concept of Dread*, transl. Lowrie. London, 1944.
Kitto, H. D. F. *Greek Tragedy*. London, 1950.
—— *The Greeks*. (Pelican) 1951.
Knight, G. Wilson. *The Imperial Theme*. Oxford, 1931.
Koht, H. *Life of Ibsen*, transl. McMahon and Larson. London, 1931.
Krutch, J. W. *The Modern Temper*. London, 1930.
Leech, Clifford. *Shakespeare's Tragedies (and other studies in seventeenth-century drama)*. London, 1950.

Lorca, F. García. *Three Tragedies.* New York, 1947.

Lucas, D. W. *The Greek Tragic Poets.* London, 1950.

Lucas, F. L. *Authors Dead and Living.* London, 1926.

—— *Tragedy.* Hogarth Press, 1927.

—— *Literature and Psychology.* London, 1951.

—— *Greek Drama for Everyman.* London, 1954.

Margoliouth, D. S. *The Poetics of Aristotle.* London, 1911.

Matthaei, B. M. *Studies in Greek Tragedy.* Cambridge, 1918.

Mortensen, B. M. E. and Downs, B. W. *Strindberg.* Cambridge, 1949.

Moulton, R. G. *Shakespeare as a Dramatic Artist.* Oxford, 1893.

Murray, Gilbert. *Aeschylus, the Creator of Tragedy.* Oxford, 1940.

—— *The Classical Tradition in Poetry.* Oxford, 1927.

—— *Myths and Ethics.* London, 1944.

Nicoll, Allardyce. *The Theory of Drama.* London, 1931.

Niebuhr, Reinhold. *Beyond Tragedy.* London, 1938.

—— *The Nature and Destiny of Man* (Gifford Lectures, 1939). London, 1941.

—— *The Irony of American History.* London, 1952.

Nietzsche. *Collected Works,* ed. Levy. Edinburgh, 1909–13.

Northam, J. R. *Ibsen's Dramatic Method; a Study of the Prose Dramas.* London, 1953.

Norwood, Gilbert. *Euripides and Shaw.* London, 1921.

O'Neill, Eugene. *Collected Plays.* New York, 1924.

Raglan, Lord. *The Hero.* London, 1936.

Rank, Otto. *The Myth of the Birth of the Hero: a Psychological Interpretation of Mythology.* New York, 1914.

Richards, I. A. *Principles of Literary Criticism.* London, 1925.

Russell, Bertrand. *Human Society in Ethics and Politics.* London, 1954.

Schweitzer, A. *My Life and Thought,* transl. C. T. Campion. London, 1954.

Sedgwick, W. E. *Herman Melville.* Harvard, 1944.

Sewell, W. A. *Character and Society in Shakespeare.* Oxford, 1951.

Sikes, E. E. *The Greek View of Poetry.* London, 1931.

Smart, John S. *Tragedy* (Essays and Studies of the English Association, Vol. VIII). Oxford, 1922.

Southworth, J. G. *The Poetry of Thomas Hardy.* New York, 1947.

Spencer, Theodore. *Death and Elizabethan Tragedy.* Harvard, 1936.

—— *Shakespeare and the Nature of Man.* Cambridge, 1943.

Strachey, Lytton. *Books and Characters.* London, 1927.

Strong, L. A. G. *The Sacred River.* London, 1949.

Stuart, D. C. *The Development of Dramatic Art.* London, 1928.

Temple, W. *Mens Creatrix.* London, 1949.

Tennant, F. R. *The Concept of Sin.* Cambridge, 1912.

Tennant, P. F. D. *Ibsen's Dramatic Technique.* Cambridge, 1948.

Thelen, M. F. *Man as Sinner.* New York, 1946.

Thompson, A. R. *The Anatomy of Drama.* Univ. of California, 1942.

—— *The Dry Mock.* Univ. of California, 1948.

Thorndike, A. H. *Tragedy.* London, 1908.

Tuve, R. *Elizabethan and Metaphysical Imagery.* Chicago, 1947.

Unamuno, M. de. *The Tragic Sense of Life.* London, 1921.

Ussher, Arland. *Three Great Irishmen.* London, 1952.

Vaughan, C. E. *Types of Tragic Drama.* London, 1924.
Volkelt, J. *Aesthetik des Tragischen.* Munich, 1923.
Wade, Allan. *The Letters of W. B. Yeats.* London, 1954.
Watts, A. W. *Myth and Ritual in Christianity.* London, 1953.
Weil, Simone. *Waiting on God*, transl. E. Crauford. London, 1951.
Weisinger, H. *Tragedy and the Paradox of the Fortunate Fall.* London, 1953.
Welsford, E. *The Fool, His Social and Literary History.* London, 1935.
Wheelwright, Philip. *The Burning Fountain.* Indiana University, 1954.
White, Victor. *God and the Unconscious.* Foreword by C. G. Jung. London, 1952.
Whitehead, A. N. *Process and Reality* (Gifford Lectures, 1927–8). Cambridge, 1929.
—— *Adventures of Ideas.* Cambridge, 1933.
Wickes, F. G. *The Inner World of Man.* London, 1950. (New York, 1948.)
Williams, Charles. *The Figure of Beatrice.* London, 1943.
Yeats, W. B. *Essays.* London, 1934.
—— *Dramatis Personae.* London, 1936. (Dublin, 1935.)
—— *Plays and Controversies.* London, 1923.

Index

Date Due

NOV 6 '63	MAR 15 1974		
DEC 18 '64	DEC 2 0 1979		
9-6-66	6 July 82		
DEC 5 '66	SEP 2 6 1998		
DEC 16 66			
JAN 17 '67			
FEB 2 2			
MAR 8 '67			
MAR 2 0			
MAR 2 4 '67			
NOV 11 '67			
FEB 2 9 1968			
APR 1 7 1968			
4-9-68			
APR 2 6 1968			
Oct 6, 70			
JAN 7 1970			
MAR 1 5 1972			
	PRINTED	IN U. S. A.	